SALES MANAGEMENT

concepts, practices, and cases

001441

Manufactured in the United States of America.

Published simultaneously in Canada.

Library of Congress Catalog Card Number 74-77773

This book is in the General Learning Press marketing series under the consulting editorship of Stanley Hollander.

TO OUR FAMILIES

FOREWORD

What response should a student give if he encounters the following true-false question on an examination: "Nothing really happens in business until there is a sale."? As any marketer knows, this statement is clearly false in two respects; yet as any successful marketer also knows, it is in one important sense very true.

The statement is a gross oversimplification in view of the fact that our entire economic system is organized around the concept of production in advance of sale. A host of organizational and marketing functions must precede any agreement to transfer goods or services from buyer to seller. Moreover, responsible businessmen realize that their obligations often extend long beyond the time and locus of sale. Suppliers may have to help middlemen and endproduct manufacturers solve their own subsequent selling problems; all three groups may have postsales warranty and/or financing commitments to final purchasers.

The concept of sales management explains the second respect in which much activity must occur before and after the sale. Sales don't just happen. Sales programs must be developed; sales staffs must be recruited, selected, and trained. Selling efforts must be deployed in line with sales opportunity, and sales supporting services must be provided. Then, after the event, sales efforts must be rewarded. Salesmen must be compensated and recognized and simultaneously encouraged to provide all appropriate postsales service.

But, aside from the organizational and sales management activities, in one sense nothing does happen until there is a sale. As George Burton Hotchkiss pointed out in his *Milestones of Marketing*:

> For the past five hundred years, at least, fear of scarcity was far
> less common than fear of surplus. . . . Only for short periods, or in

limited groups, were producers ever free from worry regarding the marketing of their merchandise and services.*

The sales transaction is the great energizer of the commercial system. Sales management is not an activity that is carried on for its own sake, nor are sales force recruitment and compensation ends in themselves. The prime objective of sales management is to produce a profitable volume of sales over the long run. Emphasis on long-term results is important because it demands attention to such considerations as customer satisfaction and standards of commercial morality. Emphasis on profitability is important because the commercial enterprise cannot survive without profits.

The discussion in *Sales Management: Concepts, Practices, and Cases* constantly remains aware of these parameters. Professors Dunn, Johnson, and Kurtz have steadily focused on sales management's true function within the firm and within the economic system. In the expository sections, discussion questions, and case studies, they have ably dealt with the planning, coordinating, leadership, supportive, and control tasks that every sales manager faces. The entire text was conceived to offer the student a realistic learning experience that would encourage flexibility in handling sales problems.

The student who has faithfully worked through this book will know how the opening question should properly be answered. He will know that the two indicated answers, "true" and "false," are both really inappropriate, and that instead he really should write, "It depends." And he will know what it depends upon.

Stanley C. Hollander

---

*New York: Macmillan Co., 1938, p. xvi.

PREFACE

Selling is the most *public* of all business activities. Many people form their opinions of a company from their impressions of the firm's sales force. As a result, salesmen receive a substantial part of the criticism that actually should be directed toward other areas of the organization. If a consumer is dissatisfied with some aspect of a company's procedure—whether it is an accountant's handling of his account, a quality control engineer's standard of product reliability, or a personnel officer's decision not to hire a favorite nephew—he most likely will voice his objections and discontent for the firm's *public representative:* the salesman!

At the same time, selling is the most *dynamic* field of business. The environment for the selling process is constantly changing. A sales manager of a decade ago would have had difficulty visualizing the marketing decisions precipitated by the ecology movement, consumerism, unit pricing, and the like. Similarly, the sales manager of the immediate future may have to deal with problems involving conversion to the metric system or the continued rationing of fuel oil and gasoline.

From the viewpoint of sales education, the primary question has always been how to best communicate the need for flexibility in dealing with sales problems and, at the same time, present accepted concepts and practices. Basically, authors of sales management texts are faced with the question of how to structure the material to maximize the learning experience.

Sales Management: Concepts, Practices, and Cases was designed to provide students in personal selling and in sales management classes with a textbook that realistically meets student needs. The book is a relatively complete learning/teaching tool. In addition to organizing the large body of sales knowledge into a manageable number of chapters and pages, the book provides classroom users with a comprehensive series of discussion/review questions and with thirty-six case studies based on actual business experiences.

The volume is also appropriate for sales management development sessions and for executive reading programs. Its length allows complete coverage of the material within normal time constraints.

The text has been thoroughly classroom tested by the authors. Student reaction toward the material has been uniformly positive. We are deeply appreciative of the many constructive comments received from our students. Many of these suggestions have been incorporated in this manuscript.

Albert H. Dunn
Eugene M. Johnson
David L. Kurtz

Newark, Delaware
Kingston, Rhode Island
Ypsilanti, Michigan

ACKNOWLEDGEMENTS

The authors would like to gratefully acknowledge the contributions of various people who have assisted us in preparing this book. First, we would like to thank those individuals and organizations who have permitted us to reprint published material. A special word of thanks is given to Professor James P. Jennings of the University of Detroit for providing much of the information on sales forecasting. Professor Jennings is a well-qualified consultant on this subject and has been a valuable contributor to *Sales Management: Concepts, Practices, and Cases.*

Professors Anthony G. Eonos of Suffolk University, Milton M. Pressley of the University of North Carolina at Greensboro, and Stanley C. Hollander provided enlightened reviews of our early manuscript drafts. Their criticisms, comments, and suggestions played a crucial role in shaping the final product. The authors are sincerely grateful for their effort. For her assistance in preparing the manuscript, the authors would also like to thank Tonia M. Marcaccio.

A.H. D.
E. M. J.
D. L. K.

CONTENTS

PART ONE

THE PERSONAL SELLING FUNCTION

Chapter 1   The Sales Management Process: An Overview,   3

The role of selling. Marketing mix. Demand Creation. Selling and sales management. Evolution of sales management. The salesman as problem solver. The marketing concept. The process of management. Management defined. The job of the sales manager. Services and sales management. Sales management as an integrated, interrelated process. Uniqueness of the sales manager's job. Planning as a critical sales management responsibility. Sales management as part of the total marketing effort. A final word about the study of sales management. Summary.

Chapter 2   The Historical Development of Professional Sales Force,   27

Earliest times. The development of salesmanship in England, 700–1775. The American Experience, 1650–1900. Major contributions of early American salesmen. The American experience since 1900. Future outlook. Summary.

xi

Chapter 3   The Environment of Selling,   43

Environmental constraints on sales management. The market environ-
ment. Public and legal environment. Antitrust legislation. The Federal
Trade Commission. Pricing legislation. Consumer protection laws.
Economic environment. Physical and technological environment.
Societal environment. Social issues. Ethical issues. Bribes, gifts, enter-
tainment. Preserving employer and customer secrets. Expense ac-
counts. Sales management's relationship with subordinate personnel.
An environmental checklist. Summary.

Chapter 4   Essentials of the Sales Function   77

Salesmanship: the traditional viewpoint. The buyer-seller dyad: the
modern viewpoint. A classification system for the sales function. Sales
tasks. Purchasing decisions. Toward effective selling. Steps in the sales
process. Pre-approach. Approach. Presentation. Demonstration. Identifying and handling of objections. Closing. Follow-up. Second-effort
review. Increasing sales volume. Summary.

Cases for Part One

PART TWO

PLANNING AND ORGANIZING FOR SALES MANAGEMENT

Chapter 5   Introduction to Sales Forecasting,   131

Importance of sales forecasting. Use of sales forecasts. Setting sales
quotas. Sales budgeting. Market potential and sales potential. Moni-

toring market and sales potentials. Estimating market and sales potentials. Basic steps in sales forecasting. Organization of the forecasting function. Evaluation of the sales forecast. Methods of evaluation. Responsibility for evaluation. Summary.

Chapter 6 Forecasting Methodology, 155

Judgmental methods. Jury of executive opinion. Delphi technique. Sales force composite. Factor listing. Survey of consumer buying intentions. Quantitative methods. Continuity extrapolation. Trend and cycle analysis. Standard error of the estimate. Exponential smoothing. Correlation analysis. Lead-lag series. Econometric models. Synthesizing forecast methodology. Summary.

Chapter 7 Organization of the Sales Force, 173

The importance of organization to sales management. Developing the sales organization. Formal and informal organizations. Horizontal and vertical organizations. Centralized and decentralized organizations. Line and staff components of the marketing organization. Size of the sales organization. Concepts of effective organization. Sales activities should be organized, not people. Similar functions should be grouped together. Sales organizations should be coordinated, balanced, and flexible. Basic types of sales organizations. Customer specialization. Product specialization. Geographical specialization. The first level sales manager. Territory decisions. Establishing territories. Call frequency. Scheduling. Routing. Measuring the effectiveness of the sales organization. Summary.

Cases for Part Two

PART THREE
DEVELOPING THE SALES FORCE

PART FOUR

DIRECTING THE SALES FORCE

Chapter 11 Leadership and Supervision in Sales Management, 339

Understanding behavior. Elements of behavior. Theories of motivation. Primary and secondary needs. Rational and emotional needs. A hierarchy of needs. The management of motivation. Job challenge. Participation. Being part of the company. Morale. Discipline. Sales management leadership and supervision. The basic condition on sales supervision. The critical importance of salesmen's cooperation. The costs of less than complete cooperation by salesmen. The essence of sales leadership. The environment of sales management leadership. The sales manager's leadership roles. The salesman's role in the command hierarchy. Followership as a contractual relationship. What the salesman gives under the followership contract. The follower's prices for his cooperation. Basic human relations skills. Perception. Conceptual ability. Communication skills. Self-awareness. Summary.

Chapter 12 The Evaluation of Salesmen, 371

Why evaluate salesman performance? Characteristics of a good salesman evaluation program. Obstacles to salesman evaluation. Isolation of the salesman. Finding and relating criteria. Lack of control over some performance conditions. Evaluation facts and evaluation judgments. Developing the salesman evaluation program. The use of a single standard. The use of several standards. Commonly used measures of performance. ROI—another evaluation tool. Information sources for evalutaion. Summary.

Chapter 13 Operation of the Evaluation Program, 391

Who should evaluate salesman performance? Frequency of evaluation. Evaluation follow-up. Degree of salesman involvement in his own evaluations. Methods of involving the salesman in his evaluation. Evaluation interviews. Evaluation of the program by salesmen. Self-evaluation by salesmen. Training the evaluators. Summary.

Types of incentives. Nonfinancial incentives. Financial incentives. Sales meetings and conventions. Planning. Participation. Evaluation of meetings. Sales contests. Planning the contest. Criticisms of sales contests. Why contests work. Honors and recognition. Communication. Compensating salesmen. Trends in salesmen's compensation. Criteria for a sound compensation plan. Developing a compensation plan. Job review. Establish objectives. Level of compensation. Method of compensation. Salary. Commission. Bonus. Combination plans. Implementing the plan. Sales expenses. Need for control. Current practices. Summary.

Cases for Part Four

PART FIVE
EPILOGUE

The advancement of marketing thought. A changed environment for selling. Consumer education. Societal changes. Increased government regulation. Technological changes. Expanded competition. Increased selling costs. Need for better sales intelligence. Dealing with a changed selling environment. Trends influencing the sales function. Summary.

Cases for Part Five

PART ONE: THE PERSONAL SELLING FUNCTION

CHAPTER ONE
THE SALES
MANAGEMENT
PROCESS
an overview

A strong, dynamic sales force is the backbone of a successful company. Such a sales force does not just happen spontaneously; it must be carefully developed and nurtured. This book presents guidelines for managing salesmen. It is oriented toward the problems that the sales manager will have to face, since he is often on the firing line of his firm's marketing effort.

THE ROLE OF SELLING

Some preliminary definitions and concepts are in order. Before sales management can be examined, it is important to distinguish between marketing, promotion, and selling and to define the role of selling within the context of marketing.

Marketing Mix

Marketing is a broad term. As defined by the American Marketing Association's Committee on Definitions, *marketing* is "the performance of business activities that direct the flow of goods and services from producer to consumer or user."[1] *Marketing management* deals

---

[1]Committee on Definitions, *Marketing Definitions: A Glossary of Marketing Terms* (Chicago: American Marketing Association, 1969), p. 15.

with the planning, implementation, and control of these activities.

A convenient concept for explaining a company's marketing activities is *marketing mix,* or the combination of variables that the marketer uses to direct his goods and services to the consumer. The major components of a company's marketing mix are product, distribution, price, and promotion.

Product refers to what the company sells. All pertinent questions related to the company's goods and services must be considered in product management decisions. For example: What features should the product have? What form of packaging should be used? How many models are required? How important is quality? Should a brand or trademark be used?

Distribution is concerned with the actual movement of goods and services. In particular, where and by whom are products to be offered for sale? Sales managers are especially concerned with channels of distribution—those wholesalers, distributors, retailers, salesmen, and others who are responsible for getting goods and services ultimately to the consumer.

Price, or what the company will charge for the product, is the third element of the marketing mix. Price is the exchange value of a good or service. Economic, legal, and marketing considerations are involved in setting prices for products. The price charged must provide a fair return on the company's investment, and yet it must not exceed the buyer's financial resources.

Promotion includes advertising, personal selling, and sales promotion (including public relations and product publicity). Two prime objectives are achieved by effective promotion:

1. **Information.** Promotion is a form of communication in that it informs the public of the availability of a product or seller.
2. **Persuasion.** Promotion is persuasion; it attempts to influence people to do something, such as buy a Buick, prevent a forest fire, join the U.S. Army, or purchase a new home.

Demand Creation

The elements of the marketing mix are blended together to create a total *package* that will best satisfy the customer's needs. *Demand cre-*

4

ation, which is the prime focus of marketing in today's highly competitive marketplace, includes a company's efforts to create among consumers a preference for a given product, service, or seller. This process might more appropriately be called *demand stimulation*, since marketing is aimed, not at creating demand, but at increasing or bringing to the surface the buyer's needs.

When viewed from the economist's perspective, there are two ways a company can stimulate sales. First, sales can be increased by a *price reduction* as shown in Figure 1–1. According to the *law of demand*, quantity sold will increase as price is reduced. Figure 1–1 shows that as price is reduced from P_1 to P_2, the quantity demanded moves from Q_1 to Q_2.

FIGURE 1–1
Increasing Sales Through Price Reductions

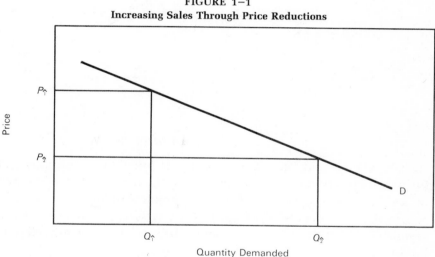

The other method of increasing sales is *nonprice competition*. The businessman attempts to shift the demand curve to the right (Figure 1–2). In other words, he hopes to increase the demand for his product so that buyers will purchase either a greater quantity (Q_2) at the same price (P_1) or the same quantity (Q_1) at a higher price (P_2).

There are many forms of nonprice competition. Efforts can be made to stimulate demand through the channels of distribution. Incentives,

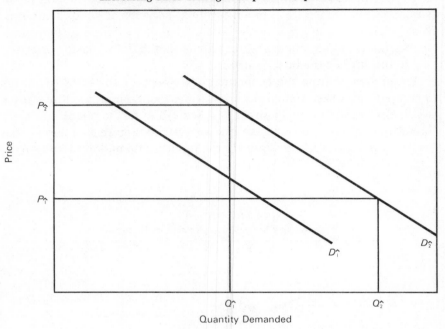

FIGURE 1–2
Increasing Sales Through Nonprice Competition

such as higher margins and special dealer promotions, are provided to encourage middlemen to push the company's products. Product or service policies can also be used. Product differentiation, packaging, and customer services are just a few of the ways in which a company will try to make its products or services more attractive to buyers.

The final form of nonprice competition is *promotion* or, in other words, a direct attempt to persuade the buyer. *Personal selling*, as the term implies, involves individual, face-to-face contacts with buyers, while *advertising* utilizes the techniques of nonpersonal, mass communication. *Sales promotion* is a general term that includes all promotion activities that supplement advertising and personal selling, such as public relations, product publicity, trading stamps, point-of-purchase displays, contests, samples, and premiums.

6

Selling and Sales Management

The primary characteristic of personal selling as a marketing tool is the face-to-face relationship. Two-way communication between buyer and seller is essential for many products. Since ideas flow directly from the buyer to a company representative, the responses of the buyer can be used immediately to modify promotion strategy.

Selling, then, is a major form of marketing communication and an important method of nonprice competition. One study found that selling was considered the most important element of marketing communication in all product markets researched (see Table 1–1). The role of personal selling in the marketing mix varies with the resources of

TABLE 1–1*
Relative Importance of
the Elements of Marketing Communications

Sales Effort Activity	Producers of		
	Industrial Goods	Consumer Durables	Consumer Nondurables
Sales Management and Personal Selling	69.2	47.6	38.1
Broadcast Media Advertising	0.9	10.7	20.9
Printed Media Advertising	12.5	16.1	14.8
Special Promotional Activities	9.6	15.5	15.5
Branding and Promotional Packaging	4.5	9.5	9.8
Other	3.3	0.6	0.9
Total	100.0	100.0	100.0

*The data are the average point allocations of 336 industrial, 52 consumer durable, and 88 consumer nondurable goods producers. Nine responses are excluded because of point allocations which did not equal 100. [Note: Firms were asked to rate the relative importance of each of the above elements in the promotional mix, using a scale of 100.]

Source: Jon G. Udell, Successful Marketing Strategies in American Marketing (Madison, Wis.: Mimir Publications, Inc., 1972), p. 47.

the company, with the dimensions of the market, with the needs of the product, and with the time period involved. Personal selling will dominate if the company has inadequate funds to carry on an effective advertising program. Also, if the market is concentrated in a particular geographical region, selling will be a more efficient promotional technique.

For many goods and services, personal selling is required to establish rapport with customers and to create confidence in the product. For example, personal selling is more vital to the sale of life insurance or computers than to the sale of toothpaste or razor blades. Personal selling dominates if the product has a relatively high price, is purchased infrequently, requires demonstration, or must be adapted to a customer's individual needs.

FIGURE 1−3
Relative Importance of Advertising and Selling

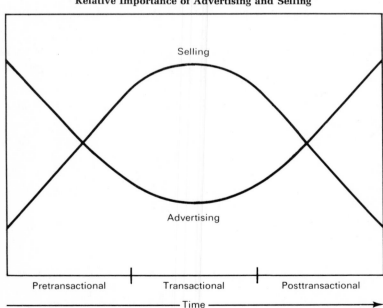

Source: Harold C. Cash and W. J. E. Crissy, "The Salesman's Role in Marketing," *The Psychology of Selling* (Flushing, N.Y.: Personal Development Associates, 1965). Reprinted by permission of Personal Development Associates (Station A, P.O. Box 36, Flushing, New York, 11358).

The importance of selling is also related to the time period involved (see Figure 1 – 3). During the *pretransactional* period (the period prior to the actual sale), advertising is usually more important than personal selling. Selling assumes primacy during the *transactional* phase since it becomes the mechanism for actually closing the sale. Advertising again becomes relatively more important during the *post-transactional* stage, as it then performs a reminder function.

Sales management, or more appropriately the management of personal selling, involves the planning, implementation, and control of the selling effort. As a starting point, management must determine the optimum role for personal selling in the marketing mix. Further, sales managers must be prepared to modify personal selling techniques and activities. Selling is only one part of the total marketing mix and must therefore be changed as advances and alterations are made in other forms of demand creation.

EVOLUTION OF SALES MANAGEMENT

Although selling has been a productive business activity since the beginning of modern civilization, formal study of selling and sales management did not begin until the early 1900s, when courses in the distributive trades were first offered.[2] It was during this period that businessmen recognized the importance of demand creation. As production facilities expanded, and as new products were introduced, conventional sales practices became inadequate. The twentieth century called for creative, dynamic approaches to selling and sales management.

Early thoughts on the management of salesmen developed along contrasting lines. One viewpoint emphasized the independence of salesmen and considered them to be almost independent businessmen, exempt from supervision. Other early authorities took an opposite stand. Rather than viewing the salesman's job as independent from his company, they suggested that a salesman's activities must be regulated by the company. Further, the belief that mastery of selling techniques leads to sales success resulted in growing demands for

---

[2]For an informative review of the history of sales management, see Robert Bartels, *The Development of Marketing Thought* (Homewood, Ill.: Richard D. Irwin, Inc., 1962).

FIGURE 1-4
The Field Sales Executive's Pivotal Position

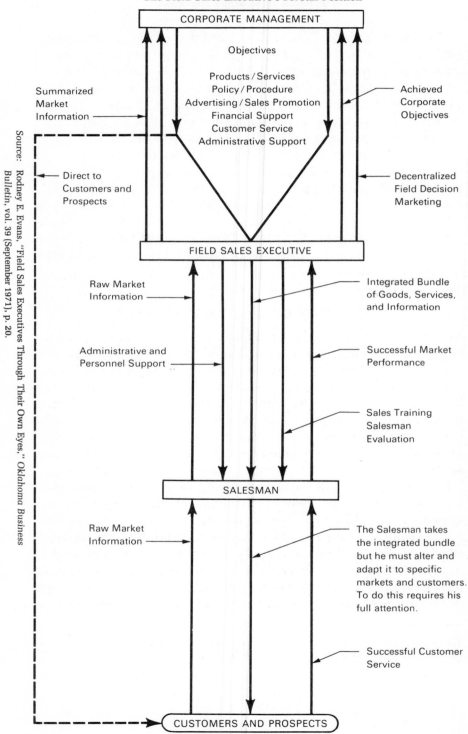

sales training. As this viewpoint was accepted, the sales manager emerged as the link between salesmen and the company.[3] Figure 1–4 demonstrates this relationship.

It should be noted that our current marketing system still contains a large component of independent salesmen. These are the various brokers, agent middlemen, and manufacturer's representatives who perform the selling function in many areas of industry. Essentially, these salesmen are independent businessmen working on a straight commission compensation plan. While this text deals primarily with company-organized field sales forces, most of the concepts and practices described are equally applicable to the independent segment of sales.

The next historical development was the recognition that personal selling is an integral part of the total marketing effort. Within this complex structure, the sales manager is essential, since he is responsible for coordinating the company's sales effort.

Since World War II, even broader interpretation has been given to sales management. Two major developments in thought are responsible.—the view of salesmen as problem solvers and the emergence of what is known as the *marketing concept*.

The Salesman as a Problem Solver

The modern view of selling portrays the salesman as more than an accomplished persuader. As a problem solver, a salesman must be able to think on his feet, in order to meet the individual needs and problems of customers. In his well-known book, *The Vanishing Salesman*, E. B. Weiss suggests that personal selling must be creative, that it must involve a great deal more than personal persuasion. Weiss argues that companies must revise their methods of hiring, training, and organizing salesmen, in order to accommodate new market conditions.[4] This changed viewpoint has substantially improved the effectiveness of today's salesmen. One survey of buyers reported that a majority (64 per cent) believed that modern salesmen are more effec-

---

[3]The sales manager's role as a linking mechanism between salesmen and corporate management has been pointed out in Rodney E. Evans, "Field Sales Executives Through Their Own Eyes," *Oklahoma Business Bulletin*, vol. 39 (September 1971), pp. 14–21.

[4]E. B. Weiss, *The Vanishing Salesman* (New York: McGraw-Hill Book Company, 1962).

tive than their counterparts of fifteen or twenty years ago.[5]

Also related to the salesman's role as problem solver is the recognition that personal selling is more than making a sale. Writing in *Fortune*, Carl Rieser comments:

> Whereas the old-time salesman devoted himself primarily to pushing a product, or a line of products, the new-era salesman is involved with the whole distribution pipeline, beginning with the tailoring of products to the customer's desire and extending through their promotion and advertising to final delivery to the ultimate consumer.[6]

With each changing view of the salesman's role, sales management has become a more vital activity.

The Marketing Concept

In the early 1950s, concepts of management changed. The General Electric *Annual Report* of 1952 described the new philosophy this way.

> The [new] concept . . . introduces the marketing man at the beginning rather than at the end of the production cycle and integrates marketing into each phase of the business. Thus, marketing, through its studies and research, will establish for the engineer, the design and manufacturing man, what the customer wants in a given product, what price he is willing to pay, and where and when it will be wanted. Marketing will have authority in product planning, production scheduling, and inventory control, as well as in sales distribution and servicing of the product.[7]

Known as the *marketing concept*, this philosophy is based on the proposition that a customer orientation should characterize all business planning and actions.

---

[5]"How Buyers Rate Salesmen," *Sales Management* (January 15, 1971), p. 21.
[6]Carl Reiser, "The Salesman Isn't Dead—He's Different," *Fortune* (November 1962), p. 124.
[7]*1952 Annual Report* (New York: General Electric Company, 1952), p. 21.

Customer orientation is the key to the marketing management concept. A sales manager must shift from an internal company perspective to the customer's viewpoint. Successful marketing requires a complete understanding of the buyer—his needs, attitudes, and buying behavior. Thus, the car salesman who knows that his customer is a family man on a tight budget will realize that a sleek sportscar does not fit this particular customer's needs.

Two examples from business history emphasize the importance of customer orientation and marketing insight. In the nineteenth century, both Obed Hussey and Cyrus McCormick invented reapers to harvest grain. McCormick's company became International Harvester, which remains today a leading producer of farm equipment. By contrast, although Hussey's machine was just as good, its inventor has faded into complete obscurity. As to why McCormick succeeded where Hussey failed, the answer is simple: McCormick was the superior businessman. He moved his factory to Chicago, close to grain country; he maintained an adequate inventory for rush orders; and he allowed farmers to pay on an installment plan related to harvest conditions. He established a fair price and stuck by it; he guaranteed his products; and he built an excellent reputation as a friend of the farmers. Although these customer-oriented practices are not unusual today, they established McCormick as the leading farm-equipment producer of his time.

The second example involves another familiar name, Isaac Singer. Although Elias Howe is given historical credit for inventing the basic sewing machine, Singer utilized the more effective marketing techniques. His company developed a consumer installment plan and a franchised agency system. Also, Singer was one of the first American businessmen to recognize the importance of international marketing. The Singer sewing machine is now known throughout the world and Singer Sewing Centers, rather than Howe Sewing Centers, exist in every major city in the United States.

Another facet of the marketing concept is *coordination*. There must be close cooperation between all components of a business. When a salesman writes a large order, for example, he must be sure that production schedules will permit the order to be filled.

The marketing concept also stresses that customer orientation is the path to *profitability*. Consequently, customer orientation is the logical focal point for profit planning.

13

THE PROCESS OF MANAGEMENT

This book is concerned with the job of the sales manager, with his skills, perceptions, responsibilities, problems, and functions. However, before we consider the sales manager's job *per se*, it is desirable to develop some basic notions about the management process in general.

Management Defined

Broadly defined, *management* is that process required to optimize the return from a particular commitment of the company's assets (technical, financial, human, and mechanical), when other possible alternative commitments exist. Information concerning the commitment is incomplete, and the conditions under which the commitment will be fulfilled are uncertain. Within the management process, there are also subprocesses, such as planning, forecasting, decision making, and evaluation; these will be considered later in some detail.

Because of the increasing use of computers, models, and sophisticated problem analysis techniques, one is tempted to conclude that the management process can be analyzed with total objectivity, as a science in which human skills, experience, and insights play no part. Such will never be the case for the following reasons:

1. The management process importantly involves people—their feelings, emotions, and prejudices. Personal reactions and behavior patterns can never be completely and scientifically forecasted or programmed.
2. In a dynamic economic system, all management must take place under conditions of uncertainty and constant change.

Thus, when the management process is viewed realistically, it is seen to include variables, both human and economic, that cannot be measured with mathematical precision. It is an *art* rather than an exact science—an art in which scientific observations and apparatus can be used nonetheless to great advantage. These observations on the management process lead to two important conclusions:

14

1. Management can be learned.
2. Management is essentially a process of getting things done through people.

Since a good deal of management involves making decisions and acting under conditions of incomplete knowledge, *learning* is an important aspect of the manager's job. This learning takes two forms: *formal* learning, from sources like this book, and on-the-job learning from *experience*. In the formal learning of management, the manager explores the condensed experiences, knowledge, and research findings of a number of other managers and teachers of management, in order to profit from their observations and conclusions. Learning from experience is a continuing process by which the manager seeks to make his own experiences teach him something more about himself and his management job.

In only the very smallest companies is it possible for the manager to do everything himself. In fact, studies show that this is precisely the major cause of failure in small business—lack of *management depth*. To be effective and to succeed, *the manager must magnify himself through his people by delegating authority and responsibility to the lowest possible level* and by involving his subordinates as deeply as possible in the operations of the enterprise.

THE JOB OF THE SALES MANAGER

The sales manager's duties and responsibilities can be summarized into four major categories, as shown in Table 1–2.

Table 1–3 shows how field sales executives allocate their work week. Unfortunately, too many sales managers must focus their time on *present-oriented* tasks, such as selling to personal accounts, and disregard *future-oriented* activities, such as planning.[8] However, effective sales management should be future oriented if it is to achieve optimal results.

All of the duties and responsibilities outlined in Table 1–3 are discussed in another section of this book. However, several observations

[8]This has been pointed out in the previously cited study by Evans (1971), pp. 14–21.

15

TABLE 1–2
The Sales Manager's Duties and Responsibilities

To Plan for the immediate situation and for the long run:
1. establish specific objectives to be obtained and set up policies, procedures, and plans to attain these
2. transmit objectives, policies, procedures, and plans to subordinate sales supervisors and salesmen

To Organize the sales force to achieve the objectives:
1. break down the whole selling job into operational parts (jobs)
2. create specific job descriptions for these parts
3. recruit and select personnel for these jobs

To Oversee the performance of the sales force and to *improve* its operation:
1. issue the necessary orders and directions
2. motivate salesmen for high performance
3. train men for better selling performance
4. communicate information about sales and market conditions to general marketing management

To Evaluate sales performance:
1. create performance standards and measurements
2. collect and analyze performance information in comparison with standards
3. take indicated remedial action

TABLE 1–3
Activities Ranked by Field Sales Executives
According to the Average Weekly Time Consumed

MARKETING (18.1 per cent)[2]

A. Reviewing competitive activity
*B. Communicating corporate information to salesmen
*C. Analyzing sales data
D. Participating in the formulation of overall marketing policy
*E. Digesting information received from management
F. Advising on changes in price, delivery arrangements, products or on new product development
G. Summarizing sales and customer information for communication to management.
H. Managing advertising and/or other nonselling promotional activities

16

  I. Forecasting future sales in your district
  J. Reviewing district sales coverage and salesmen's territory alignment

SELLING (36.6 per cent)

*A. Personal selling to your own accounts
*B. Handling problem accounts
  C. Expediting customer orders
*D. Making sales calls with your salesmen
  E. Deciding on a customer's request for special terms of sale

FINANCIAL (7.4 per cent)

*A. Analyzing selling expense data
  B. Controlling inventory and warehousing costs
  C. Preparing budgets
  D. Controlling costs of branch office operation
  E. Advising on the need for additional capital expenditure in your district
  F. Watching the trend of costs expanded in relation to profits generated in
      your district

PERSONNEL (20.4 per cent)

*A. Training salesmen
*B. Establishing standards of salesman performance
  C. Recruiting and selecting new salesmen
  D. Planning and holding sales meetings
  E. Handling problem salesmen
  F. Forecasting future personnel needs in your district
  G. Advising salesmen on personal problems
  H. Reviewing compensation programs for salesmen
  I. Revising man specifications required for the sales position

ADMINISTRATIVE (18.2 per cent)

*A. Managing the field office
  B. Keeping records
  C. Working with dissatisfied customers
*D. Writing reports on various aspects of district operations

---

*Activities to which the greatest amount of time is devoted
[1]These activities are listed in the same words and order in which the respondents saw them.
[2]Numbers in parentheses are percentages of the average work week spent on that functional group.

Source: Evans (1971), p. 16.

about the sales manager's job should be made here, as groundwork for the more detailed considerations in the chapters to follow.

Services and Sales Management

An economic development of special interest to sales management has been the shift to increased spending for services. Consumer services — ranging from necessities such as electric power and medical care to luxuries such as foreign travel and extravagant beauty treatments — now account for two-fifths of the average consumer's spending. In addition, the increasing complexity of modern business has created almost unlimited growth opportunities for business service firms like Arthur Andersen and Company (certified public accountants), A. C. Nielsen (market research), and Brinks, Inc. (protection). For most consumer and business services, personal selling is a major element of the marketing mix.

Intangibility is the major difference between goods and services, and many authorities feel that selling intangibles is more difficult than selling tangible goods. Since the service salesman cannot rely on tangible product features to make a sale, he must use other techniques to make intangible values seem real to the buyer. Perishability and the lack of standardization also contribute to the difficulty of selling services. Unless the service is very simple or highly standardized, the salesman will be required to play a dominant role in the marketing process.

In general, the differences between goods and services affect the means by which the sales management process is performed rather than the process itself. The sales manager's duties and responsibilities (Table 1–2) are similar for service selling. However, the increased importance of personal selling places more pressure on the sales manager. Great care must be exercised to select, develop, and stimulate creative, imaginative service salesmen. There is little room for unimaginative selling and sales management in service marketing.

Sales Management as an Integrated, Interrelated Process

Later chapters will discuss the individual subelements of the sales manager's job — the recruiting and selection of salesmen, their compensation, motivation, evaluation, and supervision. These areas can be usefully considered as *subsystems* within the *total sales management process*, such as the recruitment and selection *system*, the training *system*, and the evaluation *system*. In regard to these subsystems, two important observations can be made:

1. Each is interrelated with, and dependent upon, the others and affects their efficiency and effectiveness.
2. Each must contribute its part to the attainment of the goals of the total selling program.

Consider these actual examples: (1) A small chain of garden supply retail stores had an excellent recruitment and selection program; however, personal supervision of the clerks was virtually nonexistent. The result was a poor total selling program. (2) A small mill supply firm had excellent personal supervision of its outside salesmen, but a very unsatisfactory compensation plan. The result was an ineffective selling program.

What the good sales manager is managing, and what is being examined here, is a total, integrated, interactive system, each part of which contributes to the common goals of the sales group.

Uniqueness of the Sales Manager's Job

In most companies, the sales manager's job differs in important ways from the jobs of other managers. The sales manager spends much of his time in the field (some studies indicate as much as 60 percent of his working time); although he can only see his subordinate salesmen infrequently, he is responsible for their performance. He regularly entertains customers; he regularly works evenings and weekends. Customers hold him responsible for delivery failures and for other problems over which he has no direct control. He is the first-line (or initial level) of supervision that links his company to its outside environment, since he and his men represent the company to customers, to competitors, and to the general public with whom they come in contact. He is responsible for coordinating the personal selling efforts

19

of his salesmen with advertising, publicity, and sales promotion — in short, with all of the efforts his company may undertake to promote sales. He must also coordinate the activities of his salesmen with other functional specialties in the company, such as warehousing, personnel, delivery, and credit. Finally, he must coordinate all of his own efforts and those of his salesmen with the common company goals. It is little wonder, then, that the sales manager often becomes the kind of target illustrated in Figure 1−5.

Other managers in the company do not usually work under these stringent conditions or under the pressures that they generate. The sales manager's job is indeed unique and difficult.

Despite these diverse responsibilities, sales management is an extremely attractive career path. Sales managers are typically among the highest paid executives in any company. Their positions usually carry generous fringe benefit packages, which are at least equal to those of other functional managers at the same organizational level. However, the most important benefit of a sales management career is probably the opportunity for advancement to higher executive positions. Studies have shown that sales managers are prime candidates for such upward moves.

The starting point for a sales management career is usually a selling position in the field. Then, the salesman typically works through a series of sales management positions — such as sales supervisor, dis-

FIGURE 1−5.

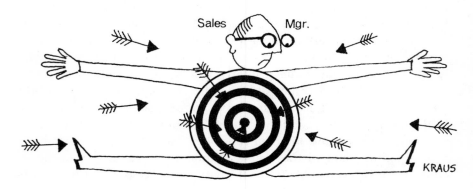

trict sales manager, regional sales manager, and zone sales manager — to top sales management. The road is rough, since young sales managers are called upon to prove their effectiveness and qualifications at nearly every turn. For those who succeed, however, the rewards — both financial and personal — are plentiful.

Planning as a Critical Sales Management Responsibility

Simply defined, *planning* is nothing more or less than the systematic process by which a person decides *what* in the present will be done in the future and *how* it will be done. There is something about planning that encourages most people to neglect it, to put it aside for another day (a day which rarely ever comes). Perhaps this stalling occurs because planning forces people to question their assumptions, to look into the future, and to make firm decisions — all difficult to do — and because everyone knows from experience that no plan works out perfectly in practice! But whatever the reasons, people tend to neglect planning, and for the sales manager such an omission can be disastrous.

The sales manager must plan for the maximum allocation of all of the resources that have been put at his disposal: his time and that of his men, company money, advertising and sales promotion aids. He must plan in order to be well prepared for future market changes, in order to respond quickly and effectively to competitive moves, and in order to coordinate the work of his sales group with other company activities. Regardless of his organizational level, planning is a prime responsibility of the sales manager.

Sales Management as Part of the Total Marketing Effort

It is vital to remember that the sales program does not operate independently of the rest of the company. It has responsibilities to other corporate units, and it draws support from these units.

All organizations have two primary functions that must be performed, which are often called the *line* functions of the organization. Every organization must *produce* a product or service, and it must then *sell* it. This is true regardless of whether the organization is a business firm, a hospital, a professional football team, or the U.S. Postal Service.

21

Selling is the line aspect of the total marketing function, which also includes such supporting, or *staff*, departments as marketing research, advertising, dealer relations, and customer service. The sales force must then interface with other marketers in the parent organizations. Coordination is necessary if the salesman is to do an effective job in the field.

Sales personnel must also interact with persons in other functional areas within the company. They must discuss production schedules with those responsible for this activity, design problems with engineers, delivery schedules with the transportation and shipping departments, credit terms with the accounting staff, and sales force vacancies with the personnel department. Salesmen and sales managers cannot operate in a vacuum. Their success is closely tied to that of other elements in the parent organization.

Unfortunately, too many sales personnel do little to nurture and develop effective working relationships with other marketers and with other functions in their company.[9] One explanation for this failure is the normal rivalry between different departments or divisions, which results when each person tries to do his job as efficiently as possible. Another reason is the physical distance that often exists between the field sales force and the parent organization. But, regardless of the cause, effective coordination between sales and other organizational elements is an absolute necessity if overall company goals are to be achieved.

A FINAL WORD ABOUT THE STUDY OF SALES MANAGEMENT

The principles, observations, research findings, and business experience on which this book is based can be universally adapted. They are applicable to selling products as well as to selling services. They can be adapted to meet the needs of industrial, commercial, and consumer customers, of government buyers, and of the import and export trade. They can be utilized for large and small selling organizations, which sell directly or through middlemen, and which handle inexpensive or big-ticket items.

---

[9]See, for example, Robert J. Boewadt, "The Inside Salesmen's Revolt," *Sales Management* (February 1, 1971), pp. 19–20.

The principles themselves are *universal*, but their adaption to a particular industry, company, product line, sales force size, price structure, or channel of distribution must rest with each company or sales group. As with every form of learning, the learner must assimilate what is being taught and then adapt it to his own particular situation and problems. For example, one could teach the Law of Gravity, what it is and how it works. But it would be up to the learner to understand how the Law of Gravity applied specifically to the production of petroleum products or, in quite a different way, to the manufacture of aircraft frames. Similarly, although the principles of sales management are universal, their application varies. A company that specializes in the door-to-door sale of cosmetics will adapt these principles in one way, while a company that sells atomic power generation equipment to public utilities will modify the same principles in quite a different fashion.

Each student who utilizes the sales management principles in this book must apply them to himself and to the varying selling situations that face him in this most dynamic of all business functions. The remainder of Part I will discuss the sales management process, its development and the constraints in which it now operates. Specifically, Chapter 2 will consider the historical development of professional sales forces, Chapter 3 ·the environmental influences on selling, and Chapter 4 the actual functioning of the personal selling process.

SUMMARY This chapter has presented an overview of the sales management process. Basic definitions and concepts — such as marketing, marketing mix, marketing management, product, distribution, price, and promotion — were described. *Personal selling* was defined, and it was considered as one aspect within a promotional package that also includes advertising and sales promotion. All parts of the promotional effort are designed to achieve two basic objectives: (1) to provide information about the availability of a product or seller, and (2) to persuade someone to do something, such as buy a particular product. Selling was also described as an important aspect of marketing communication and contrasted to advertising at different stages of the sales transaction.

The era following World War II has seen two developments in business thought that have greatly influenced the sales management process. The first was the concept of salesmen as problem solvers, and the second was the emergence of the marketing concept. The importance of these factors to sales management has been detailed in Chapter 1.

The duties and responsibilities of sales management were also discussed, and they were categorized into four principle groups: to plan, to organize, to oversee, and to evaluate.

The final section of this chapter dealt with
——sales management as an integrated, interrelated process,
——the uniqueness of the sales manager's job,
——the importance of planning the relation of sales management to other functional areas in the business organization, and
——general comments about the study of sales management.

These sections will provide the necessary perspective for enlightened reading of later chapters.

DISCUSSION/REVIEW QUESTIONS

1. Consider a sales manager you know. Is his job about the same or different from the jobs of other managers in his company?
2. What should be the role of personal selling in the marketing mixes of the following companies?
   (a) a major producer of household cleaning products,
   (b) a manufacturer of expensive machine tools,
   (c) a local travel agency,
   (d) an automobile insurance company.
3. "Sales planning is too expensive—both in terms of money and time. And everyone knows that business plans usually end up missing the mark. Hence, no effective sales manager should spend very much time on this wasteful activity." Comment on this statement.
4. Differentiate between marketing, promotion, and selling.
5. List and compare the elements of the marketing mix.

6. Show in what specific ways the sales manager's job differs from the job of other managers in his company.
7. How can a company stimulate sales? Discuss.
8. Trace the historical evolution of sales management.
9. The field sales manager has been described as a "linking mechanism" in the sales organization. Explain.
10. Is management an art or a science? Discuss.
11. Identify the various subsystems of the total sales management process.
12. Identify and briefly explain the following:
    a. marketing
    b. marketing management
    c. marketing mix
    d. product
    e. distribution
    f. price
    g. promotion
    h. personal selling
    i. advertising
    j. sales promotion
    k. sales management
    1. marketing concept
    m. management

CHAPTER TWO
THE HISTORICAL
DEVELOPMENT OF
PROFESSIONAL
SALES FORCES*

History is one of man's greatest teachers. By studying what has happened in the past, one can begin to understand the changes occurring in a contemporary environment. Commercial history is no exception to this basic generalization. Many current business practices can be explained in terms of evolutionary processes that have been under way for decades, and even centuries. One of the clearest examples of this is the increased professionalization of the modern sales force. This chapter will provide a historical perspective for the study of personal selling and sales management. It will outline the growth and development of the professional sales force, from earliest times to the current era.

EARLIEST TIMES

The sales function has always been an integral part of commercial activity. As Robert Bartels has pointed out in *The Development of Marketing Thought:*

> Historical accounts of trade lead one to conclude that marketing has always existed. More than six thousand years of recorded his-

---

*This chapter is based on article by one of the present authors. See David L. Kurtz, "The Historical Development of Professional Selling," *Business and Economic Dimensions*, vol. 6 (August 1970), pp. 12–18.

tory shows the roots of both Western and Eastern civilization to have included various forms of trade.[1]

Such marketing activity was the natural outgrowth of production surpluses. Man left the subsistence stage by adopting the techniques of work specialization, whereby each person concentrated on the activity in which he was most efficient. This created a surplus of goods which necessitated the process of exchange. Wroe Alderson, the marketing theorist, has stated that "it seems altogether reasonable to describe the development of exchange as a great invention which helped to start primitive man on the road to civilization."[2] Few marketers would disagree with this contention.

However, trading was not highly regarded in ancient societies. Agricultural pursuits were held in highest esteem, since it was believed that all value originated from the land. Even the nascent manufacturing sector ranked higher than trading, which was regarded as basically an immoral activity. In *The Republic*, Plato describes the salesmen of his day in particularly unflattering terms:

> Suppose now, that a husbandman, or an artisan, brings some production to market, and he comes at a time when there is no one to exchange with him – is he to leave his calling and sit idle in the market place?
>
> Not at all; he will find people there who, seeing the want, undertake the office of salesman. In well-ordered States, they are commonly those who are the weakest in bodily strength, and therefore of little use for any other purposes. . . .[3]

While trading started the evolutionary development of the marketing system, one must be careful in characterizing correctly these ancient traders and the functions they performed. The early traders usu-

---

[1]Robert Bartels, *The Development of Marketing Thought* (Homewood, Ill.: Richard D. Irwin, Inc., 1962), p. 4.

[2]Wroe Alderson, *Marketing Behavior and Executive Action* (Homewood, Ill.: Richard D. Irwin, Inc., 1957), p. 292.

[3]Plato, *The Republic*, Book II (New York: Charles Scribner's Sons, 1928), p. 67.

ally purchased their goods in one area and then resold them in another geographical location. Since the chief marketing function that they performed was one of *physical distribution* (in which personal selling was only an incidental activity), these traders could actually be considered predecessors of today's merchant wholesalers. In other cases, they (or their immediate families) actually produced the goods which were offered for sale. There was no significant separation of the production and marketing functions. For these reasons, *the early traders cannot legitimately be classified as true sales personalities.* The marketing system characterized by these traders existed for many centuries, and it was not until seventh-century England that further significant developments occurred in the history of personal selling.

THE DEVELOPMENT OF SALESMANSHIP IN ENGLAND, 600–1775

Business historians often use the term *town economy* to describe the economic organization of medieval society. Most commercial activities were centered around the various population centers, because the existing political and social organization was quite fragmented, and because adequate means of transportation were nonexistent. This required that economic activity be organized primarily on a local level. Each town (along with its surrounding trade area) became what was essentially a self-sufficient economic system. At the core of this system was the local marketplace, where goods were exchanged primarily on a barter basis. Traditionally, a specific day of the week was set aside as market day. An inadequate road network, however, prevented many farmers from bringing their produce to the central market. This led to an emergence of an important marketing intermediary: the *agricultural middleman*. This early businessman purchased staple farm products in the countryside and transported them to the town market for resale. The agricultural middleman was significant to sales history because he symbolized the final separation of personal selling from production.

Another noteworthy marketer who emerged at approximately the same time was the *chapman*, who dealt primarily in specialty goods which were secured from importers who were sometimes called

29

commercial adventurers. The chapman then sold his newly acquired wares on a door-to-door basis. It should be noted that his supplier— the commercial adventurer—was quite often a pirate on the high seas, who became a respectable businessman only when it was time to sell his booty.

Britain, along with the rest of Europe, continued to be characterized by a fragmented and localized economic organization for some time. Gradually, however, the chaotic conditions were replaced by a more stable business environment, one that was dominated by guilds (circa 1200–1500).[4] This system provided the background from which the first industrialized society was to emerge.

The first true salesman appeared in the late eighteenth century, at the time of the Industrial Revolution in England. These first salesmen, called bagmen, were instrumental in the economic growth of the period, since they successfully marketed the goods produced by the developing factory system. Probably the first manufacturers to establish such a sales force were the Manchester (England) textile firms. As a result, the term Manchester man was often used interchangeably with bagman.

The bagmen were the first real salesmen, since they were charged with performing the sales function by firms in which they typically did not have an ownership interest. This is the origin of professional selling as we know it today. It is interesting to note that the term bagman was derived from the fact that these salesmen were the first to sell from bags of samples. While this point is often overlooked, it is significant because it indicates a marked change in consumer attitudes. Customers no longer insisted upon personal inspection of the goods, which had been common practice in earlier times. This change also implies that much of the historical criticism of sales ethics was really directed at the quality of the available merchandise rather than at deceptive sales practices.

THE AMERICAN EXPERIENCE, 1650–1900

The historical development of personal selling in the United States can be traced in Figure 2–1. As this diagram shows, American sales-

---

[4]An excellent discussion of the guilds is contained in William T. Kelly, "The Development of Early Thought in Marketing and Promotion," Journal of Marketing, vol. 21 (July 1956), pp. 62–69.

manship began with the early exploits of the *Yankee peddler*, sometime during the late seventeenth century. These salesmen — often called *pack peddlers* — were traditionally based in New England. One popular description of the origin of these peddlers states that:

> Like baked beans on Saturday night and pie for breakfast, the Yankee peddler undoubtedly has his origin in staid old Boston in the late seventeenth century; at least the city fathers have never successfully denied it.[5]

As America's population began to shift, prior to the Revolutionary War, Connecticut seems to have become the home state for these peddlers. In fact, "Connecticut is still called 'the nutmeg state' because so many of these Yankee peddlers sold wooden nutmegs to unsuspecting housewifes in place of the real article."[6]

These itinerant peddlers sold their wares to the settlers of the hinterland. Wherever our pioneers went, the peddler soon followed. At first, upstate New York and parts of New Jersey were considered fertile sales territories but, as competition increased, many Yankee Peddlers moved on to the West and to the South. By the time of the Revolutionary War, they were operating in the Mississippi River Valley.

These pack peddlers originated from several sources. In some instances, they were young men who were seeking the adventure of travel to distant places and who frequently came from relatively wealthy families. In other cases, the pack peddlers were indentured servants who had fulfilled their contractual servitude. Perhaps the most important group, however, were the immigrants. In the final stages of this era of American salesmanship, immigrant peddlers substantially outnumbered the native born. As a result, the composition of the colonial sales force typically consisted of the latest ethnic wave of immigrants. As each new ethnic group entered the labor force, the earlier peddlers gravitated to more permanent occupations.

Sometime after about 1810, a dichotomy developed in personal selling. Some of the pack peddlers modified their selling methods, by switching to the use of horse-drawn wagons capable of carrying sever-

---

[5]From *The Yankee Peddlers of Early America* by J. R. Dolan. © 1964 by J. R. Dolan (p. 15).
[6]From *Textbook of Salesmanship* by Frederick A. Russell and Frank Herman Beech. © 1941 (p. 36).

FIGURE 2−1
The History of American Salesmanship

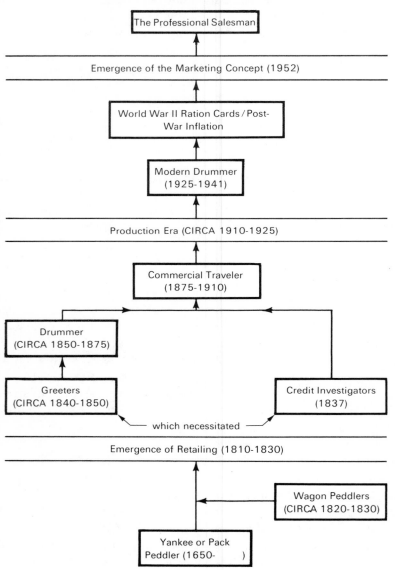

al tons of merchandise. It was common practice for these salesmen, now called *wagon peddlers*, to leave home in the early spring, to work their territory, and then to return by late summer. The wagon peddler was a well-known character on the American scene throughout the nineteenth century. In fact, they can legitimately be traced into the late 1920s, when the *cart peddler* made his final appearance on the streets of major cities.

The other branch of the early peddlers became our first *retailers*, as is shown in Figure 2-1. One of the primary causes of this transition was the increased use of strict local licensing requirements for peddlers. Retail stores, as we know them, did not exist until the early nineteenth century. Prior to this, the retail function was performed via small shops operated by local craftsmen, such as silversmiths.

The growth of retailing was a causal factor in the next era of personal selling. The country stores of the early nineteenth century were typically granted liberal credit terms by their suppliers. The financial panic of 1837, however, caused a tightening of credit. As a result, the suppliers began to send out *credit investigators* who, in addition to evaluating a retailer's credit rating and performing the collection function, were charged with developing good will. In time, these men began to actually sell merchandise to the rural stores: "As credit problems diminished and as the realization of the possibilities of this type of selling grew, more and more credit investigators became salesmen."[7] Later, the term *commercial travelers* was used synonymously with *credit investigators*.

These representatives, however, could not supply all of the needs of our developing retail system. Therefore, it was customary for the store owners to make a pilgrimage at least once a year to the nearest large city to purchase merchandise for their stores.[8] These buying trips led to the development of America's best known salesmen—the *greeters* or *drummers*. Much of the historical prejudice directed against salesmen resulted from the sales techniques employed by these individuals. Their often unethical tactics helped to form the basis for much of the traditional antagonism toward *high pressure* sales presentations.

The term *greeter* originally developed because these salesmen

---

[7]Alfred Gross, *Salesmanship*, 2d ed. (New York: The Ronald Press Company, 1959), p. 554.

[8]Examples of such wholesale centers included Boston, Chicago, New York, Philadelphia, and St. Louis.

would meet the visiting retailers at their hotels to solicit business for the various supply houses. Although they later shifted their base of operations to the railroad stationhouses, the greeters remained a permanent fixture in trading centers of the day. Unfortunately, keen competition and the wide use of a straight commission system of compensation induced them to resort to some rather dubious sales practices.

As competition continued to increase, some enterprising greeters adopted the custom of boarding the trains outside the city, in order to make sales presentations before the competition had an opportunity to lure away the prospective buyers. Eventually, the greeters simply journeyed to a merchant's place of business. At this point, the term *drummer* began to replace *greeter* in America's sales vocabulary.

The literature suggests two possible derivations of the term *drummer*. According to the first, it comes from the fact that these men *drummed up trade* for the manufacturers and wholesalers. The second explanation suggests that the term was derived from the large trunks carried by these salesmen. These trunks — often weighing several hundred pounds — were used to transport the salesman's samples as well as his personal items, during the long journeys which often lasted several weeks or months. The round shape of these trunks caused them to be labeled *drums*. Because the drums were closely associated with the traveling salesman of the period, this seems to be a plausible explanation for the evolution of the term *drummers*.

Admittedly, the public's attitude toward the drummers always bordered on suspicion, or outright distrust. The nineteenth-century drummer was characterized by a flamboyant manner and boisterous behavior, and his reputation was the basis of some of today's humor about "traveling salesmen." However, the drummers and their predecessors — the early peddlers — were not entirely despicable characters. Their sales methods were considered appropriate at that stage of the development of our business system. In fact, a comparison of their methods with those of their contemporaries in manufacturing, retailing, and finance suggests that the salesman receives relatively high grades in terms of ethical standards. Many of these early salesmen went on to become prominent figures in business and public life. Marshall Field, Aaron Montgomery Ward, and King C. Gillette all had their start as peddlers or drummers.

Major Contributions of Early American Salesmen

The major contributions of the first two hundred and fifty years of American salesmanship (1650–1900) can be outlined as follows:

1. The early salesman was an important factor in improving the nation's standard of living, since the goods which he sold were otherwise unavailable to the bulk of the citizenry located away from the principal urban centers. A relatively efficient sales function also allowed the rapid expansion of the country's newly developing manufacturing sector. Alexander Hamilton, for example, recognized the important role of the early salesmen, when he requested in 1791 that Congress investigate the way England had spread "her factories and agents (Salesmen) over the four quarters of the globe."[9]
2. The sales function served as a vehicle for upward economic and social mobility. This was certainly true in the seventeenth and eighteenth centuries, and particularly for thousands of immigrants. Peddling provided the opportunity for an individual to improve his economic position in society.
3. A closely related contribution is that selling served as a rigorous training ground for future entrepreneurs. Peddling was dominated by young men who later moved to other types of business careers. It is interesting to point out that many of today's top marketing executives continue to regard sales as the best available management development program.
4. The Yankee peddler performed another essential function on the nation's frontier: he was the only source of information concerning important news events. The peddlers were also well known as story-tellers, which was one of the most popular forms of entertainment of the era, and originated much of American folklore. Later, the drummer performed similar functions for rural America.

THE AMERICAN EXPERIENCE SINCE 1900

The drummers did not disappear at the turn of the century; many existed until the late 1920s. Personal selling, however, changed during

---

[9]See Donald Robinson, *The Salesman: Ambassador of Progress* (New York: Sales and Marketing Executives—International, 1967), p. 4.

the twentieth century. This was the era of tremendous growth in heavy manufacturing, and much of the emphasis in business was concentrated in producing the product rather than marketing it. Perhaps the most characteristic development of the *Production Era* was Frederick W. Taylor's introduction of the concept of *scientific management* (1911). Taylor's philosophy was widely acclaimed, and its popularity resulted in a reduced emphasis on marketing in general, and on personal selling in particular. This is not to say, however, that Taylorism was totally ignored in sales. In fact, the original approach to sales management and sales organization was based on Taylor's work.[10]

The Production Era probably reached its apex with the introduction of mass assembly techniques by Henry Ford. Ford's attitude toward marketing, which was typical of industry at that time, was reflected in his widely quoted remark about the purchasers of his automobile: "They can have any color they want as long as it is black." Production management reigned supreme, and selling was regarded merely as an auxiliary (although necessary) business function.

The success of the new manufacturing methods eventually led to production surpluses and, in some degree, to a buyer's market in the late 1920s. The net result was a re-emergence of the sales function and the beginning of a stage that might be called the *Era of the Modern Drummer*. Sales practices had changed very little since those of the drummer of the 1880s, and *canned* (or memorized) presentations — originally developed by John H. Patterson of National Cash Register[11] — became very much in fashion. While the selling process had lain dormant throughout the Production Era, the *modern drummer* became characteristic of selling until the beginning of World War II. The war years, of course, forced selling efforts to take a back seat to government ration cards.

Two significant events took place during the years before World War II (1925 – 1941). First, the *Great Depression* of the 1930s shook the very core of the American free enterprise system. During this economic catastrophe, the sales function assumed a more aggressive posture. Management seems to have favored expanding, or at least main-

---

[10]Bartels (1962), p. 93.
[11]An interesting account of Patterson's career appeared in C. Westenboker, "Patterson's Marvelous Money Box," *Saturday Evening Post* (September 19, 1953), p. 28.

taining, the sales effort during a time when *cost cutting* and *layoffs* were the bywords in the other functional areas of industry. For example, government figures "show that more salesmen were employed twelve-months-a-year during the depression of the 1930's than were people in any other line of endeavor."[12] This was a significant development in the growth of professional salesmanship because it marked a milestone in management's acknowledgement of the inherent necessity to successfully market a product.

The second event was the *creation of the various marketing staff departments*, such as marketing research and sales promotion, which developed rapidly in this period. Industry came to accept the need for staff support of their sales function. Previously, many of these marketing service activities were performed by sales personnel who had no interest and/or ability in the area. The recognition of this problem was crucial in the development of professional sales forces.

By about 1947–1948, a state of economic normalcy had returned. This was the environment in which sales professionalism developed. The public had spent the excess liquidity built up from 1941–1945, and the inflation of the immediate postwar era had begun to subside. This was the beginning of the *Modern Sales Era*—the time of the truly *professional salesman*. This era cannot be disassociated from the emergence of the marketing concept, which can be described as an emphasis on *a company-wide consumer orientation to achieve long-run profit objectives*. The development of the marketing concept led to a major organizational change, in which all marketing functions were centralized under a director of marketing.[13] Sales, of course, remained the only line function within the marketing organization, but now the service functions were coordinated to an extent which had not previously existed. The formation of technically qualified sales support departments aided in the professionalization of the field sales force. There is little doubt that the nature of salesmanship has changed significantly in recent years. Salesmen have become more professional, and they have become more customer-oriented in line with the tenets of the marketing concept.

---

[12]Robinson (1967), p. 10.

[13]The term *director of marketing* is used here to refer to the top marketing executive. A synonymous title would be *vice-president for marketing*.

FUTURE OUTLOOK

While lacking such things as an established code of ethics, sales has certainly become professionalized to the extent that the emphasis is now on *helping the customer to buy, rather than attempting to sell him something.* It remains for us to consider the future outlook for personal selling in regard to this trend. Will professionalization continue to increase or will certain factors reverse this trend?

Admittedly, there are several existing factors which tend to retard professionalization, such as the relatively poor historical image of salesmen and the lack of formalized educational requirements. On balance, however, an impartial assessment would suggest that the trend toward professionalization will continue into the foreseeable future. *The real question concerns the rapidity of its development.* On this score, it would seem that the facts argue for accelerated movement. The sales function should become increasingly professionalized, as *marginal sales activities* — which account for a large portion of the techniques and methods tending to retard professionalization — are forced out by escalating selling costs. A legitimate argument can be made that competitive pressures have caused unacceptable practices to be used by certain sales types. Rising costs, however, will eventually reduce these marginal sales activities.

Other factors which would suggest an acceleration of professional selling can be summarized as follows:

1. *Continuation of a Buyer's Market.* Unless a sudden shift in the economy occurs, it seems reasonable to suppose that a buyer's market will continue. This will necessitate an emphasis on the sales function.
2. *Increased Sophistication of Buyers.* This results primarily from expanded efforts in the area of consumer education. The net result should be a rejection of the *modern drummer* in the marketplace.
3. *Further Professionalization of Purchasing Management.* It is doubtful that any other occupational group has done more to improve its status in recent years. This trend has affected as well the sales personnel who deal with the modern purchasing agent.

38

4. *Wider Adoption of the Marketing Concept.* A firm's acceptance of the premises the marketing concept requires that the field sales force update its policies, procedures, and practices.

The history of personal selling is crucial to understanding contemporary developments in the field. Today's rapid movement toward a professionalized sales force can be traced to earlier decades, when this part of the business organization was regarded primarily as a peripheral activity to be performed after "the better mousetrap" had been built.

SUMMARY Marketing activity is a function of the exchange process. Man left the subsistence stage by adopting the techniques of work specialization, and this then necessitated the exchange process and marketing.

Early marketing was dominated by traders whose primary function was that of physical distribution; personal selling was only incidental. In some cases, the traders (or their immediate families) actually produced the goods which were offered for sale. There was no significant separation of the production and marketing functions.

A later era (600–1775) saw the emergence of three sales functions in England. The agricultural middleman purchased staple farm products in the countryside and then transported them to the town for resale. The chapman purchased speciality goods from importers and resold the items on a door-to-door basis. The first true salesmen—the bagmen—appeared at the time of the Industrial Revolution in England. These representatives sold for firms in which they typically did not have an ownership interest. The bagmen were instrumental in the economic growth of the period since they successfully marketed the output of the developing factory system.

The first American sales personality was the Yankee peddler, or pack peddler, who spread the infant marketing system to the farthest reaches of the frontier. Later, the pack peddlers were replaced by retailers and by wagon peddlers. The financial panic of 1837 caused many suppliers to send credit investigators into the field. When the credit problem was alleviated, these employees became field salesmen.

The greeters were nineteenth-century salesmen who serviced retailers during their annual buying trips. Eventually, these salesmen began calling upon the retailers at their stores. At this point, the term *drummer* replaced *greeter* in the marketing vocabulary. The selling strategies and practices of the drummers existed well into the twentieth century. Modern professional sales forces did not emerge until after World War II.

Chapter 2 concludes by predicting that the trend toward the professionalization of the sales function will continue. Several factors for the acceleration of this trend are:

1. reduction of marginal sales activities;
2. continuation of a buyer's market;
3. increased sophistication of buyers;
4. further professionalization of purchasing management;
5. wide adoption of the marketing concept.

DISCUSSION/REVIEW QUESTIONS

1. Briefly identify each of the following:
   - (a) town economy
   - (b) agricultural middleman
   - (c) chapman
   - (d) commercial adventurer
   - (e) bagmen
   - (f) Yankee peddler
   - (h) wagon peddler
   - (i) credit investigator
   - (j) greeters
   - (k) drummers
   - (l) Production Era
   - (m) scientific management
   - (n) Era of the Modern Drummer
   - (o) Modern Sales Era
2. Why were early marketers held in low regard by ancient societies? Discuss.
3. Distinguish the early traders from the salesmen who emerged after the Industrial Revolution.

4. Why did the bagman's use of sample merchandise indicate a significant change in consumer attitudes?
5. Describe the origin of the pack peddler.
6. Describe the role of the greeter/drummer in the history of American salesmanship.
7. List the major contributions of American salesmanship prior to 1900.
8. Two significant events took place during the Era of the Modern Drummer: (1) the Great Depression and (2) the emergence of marketing staff departments. Illustrate how these events influenced the development of professional sales forces.
9. Trace the factors that will affect the future outlook for professional selling.
10. "The study of sales history can help one understand the changes occurring in the contempory selling environment." Do you agree with this statement? Why? Why not?
11. Contrast selling ethics in the various eras discussed in this chapter.

CHAPTER THREE
THE ENVIRONMENT
OF SELLING

A sales manager must learn to be effective in the dynamic environment of selling. Arthur M. Weimer, former Dean of Indiana University's School of Business, compares the influence of the environment on a manager to the influences of weather on an airplane pilot.[1] Before he takes off, a pilot checks the weather conditions and plans his flight accordingly. He may, for example, decide to detour around a thunderstorm. When severe weather conditions persist, he may even be forced to postpone or cancel the flight.

Just as the weather influences a pilot's flight plans, the environment affects the sales manager's decisions. However, a sales manager has more options than a pilot, who must always adapt his own plans to the conditions of the weather. A sales manager can choose one of three options — he can adapt his operations to the environment, he can move contrary to established trends, or he can attempt to change the environment.

Adaptation.   The easiest and safest course of action is to try to adapt sales plans to changes in environmental conditions. Many examples of this strategy can be identified. More working wives and changing patterns of work and leisure have resulted in extended evening store hours for suburban shoppers. Relaxed moral and social standards have brought about changes in motion pictures and dress. Domestic car manufacturers began to produce economy models in response to demands for lower-priced automobiles.

---

[1]Arthur M. Weimer, *Business Administration: An Introductory Management Approach* (Homewood, Ill.: Richard D. Irwin, Inc., 1966), pp. 76–77.

43

There are also abundant examples of firms that failed to adjust to changed environmental conditions. For instance, Mattel's immensely popular Barbie Doll failed to crack the European toy market "because no one had thought to provide her with a wardrobe of costumes peculiar to European countries."[2]

Movement Contrary to Established Trends. This course of action involves more risk, but the payoff is greater. Volkswagen is one company that successfully countered an established trend more than a decade ago. When Volkswagen entered the U.S. auto market, there were formidable domestic competitors. American car buyers were conditioned to large cars with many extras, such as plush interiors, automatic transmissions, and yearly style changes. But Volkswagen's "Beetle," which lacked these extras, became a major factor in the American car market. Volkswagen had reasoned correctly that the American car buyer was also interested in economy and would accept a low-priced car without costly extras.

Attempts to Change the Environment. Unlike the weather, which usually cannot be changed, the sales manager's environment can sometimes be altered. Powerful public relations and promotion tools can be used to create changes in the business environment. For instance, many industries employ lobbyists who are successful in their efforts to influence public policy-makers.

Two similar attempts to change consumers' buying behavior—one a success, the other a failure—illustrate the role of promotion. Until several years ago, men's fashions had defied change. Although a few men were fashion conscious, many males were content to wear the same clothes until they wore out. This is no longer true. A concerted effort by the men's fashion industry has resulted in drastic changes in men's attitudes toward clothing.

The women's fashion industry had no such success when leading fashion designers and clothing manufacturers tried to push the *midi* on the American woman. She rebelled, and many stores were left with fashions they could not sell.

---

[2]James F. Carberry, "How Mattel, Inc. Went From Thriving Concern to Not-So-Thriving One," *Wall Street Journal* (June 20, 1973), p. 16.

ENVIRONMENTAL CONSTRAINTS ON SALES MANAGEMENT

The selling environment is really a composite of many environments. To simplify the discussion, five major forces have been designated: the market environment, the public and legal environment, the economic environment, the physical and technological environment, and the societal environment. All of the aspects of the sales manager's job are influenced by these environmental factors, as is shown in Figure 3–1.

FIGURE 3–1
The Sales Management Tasks Are Performed Within Environmental Constraints.

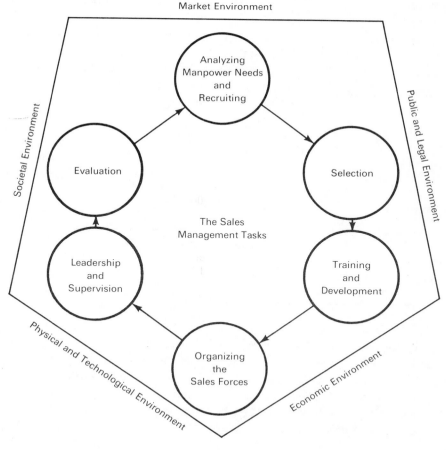

THE MARKET ENVIRONMENT

Customers are the most important part of any company's selling environment, and every sales manager must try to learn as much as he can about them. In recent years, sophisticated marketing research tools have been applied to the prediction of consumer behavior. And yet, because of the complexity of human behavior, the market environment remains the most difficult to evaluate.

The first and most essential issue is to determine who are the customers for a particular product or service. Although this may seem obvious, it is a question which is often overlooked or grossly simplified. One of the greatest mistakes made by marketers is to assume that everyone is a potential customer. In actuality, consumers are highly selective in their purchase behavior.

The marketplace is divided into numerous market segments, each with a different probability of buying a particular item. The sales manager's job is to select the markets with the greatest expected sales. Consider the example shown in Table 3–1.

TABLE 3–1
Analysis of the Market Environment

Market Segment	Cost of Market Penetration	Potential Market Size	Per cent Probability of Purchase	Expected Sales
A	$1,500,000	$10,000,000	10	$1,000,000
B	$1,500,000	$ 8,000,000	30	$2,400,000
C	$1,500,000	$ 7,000,000	20	$1,400,000
D	$1,500,000	$ 3,000,000	70	$2,100,000

If the cost of market penetration remains constant at $1.5 million, only market segments B and D would be profitable for this particular firm. Potential market size and the probability of purchase vary among market segments. This information, which can be derived from proper marketing research, should then be compared with the cost of market penetration for each segment. While the method of analysis may vary, this is the type of reasoning that allows the sales manager to deal effectively with the market environment.

Another way to approach this question is to divide the market into *consumer, industrial,* and *trade* segments. This segmentation is based on *end use.* Consumers purchase a given product for their personal use. The housewife who buys orange juice is purchasing it for her family's consumption. Industrial buyers purchase goods and services to use in the production of other goods and services. Tires that are bought by an automobile manufacturer for new cars are industrial goods. Of course, many products are sold to both consumers and industrial buyers. A restaurant purchases orange juice to serve to its customers, and consumers buy tires for their personal cars. The trade market includes retailers, wholesalers, distributors, and the like who resell goods and services to consumers and industrial buyers.

Having determined who customers are, the other information needed will depend on the product and its buyers. Some general questions involve *why* the product is purchased, *when* it is bought, *where* the customers are located, *who* is involved in the purchase decision, and *how* the product is bought. The answers to these and similar questions are essential to sales planning.

Effective marketing requires a continual monitoring of consumer information. Even slight shifts in the market environment can affect the results of sales management decisions. For example, consider how coffee and tea distributors might be affected by the recent trend toward drinking Coca-Cola and Pepsi Cola for breakfast in some southern states.[3]

The marketing function has essentially two ways to present its product offering to the marketplace: market segmentation or product differentiation. *Product differentiation* attempts to isolate profitable market segments that are not now being satisfied by competitive offerings. The firm then tries to reach the market segment by stressing the important features of the product. Promotion such as personal selling and advertising play an important role in this marketing strategy. The use of the Rock of Gibraltar as a trademark by the Prudential Insurance Company conveys a sense of strength and permanence, while the

---

[3]"More Critics Assail Soft Drinks for Ingredients and Labeling, but Makers Call the Attack Unfair," *Wall Street Journal* (January 20, 1972), p. 30.

lion associated with the Dreyfus Fund suggests that it is "the king" of mutual funds.[4] The ethnic appeals used in some beer promotions are another example. By contrast, a policy of *market segmentation* tries to design a unique product for a particular market. The introduction of the Gremlin, Pinto, and Vega automobiles is an example of this adaptation of a product to fit the needs of a market segment. But, the product still must be promoted, and the consumer must be made to feel that it meets his particular needs. In both market segmentation and product differentiation strategies, the sales manager plays an important role in the planning and implementation stages.

PUBLIC AND LEGAL ENVIRONMENT

The firm's public environment includes formal *legal constraints* on a firm's operations and informal constraints in the form of *public opinion*. In some cases strong public opinion forces will lead to legal action. For example, Ralph Nader and his colleagues spurred Congress to act on safety standards for automobiles. Similar public opinion pressure resulted in cigarette commercials being taken off radio and television.

Public opinion is important to all marketing efforts—domestic or international. In Thailand, for example, Helene Curtis was forced to switch to *black* shampoo because Thai women believed that it made their hair glossier.[5] A large American coffee manufacturer's slogan "America's Finest Coffee" was soundly rejected by public opinion in Holland whose 300 year history in this industry led the Dutch to regard Americans as amateurs in the business.[6] Domestically, public opinion varies by region. Surveys show that nearly 70 per cent of eastern consumers have never eaten catfish, the popularity of which is based primarily in the South and Midwest.[7] Similar examples are abundant. As a result, every sales manager must be especially careful

---

[4]These examples are suggested in Ronald D. Michman, "Behavioral Theories and Alternative Strategies of Product Differentiation and Market Segmentation," *Business Perspectives*, vol. 6 (Winter 1970), pp. 24–27.

[5]See "Why A Global Market Doesn't Exist," *Business Week* (December 9, 1970), pp. 140, 144.

[6]John K. Kracmar, *Marketing Research in the Developing Countries* (New York: Praeger Publishers, 1971), p. 117.

[7]"Catfish Farming not in Big Time Yet," *The Press* (September 26, 1972), p. 11.

to weigh contemporary public opinion in all of his marketing decisions. Sales management decisions cannot be isolated from the public environment in which they are made.

Many federal, state, and local laws affect a sales manager's decisions. The stated purposes of these laws are to protect the public and to preserve competition.[8] These regulations form another parameter within which sales management decisions must be made. The origin of these mandates was typically an unfavorable public opinion of certain business and marketing practices.

Antitrust Legislation

The first national laws that affected sales management were the anti-monopoly regulations of 1890 and 1914. These ordinances were essentially designed to maintain a competitive marketing system in the United States. The *Sherman Antitrust Act* of 1890 prohibited restraints of trade and attempts to monopolize. Many writers have noted that the Sherman Act resulted from the public clamor over large business *trusts* such as the Standard Oil Company. This bill provided for equity suits as well as for the prosecution of responsible parties for misdemeanors.

In 1914, Congress enacted the *Clayton Act* to restrict practices such as price discrimination, exclusive dealing, tying contracts, and interlocking boards of directors, where the effect might "substantially lessen competition or tend to create a monopoly." This legislation expanded the provisions of the Sherman Act by outlawing many sales and marketing practices that could eventually become Sherman Act violations.

It is interesting to note that the United States' policy of maintaining competitive markets (as espoused in the Sherman and Clayton Acts) is in direct opposition to the philosophy held in many foreign countries, where monopolistic practices are tolerated, if not encouraged, in an attempt to further productive efficiency.[9] In response to this situation,

---

[8]An expanded discussion of the legal environment for American business is contained in Louis E. Boone and David L. Kurtz, *Contemporary Marketing* (New York: Dryden Press, 1974), pp. 32–41.
[9]An interesting discussion of American and British antitrust policy is contained in Robert S. Raymond, "Consumer Protection in Great Britain and the United States," *Marquette Business Review*, vol. XIII (Winter 1969), pp. 151–158.

Congress passed the *Webb-Pomerene Export Trade Act* of 1918. This legislation exempted voluntary American export trade associations from the Sherman Act restrictions, provided that these associations were extending foreign trade and not fixing prices domestically.

The Federal Trade Commission

Of particular importance to sales managers is the *Federal Trade Commission Act* of 1914. This law prohibited "unfair competitive practices," and it established the Federal Trade Commission (FTC) to serve as a quasijudicial agency (an agency with some powers that resemble those of the judiciary) to monitor the various laws dealing with business operations.

Through the years, the FTC has played an increasingly more important role in regulating business. Originally, the Commission had to show "injury to competition" before a marketing practice was declared "unfair." This was changed in 1938 with the adoption of the *Wheeler-Lea Act*, which banned all deceptive or unfair marketing practices per se. The Wheeler-Lea Act was specifically developed to restrict deceptive promotional and sales practices.

In recent years, the FTC has moved aggressively in pursuing consumer protection goals. Rather than formal legal action, the Commission has relied upon company or industry conferences and consent agreements to curb unfair trade practices. The *conference method* seeks voluntary compliance from a company or industry with mutually acceptable rules and regulations. The *consent method* secures a specific agreement from a company or industry to abandon a particular unfair trade practice.[10]

Pricing Legislation

The sales manager's prerogatives in regard to pricing are restricted by several provisions at both the state and national levels. It should also be noted that much of our pricing legislation was formulated during the Great Depression of the 1930s, when legislative attention was di-

---

[10]These methods are discussed in Vernon A. Mund, *Government and Business* (New York: Harper & Row, Publishers, 1960), pp. 294–299.

rected toward preserving employment levels. Marketers, who emphasized pricing in a competitive strategy such as the rapidly expanding chain stores, were seen as a threat to already scarce jobs. Hence, it can be reasonably argued that these laws were more a result of practical economics than they were a concern over maintaining a viable competitive marketing system.

The *Robinson-Patman Act* of 1936, which was technically an amendment to the Clayton Act, prohibited price discrimination that was not based on a cost differential.[11] It also prohibited selling at an unreasonably low price in order to eliminate competition. The bill, which was popularly known as the *Anti A & P Act*, was based on the premise that large purchasers, such as the chain stores, might be able to secure discounts not available to smaller, independent stores. Again, note the emphasis on protecting jobs.

Three defenses to Robinson-Patman Act charges have been held permissible by the courts:[12]

1. That products are not of like grade and quality (as required by the act).
2. That the alleged price discrimination occurred in a legitimate attempt to *meet* competition.
3. That the price discounts are justified by cost differentials, such as *reasonable* volume discounts.

The variety of possible defenses coupled with uncertain interpretations qualifies the Robinson-Patman Act as one of the vaguest laws affecting the sales management process. The net result is that sales managers have tended to avoid price competition where a Robinson-

---

[11]See, for example, Charles C. Slater and Frank H. Mossman, "Positive Robinson-Patman Pricing," *Journal of Marketing*, vol. 31 (April 1967), pp. 8–14; Lawrence X. Tarpey, "Indirect Price Discrimination and Robinson-Patman," *Journal of Marketing*, vol. 27 (January 1963), pp. 68–70; John R. Davidson, "FTC, Robinson-Patman, and Cooperative Promotional Activities," *Journal of Marketing*, vol. 32 (January 1968), pp. 14–17.

[12]These defenses have been examined in such articles as Jacky Knopp, Jr., "What Are 'Commodities of Like Grade and Quality,'" *Journal of Marketing*, vol. 27 (July 1963), pp. 63–66; Robert A. Lynn, "Is the Cost Defense Workable?" *Journal of Marketing*, vol. 29 (January 1965), pp. 37–42; Morris L. Mayer, Joseph B. Mason, and Einar A. Orbeck, "The Borden Case—A Legal Basis for Private Brand Price Discrimination," *MSU Business Topics*, vol. 18 (Winter 1970), pp. 55–63.

Patman violation might be inferred. Hence, it can be argued that the law has had the effect of maintaining consumer prices at levels higher than might otherwise be the case.

The depression years also saw state legislatures active in passing pricing regulations. In 1931, California became the first state in the nation to adopt a *Fair Trade Law*.[13] Soon, only Missouri, the District of Columbia, Vermont, and Texas had not passed similar legislation. Fair trade laws permitted manufacturers to specify a minimum retail price for a product. Retailers were required to sign contracts agreeing to abide by these prices. These laws were based on the premise that a product's image, as implied by its price, was a property right of its manufacturer. The producer should be able to protect this right through pricing policies. In 1937, congressional passage of the *Miller-Tydings Resale Price Maintenance Act* exempted interstate fair trade contracts from compliance with antitrust requirements.

Many states later included *nonsigner clauses* in their fair trade laws. These provisions specified that a price maintenance contract between a manufacturer *and a single retailer* made all retailers in that state subject to the agreement. The effect of this clause was to allow manufacturers to exert substantially greater authority over the retail price of their product. In 1951, the Supreme Court temporarily voided the nonsigner provisions in the *Schwegmann decision*. The following year, however, Congress reinstated the clause when it passed the *McGuire-Keough Act*.

In more recent years, the fair trade concept has declined in importance because of (1) repeals by state legislatures; (2) unfavorable decisions by state courts; and (3) the growth of chain discount stores, which made it unwise for manufacturers to continue to enforce these provisions. Periodically, however, a federal fair trade law is proposed in Congress. This proposal, which is usually called a *Quality Stabilization Act*, would require *mandatory* fair trade, rather than merely *permitting* fixed prices as under the Miller-Tydings Act. From the consumer's viewpoint, it is probably fortunate that this proposal has received little congressional support.

---

[13]Excellent reviews of the fair trade laws are contained in Louis E. Boone and Robert Stevens, "Resale Price Maintenance in Theory and Practice," *Business Ideas and Facts*, vol. 3 (Winter 1970), pp. 13–15; and Stewart Monro Lee, "The Impact of Fair Trade Laws on Retailing, *Journal of Retailing*, vol. 41 (Spring 1965), pp. 1–6.

Another piece of pricing legislation passed at the state level has been the *unfair trade laws*, which set price floors for *comparable* merchandise. The minimum prices were usually set at cost (for merchandise and transportation) plus 6 or 8 per cent. The underlying purposes of these laws were to protect small specialty shops and to preserve jobs. As such, the laws are another example of depression era pricing legislation. The affluency of recent years has caused the unfair trade laws to decline in importance.

Consumer Protection Laws

The sales manager must also be aware of the various consumer protection laws that exist at national, state, and local levels. The sales manager is often faced with urgent decisions involving these laws. Consider a district sales manager's plight when he must decide whether to halt a shipment of thousands of dollars of a soap product because of a local ordinance banning phosphates. He may believe, for example, that the ordinance is unenforceable because of a jurisdictional conflict with state consumer protection laws. However, a decision to deliver the product may result in arrest and in adverse local publicity. As this situation illustrates, consumer protection is probably the most dynamic and uncertain area of the sales manager's legal environment. Society is still reaching for a workable solution to many environmental, ecological, and ethical problems. The net result is a highly uncertain environment for many sales management decisions.

The *Pure Food and Drug Act* of 1906 was the first major consumer protection law passed in the United States. The act, which was a direct result of the exposures of the meat packing practices of Chicago stockyards, prohibited the adulteration and misbranding of food and drugs in interstate commerce. Through the years, the Food and Drug Administration has been given increased regulatory authority in such matters as product development, branding and advertising.

The various disclosure laws are also important to the sales manager:
Wool Products Labeling Act (1939) — requires that labels must identify the kind and percentage of each type of wool.

Fur Product Labeling Act (1951)—requires that labels must state the animal from which the product was derived.

Flammable Fabrics Act (1953)—outlaws the interstate sale of flammable fabrics.

Fair Packaging and Labeling Act (1967)—requires the disclosure of product identity, name and address of manufacturer or distributor, and information on the quality of the contents.

Consumer Credit Protection Act (1968)—popularly known as the *Truth-in-Lending Law*—requires the disclosure of the annual interest rates on loans and credit purchases.

It also appears that the consumer protection laws will be substantially expanded in the future. In addition, marketers may expect to see

FIGURE 3–2

"Looks like they're really putting teeth in the 'Truth-in-Lending' law."

Source: Reprinted by permission from *Sales Management*, The Marketing Magazine. Copyright 1972.

more *liberal* interpretation of existing consumer legislation, as the regulatory agencies seek to provide a greater degree of protection to buyers.

The expansion of consumer protection is most evident at the state and local levels. One study, for instance, reported that many states have restricted the *holder-in-due-course doctrine* in their legal system or have removed the provision entirely. This provision allows a finance company or bank to disclaim any responsibility for consumer complaints against the original holder of commercial paper (debt agreements). The holder-in-due-course concept denies any customer claims against a financial institution that has purchased a loan agreement from the original seller of merchandise or a service. Hence, the consumer is sometimes left without recourse.[14]

Strict prohibitions against disposable packaging have been passed in other localities. Some cities have *Green River Ordinances* which restrict door-to-door solicitation by salesmen. Sales schemes based on pyramid distributorships have also been banned in most areas. The complexity and diverse nature of these requirements means that each individual field sales manager must remain constantly aware of the regulations in his district or region.

Finally, the legal environment for selling also includes the basic apparatus of the law of contracts, negotiable instruments, and related matters. This assures an orderly market system and protects both consumer and seller.

ECONOMIC ENVIRONMENT

The *economic environment* of selling consists of those factors and processes that relate to the satisfaction of human needs through material goods and services, and it includes the resources used to provide this satisfaction. In a free-enterprise economy, resources are allocated to needs by the marketplace. The sales manager must understand this process and the economic implications for selling.

An important aspect of the economic environment is *competition*. Although a sales manager has little, if any, control over his competi-

---

[14]Louis E. Boone and David L. Kurtz, "The Consumer Versus the Holder in Due Course Doctrine," *Bulletin of Business Research*, vol. XLVII (August 1973), pp. 1–3, 6.

tors, they are a major restraining force on company sales. Most American industries, except for regulated public utilities, are faced with keen competition. The sales manager must assess the intensity of competition as well as its form. While the term *competition* normally implies *price* competition, *nonprice* competition—such as product differentiation, promotion, and channel strategy—is also important.

The economic environment is extremely complex in that its fluctuations exhibit rapid, and sometimes extreme, variation. Selling strategy, which is dependent upon the prevailing economic climate, must change in response to altered environmental constraints.

While business and economic fluctuations are dynamic, they tend to follow a cyclical pattern. Sales management strategy will, of course, vary with each stage of the cycle. Four separate stages can be identified in business cycles:

1. prosperity
2. recession
3. depression
4. recovery

Figure 3–3 demonstrates these four component stages. A more aggressive selling effort is usually required during a recession or depression, when consumers feel threatened by work force cutbacks and tend to resist or postpone all but necessary purchases. The sales manager's use of competitive pricing tactics also becomes relatively more important.

By contrast, prosperous times find consumers more willing to acquire additional goods and services. As a result, sales management strategy also changes. Nonprice competition receives greater emphasis in the marketing mix. The overall selling effort adopts a less aggressive approach, with greater attention to customer service and to the building of long-term vendor-buyer relationships.

One important task is to analyze the demand for goods and services. The economist defines *demand* as the various amounts of a product which customers will buy at different prices during a given period of time. Three determinants of demand must be considered: the cus-

FIGURE 3–3
Stages of the Business Cycle

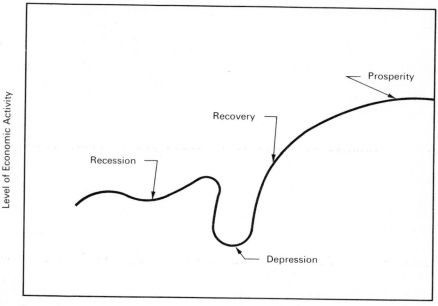

tomer's needs and wants, his ability to buy, and his willingness to buy. All three of these conditions must be present if there is to be demand for a product.

Techniques of forecasting future sales are presented in Chapters 5 and 6. Suffice it to say that although sales figures tend to experience cyclical variations, a successful firm will probably have a positive sales trend over the long run (see Figure 3-4).

The effective sales manager is able to evaluate intuitively any movement in sales figures. He must also correctly delineate and define new potential markets for his company's products. This is the subjective aspect of sales forecasting, which is crucial to the future well-being of the organization.

The final concern is an analysis of the *costs* of resources. Maximum economic efficiency is attained by minimizing the costs of resources used to produce and distribute goods and services. A manager's dis-

FIGURE 3-4:

Sales Figures Usually Exhibit Both a Long-Run Trend and Cyclical Variations.

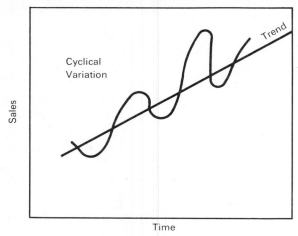

Time

trict, region, or zone will not realize a profit unless costs are kept in line. Because it is expensive to maintain a field sales force, every sales manager must understand fully the nature of the costs for which he will be responsible. The costs of selling are discussed in several places in this book. But, it is important to note here that these expenses are increasing rapidly. In many cases, they are rising faster than the costs associated with the other aspects of promotional strategy. It seems reasonable to conclude that the cost of obtaining sales resources will play an even larger role in sales management decisions in the decades to come.

Several other aspects of the economic environment exert a substantial influence on sales management decisions. One of the most recent has been the inflationary trend in our economy. *Inflation*, which is a rising price level that reduces consumer purchasing power, has reached 6 per cent and more in recent years in the United States. This is indeed a serious problem since continued inflation dampens incentive and leads to curtailed business investment. It also results in social inequities, such as a reduced standard of living for those individuals with fixed incomes. The United States and Canada no longer seem exempt from the bitter aftermaths of uncontrolled inflation.

To the sales manager, inflation presents several related marketing problems. Consumers generally become more price-conscious, thus forcing the marketer to place greater reliance on the element of pricing strategy. This is particularly true where recent price increases have been dramatic, sudden, and/or extensive. Furthermore, government attempts to alleviate inflationary pressures often drastically influence marketing and sales decisions.

Attempts to combat inflation are typically based on the use of fiscal and/or monetary policy implementation. *Fiscal policy* deals with the expenditures and receipts of government. An anti-inflationary government policy would call for reduced government expenditures or increased tax revenue, or a combination of both. *Monetary policy* concerns the regulation of the money supply and of the interest rates. Purchasing can be restrained by reducing the money supply and raising market rates of interest.

Both fiscal and monetary policies have important implications for marketing and sales management. Lower government expenditures can reduce the market for some products and services. Direct fiscal controls, such as the 1971 price freeze, can substantially limit the sales manager's area of discretionary decision-making. Higher interest rates can have a critical impact on the housing, construction, and banking industries.

The net effect is that sales management must take account of the economic environment in the development of its competitive strategy. A current assessment of the existing economic climate is absolutely essential to effective decision-making. In addition, the sales manager must be aware of the short, intermediate, and long-run impact of the government's economic policies.

PHYSICAL AND TECHNOLOGICAL ENVIRONMENT

A company's physical and technological environment includes various aspects, natural or man-made, which surround the selling operation. The natural physical environment consists of factors such as climate, geographic location, and natural resources, all of which must be considered when sales plans are developed. For example, a producer of boating supplies would probably want to locate his regional sales headquarters close to major bodies of water. The paper industry is concentrated in the South and Northwest because these regions have a ready availability of the basic raw material — wood. Many technically oriented industries are located in general proximity of major universities, where the necessary technical experts are available. Palo Alto, California; Boston, Massachusetts; Ann Arbor, Michigan; and the Research Triangle area of North Carolina are examples.

Geographic concentration or dispersion of potential buyers can create contrasting, but critical, sales management problems for the vendors serving these industries. Certainly, this factor must be considered when developing one's promotional strategy.

Technology is used to create the *man-made* physical environment. Unlike other living things, man is able to modify the effects of his natural environment. Rapid technological change is an accepted phenomenon of our society, to the extent that over 26,000 new products are introduced every year. These newer, more complex products have great impact on our lives and business decisions. To illustrate this, let us concentrate on just two important new products of the twentieth century — the automobile and television.

The automobile revolutionized the American way of life. People are much more mobile than they were half a century ago. Entirely new industries have emerged to serve the needs of automobile owners. Retailing has become automobile-oriented, with the emergence of drive-in restaurants, movies, and banks that cater strictly to the automobile owner. From the sales manager's viewpoint, the automobile provides salesmen with a flexibility of movement unequaled by other forms of transportation.

The introduction of television also altered the living patterns of Americans. Entertainment needs are now largely satisfied in the home, and the businessman has found a powerful advertising medium with unlimited selling possibilities. Television, which is only one of the revolutionary new media, has developed into such an important marketing tool that many segments of society have called for the establishment of curbs to its potential. The ban on cigarette advertising, regulation of political announcements, and provisions against deceptive advertising are a few examples.

Not all products, however, are successful. It has been estimated that 90 per cent of all new products fail within four years of their induction. A study undertaken by Booz, Allen, and Hamilton found a 40:1 ratio from the screening stage to the successful introduction of new product ideas.[15] Similar statistics exist in other sources.

One of the major reasons why the introduction of new products and the adoption of new technology are often unsuccessful is simply that the firm has failed to adopt a basic consumer-orientation among its management. It has been noted that:

> . . . there is an important and critical interrelationship between marketing and the effort to produce technological innovations. A marketing orientation, properly employed in management decision, could make a major contribution toward improving the efficiency of research efforts and accelerating the adoption and use of technological innovations.[16]

Venture teams have been suggested as a possible method of overcoming this type of problem. These are separate, temporary organizations within the normal corporate structure, whose goal is to successfully introduce a new product or product category. Seven structural characteristics have been found to be common to these teams:

1. organizational separation;
2. multi-disciplinary concerns;
3. diffusion of authority;
4. environment of entrepreneurship;
5. top management linkage;
6. broad mission;
7. flexible life span.[17]

Under this concept, sales management is no longer divorced from the development of new product ideas. The sales function would par-

[15]*Management of New Products* (Chicago: Booz, Allen, and Hamilton, 1960), p. 11.

[16]William V. Muse and Robert J. Kegerreis, "Technological Innovation and Marketing Management: Implications for Corporate Policy," *Journal of Marketing*, vol. 33 (October 1969), p. 9.

[17]Richard M. Hill and James D. Hlavacek, "The Venture Team: A New Concept in Marketing Organization," *Journal of Marketing*, vol. 36 (July 1972), pp. 46–47. See also Rick W. Diehl, "Achieving Successful Innovation," *Michigan Business Review* (March 1972), pp. 6–10.

ticipate in these new organizational structures rather than being the final step in the traditional sequence:

Design → Production → Marketing

The venture team concept is demonstrated in Figure 3–5. The marketing function plays an equal role with manufacturing, engineering, and finance in the development of new products.

It can be concluded that the technological factor is an important

FIGURE 3–5
Innovative Matrix Organizational Structure

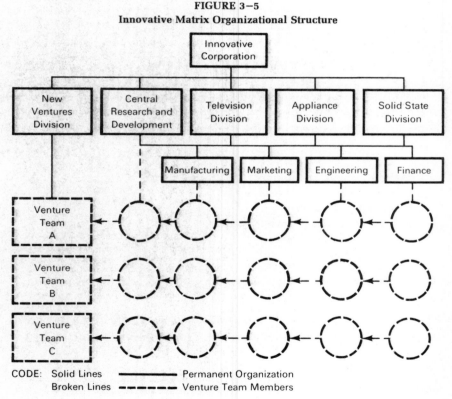

CODE: Solid Lines ——————— Permanent Organization
       Broken Lines ——————— Venture Team Members

Source: Richard M. Hill and James D. Hlavacek, "The Venture Team: A New Concept in Marketing Organization," *Journal of Marketing*, vol. 36 (July 1972), p. 47. Published by the American Marketing Association.

part of the sales management environment. In fact, one study has noted that for a high technology industry like peripheral data processing equipment, personal selling receives the largest share of the promotional budget (see Table 3-2).

TABLE 3-2

Percentage Allocations of Promotion Budget to Promotional Technique — Peripheral Data Processing Equipment Industry

Technique	Average Percentage	Range Percentage	Median Percentage
Advertising	20	0-67	13
Personal Selling	62	4-98	60
Publicity	7	0-30	4
Trade Shows	8	3-60	10
Catalogs	6.6	0-31	5
Displays	7	0-22	4

Source: Martin R. Schlissel, "Promotional Strategy in a High Technology Industry," *Journal of Economics and Business*, volume 26, no. 1 (Fall 1973).

SOCIETAL ENVIRONMENT

The societal environment is probably the most dynamic of the external factors facing sales management.[18] This factor is subject to constant change and has an important influence on contemporary marketing activity.[19]

In recent years, the public has sometimes called for sweeping changes in marketing practices and for socially oriented objectives as a part of standard business philosophy. In most cases, this has already

---

[18]See Dale L. Varble, "Social and Environmental Considerations in New Product Development," *Journal of Marketing*, vol. 36 (October 1972), pp. 11-15.

[19]The importance and scope of the societal environment is pointed out in such articles as Leonard L. Berry, "The Challenges of Marketing: A Field in Transition," *Southern Journal of Business*, vol. 6 (January 1971), pp. 75-84; Lawrence P. Feldman, "Societal Adaptation: A New Challenge for Marketing," *Journal of Marketing*, vol. 35 (July 1971), pp. 54-60; Edward M. Mazze, "Current Marketing Practices: Some Societal Implications," *Marquette Business Review*, vol. XV (Summer 1971), pp. 86-89; Leslie M. Dawson, "Marketing Science in the Age of Aquarius," *Journal of Marketing*, vol. 35 (July 1971), pp. 66-72.

been done *to a certain extent.* For instance, although some top corporate executives are prone to espouse new affirmative action programs that catch the attention of the news media, their subordinates continue to follow the hiring procedures they adopted twenty years ago. The basic problem is not one of *acceptance,* but one of *implementation.* Modern, effective companies have included various social objectives in their adoption of the marketing concept at all organizational levels.

A very real problem for sales and marketing executives is how to measure the accomplishment of societal objectives. Simple awareness of the societal environment is not enough; one has to be able to evaluate a firm's performance in this area.[20] To date, no one has developed a generally accepted measurement tool. The development of such a measuring device is one of the major challenges that face marketing.

The societal environment for sales management may be divided into two sub-classifications: social issues and ethical issues. Both are closely related and often similar in meaning and impact. Generally, however, social issues are somewhat *broader* in that they are usually directed to all functional areas of business enterprise. By contrast, it is possible to isolate *specific* ethical issues.

Social Issues

In most discussions of the subject, three clearly identified topics stand out as the most pressing social issues facing business today:

1. the consumerism movement;
2. concern over ecology and the preservation of our natural environment;
3. the adoption of a humanistic philosophy by management.

Consumerism can be described as "a protest against abuses and malpractices in our marketing system and may be a part of a broader movement that seeks increased social responsibility in many sectors

---

[20]This matter is examined in Robert S. Raymond and Elizabeth Richards, "Social Indicators and Business Decisions," *MSU Business Topics,* vol. 19 (Autumn 1971), pp. 42–46. Also see M. Neil Browne and Paul F. Hass, "Social Responsibility and Market Performance," *MSU Business Topics,* vol. 19 (Autumn 1971), pp. 7–10.

of our society."[21] Its basic premise is that marketers should pay increased attention to consumer wants. The consumerism movement advocates direct protection of consumer interests rather than the *preservation of competition* espoused in such legislation as the Sherman and Clayton Acts. The consumerism movement is *activist* and *involvement-oriented*. Marketing decisions are no longer considered the *sole* domain of sales and marketing managers. Direct consumer input has become a fact of life in modern marketing decision-making, and this trend is likely to accelerate in the future.

Perceptive sales managers have accepted and encouraged the constructive elements of the consumerism movement. A survey of 1400 members of the American Marketing Association found that 80 per cent of the respondents disagreed with the statement that "the 'Consumer Movement' is likely to result in more harm than good for society." Only 16 per cent of the marketers agreed with this viewpoint.[22]

Admittedly, not all consumer demands can be met, because of the necessity to maintain reasonable profit objectives. The basic question then concerns what the consumer should have a right to expect from our marketing system. President Kennedy replied directly to this question when he identified four basic consumer rights in 1962:[23]

1. the right to safety;
2. the right to be informed;
3. the right to choose;
4. the right to be heard.

Since that time, these rights have become the recognized objectives of the consumerism movement, and most recent consumer protection

---

[21]Boone and Kurtz (1974), pp. 392–399. See also George S. Day and David A. Aaker, "A Guide to Consumerism," *Journal of Marketing*, vol. 34 (July 1970), pp. 12–19; David W. Cravens and Gerald E. Hills, "Consumerism: A Perspective for Business," *Business Horizons*, vol. XIII (August 1970), pp. 21–28; Rom J. Markin, "Consumerism: Militant Consumer Behavior: A Social and Behavioral Analysis," *Business and Society*, vol. 12 (Fall 1971), pp. 5–17; John F. Willenborg, "The Emergence of Consumerism as a Social Force," *Business and Economic Review*, vol. XVIII (December 1971), pp. 2–6.

[22]"Consumers Not Well-Protected, Back Standards if Safety Periled," *Marketing News* (Mid-November 1971), p. 2.

[23]See, for instance, E. B. Weiss, "Marketers Fiddle While Consumers Burn," *Harvard Business Review*, vol. 46 (July–August 1968), pp. 45–53.

legislation has been directed toward the preservation of these standards. Undoubtedly, marketers will see increased consumer activism in the years ahead.

Ecology has become a growing concern for many segments of the consumerism movement. This concept can be applied to all relationships between man and his environment[24] and can be broken down into two relevant aspects:

1. concern with pollution, both environmental and cultural
2. the preservation of economic resources

Environmental pollution — the contamination of water and air — receives the bulk of the attention in the popular press. While consumers typically recognize these problems, they are not always willing to pay for corrective action. This, of course, leaves legislative bodies and government regulatory agencies in a quandary. The costs of combating pollution can be assessed in various ways but, in the long run, the consumer will usually have to pay the bill. This dilemma emphasizes an increasingly obvious deficiency in the business/society interface: the inadequate use of existing benefit-cost analysis techniques. All ecological decisions should be subject to a thorough benefit-cost study, which would determine whether the benefits emanating from the decision would be worth the costs related to the action. This has not been the usual case in previous decisions of this nature.

Cultural pollution, while not as well recognized as environmental pollution, may prove to be the more troublesome of the pair. It may be defined as any disruption, or retardation, of our cultural heritage, and it is of direct concern to marketers. Cultural pollution can result from low-level advertising, from excessive commercialization of the media, or from a *lack of professionalism in the personal selling function*.

---

[24]Several excellent articles have dealt with the relationship between marketing and ecology. See, for example, Harold W. Fox, "Ecological Challenges to Marketing Strategy," *Baylor Business Studies* (February/March/April 1972), pp. 29–47; Robert A. Peterson, "The Marketing-Ecology Interface," *Marquette Business Review* (Fall 1971), pp. 167–172; Robin T. Peterson, "Selling the Ecology Theme," *Idaho Business and Economic Bulletin*, vol. 2 (November 1971), pp. 16–19; Harold H. Kassarjian, "Incorporating Ecology into Marketing Strategy: The Case of Air Pollution," *Journal of Marketing*, vol. 35 (July 1971), pp. 61–65.

The *preservation of economic resources* is another aspect of ecology, and one that includes some of the most perplexing issues:

Planned obsolescence: the need to maintain employment versus
  the waste of making objects with a short life-span;
The energy crisis: the need for additional energy, such as oil, versus
  the danger of further environmental pollution;
Recycling: the advantages of reusing materials versus the costs
  and effort required to do so.

In many cases, these questions require a trade-off between the preservation of an economic resource and some other social cost. Future marketers will have to face these questions and problems squarely if they are to survive.

The third of the basic social issues is the need for firms to adopt a more *humanistic philosophy*. This is of particular concern to sales management. A later chapter (Chapter 15) will point out that personal selling lags behind other areas when it comes to providing equal employment opportunities, both for minority groups such as blacks and for women. Expanded *affirmative action* hiring programs for sales personnel would go a long way toward removing the bias that exists.

Total human resource development has become the proper role for a sales manager.[25] Not only must he work to provide equal employment opportunity to all, but he must also consider the personal development of the existing sales force. This requires the implementation of a humanistic managerial philosophy in place of the previous emphasis on short-run profitability and control.

A humanistic philosophy is also applicable to sales management's dealings with persons outside the firm, an example of which would be a company's relationship with disadvantaged consumers. In many ghetto areas, there is a definite need to restore public confidence in the marketing function. Sales managers should recheck their operations in low-income areas so as to remove any vestiges of discriminating selling and pricing practices.

---

[25]See Leslie M. Dawson, "Toward a New Concept in Sales Management," *Journal of Marketing*, vol. 34 (April 1970), pp. 33–38.

Ethical Issues

Ethical issues form the other side of the societal environment. This is a complex area that is characterized by the conflict between idealism and realism. The ethics of a sales situation can be evaluated in terms of the act's consequences or motives or in terms of general standards of conduct.[26] The fact that sales management decisions are subject to *some ethical evaluation* is far more important than the method used to conduct the evaluation.

Ethical evaluation should also take the long-run viewpoint. What may appear to be an ethical decision today, may have dire long-run consequences. Various time periods should be considered in ethical

FIGURE 3-6
Ethical Evaluation of Sales Management Decisions

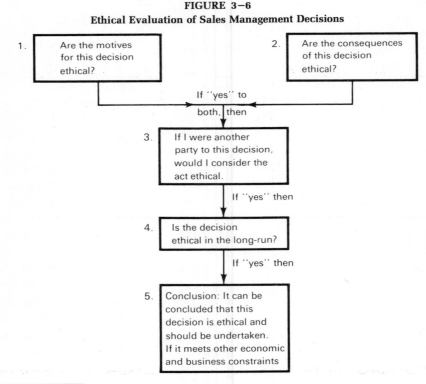

[26]See Philip Kotler, *Marketing Management: Analysis, Planning and Control* (Englewood Cliffs, N.J.: Prentice-Hall, Inc., 1972), p. 840.

assessments. The process of ethical evaluation is demonstrated in Figure 3–6. If the sales manager can legitimately answer "yes" to the four questions posed in this diagram, then his proposed decision has met any reasonable ethical constraint.

Personal selling has been the subject of criticism on ethical grounds since the beginning of recorded history. The ancient regulations prohibiting excessive puffing (extolling a product's virtues) by early traders are an example of the public's general concern over sales ethics. The Yankee peddlers of the eighteenth century, the drummers of the nineteenth century, and the used car and door-to-door salesmen of the twentieth century have done little to alleviate the public's concern.

The specific practices that are the source of ethical issues[27] can be outlined as follows:

1. bribes/gifts/entertainment;
2. the preservation of employer and customer secrets;
3. expense accounts;
4. sales management's relationship with subordinate personnel.

Bribes / Gifts / Entertainment

Bribes paid to persons responsible for purchasing goods and services are clearly unethical. Most firms have well-established policies that call for immediate dismissal of sales personnel offering bribes to potential customers. No professional sales manager would condone bribes as a legitimate sales practice.

The really complex ethical issues center on the use of *gifts* and *entertainment* in business. When does a gift become a bribe? Is there a certain dollar figure that allows management to make this type of ethical evaluation? Some companies have established specified limits on the value of business gifts that their employees can receive or give. The Internal Revenue Service regulations state that business gifts are limited to $25 a year per recipient. Annual gifts in excess of $25 are

---

[27]Examples of unethical sales practices are given in "Flimflam, the 10 Most Deceptive Sales Practices of 1968 — So Far," *Sales Management* (September 15, 1968), pp. 33–36. Also see Del I. Hawkins and A. Benton Cocanougher, "Student Evluations of the Ethics of Marketing Practices: The Role of Marketing Education," *Journal of Marketing*, vol. 36 (April 1972), pp. 61–64.

not tax deductible. The regulations exempt from the $25-limit any item valued at less than $4 with the giver's name on it. These items are classed as *specialty advertising*.

Similar questions can be raised in the case of entertainment. When and how much entertainment (if any) qualifies as an ethical sales practice? Some firms have even prohibited their employees from accepting a modest lunch from salesmen.

The best policy is for sales personnel to be well informed as to the gift and entertainment regulations of the firms with which they deal. It is their responsibility to closely monitor this aspect of the sales process. In some cases, the salesman's own firm will have limits or regulations as to gifts and entertainment. Where these rules conflict with those of the buyer, the *strictest* limits should be followed.

Preserving Employer and Customer Secrets

The salesman and sales manager are often party to trade secrets of both their own company and their customers. Preserving these trade secrets is an important aspect of selling ethics.

Trade secrets would include such items as delivery schedules, price changes, planned entries into new markets, new promotional themes, and future plant expansions. All information about a customer's business operation—particularly, if the firm's representative notes it as being privileged information—should be treated as *confidential* by the salesman. Aside from the obvious ethical standard, the preservation of another person's confidence *is simply good business*. Over the long run, violations of such trust will result in reduced sales for the offending party.

In his relationships with his employer, the salesman must also maintain confidential trade information, even if its release would gain him a temporary advantage over his competition. Long-run considerations are relevant here.

Expense Accounts

Expense accounts are used to reimburse sales personnel for legitimate business expenses such as travel, lodging, meals, and entertainment. In practice, however, there is probably no other area that is more prone to various ethical questions.

Some salesmen *pad* their expense accounts by claiming reimbursement for expenses that they did not incur or expenses that were of a personal nature. Certainly, this type of *padding* is highly unethical. Mitigating circumstances, however, play an important part in such ethical assessments. Consider the case where automobile mileage is reimbursed at 10 cents a mile when recent figures show that actual costs are about 13 – 14 cents per mile. Salesmen in this situation will tend to report extra mileage in order to recover the 3 – 4 cent difference. In their minds, this is an ethical practice because the mileage rate is inadequate. The *basic fault lies with sales management* since they failed to adjust the the reimbursement policy as costs increased.

Most ethical questions related to expense accounts can be resolved by proper management attention to this area. Companies should pay all reasonable selling expenses. If allowances are used, they should be adequate to cover all *actual* costs. If these inequities are eliminated, then examples of expense account abuse should be dealt with firmly.

Sales Management's Relationship with Subordinate Personnel

Ethical questions also arise in the sales manager/salesman interface. Hiring decisions, promotions, demotions, territory assignments, quota allocations, dismissals, bonus arrangements, expense accounts, travel arrangements, and the like can provide the framework for various ethically related issues.

These relationships require a careful balancing on the part of the sales manager. In some cases, the sales manager is torn between the dictates of a higher-level of management and the desire to provide a totally supportive work environment for his personnel. Consider the case of a district sales manager who is ordered by the director of marketing to equalize sales territories within the district. The sales manager, however, recalls that his senior representative had originally *pioneered* the district years before and had been promised preferential treatment in future territory assignments. This presents a serious ethical question to sales management.

Generally, the wisest policy would be to apply a *Golden Rule* type of standard to these decisions. The sales manager must be supportive of his subordinates, but this does not necessarily mean that the manager should disregard instruction issued by a higher level of management. Instead, he should work within organizational channels to obtain an acceptable and ethical solution to the problem. This is probably one of the most important tasks that the sales manager performs.

AN ENVIRONMENTAL CHECKLIST

This chapter has pointed out the considerable influence that environmental forces exert on sales management decisions. But, how should the individual sales manager evaluate and deal with these environmental factors?

One way of handling this situation is to condense the relevant factors into a checklist such as the one shown in Figure 3–7. This type of approach allows the manager to deal with the following questions: What are the environmental forces in a particular selling situation? What is the impact of these forces? How should sales management react to each separate factor?

FIGURE 3–7
Environmental Checklist

Force	Impact	Reaction
A. Market Environment		
1. Who? _____	_____	_____
_____	_____	_____
2. Why	_____	_____
3. When ⎱ buy? _____	_____	_____
4. Where ⎰ _____	_____	_____
5. How _____	_____	_____
B. Public and Legal Environment		
1. Public Opinion: _____	_____	_____
_____	_____	_____
2. Legal: _____	_____	_____
_____	_____	_____
C. Economic Environment		
1. Demand: _____	_____	_____
_____	_____	_____
2. Competition: _____	_____	_____
_____	_____	_____
3. Costs: _____	_____	_____
_____	_____	_____

4. Government economic
   policy: _____   _____   _____

_____   _____   _____

D. Physical and Technological Environment
   1. Natural: _____   _____   _____

_____   _____   _____

   2. Man-Made: _____   _____   _____

_____   _____   _____

E. Societal Environment
   1. Consumerism: _____   _____   _____

_____   _____   _____

   2. Ecology: _____   _____   _____

_____   _____   _____

   3. Human Concerns: _____   _____   _____

_____   _____   _____

   4. Selling Ethics: _____   _____   _____

_____   _____   _____

SUMMARY Chapter 3 identifies five environmental constraints on sales management decisions:

1. Market environment
2. Public and legal environment
3. Economic environment
4. Physical and technological environment
5. Societal environment

A sales manager must adapt his operations to the environment, move contrary to established trends, or attempt to change the environment.

Each of the five environmental constraints are discussed in this chapter. The market environment section examines how to identify and reach customers. Next, Chapter 3 considers the formal legal constraints on a firm's operation and the informal constraints in the form of public opinion. The economic environment section discusses competition, stages of the business cycle, inflation, and monetary and fiscal policy. A company's physical and technological environment includes various aspects surrounding the selling operation—both natural and man-made. Suggestions for coping with these environmental constraints are offered. The societal environment is divided into two major areas: social issues and ethical issues. The relationship of these issues to sales management is considered. The chapter concludes with an environmental checklist, which can assist a sales manager in evaluating and dealing with these factors.

DISCUSSION/REVIEW QUESTIONS

1. Think about a company with which you are familiar. What important environmental changes have happened over the past year? How did the company's management react?
2. Evaluate the following statement: "The most effective environmental strategy is to try to change the environment through promotion."
3. "Technology has had a major impact on the environment of selling." Discuss.
4. "Public opinion is of little importance to sales management since individual citizens have no real influence over public policy." Comment.
5. Describe the sales manager's three options in dealing with environmental factors.
6. How would you go about determining whether a particular sales management decision met minimum ethical standards?
7. List and describe the various environmental factors affecting the personal selling function.
8. Explain the alternative marketing strategies of *market segmentation* and *product differentiation*.
9. What are the three acceptable defenses to Robinson-Patman Act allegations? Discuss.
10. Draw a graph demonstrating a typical business cycle. Correctly label each stage of the cycle.
11. What is meant by a *venture team*? Discuss.
12. "The consumerism movement is activist and involvement-oriented." Comment.
13. Differentiate between environmental and cultural pollution. Cite examples of each.

14. President Kennedy identified four basic rights of consumers. Show how each of these rights have been incorporated into legislation since 1962.
15. Briefly identify each of the following:
    (a) consumer market
    (b) industrial market
    (c) trade market
    (d) Sherman Act
    (e) Clayton Act
    (f) fair trade laws
    (g) unfair trade laws
    (h) nonsigner clause
    (i) Robinson-Patman Act
    (j) Webb-Pomerene Export Trade Act
    (k) Wheeler-Lea Act
    (l) Pure Food and Drug Act
    (m) holder-in-due-course doctrine
    (n) Green River Ordinance
    (o) inflation
    (p) monetary policy
    (q) fiscal policy

CHAPTER FOUR
ESSENTIALS
OF THE SALES
FUNCTION

This chapter will examine the essentials of the sales function. It will focus on the interaction between the salesman and potential customer, since this is the area in which the sales manager will make a contribution. Successful sales managers are able to improve salesman effectiveness in these situations. It is worth noting that personal selling experience is often considered necessary for those who hope to advance to positions in marketing management, particularly if these positions involve direct customer contact and public exposure. Chapter 2 has pointed out that selling has been a traditional training ground for those aspiring to business leadership. Personal selling also provides invaluable experience to persons entering other fields of endeavor. For example, Lefty Driesell, the successful basketball coach of the University of Maryland, attributes his success in player recruitment to his experience as an encyclopedia salesman.[1] Similar, although less dramatic, examples are abundant.

An examination of the actual operation of the sales function is a vital prerequisite to the study of its managerial aspects. Selling is constantly changing, and an effective sales manager cannot isolate himself from this flux. One of the most marked changes has been a shift in general attitude toward the sales process itself. The following sections reveal how this factor has developed in recent years.

---

[1]"Hardwood Huckster," Time (January 22, 1973), p. 41.

SALESMANSHIP: THE TRADITIONAL VIEWPOINT

The traditional view of the sales function was what might be called the *salesmanship approach*. The salesman's behavior was regarded as the key ingredient to the sales process. Whether or not a sale resulted from the salesman's call depended almost entirely upon the way the representative handled the prospect. *Canned* (memorized) presentations, or *correct* ways to sell, were considered to be a fixed aspect of the process. The prospect was treated as essentially passive.

Stimulus-response theories dominated selling strategies. The basic premise was that prospects were keyed to buy upon hearing a certain set of statements — provided that the statements were presented in the correct manner:

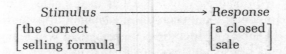

$$Stimulus \longrightarrow Response$$
$$\begin{bmatrix} \text{the correct} \\ \text{selling formula} \end{bmatrix} \qquad \begin{bmatrix} \text{a closed} \\ \text{sale} \end{bmatrix}$$

The salesmanship approach stressed *correct* selling formulae. A typical example was Arthur Frederick Sheldon's formula published in 1902: AIDR (Attention, Interest, Desire, Resolve).[2] Prior to 1902, only nine books had ever been published that dealt with this field. The Sheldon selling course, the first comprehensive course of this type, went through numerous revisions and became the accepted procedure for effective selling. The basis was Sheldon's argument that the prospective buyer went through four identifiable stages — *attention, interest, desire, resolve* — on his way to a purchase decision. It is interesting to point out that many modern marketing textbooks refer to the AIDA (attention, interest, desire, *action*) approach toward personal selling or advertising. AIDA is simply an update of Sheldon's AIDR concept. Apparently, the word *action* is regarded as more contemporary than *resolve*. Regardless of the designation, the strategy emphasizes persuasive ability, in proposing that the salesman should be able to lead the prospect through each of these stages. A 1908 brochure entitled *What is Salesmanship?* described the Sheldon method in this manner:

---

[2] A. R. Hahn, "Selling's Path-finder," *Sales Management* (December 15, 1952), pp. 96–97.

You can take two men of apparently equal ability, teach them both the same facts about any line, send them out, and one man will sell twice as much as the other. The one didn't know the goods any better than the other, but he knew better how to appeal to the minds of his customers. He could persuade.[3]

In 1924, the Sheldon course defined successful selling as "the art of inducing conscious, willing agreement, resulting in a sale mutually beneficial to buyer and seller."[4] This definition again emphasized selling as an *art* that is performed by the salesman. The phrase "inducing conscious, willing agreement" is descriptive of the salesmanship viewpoint of the sales function.

Another way to consider the traditional approach is presented in Figure 4−1.

FIGURE 4−1
Traditional View of the Personal
Selling Function

Source: Barry J. Hersker, "The Ecology of Personal Selling," *Southern Journal of Business*, vol. 5 (July 1970), p. 42.

As this diagram shows, an effective sales presentation has the salesman seeking to match the perceived needs of his customers with his product's unique characteristics. According to the traditional viewpoint, the only determinants of an effective sales presentation are product qualities and customer needs. This approach is extremely

---

[3]Quoted in Hahn (1952), p. 97.
[4]Hahn (1952), p. 96.

simplistic, since it ignores the fact that the sales function is performed within the context of some ecological milieu or environmental condition.[5] As one writer has observed: "The salesman does not ply his trade in a vacuum—he is profoundly affected by the ecology of personal selling."[6]

Reservations of this nature led to the modern viewpoint that the sales function could better be described in terms of buyer-seller interaction.

THE BUYER-SELLER DYAD: THE MODERN VIEWPOINT

The term *buyer-seller dyad* represents a situation in which two people interact. The basis of the modern viewpoint toward personal selling, it differs in several ways from the traditional *salesmanship* approach. First, the concept of the buyer-seller dyad recognizes that external factors such as repeat-sale potential influence the sales methodology. These external factors form the ecological milieu or environment men-

FIGURE 4–2
The Three Determinants of an
Effective Sales Presentation

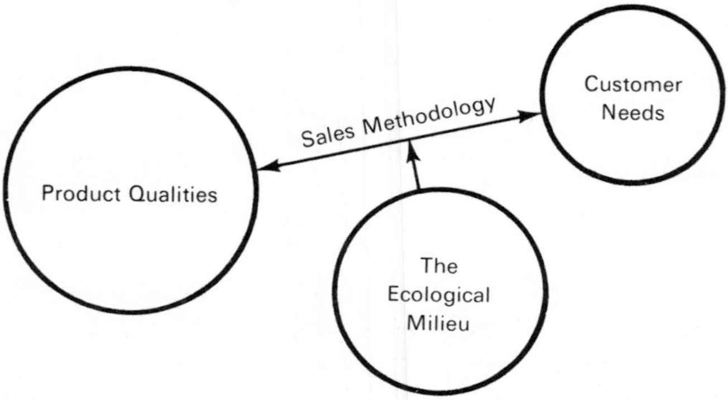

Product Qualities

Sales Methodology

Customer Needs

The Ecological Milieu

Source: Hersker (1970), p. 43.

---

[5]Barry J. Hersker, "The Ecology of Personal Selling," *Southern Journal of Business*, vol. 5 (July 1970), pp. 41–46.
[6]Hersker (1970), p. 42.

tioned in Chapter 3 and constitute a third determinant to effective selling. The interrelation of these three elements is shown in Figure 4–2.

Second, the modern view holds selling to be an interpersonal communications process with a *feedback mechanism* (Figure 4–3).

FIGURE 4–3
Selling as an Interpersonal Communication Process

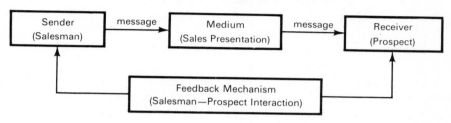

The sender (salesman) transmits his message through a medium (his sales presentation) to the receiver (prospect). The resulting salesman-prospect interaction provides the necessary feedback mechanism and closes the communication system. While this description is admittedly simplified, it points out the fact that the prospect is no longer viewed as being passive. He is now seen as playing an active role in the sales process. The prospect responds, interacts, and communicates with the salesman. This differs drastically from the earlier stimulus-response viewpoint.

Selling is an interpersonal process, one that is conditioned by the interaction between the parties to the dyad. Generally, the greater the similarity between seller and prospect, the greater the possibility of a sale. The widely cited study of life insurance selling, undertaken by F. B. Evans, found that the more alike the salesman and prospect were, and the more the prospect knew about the salesman and his company, the more likely the prospect was to buy the insurance.[7] Another study of life insurance selling concluded that salesmen tend to concentrate on prospects with similar characteristics such as age, that they appar-

[7]F. B. Evans, "Selling as a Dyadic Relationship," *The American Behavioral Scientist,* vol. 6 (May 1963), pp. 76–79.

ently recognize the importance of the similarity factor to selling interaction.[8]

The sales process is a highly structured interaction system. Roles of both salesman and buyer are rather clearly delineated and are usually understood by both parties. In some cases, however, either the salesman or the buyer attempts to disguise his role from the other party. The *door-to-door salesman who poses as a survey interviewer*, and *the customer who enters a car dealership to get some prices for a nonexistent friend* are common examples. It is important to observe that this relatively rigid structure does not alter the importance and necessity of the dyad's interaction.

There is another dimension of the personal selling function. The salesman is accomplishing an interorganizational link between a selling organization and a purchasing organization.[9] This link is shown in Figure 4–4, which applies Robert Durbin's theory of organization to selling behavior.[10] In this view, power, authority, and status relations flow laterally between similar sections of the selling and purchasing organizations. The salesman is the linking pin between the organizations. One writer concludes that:

> The function of an outside salesman is to establish and maintain the exchange relationship between organizations. Salesmen set up a patterned interaction with members of customer organizations, such patterns of interaction being an extension of the human relations that take place within an organization. A salesman's behavior at his customer's place of business can be understood in terms of power, authority, and status, which can be seen to flow between organizations linked in a channel of distribution, characteristically in lateral flows, the lateral nature of which in part determines the particular characteristics of those basic flows. Salesmen serve as the linking pins between functionally independent organizations, acting as conductors of these flows. For this reason,

---

[8]M. S. Gadel, "Concentration by Salesman on Congenial Prospects," *Journal of Marketing*, vol. 28 (April 1964), pp. 64–66.
[9]Henry O. Pruden, "The Outside Salesman: Interorganizational Link," *California Management Review*, vol. XII (Winter 1969) pp. 57–66.
[10]See Robert Durbin, *The World of Work: Industrial Society and Human Relations* (Englewood Cliffs, N.J.: Prentice-Hall, Inc., 1958), Chapters 2–5. Durbin's theory is also discussed in Pruden's (1969) article (see footnote 9).

FIGURE 4–4

The Outside Salesman as an Interorganizational Linking Pin

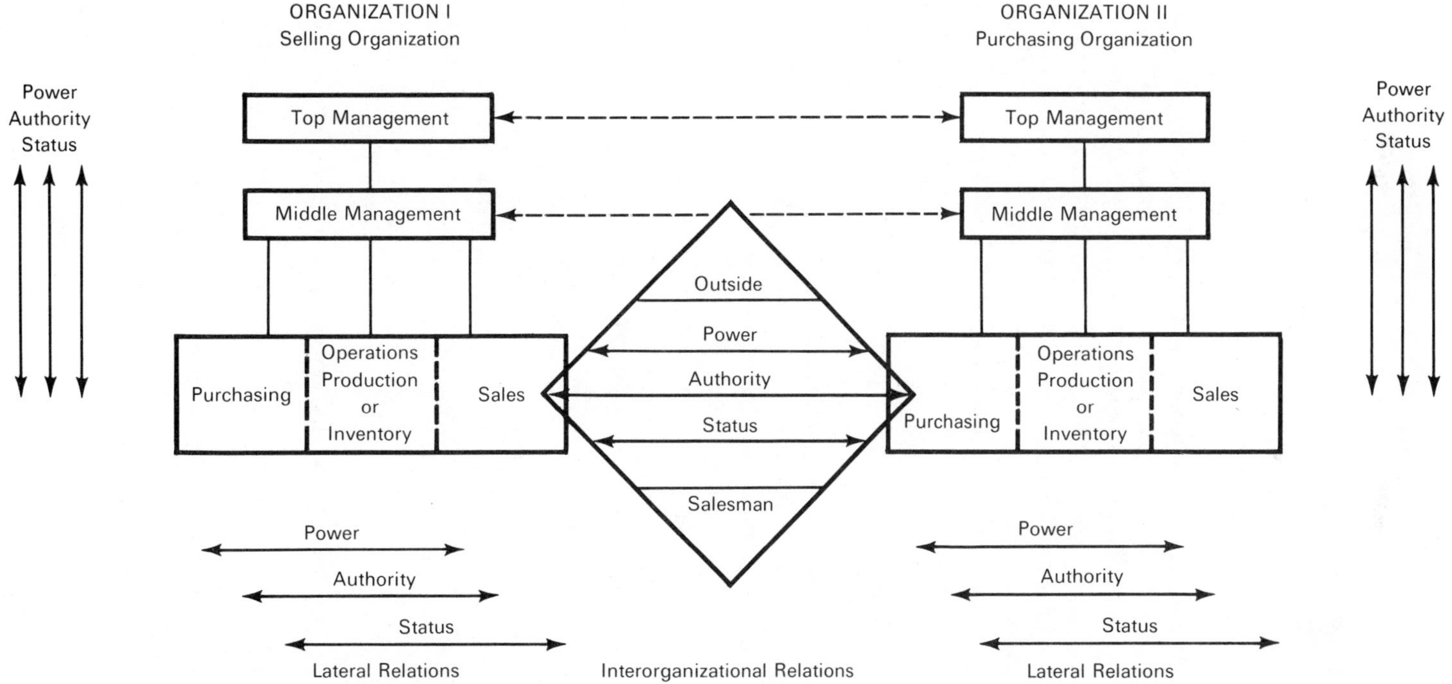

Source: Pruden (1969), p. 58.

83

the role of the salesman can be described as a "man-in-the-middle" accommodation to the pressures growing out of these lateral flows.[11]

As was discussed above, the concept of selling has changed significantly over the years. The traditional viewpoint visualized the salesman as performing some persuasive action upon an essentially passive prospect. Sales management would identify certain attributes that would make sales recruits successful and would then *teach* the new personnel to follow some *tested* formula for effective selling. By contrast, the more recent view has studied selling via the interaction within a buyer-seller dyad. The prospect has been shown to play an active role in the selling function. Sales managers now advocate that salesmen make their sales presentations flexible so that they can respond to feedback from the prospect.

What is needed is an integrated approach that combines the better features of both the traditional and the modern conceptual schemes. Salesmen and prospects do interact; many external factors influence the sales process; and frames of reference are relevant to purchase decisions. However, there are certain guidelines that should be followed in nearly all selling situations. Although they are usually altered to fit particular prospects and situations, these guidelines remain valid as basic generalizations. Hence, it can be concluded that both traditional and modern concepts can be useful to today's salesmen and that contemporary marketing should implement a delicate balance between the old and the new. It behooves sales managers to continually study the selling process in order to better understand its operational complexities.

A CLASSIFICATION SYSTEM FOR THE SALES FUNCTION

Although increased *specialization* has long characterized many functional areas such as engineering and production, it has been largely ignored in marketing. Most firms have persisted in full-line selling with a minimum of staff assistance, and only recently has the trend

---

[11]Pruden (1969), p. 64.

toward specialization begun to appear among sales personnel. In 1973, it was noted that:

> Today's three basic levels of selling — manufacturing, wholesaling, and consumer and industrial services — are spawning dozens of highly-specialized sub-categories aimed at shortening the lines of communication between buyer and seller. IBM is even experimenting with administrative specialists who help its sales specialists handle order preparation, scheduling, collections, and other paperwork.[12]

At the same time that sales personnel are becoming more specialized, the product concepts they sell are often being expanded. *Systems selling* has been widely accepted, which means that in certain situations salesmen will seek to sell a total system, rather than individual component parts. Systems selling is fine, except that it must be implemented effectively. Consider the case of a company where management neither defined the situations appropriate to system selling nor trained salesmen in this more complex approach. The net result was that the sales personnel did not attempt to sell systems, but they concentrated on selling system components instead. When management criticized sales force performance, morale declined significantly.[13] In this case, a good concept failed because of poor implementation by sales management.

Sales Tasks

Any classification system of salesmen depends in large part on the sales tasks that are performed. *Sales tasks* are the job activities performed by salesmen; they can be classified into various categories. The simplest, two-way classification is to divide selling activity into creative selling and service selling. *Creative selling* deals with arous-

---

[12]"The New Supersalesman: Wired for Success," *Business Week* (January 6, 1973), p. 46.
[13]B. Charles Ames, "Build Marketing Strength Into Industrial Selling," *Harvard Business Review* (January-February 1972), p. 53.

FIGURE 4–5
Continuum of Sales Tasks

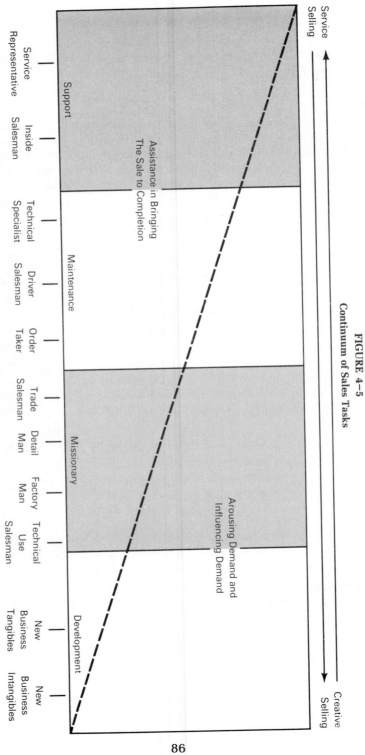

Service
Selling

Creative
Selling

| Support | Maintenance | Missionary | Development |

| Service Representative | Inside Salesman | Technical Specialist | Driver Salesman | Order Taker | Trade Salesman | Detail Man | Factory Man | Technical Use Salesman | New Business Tangibles | New Business Intangibles |

Assistance in Bringing
The Sale to Completion

Arousing Demand and
Influencing Demand

Source: H. Robert Dodge, "The Role of the Industrial Salesman," *Mid-South Quarterly Business Review*, vol. IX (January 1972), p. 13.

ing demand and influencing patronage. *Service selling* aids the customer in bringing the sale to completion.

A more finite classification might include four types of sales tasks: *development, missionary, maintenance,* and *support.*[14] These can be arranged on a spectrum with examples of each type of sales task (see Figure 4-5). *Sales development* concerns the creation of customers, through methods such as motivating a customer to change vendors. *Missionary salesmen* pull the product through the marketing channel by providing low-key personal selling assistance. *Maintenance selling* involves the development of sales volume from existing customers. A *support salesman* provides continuing service to the buyer. In some cases, the support salesman also sells directly by suggesting a replacement item rather than repair of an older product.[15] All of these tasks are important, since each makes a significant contribution to the total marketing effort.

A Classification System

What has been described above is actually a series of selling situations. The field salesman's job usually involves a blend of these various tasks, while the sales representative may perform all four of these tasks at some point in his daily routine. Salesman A might spend 45 per cent of his time in sales development work, 25 per cent in missionary sales, 20 per cent in sales maintenance, and 10 per cent in sales support. Salesman B might have a different mix of activities: development, 5 per cent; missionary, 15 per cent; maintenance, 60 per cent; and support, 20 per cent. While most salesmen perform all of these tasks to some extent, it is still reasonable to classify salesmen by the activity in which they spend the bulk of their time. Salesman A would be a sales development specialist, and person B would be classified as a maintenance salesman.

In those cases where the person's selling efforts are equally divided between two tasks, the broader classifications—creative and service selling—would probably be useful. Hence, a salesman with the following mix:

---

[14]H. Robert Dodge, "The Role of the Industrial Salesman," *Mid-South Quarterly Business Review,* vol. IX (January 1972), pp. 11–15.
[15]Dodge (1972), p. 13.

40 percent sales development

40 percent missionary sales

15 percent maintenance selling

5 percent sales support

could best be classified as involved in *creative selling.*

Certainly, it can be concluded that the classification of salesmen is not a rigid system. The terminology varies according to the users and the selling situation. It is well to consider this when describing sales activities.

PURCHASING DECISIONS

Salesmen must be knowledgeable about the purchasing process of customers. Here, the reference is primarily to field salesmen dealing with industrial purchasing decisions. However, it should be noted that the same process is applicable to wholesale and retail buyers. While they may not be as complex, individual consumers also follow certain patterns in making purchase decisions.

A model of the industrial adoption process is shown in Figure 4–6. This model was based upon a study of 106 paper users, but its applicability to other purchasing decisions is evident. The schema shows that purchasers go through three distinct stages in the adoption process. First, they determine which product is suitable for the particular job. Next, the buyer determines which vendors will receive trial orders. Third, the trial orders are evaluated and a decision is made on whether to retain or drop a supplier.

At each stage in the adoption process, there are different buying influentials. While purchasing and top management are always involved to some extent, the other participants vary from stage to stage. The salesman's job is to be able to identify and isolate the key buying influence under varying circumstances.[16]

Many salespersons are simply unable to spot the decision-makers in purchasing situations. As a result, much of their activity and sales ef-

---

[16]See Steve Blickstein, "How to Find the Key Buying Influence," *Sales Management* (September 20, 1971), pp. 51–54.

FIGURE 4−6
The Industrial Adoption Process

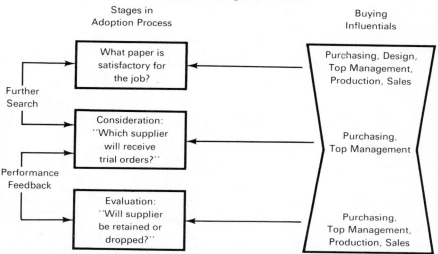

Source: John A. Martilla and James R. Schmelzer, "More Than Just a Foot in the Door?" *Sales Management* (January 10, 1972), p. 31. Reprinted by permission from *Sales Management*, The Marketing Magazine, Copyright 1972.

fort is wasted. Edward J. Feeney, vice-president of the Systems Performance Division of Emery Air Freight Corporation, has observed that:

> Selling is very, very inefficient compared to what it could be. Most salesmen are sitting in lobbies. They're calling on wrong accounts. They're calling on accounts that give them all the business that they can. They're calling on people they think can make the buying decision, when, in fact, they do not or cannot make much of it at all. . . .[17]

A basic problem is the fact that some purchasing decisions are stretched over several months and involve many different people. One computer order, for instance, took about two years from conception to

---

[17]Quoted in "The New Supersalesman" (1973), p. 45.

FIGURE 4–7
Diagram of a Computer Purchase Decision

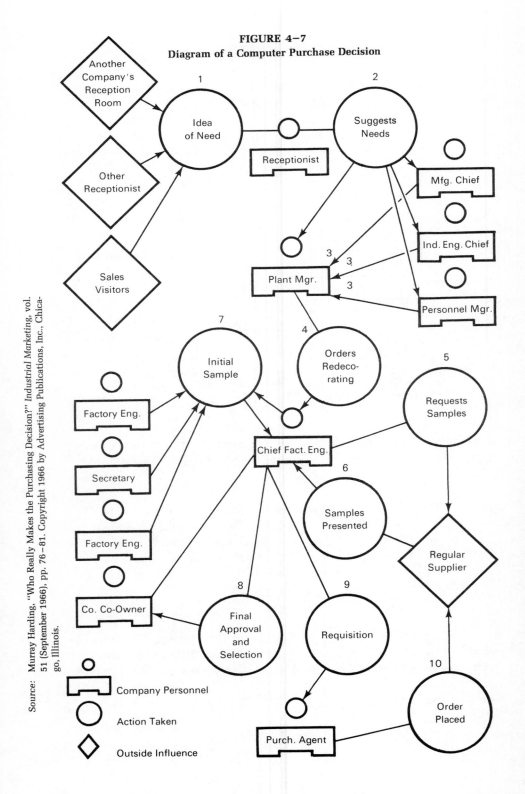

Source: Murray Harding, "Who Really Makes the Purchasing Decision?" Industrial Marketing, vol. 51 (September 1966), pp. 76–81. Copyright 1966 by Advertising Publications, Inc., Chicago, Illinois.

order placement. The path this order followed is shown in Figure 4 – 7. It is not difficult to visualize how a salesman in such circumstances would have problems in isolating the key buying influences. But, regardless of the hindrances involved, the field salesman must be able to get to the core of the purchasing decision in each selling situation he faces.

The purchasing mix is a useful tool in making such an analysis. A *purchasing mix* is a blend of purchasing elements that will offer the customer what he wants.[18] The elements of the purchasing mix are interrelated, as are the subelements within each class.

Table 4–1 outlines the elements of a purchasing mix for industrial buyers. An examination of this list reveals the various factors involved in most purchasing decisions. It can serve as a valuable checklist for field salesmen in their quest to understand purchasing decisions.

TABLE 4–1
Elements of a Purchasing Mix for Industrial Buyers

1. Product Elements
   1.1 Rate and continuity of production (both buyer and supplier)
   1.2 Design of production equipment (both buyer and supplier)
   1.3 Quality control consistency of quality of materials, workmanship, design, completeness of line, new product policies. Packaging — protection, convenience, identification, economy through material size, shape, construction
   1.4 Service — installation, repair, delivery, credit, returned goods, guarantees
   1.5 Indications of shifts in product elements

2. Supply Elements
   2.1 Frequency of purchase and volume
   2.2 Rapidity of consumption
   2.3 Seasonality of use
   2.4 Supplier development costs, such as tools supplied by buyer
   2.5 Reciprocal propensity

[18]G. E. Kiser, "A New Conceptual Framework for the Purchasing Function," *Business Studies*, vol. IX (Fall 1970), pp. 5 – 9.

3. Delivery Elements
   3.1 Mode and cost of transportation
   3.2 Suppliers' stock locations, variety, and quantity
   3.3 Degree of selectivity (differentiation) between suppliers
   3.4 Transactional elements—order-handling systems and other facilitating activities necessary to transfer title and take custody of goods
   3.5 Indications of shifts of relative importance of channels and members

4. Price Elements
   4.1 Unit price
   4.2 Discounts—functional, quantity, cash, other
   4.3 Service charges
   4.4 Negotiation costs and length of contract period
   4.5 Trends in price behavior

5. Possession Elements
   5.1 Adequacy of storage facilities
   5.2 Cost of storage
   5.3 Location of buyer's warehouses by type and design
   5.4 Indications of trends in possession elements

Source: G. E. Kiser, "A New Conceptual Framework for the Purchasing Function," *Business Studies*, vol. IX (Fall 1970), pp. 6–7.

TOWARD EFFECTIVE SELLING

Selling is a difficult task because of the multitude of variables that affect the sales function. Buyer-seller interaction is a complex communication system that often frustrates attempts at analysis. Despite this element of elusiveness, certain general comments can be made about selling. First, it is a *universal* function. Everyone is required to sell something at some time or another—their ideas, philosophies, personalities, or products. Regardless of the product or concept involved, the function of personal selling is universal.

The second factor related to effective selling is that at least some of the characteristics of successful selling are known. This knowledge allows the sales force to take some tentative steps toward improved sales performance. One approach is to consider the reasons why salesmen fail. A survey of sales managers (Table 4–2) indicated that the

TABLE 4–2
Why Salesmen Fail

Cause of Failure	Percent
Lack of Initiative	55
Poor Planning and Organization	39
Inadequate Product Knowledge	37
Lack of Enthusiasm	31
Salesman Not Customer-Oriented	30
Lack of Proper Training	23
Inability to Get Along with Buyers	21
Lack of Personal Goals	20

Source: Adapted from Charles Atkinson Kirkpatrick, *Salesmanship*, 5th ed. (Cincinnati: South-Western Publishing Co., 1971), p. 131.

lack of initiative was the leading cause of salesmen failure, followed by *poor planning and organization* and by *inadequate product knowledge*. It is important to observe that all of these factors are also crucial to other functional areas in the firm.

If the basic characteristics of successful selling—such as initiative, proper planning and organization, and adequate product knowledge— do in fact exist, then the next step is to select the appeal appropriate to the selling situation. Buying motivation can be classified as *rational, emotional*, or *societal*, each of which can be characterized as follows:

Rational. The prospect may be considered as a sort of economic automaton, buying essentially for rational reasons (price advantages, cost-savings effects, usage benefits, and the like).

Emotional. He may be regarded as essentially a creature of subtle whims, motivated by emotional reasons (sense of pride, need to lessen fears, romantic or other feelings of love, and the like).

Societal. He may be treated as an actor, Pavlovian-conditioned into buying for social role-playing reasons (performing as expected as husband, employer, member of social class, and the like).[19]

---

[19]Walter Gross, "Rational and Nonrational Appeals in Selling to Businessmen," *Georgia Business*, vol. 29 (February 1970), p. 1.

The salesman must gear his approach and presentation to the buying motivations exhibited by the prospect. While all three buying motives influence customers at different times, usually one of these appeals tends to predominate at any particular point. Effective selling requires that the salesman be able to recognize these motivations, and develop promotional appeals that are relevant.

STEPS IN THE SALES PROCESS

While terminology will vary somewhat, most sales managers identify eight distinct steps in the sales process:[20]

1. pre-approach (prospecting and qualifying);
2. approach;
3. presentation;
4. demonstration;
5. identifying and handling of objections;
6. closing;
7. follow-up;
8. second-effort review.

Pre-Approach

The initial step in the selling sequence is termed the *pre-approach* and actually comprises two distinct aspects: prospecting and qualify-

---

[20]For a more detailed discussion of the steps in selling, see: Kenneth B. Haas, *Professional Salesmanship* (New York: Holt, Rinehart and Winston, Inc., 1966), pp. 144–346; Charles Atkinson Kirkpatrick, *Salesmanship*, 5th ed. (Cincinnati: South-Western Publishing Co., 1971), pp. 213–400; Paul W. Ivey and Walter Horvath, *Successful Salesmanship* (Revised by Wayland A. Tonning), 4th ed. (Englewood Cliffs, N.J.: Prentice-Hall, Inc., 1961), pp. 101–383; Carlton A. Pederson and Milburn D. Wright, *Salesmanship: Principles and Methods*, 5th ed (Homewood, Ill.: Richard D. Irwin, Inc., 1971), pp. 293–538; Richard M. Baker, Jr. and Gregg Phiffer, *Salesmanship: Communication, Persuasion, Perception* (Boston: Allyn and Bacon, Inc., 1966), pp. 237–417; Edwin Charles Grief, *Modern Salesmanship: Principles and Problems* (Englewood Cliffs, N.J.: Prentice-Hall, Inc., 1958), pp. 143–424; Allan L. Reid, *Modern Applied Salesmanship* (Pacific Palisades, Cal.: Goodyear Publishing Company, Inc., 1970), pp. 187–391; Willard M. Thompson, *Salesmanship: Concepts, Management and Strategy* (New York: John Wiley and Sons, 1963), pp. 315–501; H. Webster Johnson, *Creative Selling* (Cincinnati: South-Western Publishing Company, 1966), pp. 95–278; Kenneth B. Haas and John W. Ernest, *Creative Salesmanship: Understanding Essentials* (Beverly Hills: Glencoe Press, 1969), pp. 85–268; Frederic A. Russell, Frank H. Beach, and Richard H. Buskirk, *Textbook of Salesmanship*, 8th ed. (New York: McGraw-Hill, Inc., 1969), pp. 153–504.

FIGURE 4–8

"Don't forget, I'm playing under a terrific handicap.
You're a potential customer."

Source: Reprinted by permission from *Sales Management*, The Marketing Magazine. Copyright 1973.

ing. *Prospecting* involves the seeking out of potential customers (see Figure 4–8) who may come to the salesman from many sources: friends and acquaintances, other salesmen, previous customers, suppliers, nonsales employees in the firm, and social and professional contacts. The identification of potential customers is not an easy task,[21] and prospecting is often a frustrating experience, particularly for the young salesman. The immediate payoff is often minimal, and the prospecting effort is typically met with rejection. Yet, sales managers will consistently point out that good prospecting usually separates the successful from the mediocre salesperson.

Consider the often-cited case of the new graduate who enters the

---

[21]Some of the difficulties in the salesman's perception of prospects are outlined in Gordon L. Wise, "Automobile Salesmen's Perceptions of New-Car Prospects," *Bulletin of Business Research*, vol. XLVI (February 1971), pp. 2–6.

.rst year, he receives numerous sales
ᵴ to his company. Two years later, he
ᴌ. Everyone asks, *"What happened?"*
e: *the new graduate simply exhausted*
ᵎ! In other words, he was highly success-
ᵴt of prospects, but when this list ended,
new prospects. The effective insurance
searching out new prospects continuously.
part of the pre-approach, since not all prospects are ᵩ ome customers. A man who is 6'9" tall and
who weighs 300 pᴑ may strongly desire a FIAT 124 Spider but,
practically, he would be more comfortable in a full-size automobile.
Another person may want the new $60,000 colonial style house on
Honeysuckle Drive, although his $7500 income rules out this purchase.
Salesmen must determine whether a prospect is *qualified* to acquire
the product or service.

Financial resources are the primary factor involved in *qualifying* a
prospect. As a result, salesmen must be familiar with the various credit reporting agencies that exist.

Approach

The starting point for the salesman's approach is adequate information. The salesman must be knowledgeable about varied aspects of the
sales process. He must

> know his company,
> know his product,
> know his competition,
> know his customer
> AND
> know himself.

If the salesman is familiar with all factors surrounding the selling
situation, he is ready to approach the prospect.

Traditionally, the approach has been viewed as somewhat standardized. Certainly, factors such as a person's handshake, smile, poise,
and appearance are important. Customers do form initial impressions

of salesmen; and these are important in purchasing decisions. Figure 4–9 is a self-evaluation instrument that has been used in some sales training programs. Admittedly, the reader might question the statisti-

FIGURE 4–9
An Evaluative Instrument for Considering
the Personal Qualities Important to the Approach
HOW DO YOU RATE?

Personal Qualities	#1 Tremendous	#2 Good	#3 Average	#4 Poor	#5 Horrible
Appearance					
Confidence and Poise					
Dependability					
Determination and Persistence					
Enthusiasm and Interest					
Imaginative Opening Remarks					
Handshake					
Speaking Voice					
Attractive Personality					
Sincerity					

Give yourself an honest rating on each of these qualities. Then calculate your "personal qualities index" by counting as follows: 10 – Tremendous; 8 – Good; 6 – Average; 4 – Poor; 1 – Horrible.

Here is Your Index Rating

Over 90 ⟶ You've got the approach "licked"!
70–90 ⟶ Good, but don't stop trying to improve.
50–70 ⟶ Fair – work on improving!
30–50 ⟶ Your approach hurts your sales performance.
Less than 30 ⟶ Have you ever considered another line of work?

cal validity of such a device, but it does suggest the personal qualities considered important in approaching a prospect.

While personal qualities are important to the salesman's approach, they should not always be regarded in terms of a rigid format. The approach can be varied to meet the buying motivations of the prospect. Figure 4–10 presents a sales aggression spectrum, according to which the relative aggressiveness of the salesman's approach varies inversely with the repeat-sale potential of the prospect. The higher the repeat-sale potential, the *softer* the approach should be and vice-versa.[22]

FIGURE 4–10
The Sales Aggression Spectrum with Ecological Determinants

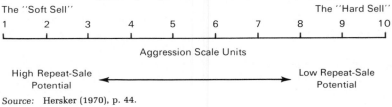

Source: Hersker (1970), p. 44.

Presentation

As one writer has noted, "a major determinant of the salesman's effectiveness is the quality of the sales presentation he delivers to the prospect."[23] The *presentation* is the core of the sales process, for this is where the salesman transmits his promotional message to the prospect. A presentation is the *medium* of the salesman-prospect dyad. The feedback mechanism of the interaction reflects how the presentation has been received, whether the response has been positive, negative, or neutral.

The disheartening fact is that so many salesmen make ineffectual sales presentations. One survey of buyers reported that four out of ten

---

[22]Hersker (1970), pp. 43–44. The effectiveness of the *hard* and *soft* sell is also studied in Richard C. Reizenstein, "A Dissonance Approach to Measuring the Effectiveness of Two Personal Selling Techniques Through Decision Reversal," *Conference Proceedings* (Chicago: American Marketing Association, 1971), pp. 176–180.
[23]Frederick E. Webster, "Interpersonal Communication and Salesman Effectiveness," *Journal of Marketing*, vol. 32 (July 1968), p. 12.

respondents classified the presentations that they generally witness as *less than good*.[24]

Sales presentations should be clear, concise, and well prepared. The usual format is for the salesman to describe the product's major characteristics, to cite its advantages, and to conclude by noting examples of customer satisfaction.

The salesman should seek agreement from the prospect on key points: "Don't you agree that this is an impressive looking car?" or "You seem to prefer the blue dress rather than the pink one," or "Do you like this particular option on the equipment?" In addition to seeking agreement on key points, the salesman should try to get the prospect to narrow the selection. Retail salesmen typically offer a prospect three choices — say, three different brands of cameras — since this lets the prospect focus on a selection of items that meet his needs. The salesman, of course, has already assessed what the prospect wants and needs in a camera purchase. The usual approach is to ask the prospect to narrow the choice to two items, which is accomplished by an analysis of the various features of the alternatives. Eventually, the selection process settles on the choice that is preferred.

Demonstration

Good demonstrations require adequate planning. The salesman should double check all parts of his demonstration before he attempts to begin a demonstration. Even a minor failure or malfunction at this critical point may convince the prospect that the product (as well as the company it represents) is totally undependable.

Demonstrations are a supplement and reinforcement for the salesman's presentation. They allow the prospect to take an active role in the sales situation. They involve the customer in the presentation, and they heighten buying interest in the product.

A basic rule in demonstrating the product is to let the prospect touch, feel, or operate the product. A clothing salesman tries immediately to demonstrate his product — "Now, let's have you slip that coat on, sir." An automobile salesman suggests a demonstration ride. An industrial salesman arranges a demonstration of his product before the

---

[24]"How Buyers Rate Salesmen," *Sales Management* (January 15, 1971), pp. 21, 23.

purchaser's technical personnel. All of these salesmen realize the value of having the prospect involved in the sales presentation.

Identifying and Handling of Objections

Some salesmen experience considerable difficulty in identifying objections. Either they become so involved in their presentation that they simply overlook the objection, or they treat the customer's action or remarks as a complete rejection of their product or service. Both reactions are wrong. In both cases, the salesman has perceived the objection incorrectly.

An objection is a logical part of the sales presentation. Comments such as "Well, I think I'll shop around before deciding" or "I had better check with my wife on this first" or "I don't like the four-speed transmission" are reasonable and should be expected. People naturally tend to postpone, delay, or avoid making purchase decisions. Salesmen should be aware of this, expect it, and learn to deal with such objections.

In many cases, objections are really disguised requests for additional information. "I don't like the four-speed transmission" often means "What other types of transmissions are available?" Objections usually indicate that the prospect has at least some interest in the product. This is an opening for the effective salesman to expand his presentation and to strengthen his selling arguments.

Closing

After the salesman has made his presentation, demonstrated the product, and handled any objections, he is ready to ask for the order. All his effort is wasted unless the salesman can get the prospect to agree to buy the product, and this is a spot where many salesmen fail. The salesman should be succinct and positive in his close. Typically, he holds back a major sales point, such as a testimonial, to assist his close.

Numerous closings are available to the salesman:

Alternative Decisions. "Will that be cash or charge?" is a traditional closing. A more recent one is "Do you prefer to use BankAmericard or Master Charge?"

Review of the Sales Presentation. Summarize the major points that were made during the presentation. Ask for agreement from the prospect as each point is covered.

Proposal of a Decision. "May I write that order up for you?" is a typical type of proposed decision. "I think you preferred the brown one, didn't you?" is another.

Many other closings are available to the salesman, but these are probably among the most useful. The crucial point is that the salesman should try several closings throughout his presentation. Better salesmen always try to close early. If they are not successful, they continue the presentation and then try a different close. Effective salesmen know that if they have completed all of the earlier steps successfully, then the prospect is certainly worth an extra effort at closing. In most cases, this simply means switching to a different type of close. Closing is the most important aspect of selling, for unless the salesman can close the sale, the other steps in the sales process are meaningless.

Follow-Up

After-sale activities are also very important. Effective sales follow-up reduces the buyer's *dissonance* or doubt, and it improves the chance that the person will become a repeat customer. Failure to follow up properly on a sale is a major complaint voiced by buyers. This was noted by 61 per cent of the respondents to a survey of buyers conducted by *Sales Management* magazine. In the words of one buyer: "Service is the first thing that gets sold, and the last thing delivered."[25]

Salesmen should check back with purchasers to determine whether they are satisfied or not and to remove any source of discontent. These callbacks also allow the salesman to gather valuable market information and to make additional sales.

Satisfied customers become good salesmen for the products they bought. For example, buyers often reduce their dissonance by promoting their purchases to their peers.[26] Any major purchase decision cre-

---

[25]"How Buyers Rate Salesmen" (1971), p. 23.
[26]See John R. Stuteville, "The Buyer as a Salesman," *Journal of Marketing*, vol. 32 (July 1968), pp. 14–18.

ates a considerable degree of anxiety in the buyer, anxiety which he can reduce by promoting the item which he eventually bought. This word-of-mouth promotion often encourages friends and relatives of the satisfied customer to desire the product also. Hence, it is important that the salesman initiate a formal procedure for following up on customers.

Second-Effort Review

Second-effort review refers to the salesman's continuing efforts to improve his performance. A salesman should conduct a post-mortem on every call he makes, by asking himself what it was that allowed him to close that sale or what caused him to lose it. Another useful practice is to review the checklist shown in Table 4–3 at the start of each selling day.

Regardless of the procedure that is followed, every salesman should

TABLE 4–3
A Checklist for Effective Selling

CUSTOMERS LIKE THE SALESMAN WHO

1. Exhibits thoughtfulness and consideration in scheduling his calls.
2. Keeps appointments and promises.
3. Conducts his business efficiently and then leaves promptly.
4. Has authority for any commitment he makes.
5. Knows prices and terms, and quotes them in a clear, understandable, complete manner.
6. Tells a concise, coherent, well-organized sales story.
7. Can answer all questions he should be able to answer.
8. Displays genuine interest in helping the customer better himself.
9. Continues to be interested even after changing a prospect into a customer.
10. Makes the customer feel important.
11. Respects confidences, beliefs, and intelligence.
12. Refrains from going behind or over the head of the customer without the customer's knowledge.
13. Does not allow himself to become too familiar or too aggressive.
14. Keeps friendship and business in their proper places.

Source: Kirkpatrick (1971), p. 350.

make a serious effort to assess his own performance. Second-effort review allows the person to become a better salesman.

INCREASING SALES VOLUME

Effective selling means that the salesman not only makes the sale, but also maximizes the volume of the sale to the extent feasible with long-run company objectives and profit considerations. In other words, the salesman would want neither to harm long-term relationships with the customer nor to generate increased volume that was profitless. If these constraints are fulfilled, then increased sales volume should be the goal of every successful salesman.

One way to accomplish this objective is through *suggestion selling*. Once an initial sale is closed, the salesman attempts to have the customer broaden the original purchase with related products, special promotional items, and holiday or seasonal merchandise. The underlying premise is that the salesman should not attempt to sell products the customer does not need or want. However, it is an ethical sales practice to help the customer become aware of additional needs. In fact, it seems reasonable to argue that the salesman should point out additional items that would enhance the consumer's enjoyment of the original purchase.

The term *selling-up* means persuading a customer to buy an item that is higher in price than the one he originally intended to purchase. For example,

> . . . one salesman sold a bereaved woman a finer casket for her dead husband by pointing out that it had coil springs under the pad so that the body would be supported in greater comfort throughout eternity.[27]

Although the humor in this situation derives from the callous way in which the salesman has offered the woman something for which she obviously has no need, this kind of selling-up is hardly advisable.

---

[27]Baker and Phiffer (1966), p. 97.

In actuality the practice of selling-up should always be used within the constraints of the customer's real needs.

Regardless of the sales technique that is used, sales personnel should seek out ways to maximize sales volume within ethical constraints. It is an integral part of the total sales process and an important determinant of overall marketing performance.

SUMMARY Personal selling experience is often considered as necessary for those hoping to advance to a position in marketing management, particularly when the job involves direct customer contact and public exposure. Chapter 4 has outlined the basic essentials of the sales function. This examination of the actual operation of the sales function is a vital prerequisite for the study of the managerial aspects discussed in Parts II, III, and IV of this book.

Chapter 4 has contrasted the traditional salesmanship approach with the modern buyer-seller dyad viewpoint. The salesmanship approach regarded the salesman's behavior as the key ingredient to the sales process; the prospect was treated as essentially passive. By contrast, the buyer-seller dyad acknowledges personal interaction and the importance of external factors such as repeat-sale potential.

A classification scheme for the sales function was developed, based upon sales tasks. This system identified four types of sales tasks: development, missionary, maintenance, and support.

Chapter 4 then discussed purchasing decisions, the industrial adoption process, and a purchasing mix. Typical reasons for sales failures and buying motivation categories were also considered.

A major part of the chapter was devoted to discussion of the eight distinct steps of the sales process: (1) pre-approach (prospecting and qualifying); (2) approach; (3) presentation; (4) demonstration; (5) identifying and handling of objections; (6) closing; (7) follow-up; (8) second-effort review.

The chapter concluded with a consideration of increasing sales volume through suggestion selling and selling-up.

DISCUSSION/REVIEW QUESTIONS

1. Briefly identify each of the following:
   - (a) AIDR
   - (b) AIDA
   - (c) Arthur Frederick Sheldon
   - (d) systems selling
   - (e) sales tasks
   - (f) creative selling
   - (g) service selling
   - (h) purchasing mix
   - (i) suggestion selling
   - (j) selling-up
   - (k) stimulus-response theory of selling

2. Contrast the *salesmanship* and *buyer-seller dyad* viewpoints of personal selling.

3. Discuss A. F. Sheldon's conceptualization of the sales process.

4. "Selling is an interpersonal communication process." Comment.

5. Why is the sales process described as a "*highly structured interaction system*"? Discuss.

6. Apply Durbin's theory of organization to selling behavior.

7. Four sales tasks are identified in this chapter: development, missionary, maintenance, and support. Describe each of these and cite examples of salesmen performing these tasks. How can you use these categories of sales tasks to classify salesmen?

8. Explain the industrial purchasing decision.

9. Buying motivations may be classified as rational, emotional, or societal. Discuss.

10. List and briefly describe each of the eight basic steps in the sales process.

11. Describe the relationship between sales aggressiveness and repeat-sale potential.

12. Complete the self-evaluation instrument presented in Figure 4–9. How did you rate according to this test?

13. Set up a practice sales situation. Ask a friend to act as a customer, and try to sell the following items to this person:
    - (a) color television
    - (b) Ford Pinto
    - (c) electric frying pan
    - (d) room air conditioner
    - (e) sweater
    - (f) Sheaffer pen set
    - (h) a vacation trip to Hawaii
    - (i) a cocker span.el
    - (j) Frigidaire washer and dryer
    - (k) your neighbor's house
    - (l) Datsun 240 Z
    - (m) Westinghouse toaster

INTRODUCTION
TO THE
CASE STUDIES

The case studies that follow are directly related to the chapters in Part I. All cases are based upon actual events and problems. Many indicate the actual firms and persons involved, while others have been disguised to protect proprietary information. All of these cases demonstrate situations and problems faced by salesmen and sales managers every day. Throughout this book, each part division is followed by a similar series of cases; it is hoped that they will stimulate the reader to further pursue the subject of sales management.

Each case is accompanied by an assignment, by questions, and/or by problems. The authors suggest that the cases be employed to reinforce the concepts presented in the various chapters. This may be accomplished via written assignments or class discussion.

PART ONE
CASES

CASE 1
THE NEW SALES MANAGER

Bret Stanley, the district sales manager for the Northern section of New Jersey, is talking to Harvey Bianco, the general sales manager for his company. Mr. Bianco has been visiting districts on the East Coast for the past two weeks. The company is headquartered in Los Angeles.

Mr. Bianco begins the conversation:

"Needless to say, we think you have been doing a good job, Bret. That is why the company promoted you from the field force last year. Personally, I think you are going to advance rapidly in the organization.

"In fact, one of the purposes of these inspection trips is to try to help our young managers develop as soon and fast as possible. The company needs young people with innovative ideas.

"Bret, are there any problems with which I can help you? Have you had any difficulties adjusting from the role of salesman to that of sales manager?"

Mr. Stanley:

"Actually, I think the transition has been rather smooth. While my wife complains occasionally, I have met the increased workload by just putting in more hours—I can get a lot of my paperwork done here at the office on Sunday when no one else is around.

"So far, I don't have any personnel or organizational problems—that I know of! I suppose my only difficulty has been trying to find enough time to do everything. Recruiting new salesmen takes a lot of time; and, of course, I retained my seven largest customers as house accounts. I have to continue to give those fellows the same level of service I did when I was a salesman. I can do it because Veda, my secretary, does a great job of taking care of the administrative details here at the office."

ASSIGNMENT

1. If you were Mr. Bianco, how would you respond to Mr. Stanley?
2. Has Mr. Stanley made a "smooth transition" from salesman to sales manager?
3. Do you see any potential problems in the way Mr. Stanley is running his district?

CASE 2
INSTANT SWIMWEAR, INC.

Instant Swimwear, Inc., is a manufacturer of disposable, paper swimwear. The firm, located in Philadelphia, had sales of $3.5 million last year.

The company's products resemble cotton in texture and appearance, but are actually made of reinforced paper fiber. Various sizes, colors, and styles are available. The products are sold primarily in gift shops at hotels and variety stores in resort areas. Guests who have forgotten their swimwear can purchase Instant Swimwear for $3.75 (men) or $5.75 (women).

Purchasers can use the swimwear about seven or eight times before disposing of the item. But no one need worry about embarrassing accidents, since the product is designed to become completely colorless before any damage to the actual fiber occurs. The package clearly warns that the disappearance of colors means that one should dispose of the swimwear. A considerable "safety margin" is built into the "colorless warning sign."

Instant Swimwear has been distributed solely through agent middlemen specializing in variety merchandise. Recently, however, a top level management decision to build a field sales force has been made. The company will employ and train a sales force of twelve persons. Management expects the field force to be operative within four months. The agent middleman distribution network will be completely disbanded at that time.

ASSIGNMENT

Assume that you have just been given the responsibility of building Instant Swimwear's new sales force.
1. How would you go about this task?
2. What types of sales management decisions must be made?
3. How would you coordinate other promotional activities with the sales effort?

CASE 3
SAMUEL KEISBERG ASKS A QUESTION

For several years, a state university in the Upper Midwest has sponsored a Career Conference where students can hear guest speakers discuss various career opportunities for college graduates. These talks are usually limited to about 45 minutes, and they are typically followed by a question and answer period of equal length. The Career Conference has always been the subject of considerable interest. Recent discussions have centered around careers with the FBI, the Foreign Service, and the CIA, careers in teaching and in various social services; they have attracted "standing room only" crowds.

Tonight, however, the case is different. Alf Swanson, the regional manager for a national insurance company, and Dr. Charles Ainsbury, a professor in the school's marketing department, are scheduled to speak on careers in personal selling. Only about 25 students, mostly from Professor Ainsbury's sales management class, are in attendance. After some introductory remarks by Dr. Ainsbury, Mr. Swanson spends the bulk of the allocated time describing the duties and responsibilities of new salesmen.

When the group is asked if there are any questions, Samuel Keisberg, a senior majoring in history, raises his hand. Professor Ainsbury recognizes him, and Mr. Keisberg comments:

"While I enjoyed Mr. Swanson's remarks, I believe he ignored a basic problem. Quite simply, salesmen have never been held in high regard by society. I've spent four years studying the history of various times and countries, and never can I recall a salesperson rising to any level of greatness. Hence, I would have to conclude that there is something about the occupation that does not attract young people possessing leadership attributes. For example, one can cite Presidents of the United States with backgrounds in agriculture, the military, engineering, retail management, law and the like, but never one from sales!

"Is this a reasonable criticism of the field? Or did I miss something in Mr. Swanson's remarks?"

Alf Swanson, fidgeting nervously, replied:

"Well, since I have done most of the talking tonight, I'll let Dr. Ainsbury handle that question!"

ASSIGNMENT

How should Dr. Ainsbury reply to Mr. Keisberg's comment?

CASE 4
UNION STREET BARGAIN-RITE

The lease on the Union Street Bargain-Rite supermarket in Wilmington, Delaware, which had been renewed several times, was to expire in three months. Harry Culver, district sales manager, was asked by Bargain-Rite's president, John Goldman, to recommend whether the lease for the Union Street market should be renewed. Mr. Culver was familiar with food marketing in Delaware, having managed several Bargain-Rite supermarkets, including the Union Street store. He had been district sales manager for the last six years.

The store had been leased originally as a temporary facility. In January 1963, a fire destroyed a large Bargain-Rite supermarket in Elsmere, Delaware, a suburb of Wilmington. In order to continue service to the store's customers and retain patronage, Bargain-Rite rented a vacant supermarket on Union Street in Wilmington. The Union Street store was small and in need of repair, but Bargain-Rite's management considered the building adequate for a temporary move. A new Elsmere supermarket was opened nine months later, but the Union Street store continued to operate.

Bargain-Rite operated about 100 stores in Pennsylvania, Delaware, Maryland, and New Jersey, of which five were in Delaware. Three stores in suburban Wilmington had average weekly sales volumes of over $130,000; a store in Dover, 45 miles south of Wilmington, $55,000; and the Union Street store, $30,000. A sixth store was planned for another Wilmington suburb.

Bargain-Rite's operating philosophy was to offer a wide variety of merchandise, both national and private brands, at competitive prices. Breaking with traditional pricing practices, Bargain-Rite was a pioneer in single-unit pricing, establishing a trend followed by other Middle Atlantic supermarket chains. Customer service was minimal with only standard services of check cashing, bagging, and the like, available to customers. The stores operated on a net profit margin of one per cent.

Newer stores were located in high-traffic areas. Bargain-Rite's management also tried to locate a supermarket near a department store with a similar high-volume, low-margin philosophy.

Newspaper advertising was the dominant form of promotion. Cou-

112

pons had proved successful and were used extensively, but stamps and games had never been tried.

The physical condition of the Union Street store was depressing. The ceiling, walls, and floor were a mass of pipes, cracks, and peeling paint. Heating was a major problem, and the store closed several times during the previous winter because of heating failures. Parking facilities were limited, restricted to twenty spaces along the side of the store where most of the receiving was done. If the parking lot was full, trucks either waited or delivered merchandise through the front door.

Because the Union Street Bargain-Rite was located in a heavily populated urban area, customers were from the local neighborhoods. Most customers were of Italian and Puerto Rican descent. This traffic was highly immobile, with approximately 90 per cent of the customers walk-ins. The store catered to these ethnic groups by carrying a broad line of specialty food items. Purchases of private brands far exceeded national brand sales, and lower grade meat items were popular. The only competition in the immediate area was an A & P market which was scheduled to close in two months.

Management rotation was normal, although there was a stigma attached to a move to Union Street.

Pilferage was a major problem. In fact, during some recent weeks, the merchandise losses from pilferage exceeded profits.

Mr. Culver was to report to Mr. Goldman with his decision within a month.

ASSIGNMENT

1. If you were in Mr. Culver's position, what would you decide?
2. What factors should be considered in making this decision? Why?

CASE 5
THE NEW BUYERS

Henry Culver, a recent graduate of California State College, is the assistant director of purchasing at the West Coast Manufacturing Company. Culver, who is black, reports to Matt Tobchek, the director of purchasing. In addition to Culver and Tobchek, there are two secretaries and an engineer who writes specifications for many of West Coast's technical purchases.

One afternoon, Mr. Culver was in charge of the office while the director was attending a management meeting. About 3:00 P.M., Jack Stone, a salesman for one of West Coast's major suppliers, stopped in the office. Stone approached the receptionist and asked to see Mr. Tobchek. When he was told that the purchasing director was out of the office, but that he could see Henry Culver, the salesman replied, "Well, I guess I'll just skip it and come back Monday. If I see Culver, he'll want to know what my company's minority hiring record is!"

Unfortunately for Jack Stone, Culver's office door was open and he heard the salesman's remark. Henry's initial thought was to go to the outer office and confront Stone. However, upon reflection, he decided to ignore the remark. But, Culver thought, "Wait 'till that new contract comes up; I will really make it hot for that guy!"

* * * * *

Joe Willis is head of a research group at a leading industrial laboratory. As head of the research group, Joe, who is black and holds a Ph.D. in chemistry, is responsible for purchases of scientific instruments and laboratory equipment.

A member of Joe's staff had requested a special microscope that cost $5,000. The salesman brought it into the laboratory for a demonstration. Because Joe was attending a meeting, he arrived late and asked the salesman to show him the microscope. The salesman looked at Joe and said, "Look, sonny, I haven't time to go through that again. You should have been here when I started. Besides, you'll have a chance to see it work after your boss has bought it."

ASSIGNMENT

1. Assume you are the salesman's manager in each of the above cases and these incidents are reported to you. Would you discipline these salesmen? How?
2. What do these excerpts tell you about the changing environment of selling?

CASE 6
HASBRO INDUSTRIES, INC.

Hasbro Industries is one of the ten largest toy manufacturers in the United States. In the fall of 1972 Hasbro's management faced certain consumer pressures, many of which had been strongly felt by Hasbro and other toy companies in the past. The Federal Trade Commission, Food and Drug Administration, Federal Communications Commission, Consumers Union, and parents groups continued to pose challenges to the toy industry, particularly in the areas of product safety and promotional techniques.

COMPANY BACKGROUND

Hasbro Industries, Inc. began in Rhode Island in 1926. Originally, the firm was in the textile business; in the early 1930s it began to wrap school pencil boxes in cloth. In the 1940s the company entered both the pencil manufacturing and toy making industries.

Hasbro grew substantially over the years. The company now employs in its toy operations a permanent labor force of approximately 2750 persons, more than 79 per cent of whom are engaged in production. About 600 are employed in its school supplies and pencil manufacturing operations.

The tremendous growth of Hasbro was largely a result of changes in the company's management and marketing approaches. The responsibility for all day-to-day operations of the firm was assigned to Stephen Hassenfeld—Hasbro's 30-year-old executive vice president and the third generation of the founding family. Steve Hassenfeld introduced into the company a new, young group of executives, most of whom were drawn from outside the toy industry and from outside Rhode Island.

This case was adapted from a case prepared by David Loudon and Albert Della Bitta, both of the University of Rhode Island, as a basis for classroom discussion rather than as an illustration of effective or ineffective solutions to problems. All rights reserved to the authors.

According to Steve Hassenfeld, who recruited the new management team, "Five years ago we were what Wall Street would call an all-family business. We've worked hardest lately in getting the kind of management team a small family business doesn't have."

One major result was that Hasbro diversified into new fields: children's television, day-care centers, and housewares. Together with its toy and pencil business, these operations have made Hasbro a small conglomerate.

MAJOR PRODUCT LINES

Toys

The company designs, manufactures, and markets a broad line of toys, dolls, games, and accessories which are designed for children of different age groups. Over 90 per cent of the company's toy sales result from the sale of items that retail at prices from $1 to $10.

Because the company's toy business is seasonal, shipments during the second half of each calendar year are much greater than shipments during the first half. During the first half, Hasbro produces toys for inventory largely to satisfy orders calling for later delivery and, to a lesser extent, in anticipation of future orders.

Hasbro seeks to avoid large amounts of unsold toys after Christmas and after fads; therefore, the company pursues the *promotion staple*, a toy that requires only moderate advertising to sell well all year around, year after year. Hasbro also stresses the marketing of product groups bearing recognizable names rather than individual toy items, as advertising costs are not substantially greater for a whole line than for one toy.

The company's toy line now consists of approximately 450 items. The principal categories are the following:

Preschool toys, including the Romper Room line, introduced in 1970; Captain Kangaroo's Wooden Toys, introduced in 1972; and Your Baby line of infant playthings, introduced in 1972.

Action toys, including the G.I. Joe Adventure Team and accessories, introduced in 1964; and Scream'n Demons motorcycles, introduced in 1971.

116

Dolls, including the World of Love dolls and accessories, introduced in 1971.

Craft sets, including the Arts and Crafts Today line, introduced in 1971.

Staple items, including chess and checker sets, doctors' and nurses' kits, banks, and other items such as its Mr. Potato Head and Lite Brite toys.

In 1969 Hasbro effected a "repositioning" of G.I. Joe, a toy that accounts for a significant share of the company's volume. Because of an apparent waning interest in military toys, G.I. Joe's image began to emphasize adventure, rather than war. At the peak of its popularity in 1965, G.I. Joe had sales of $23 million, but by 1968 the category was producing only $4.8 million in sales. After the repositioning in 1969, the G.I. Joe Adventure Team and related accessories reassumed its importance within the industry, and in 1971 accounted for approximately $12.5 million in toy sales.

In 1970, Hasbro introduced the Romper Room preschool line in an attempt, as Steve Hassenfeld put it, "to upgrade the quality level of the products that we were then manufacturing. " This line, which consists of over 65 items, accounted for approximately $11.8 million or 22 per cent of net toy sales in 1971.

School Supplies

The company's school supplies division either manufactures or imports a broad line of black and colored pencils, pens, erasers, drawing instruments, slide rules, stationery, and related items. Hasbro's pencil market has grown from 10 to 12 per cent a year. The company has encouraged consumers to buy full sets of pencils, instead of two or three at a time.

Nursery Schools

In the fall of 1970, Hasbro opened three nursery schools in Rhode Island on an experimental basis. In the years 1970 and 1971, the operations of these nursery schools resulted in losses. The company has no plans to further expand these operations, as it does not feel that it can offer a quality service at rates currently available in the nursery school field.

Television Programming

The company, through its recently acquired and wholly owned subsidiary, Romper Room Enterprises, Inc., is involved in the production of television programs. The principal program is the Romper Room television nursery school, a 20-year-old internationally syndicated program—the oldest in the business—which is shown on approximately 85 television stations in the United States and on 55 stations in foreign countries. According to Mr. Hassenfeld, Romper Room's biggest asset is the way it encourages children in the home audience to participate, rather than passively watch the screen. The show has received commendations from parents and from the President's Council on Youth Fitness for its exercise routines that get children to use their muscles while they play.

MARKETING

Organization

Hasbro's marketing department was revamped in 1966. Because of the changing orientation at Hasbro, the company's national sales manager and its advertising director decided to leave the firm. These veteran toy marketers were replaced by men in their twenties. These new executives have helped to steer the company in new directions; they have developed new products, introduced a product manager organization, and intensified market research among children and their parents.

Product Design and Development

Success in the toy business is based to a substantial extent on the continuing development of new toy items and on the redesigning, restyling, and repackaging of existing items for improved market acceptance.

Several years ago Hasbro determined that its product lines were not in the mainstream of the industry since the company did not manufacture many products that fell within the major industry categories—preschool items, dolls, nonriding transportation vehicles, and games. The company then moved to update its product lines by giving the marketing department greater control over product development. Because of this organizational change, the company lost its director of product development, who resigned after being with the firm for thirteen years. The director of product development now reports to the marketing vice president, whereas previously the two positions were at a similar level within the company.

The company spends over a million dollars annually on activities relating to the development and design of new products (including related art work) and relating to the improvement or modification of old products. Approximately 65 employees—including designers, artists, model makers, and engineers—carry on this work. In addition to its own staff, Hasbro deals with a number of independent inventors and toy designers, for whose designs and ideas the company competes with many other toy manufacturers.

Product quality and *playability* are important concerns for Hasbro. The company utilizes laboratory tests of its products and also observes children at play with the items, the latter serving as much to determine how well the children like a certain toy as to test product quality and durability. The company also interviews parents to obtain their viewpoints.

Channels of Distribution

Hasbro's toy products are sold throughout the United States to chain stores, jobbers, and retailers by company salesmen and manufacturers' representatives. Approximately two-thirds of the firm's sales are made to independent jobbers who maintain inventories for sale to retailers. Hasbro also maintains showrooms in New York City, Oakbrook (Chicago), Dallas, and Atlanta. A manufacturers' representative independently maintains displays of Hasbro's products in San Francisco, Los Angeles, and Portland. Approximately 90 per cent of net toy sales are made by company salesmen and approximately 10 per cent by manufacturers' representatives. Hasbro's toys are also sold in numerous foreign countries by exporters and by foreign producers licensed by the company.

Promotion

Hasbro advertises its toy products on children's network television programs. The company also uses commercials on local television stations in the more important consumer markets. In 1971, Hasbro spent approximately $5.7 million for toy advertising and sales promotion, nearly all of which was used for television advertising. The promotion budget is expected to increase significantly in future years. Hasbro strategy is to advertise a few specifically selected items in its product groups in a manner designed to promote the sale of other items in those product groups. Last year product groups advertised by the firm accounted for approximately 80 per cent of the company's net toy sales.

The company's products are frequently used in premium programs. For example, Borden's has offered G.I. Joe to promote sales of its Dutch-Chocolate mix, instant coffee, and malted milk.

Hasbro also inaugurated the industry's first incentive program involving trips and merchandise prizes for jobbers and jobber salesmen.

SOCIAL ISSUES

Various facets of toy marketing have come under increasing criticism over the past few years. The areas of major concern to toy producers such as Hasbro are those related to product safety and advertising.

Product Safety

The U.S. Public Health Service has estimated that there are about 700,000 injuries involving toys every year. Because of congressional reaction to dangerous toys, toy products are now subject to the provisions of the Federal Child Protection and Toy Safety Act of 1969. The Secretary of Health, Education, and Welfare may prohibit the marketing of items intended for use by children, if, after appropriate proceedings, the items have been determined to be hazardous. In addition, the marketing of items that are deemed imminently hazardous to the public health and safety may be barred by the Secretary for limited periods without a hearing. Furthermore, manufacturers may be required to repurchase hazardous items and reimburse certain expenses, even if such items were manufactured and sold prior to the adoption of the Act. From time to time the government has issued regulations that affect the manufacture of toys, specifically with respect to such aspects as the lead content of paint and the classification of electrically operated toys. Regulations have been proposed affecting other aspects of toy manufacture. However, Hasbro is uncertain what effect such regulations, if finally adopted, will have on its business or on the entire toy industry.

Hasbro did not anticipate that some of its products would draw government and consumer criticism. For example, the company's Javelin Darts (one of a number of lawn dart games then on the market) came under government fire as a hazardous toy. Another product, Super-Dough, drew a warning to toy buyers from *Consumer Reports*, even though the product contained an elaborate instruction sheet along with warnings that the product was not for internal consumption and that children with allergies could undergo serious reactions. Hasbro removed both of these toys from the market.

In order to maintain and improve the safety of its toy products, Hasbro has instituted more extensive screening and quality control procedures. Nevertheless, there can be no assurance that the firm's products will not be investigated by the government or recalled from the market.

Violent Toys

The marketing of war toys has met with opposition from some consumer groups, and the American Toy Fair has been picketed by various anti-war-toy groups. Concern over such toys is expressed by these groups because of the potentially harmful influence which they feel such toys may have on the child's development.

The toy industry's position has been that war toys don't cause war, they only reflect it. In other words, the industry association feels that violence is learned from human example, not from things. Nevertheless, in deference to the antiwar sentiment, Hasbro's G.I. Joe, which used to be outfitted in military dress, has taken on an adventure theme. However, the company does maintain in its G.I. Joe line a replica of an Army jeep with a recoilless rifle mounted on it.

Although not classified as a violent toy, a water gun which Hasbro marketed—called Hypo Squirt—was fashioned like a giant hypodermic needle. Even though the product had been on the market for seven years, when the drug issue developed, the toy was suddenly

121

dubbed "play junior junkie" in the press and drew considerable criticism from the public. Hasbro withdrew the toy from the market.

Packaging

The Federal Trade Commission has spot checked the packaging of Hasbro's toy products as part of an investigation of "slack-filled" packaging practices within the toy industry. Although no action was taken by the FTC against Hasbro, the company has no assurance that the packaging of some of its products does not violate FTC regulations.

Advertising

Children's television advertising has come under increasing scrutiny from government, parents, and consumer groups. The focal point for criticism centers around the use (or as consumer groups term it—the misuse) of advertising on television shows aimed at children, particularly within Saturday and Sunday morning programming.

Even toy retailers have criticized the magnitude of toy advertising. According to a survey conducted among 5200 toy and hobby retailers, toy store operators dislike national television advertising, despite the fact that such advertising of toys by manufacturers has increased retailers' business.

The reason for toy retailers' dislike of television is their suspicion that the cost of television advertising is so high that manufacturers are forced to charge exorbitant prices for toys, counting on the appeal of television to children to force sales to the ultimate disappointment of children and parents and the resentment of parents against retail stores which sell toys.

Protests were made by parents and consumer groups concerning the nature of advertising on children's shows as well as the extent of such promotion. One vocal organization has been ACT (Action for Children's Television), a Boston-based citizens' group that claims 2500 members and supporters.

ACT is fundamentally opposed to commercialization of television aimed at children and has argued for the elimination of advertising during such programming. The Federal Communications Commission

(FCC) has instituted an Inquiry and Proposed Rule Making procedure in response to a petition from ACT, which requested that the FCC prohibit sponsorship and commercials on children's programs and prohibit the inclusion, use, or mention of products, services, or stores during such programs. The petition cited the Romper Room television program produced by Hasbro's subsidiary, among other programs, as being commercially oriented.

ACT argued that children were being unfairly influenced by the program's advertising since Romper Room teachers were doing the commercials. In addition, the group criticized the use of toys on the program that were also advertised on Romper Room. Even before the ACT charges surfaced, Hasbro had taken steps to counter such criticism. The company decided that no Romper Room teacher could do a commercial for any toy product. In addition, the company stopped advertising Romper Room toys used on the program.

However, this action did not appear to satisfy ACT. For example, one of ACT's directors and a mother of two stated, "I don't think Hasbro has reached the heart of the problem, which is selling to unsophisticated preschool children." By using Hasbro products on the program, she added, "they still have their commercial by having the children play with the toys on the program."

ACT and other critics also complain about the number of advertisements which typically run within children's programs shown between 7:00 A.M. and 2:00 P.M. on Saturdays and Sundays. Commercials and nonprogram material may amount to no more than 12 minutes per hour (down from 16 minutes), according to the Television Code Review Board of the National Association of Broadcasters. Critics have also advocated that commercials during the children's programs be clustered.

The FTC has brought action against several toy manufacturers (although not against Hasbro) for deceptive advertising practices. Hasbro attempts to comply with the principles established in these actions, as well as with the rules promulgated by the FTC and with the regulations prescribed by the National Association of Broadcasters. The NAB standards for toy commercials are quite specific, and before a toy commercial can be shown on television, it must be approved by the NAB.

Some firms within the industry have made moves to reduce the criticism of advertising practices affecting children. For example, Ideal Toy Company, which advertised directly to children via network television, has dropped sponsorship of Saturday morning television — where the major controversy is — and now buys early weekday evening prime time. Other toy marketers such as Fisher-Price have for some time been pursuing a strategy of targeting their message almost exclusively at parents, particularly mothers. However, Hasbro had decided to continue its present policy of weekend television advertising.

ASSIGNMENT

1. What major changes have taken place at Hasbro? What impact have these changes had on sales management?
2. Analyze Hasbro's societal environment. Which of these environmental forces are most important to sales management?
3. What strategy should Hasbro follow with respect to future government and consumer complaints?

CASE 7
SMITH AND CASTLE COMPANY

Jim Stenburg was 37, married with three children, and owned a mortgaged home in Eastland, Illinois, where he had lived for three years. Jim had been a Smith and Castle (SC) salesman for 14 years, having joined the firm immediately after discharge from the Marine Corps. Before joining the Marines, he had occupied a series of industrial jobs after graduation from high school.

Smith and Castle considered a salesman's territory to be his "kingdom." He was solely responsible for results in his territory and for planning and implementing sales programs in his area. The salesman could call on headquarters for specialized assistance, but the final results were his own responsibility. Jim's present territory covered roughly the southern half of Illinois. He was presently in his third sales territory and management considered his record as "good, approaching excellent."

Smith and Castle was 120 years old. The Smith and Castle families and descendants held 54 per cent of the voting stock; the rest was held by nonfamily executives (24 per cent), suppliers (10 per cent), and SC Treasury (12 per cent). The company was, as it had been since its founding, managed by a combination of qualified family members and carefully selected outsiders. It had a reputation of being a well-financed, solidly managed company.

Smith and Castle designed and produced in its own four plants and sold through its own sales force a full line of educational equipment staples: student and teacher desks, chairs, tables, library and laboratory shelving, file cabinets, lockers, and storage bins. The company made no special equipment (such as lighting or laboratory apparatus) but its products were designed to accommodate most of the products of special equipment manufacturers. The line was broad, and the design staff competent to accommodate virtually any special customer requirement for combining standard SC components or designing new equipment from customer specifications. Smith and Castle's price schedule was slightly above the competitive industry average.

Customers included public and private grade, secondary, preparatory, and remedial schools; colleges, universities, junior and community colleges; industrial and government training facilities.

The industry was composed of Smith and Castle and five competitors; brief descriptions of each are as follows:

1. Ajax Co.: Sales 15 per cent above SC, full line
2. Smith and Castle
3. Oberon Corp.: Sales 5 per cent below SC, full line
4. Karon Co.: Sales 15 per cent below SC, special line
5. Blaine Co.: Sales 25 per cent below SC, full line
6. Markell Corp.: Sales 30 per cent below SC, special line

Sales experience indicated that the industry was highly competitive, with none of the competing companies being the only choice for any one particular order.

At a PTA meeting in January, Jim learned from a friend that the long-considered proposal for the creation of Eastland Community and Technical College (EC&TC) had been approved by the state legislature and that plans were under way to open the college the following September. He also learned that the college was to be a two-year institution, which would admit 1000 students the first year, with a goal of 5000 students in four years. The educational plant was to be built from the ground up, but would begin in some converted airport facilities which had been bought by the state as the college's primary campus.

Jim quickly recognized that EC&TC represented a substantial piece of potential business for him—and right in his own front yard! After the PTA meeting, he went home and began to plan how he should go about getting the EC&TC business.

ASSIGNMENT

1. *Specifically* what problems must Jim Stenburg consider in planning his approach to the EC&TC sales potential?
2. What steps must he take? Why? In what sequence?

CASE 8
HOUSTON GARDEN SHOP, INC.

Texas Distributors, a hardware wholesaler, has an annual hardware show at their main distribution center in Dallas. At this show, each manufacturer displays items that it wishes to sell to the numerous retailers served by Texas Distributors. There are usually several hundred different manufacturers exhibiting their products at the show. Each exhibitor is carefully chosen to provide the retailers with a broad selection of merchandise for the fall-holiday season, as well as a preview of lines for the following spring.

Many of the manufacturers give retailers special discounts to promote their merchandise. These product promotions are often used to introduce new products in a competitive field. But if there is no competition and if the product is well advertised, the manufacturer usually sets the price of the product somewhat higher.

Literally thousands of new items are displayed at very low show prices to take advantage of the large potential market. Dealers are required to attend the show and to place all orders during the show hours.

At a recent trade show, a large national manufacturer displayed one of its latest items: a cordless lawn and shrub trimmer. This was a new item that had just come out at the end of summer 1973. It was expected to become a leading seller by the following spring. Since no other company had produced a similar trimmer, the retail price was set at a level somewhat higher than conventional trimmers.

Houston Garden Shop, Inc., purchased a display of cordless lawn and shrub trimmers with a delivery date of November 1973. Harold Sedgewick, the owner-manager, intended to sell them as Christmas gifts. But the items did not arrive in time for Christmas. Instead, they came in the middle of January 1974. By this time, other companies had come along with similar trimmers at correspondingly lower prices.

Mr. Sedgewick had already been invoiced through Texas Distributors for the tools and had paid for them at the higher price. But by the time that he had received the merchandise, the trimmers he had bought were also selling at the competitive lower price.

Sedgewick then called the manufacturer and asked for an adjustment on the trimmers. Gene Marsh, the local sales representative, was told to call on Mr. Sedgewick immediately. Mr. Marsh was given full authorization to take whatever action he thought the case merited.

ASSIGNMENT

1. If you were Gene Marsh, how would you approach Mr. Sedgewick?
2. What would you do to correct the situation?

CASE 9
SELLING: THE CRITICS' CONCEPT

Selling and sales management, along with advertising, have for many years been the favorite targets of all kinds of social critics and reformers. One such critic once said: "Selling is the art of getting people to buy things they don't need, at prices they can't afford, and on credit."

ASSIGNMENT

1. Specifically, what assumptions are contained in this statement?
2. How valid is the statement in the sales of industrial goods? Why?
3. Does the statement hold equally well for all classes of consumer goods? Why?

PART TWO: PLANNING AND ORGANIZING FOR SALES MANAGEMENT

CHAPTER FIVE
INTRODUCTION TO
SALES FORECASTING

Many executives have compared sales forecasts to the predictions that emanated from the soothsayers of ancient times. Magically, it seems, forecasts of the next period's sales come pouring out of corporate headquarters. To the field sales force, these estimates often appear to be about as dependable as crystal ball prophecies (see Figure 5–1).

In most cases, however, this view of sales forecasting is far too critical. A *sales forecast*—an estimate of company sales for a specified future period—is an important aspect of sales management. Usually, these forecasts are the result of painstaking effort, by a number of individuals and departments in the firm, and their derivation should be no more mystical than any other type of organizational planning.

FIGURE 5–1

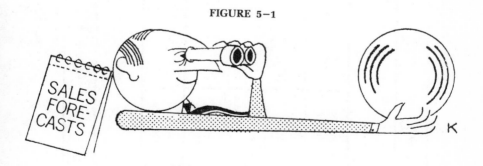

Source: Reprinted by permission from *Sales Management*, The Marketing Magazine. Copyright 1968.

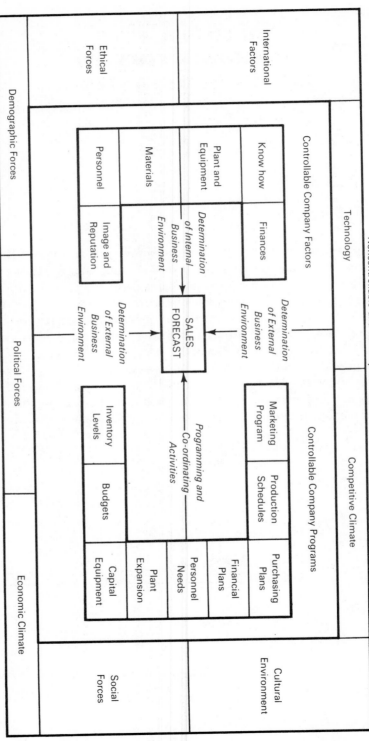

FIGURE 5-2

Sales Forecasting: A Focus for Integrative Planning

Noncontrollable and Partially Controllable External Factors

International Factors

Ethical Forces

Demographic Forces

Technology

Controllable Company Factors

Know how

Finances

Plant and Equipment

Materials

Personnel

Image and Reputation

Determination of Internal Business Environment

Determination of External Business Environment

SALES FORECAST

Determination of External Business Environment

Programming and Co-ordinating Activities

Controllable Company Programs

Marketing Program

Production Schedules

Purchasing Plans

Financial Plans

Personnel Needs

Plant Expansion

Capital Equipment

Inventory Levels

Budgets

Competitive Climate

Cultural Environment

Political Forces

Economic Climate

Social Forces

Source: William Lazar, "Sales Forecasting: Key to Integrated Management," Business Horizons, vol. 2 (Fall 1959), pp. 61–67.

IMPORTANCE OF SALES FORECASTING

Professor William Lazar, former president of the American Marketing Association, has described the importance of sales forecasting in this manner:

> Sales forecasting can aid management greatly in implementing the marketing management approach. It is the basis for developing coordinated and goal-directed systems of marketing action.[1]

The sales forecast — the framework upon which all other aspects of planning are based — is the projection of the future revenue to the organization. For example, financial budgets are typically variable in that they show different expense patterns for varying levels of production. A firm's production level is linked closely to its sales output. Therefore, the financial budget is dependent upon the sales forecast for the projected revenue figure.

Consider also the examples of manpower planning, production scheduling, and marketing planning. All functional areas of an organization have a planning task, but all of these projections and future estimates depend upon the forecasted level of sales. Professor Lazar has called sales forecasting "a focus for integrative planning." This idea is demonstrated in Figure 5–2.

Figure 5–2 shows how the sales forecast plays a major role in the determination of the controllable external and internal business environments, in addition to carrying out a function in programming and coordinating organizational activities. Sales forecasting is the most important planning task within any company — large or small.

USES OF SALES FORECASTS

The sales forecast is the basis of all other aspects of planning in an organization. For sales management, two of the most important uses of

---

[1] William Lazar, "Sales Forecasting: Key to Integrated Management," *Business Horizons*, vol. 2 (Fall 1959), p. 61.

the sales forecast are the setting of sales quotas and the developing of sales budgeting.

Setting Sales Quotas

The establishment of fair and reasonable quotas that are effective in stimulating sales is one of the most crucial tasks faced by the sales manager.[2] *Sales quotas* are the goals and objectives sought by sales management. They are the performance standards for the sales force. Comparison of actual sales with the assigned quota is the basis of much of the sales function's evaluative effort.

Sales quotas can be based on sales forecasts, on historical sales records, and/or on arbitrary management goals.[3] However, one study of 30 firms found that 24 of the companies used sales forecasts as the basis for setting quotas. This popularity of sales forecasts seems well-founded. Forecasts are the organization's *actual* prediction of what sales will be in the forthcoming time period. As a result, they should be the most reasonable foundation upon which quotas can be set. By contrast, the continuation of past sales trends may not characterize the future period, and management goals may be unrealistic in the light of contemporary business conditions. Sales forecasts are a better and fairer method of setting sales quotas.

Quotas for individual sales territories can be calculated by the following formula:

$$\frac{\text{Sales Quota for}}{\text{Territory } X} = \frac{\text{Company Sales}}{\text{Forecast}} \times \frac{\text{Sales Potential of Territory } X}{\text{Sales Potential for the Company}}$$

Assume that the firm's forecasted sales were $20 million next year, and that the sales potential for the company was $25 million, and that the sales potential for Territory X was $1 million. Then, the sales quota would be calculated as follows:

$$\text{Sales Quota} = \$20 \text{ million} \times \frac{\$1 \text{ million}}{\$25 \text{ million}}$$

Sales Quota = $20 million × .04%

Sales Quota = $800,000

---

[2]See George Risley, "A Basic Guide to Setting Quotas," *Industrial Marketing* (July 1961), pp. 88–93.
[3]Michael Schiff and Martin Mellman, *Financial Management of the Marketing Function* (New York: Financial Executives Research Foundation, 1962), p. 8.

One assumption that is implicit in the determination of any sales quota is that the sales force accepts the standards that are set. The salesmen must view the quotas as fair and reasonable, if the standards are to prove effective. This requires that members of the sales force be involved in setting the quotas by which they are to be judged. Hence, the sales force composite method of forecasting sales offers the important advantages of participative decision-making. This procedure is discussed in Chapter 6.

Sales Budgeting

Sales budgets are another important evaluative technique. A *sales budget* is a management plan for expenditures of monies in order to accomplish sales objectives. It is a blueprint for sales force action.

Sales budgets are developed at the product, product category, district, regional, zone, national, and company levels. These budgets show the share of revenue (estimated by the sales forecast) that is expected from each component part of the organization. The costs needed to reach these forecasted amounts are then estimated.

Cost standards derived from records of past performance are the usual method of budgeting selling expenses. *Cost per order* is a common standard used for this purpose. If the sales manager can reliably predict the number of orders that the organization will receive from each territory, then he need only multiply this figure by the cost per order standard.

Sales budgets are a natural extension of the sales forecasting function, and sales forecasts are essentially the revenue aspects of the sales budget. But all sales objectives require the expenditure of monies, costs which must be controlled if sales management is to be truly effective.

MARKET POTENTIAL AND SALES POTENTIAL

Pillsbury is concerned with several types of sales estimates. For instance, they would be interested in knowing how many dozen cake mix packages *could possibly be sold* in the Southeast during August. And since the retail food business is characterized by stiff competition in all geographical regions, Pillsbury would also be concerned about how many dozen units *they could possibly sell* in the Southeast during August. In other words, Pillsbury would like to be able to determine what their maximum market share would be. Finally, the company would want to know how many dozen units *they were likely to sell in that region* during this time period.

As the above situation points out, there are three levels of concern in sales forecasting: market potential, sales potential, and the actual sales forecast.

Market potential is the expected industry sales of a product or service in a specified market segment for a given time period. The market potential for the sale of widgets in California, for example, might be two million units annually. This means that the *entire* widget industry would expect to sell a maximum of two million units this year in California. Market potential might be described as the *capacity* of a sales segment.

Sales potential refers to an individual firm's share of the market potential. It might be expressed as

$$\text{Sales Potential} = \text{Market share} \times \text{Market Potential}$$

where market share is defined as the percentage of the market controlled by a particular company or product.[4] The sales potential of the Empire Widget Company might be 400,000 units in California, or a market share of 20 per cent. *Sales potentials* are the *maximum* sales that the firm could hope to obtain.

The *sales forecast*, by contrast, is the sales estimate that the company actually expects to obtain. It is predicated on the basis of market circumstances, actual company resources, and a clearly defined market plan or program. The sales forecast is usually less than the sales potential since the latter is based upon an ideal set of circumstances. For example, limited financial resources might prevent Empire from establishing an adequate dealer network in California. Hence, the company's sales forecast might be 300,000 units, or 100,000 less than its sales potential.

---

[4]This formula is suggested in Kenneth R. Davis and Frederick E. Webster, Jr., *Sales Force Management* (New York: The Ronald Press Company, 1968), p. 258.

Monitoring Market and Sales Potentials

Continuous monitoring of market and sales potentials is a premise upon which effective sales forecasting is based. Figure 5–3 suggests a grid that might be helpful in this regard.

FIGURE 5–3
Monitoring Markets Through Grid Analysis

	Present	Future	Trend
Market Industry			
Sales			
Company Share			

Source: William Crissy and William H. Cunningham, "Monitoring Markets for Profitable Growth," *Sales Management* (July 1, 1971), pp. 27, 30. Reprinted by permission from *Sales Management*, The Marketing Magazine. Copyright 1971.

Not only must a company keep track of trends in sales and market share, it must also remain alert to basic shifts in product offerings. Market and sales potentials assume that the current product offerings are relevant to a particular market. For instance, most observers would not have predicted the plight of Penn Central with over $2 billion in annual sales. But, here is a classic example of a firm that failed to modify its offering to meet a changed competitive environment.[5]

Estimating Market and Sales Potentials

Because market potentials really attempt to measure the potential *demand* for a product in a given market, they are dependent upon the consumer's *ability* to buy. For example, market potential for grinding

---

[5]William Crissy and William H. Cunningham, "Monitoring Marketing for Profitable Growth," *Sales Management* (July 1, 1971), p. 27.

machines in the machine tool industry has taken buying ability into account by including in its estimate (1) the number and size of plants using such machines, (2) the need for additional equipment, and (3) need for replacement equipment—as well as (4) the funds available for such purchases.[6]

Sales potentials, since they refer to a firm's share of the market potential, are also dependent upon consumer ability to buy the product or service.

Market potential can be estimated by various means. Important sources of data are the U.S. Bureau of the Census and *Sales Management* magazine's annual "Survey of Buying Power" issue. The *Census of Population*—published every ten years—provides extensive demographic information such as number of individuals and households, residence data, ethnic classifications, family size, and other related information. This can be used to establish the market potentials of many consumer goods and personal services. The *Census of Business* (wholesale, retail, and service industries) and the *Census of Manufacturing* can be used to estimate the market potential for many industrial goods. These censuses, which are conducted every five years, provide information such as the number, size, and basic characteristics of firms in various categories.

Sales Management's "Survey of Buying Power" is an important source of information, one that concerns the *ability* to buy. It provides population, income, and retail sales estimates for all major metropolitan areas in the United States and Canada. In addition, it presents an *Index of Buying Power*, which shows the percentage of total national sales that a marketer of consumer goods could expect to obtain in each market.[7] This information is an important determinant for the derivation of market potentials. It can also be crucial in such matters as sales force allocation decisions.

The above sources are related to the *ability* to buy. The *willingness* of a consumer to buy also influences market potential, but is a far more difficult thing to assess. The *Index of Consumer Sentiment*, which is published by the University of Michigan's Survey Research Center, is probably the best known effort in this area.[8]

---

[6]Francis E. Hummel, "Market Potentials in the Machine Tool Industry—A Case Study," *Journal of Marketing*, vol. 19 (July 1954), pp. 34–41.

[7]The development of this index is described in Davis and Webster (1968), p. 270.

[8]An interesting discussion of this index is contained in Jack H. Morris, "Pollsters Gamely Try to Measure the Moods of Volatile Consumers," *Wall Street Journal* (October 4, 1972), pp. 1, 18.

Market research studies are the most common method of estimating the effect of consumer willingness upon sales potential. Marketing research methodology is quite varied; it ranges from simple mail questionnaires to test panels to actual test marketing the product in selected localities. For example, a consumer products company might establish a test panel of consumers who will evaluate possible new products. If 15 per cent of such a *representative* panel were to indicate a willingness to switch to a new brand of coffee presented by the firm, then the sales potential of the new product would be estimated at 15 per cent of a previously established market potential. In this case, the market potential would probably be based upon average annual coffee usage over the past several years.

BASIC STEPS IN SALES FORECASTING

There are three sequential steps in the sales forecasting process:

1. a forecast of the general economic conditions;
2. a forecast of industry sales;
3. a forecast of company or product sales.[9]

All other aspects of sales forecasting must be based upon a forecast of general economic conditions. The standard yardstick for measuring *general economic activity* is the *gross national product* (GNP), which is the money value of all final goods and services produced in the country during a given year. James H. Lorie has described this step as one of the two most important problems in sales forecasting (the other problem will be examined later). Specifically, he says that economic forecasts are difficult to evaluate because of problems in determining their accuracy and their economic usefulness.[10]

Few firms actually predict national economic activity, since these forecasts are readily available from various government agencies, trade associations, private foundations, and universities. The sales

---

[9]An excellent discussion of the sales forecasting process is contained in Roger K. Chisholm and Gilbert R. Whitaker, *Forecasting Methods* (Homewood, Ill.: Richard D. Irwin, Inc., 1971).
[10]James H. Lorie, "Two Important Problems in Sales Forecasting," *Journal of Business*, vol. 30 (June 1957), pp. 172–179.

forecaster in an individual firm, however, has to be cognizant and informed as to the existing forecasts. Economic forecasts, therefore, form much of the background information upon which more specific industry and company estimates are made.

In regard to *industry estimates*, one study showed that 55 per cent of all responding companies attempted to make such predictions (see Table 5 – 1). The development of industry forecasts seems to be related to the size of the firm: smaller firms are apparently less concerned with, or less able to develop, industry sales forecasts. Industry estimates, however, are also often available from trade associations and, in some cases, from government sources. Some of the estimates are based primarily upon the relationship between industry sales and a national economic indicator such as GNP or national income. In other cases, more sophisticated techniques such as input-output analysis are used.[11]

Company and product estimates are the major areas of concern for the firm's sales forecasting function. It has been noted that:

> Prior to 1945, economic and sales forecasting tended to be merged under the general concept of business forecasting. Only since the end of World War II has there been a tendency to distinguish between economic and sales forecasting. The rapid increase in the number of economic forecasting and marketing research staffs during this period infers that sales forecasting experienced the greatest rate of development in the past twenty-five years.[12]

Company and product sales estimates are the revenue forecasts for the organization, and they form the basis for other planning activity throughout the company. The various methods for making these forecasts are discussed later in Chapter 6. The typical breakdowns for sales forecasts are shown in Table 5 – 2.

---

[11]See, for example, James T. Rothe, "The Reliability of Input/Output Analysis for Marketing," *California Management Review*, vol. 14 (Summer 1972), pp. 75 – 81.

[12]James Paul Jennings, *The Role of the Controller in Sales Forecasting*, an unpublished doctoral dissertation (Columbia, Mo.: University of Missouri, 1970), pp. 15, 17.

TABLE 5–1
Percentage of Firms Forecasting Industry Sales

Do you forecast sales of your industry?	Type of Firm					Company Sales Volume			
	Consumer Products	Petro-Chemicals	Primary, Fabricated Metals	Machinery, Electrical Equipment	All other Industries	Under $10 million	$10–$99 million	$100 million or more	Total of all Companies
Yes	40	58	47	76	63	32	45	81	55
No	60	42	43	24	37	66	51	19	42

Source: Adapted from "Sales Forecasting: Is 5% Error Good Enough?" *Sales Management* (December 15, 1967), p. 43. Reprinted by permission from *Sales Management*, The Marketing Magazine. Copyright 1967.

TABLE 5-2

Aggregation Levels in Sales Forecasts, Expressed in Per Cents

Type of Sales Forecast Breakdown	Type of Firm					Company Sales Volume			
	Consumer Products	Petro-Chemicals	Primary, Fabricated Metals	Machinery, Electrical Equipment	All other Industries	Under $10 million	$10–$99 million	$100 million or more	Total of all Companies
Individual Product	63	75	47	78	62	52	55	65	58
Product Line	53	48	63	65	62	52	51	64	56
Type of Distribution	37	31	27	49	42	27	39	39	36
Sales Territory	70	72	53	68	60	52	61	55	57
Customer	10	10	0	3	2	2	0	4	2

Source: Adapted from "Sales Forecasting: Is 5% Error Good Enough?" p. 43. Reprinted by permission from Sales Management, The Marketing Magazine. Copyright 1967.

ORGANIZATION OF THE FORECASTING FUNCTION

While it varies among firms, the organization of the sales forecasting function traditionally tends to be viewed as either a sales or a finance-accounting function.[13] The accounting department originally became involved in this activity because of its natural interest in and control over much of the internal data that is required to forecast sales. In some cases, the marketing function may have lacked the necessary interest or analytical sophistication to perform the sales forecasting task. But, times have changed.

Modern marketing management has been increasingly absorbing the forecasting function in most industrial firms. Accounting and financial officials rarely have this responsibility in modern industry. In fact, one study concluded that:

> The controller who is professionally competent to prepare or have direct responsibility for directing the preparation of sales forecasts is an exceptional individual.[14]

This study goes on to point out that:

> The two general situations in which sales forecasting tends to be a controllership function include firms in which: (1) the marketing function is minimal; or (2) the marketing personnel lack either the interest or expertise to develop scientific sales forecasts.[15]

An example of a firm in which the marketing function is minimal would be the Bristol (Tennessee) Division of Raytheon, which manufactures electrical equipment for the Department of Defense.[16] In this

---

[13]C. Merle Crawford, *Sales Forecasting: Methods of Selected Firms* (Urbana: Bureau of Business and Economic Research, University of Illinois, 1955), p. 50. Also see Vernon G. Lippitt, *Statistical Sales Forecasting* (New York: Financial Executives Research Foundation, 1969), pp. 111–112; and Robert S. Reichard, *Practical Techniques for Sales Forecasting* (New York: McGraw-Hill Book Company, 1966), pp. 3–6.

[14]Jennings (1970), p. 165.

[15]Jennings (1970), p. 165.

[16]See James P. McLaney, "Asset Forecasting: A Defense Industry Technique," *Management Accounting*, vol. 51 (September 1969), pp. 33–35. Also see Jennings (1970), p. 166.

organization, the sales forecast is really just the delivery projection of contract sales. This forecast is used primarily to construct production schedules and cash budgets.

In most firms, however, marketing has assumed responsibility for developing the sales forecast. One recent study indicated that some part of the marketing function was responsible for the sales forecast in 80 per cent of the cases studied and that the finance-accounting function was given primary responsibility in only 5 per cent (See Table 5 – 3). Furthermore, as the table indicates, the sales manager was the person most frequently responsible for this task.

While the sales manager is not always responsible for the sales forecast, he certainly has a significant input in all cases. For example, some companies have elected to make the marketing research staff responsible for sales forecasting, particularly for the quantitative analysis aspects. But, even in these situations, the sales manager is called upon to provide a judgmental evaluation. Sales forecasting remains an important part of the sales manager's job.

Most firms develop sales forecasts of varying lengths from a week or month to periods of several decades ahead. An appliance manufactur-

TABLE 5–3
Individuals Responsible for Preparing the Sales Forecast

Who has the responsibility for preparing the sales forecast?	Percentage of Companies Citing
Sales Manager	21
Marketing Manager	20
Marketing Vice-President	15
Sales Vice-President	14
President	6
Division Vice-President or Manager	6
Vice-President	5
Division or Regional Sales Manager	5
Financial Vice-President, Treasurer, or Controller	5
Market Research Manager	5

Source: Adapted from "Sales Forecasting: Is 5% Error Good Enough?" pp. 41–48. Reprinted by permission from *Sales Management*, The Marketing Magazine. Copyright 1967.

TABLE 5–4
Frequency of Sales Forecasts

Frequency of Formal Sales Forecasts (in percents)	Type of Firm					Company Sales Volume			
	Consumer Products	Petro-Chemicals	Primary, Fabricated Metals	Machinery, Electrical Equipment	All other Industries	Under $10 million	$10–$99 million	$100 million and over	Total of all Companies
Annually	43	86	63	68	65	59	70	59	63
Semiannually	27	6	7	24	14	20	19	16	18
Quarterly	37	24	33	46	42	36	38	36	37

Source: Adapted from "Sales Forecasting: Is 5% Error Good Enough?" p. 43. Reprinted by permission from *Sales Management*, the Marketing Magazine. Copyright 1967.

er might prepare monthly, quarterly, and annual forecasts, as well as long-range projections of from two to ten years. Short-term forecasting is necessary in order to formulate production, personnel, and sales plans. Long-run forecasting is used primarily to make capital expenditure decisions.

A *Sales Management* survey of 182 companies found that 63 per cent of the responding firms made formal sales forecasts annually, 18 per cent semiannually, and 37 per cent quarterly. Table 5–4 classifies these data by type and size of firm.

All forecasts are based on numerous assumptions. An annual forecast for Consolidated Edison is derived on the basis of certain assumptions concerning weather conditions, industrial activity, and residential and commercial construction. Short-range forecasts are likely to be more accurate than long-term predictions, simply because one's basic assumptions are usually more correct over the short run. Since market position is slow to change, substantial changes in sales are not likely to occur from one quarter to the next.[17]

Figure 5–4 shows that there is likely to be greater divergence with actual sales and predicted sales as the time period of the forecast increases.

The importance of the assumptions upon which future sales estimates are based cannot be stressed too much. Sales managers should pay particular attention to this aspect of the forecasting procedure. One study found that in 90 per cent of the firms, top management required a statement of assumptions underlying all sales forecasts.[18] Ill-founded assumptions can seriously bias sales estimates, and business planning is ineffective if it is based upon faulty forecasting. In 1959, for instance, Lockheed Aircraft Company made a long-run sales forecast that was based upon the twin assumptions that 1959 price levels would prevail in 1970 and that the country's GNP would be $700 billion in 1970. Both of these assumptions proved to be incorrect.[19] There was considerable inflation during this time span, and our 1970 GNP considerably exceeded $700 billion.

---

[17]This is pointed out in John J. Breen, "Determinants of Future Sales," *Carroll Business Bulletin,* vol. X (Fall 1970), pp. 15–16.

[18]See "Sales Forecasting: Is 5% Error Good Enough?," *Sales Management* (December 15, 1967), pp. 41–48.

[19]William J. Stanton and Richard H. Buskirk, *Management of the Sales Force* (Homewood, Ill.: Richard D. Irwin, Inc., 1969), p. 478.

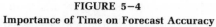

FIGURE 5–4
Importance of Time on Forecast Accuracy

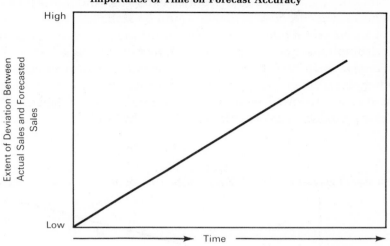

The exactness of a forecast should depend upon the time period involved. Consider how General Motors Corporation might develop sales estimates. A short-run forecast of, say, one year might specify estimates at the corporate, division, and product line levels (see Fig-

FIGURE 5–5
Forecast Exactness as a Function of the Time Period Involved

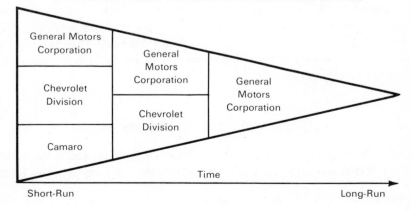

ure 5–5). An intermediate forecast of, perhaps, two to five years might warrant only corporate and division breakdowns. And in the long run, perhaps only a corporate estimate would be realistic.

If management requires greater detail for the longer forecasts, then the assumptions upon which these forecasts are based should be clearly stated. In fact, there might be *several* long-run forecasts depending upon which assumptions are chosen. The number of assumptions that are required tends to vary according to the length of the forecast period. This is demonstrated in Figure 5–6.

FIGURE 5–6
Number of Forecasting Assumptions as a Function of the Time Period Involved

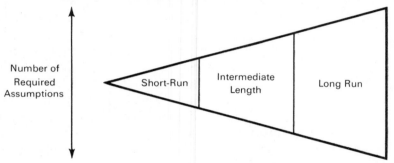

The above discussion also points up the need to continually revise sales forecasts. All such predictions should be reassessed as new information becomes available. General Mills, for example, revises *daily* their end-of-month forecasts for each major brand.[20] This type of reevaluation is needed if sales forecasts are to be the key to planning throughout the organization.

EVALUATION OF THE SALES FORECAST

A *Sales Management* survey of sales forecasting in 182 companies indicated that the difference between forecasted and actual sales aver-

---

[20]Phyllis Daignault, "Marketing Management and the Computer," *Sales Management* (August 20, 1965), p. 54.

aged 5 per cent (Figure 5–7). However, the deviation varied rather significantly according to industry category of the respondent and by size of the firm (in terms of sales volume). Larger companies have better sales forecasting records, probably because of greater resource allocation to this task. The consumer goods companies also appear to have more accurate sales forecasts, largely because of the volatility associated with the other industries studied.[21]

FIGURE 5–7
Average Deviation Between Sales Forecast and Actual Results

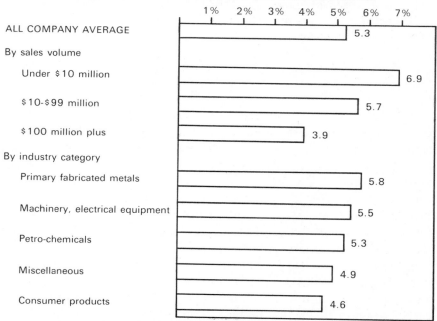

Source: "Sales Forecasting: Is 5% Error Good Enough?" pp. 41–48. Reprinted by permission from *Sales Management*, The Marketing Magazine. Copyright 1967.

Methods of Evaluation

Three objective criteria can be employed for assessing the accuracy of sales forecasts:[22]

---

[21]"Sales Forecasting: Is 5% Error Good Enough?" (1967), pp. 41–48.
[22]These criteria are suggested in John L. Clark and Pieter T. Elgers, "Evaluating the Sales Forecast," *Michigan Business Review*, vol. 20 (May 1968), pp. 14–18.

1. *Comparison with Total Sales.* This approach matches fore-casted with actual sales performance, as was done in the *Sales Management* survey.
2. *Comparison with Actual Change in Total Sales.* Here, the forecast's anticipated change is compared with the actual change. For example, if sales are expected to increase from $200 million to $230 million, and if they in fact only go up to $215 million, then the sales forecast has failed to predict 50 per cent of the real change.
3. *Comparison with Other Techniques of Projection.* Another evaluative approach would be to compare a firm's actual sales forecast with the results obtained through some *naive* method of estimating future sales, such as extrapolating the last incre-ment of change in sales.[23] This approach allows the firm to assess whether or not a more sophisticated technique is bene-ficial.

While assessing the accuracy of sales forecasting is of extreme importance to business planning, the measurement of the economic consequences of forecast error may be even more crucial. To cite some analogies: A 0.0001 per cent error may be intolerable in medical re-search, where it might incur a loss of lives. By contrast, a 5 – 10 per cent error in an IQ test administered by an educational psychologist may be permissible, since it would probably cause little harm to the future education of the child involved. Thus, the degree of acceptable error in forecasting varies from situation to situation.

In the case of a sales forecast, the degree of acceptable error really depends upon the *costs* associated with that error. Did the firm make an expensive commitment to buy new equipment because of the fore-cast? Can corrective action be taken immediately? Are these expendi-tures sunk? Recoverable? These are sometimes difficult but necessary questions.

Responsibility for Evaluation

The sales manager is often given the responsibility for periodically evaluating the sales forecast. In other cases, higher level management

---

[23]Elisha Gray II, Chairman of the Board and Chief Executive Officer of Whirlpool Corporation, pre-sents an interesting discussion of sales forecast evaluation in "A Decision-Maker Looks at Forecast-ing," *MSU Business Topics* (Summer 1966), pp. 7 – 11.

is charged with this duty, as is shown in the *Sales Management* data that appear in Table 5–5. This same survey also concluded that the forecast review was usually done on a quarterly basis (57 per cent of all responses), with 22 per cent of the respondents reporting monthly reviews.[24]

TABLE 5–5
Responsibility for Evaluating the Sales Forecast
Who Makes Periodic Reviews of the Sales Forecast?

Title	Percentage of Companies Citing
Sales Manager	17
Marketing Manager	18
Marketing Vice President	10
Sales Vice President	10
Div. Vice President or Manager	10
Vice President	8
President	7
General Manager	6
Financial Vice President, Treasurer, or Controller	5
Product Manager	4
Market Research Manager	4
Marketing or Sales Department Staff	4

Source: Adapted from "Sales Forecasting: Is 5% Error Good Enough?" pp. 41–48. Reprinted by permission from *Sales Management*, The Marketing Magazine. Copyright 1967.

SUMMARY Chapter 5 has introduced the reader to the important subject of sales forecasting. All organizational planning is dependent upon an accurate projection of future revenues to the firm. Sales forecasting is the most important planning task within any company — large or small — since it is the basis of all other planning. For example, two of the most important uses of sales forecasts are for establishing sales quotas and for sales budgeting.

There are three levels of concern in sales forecasting: *market poten-*

---

[24]"Sales Forecasting: Is 5% Error Good Enough?" (1967), pp. 41–48.

tial (or maximum possible industry sales), *sales potential* (a firm's maximum market share), and the *sales forecast* (the market share the firm actually expects to obtain).

Chapter 5 notes that there are three basic steps in the sales forecasting process:

1. the forecast of general economic conditions;
2. the forecast of industry sales;
3. the forecast of company or product sales.

Aggregation levels in sales forecasts (by type of firm and sales volume) were also reported.

Sales forecasting responsibility varies by firm, but is now usually placed in the marketing department. One study reported that the marketing function was responsible for the sales forecast in 80 per cent of the cases studied.

The chapter concluded by considering the importance of time on forecast accuracy and by examining methods of evaluating forecasts. Chapter 6 will deal with forecasting methodology.

DISCUSSION/REVIEW QUESTIONS

1. What does William Lazar mean when he calls the sales forecast "a focus for integrative planning"? Discuss.
2. How are sales quotas typically set? What role does sales forecasting play in the establishment of these quotas?
3. How are cost standards used in sales budgeting?
4. What three objective criteria can be employed for assessing the accuracy of sales forecasts? Explain each of these. Cite possible examples of each.
5. Who should be responsible for evaluating the sales forecast?
6. Describe the basic steps in sales forecasting. Who should be responsible for each stage of forecasting?
7. "Continuous monitoring of market and sales potentials is a premise upon which effective sales forecasting is based." Comment.

8. Estimate the total market potential for the following items:
   (a) color television sets
   (b) automobiles
   (c) rolled steel
   (d) flour
9. Discuss the organization of the sales forecasting function. Describe the duties and responsibilities of the (a) sales manager, (b) marketing research staff, and (c) controller.
10. How does the length of the forecast period influence the accuracy of the forecast?
11. "The number of forecasting assumptions is *inversely* related to the degree of forecast exactness." Comment.
12. Briefly identify each of the following:
    (a) sales quota   (e) sales forecast
    (b) sales budget   (f) market potential
    (c) cost per order   (g) sales potential
    (d) GNP   (h) *Index of Buying Power*
13. How would you go about implementing a sales forecast evaluation procedure for a large appliance manufacturer? What type of organizational structure, resources, and manpower would this task require?

CHAPTER SIX
FORECASTING
METHODOLOGY

Chapter 5 introduced the concept of sales forecasting to the reader. It pointed out the importance of sales forecasting, general approaches to the task, organization of the forecasting function, and methods of evaluation. The current chapter will look at the various methodologies employed in developing an actual sales forecast.

James H. Lorie's discussion of the important problems in sales forecasting (see Chapter 5) cited the difficulties of combining statistical analysis with subjective judgment in making forecasts.[1] This argument suggests that there are several different tracks that can be followed in making a sales forecast. Table 6-1 compares the sales forecasting methods used by 32 large corporations.

TABLE 6-1
A Comparison of Sales Forecasting Methods Among
Thirty-Two Large Companies

Method	Total
Jury of Executive Opinion	3
Sales Force Composite	5
Users Expectations	1
Analysis of External Conditions	7
Time Series	6
Correlation	4
Mathematical Models	4
Exponential Smoothing	2
Total	32

Source: James Paul Jennings, *The Role of the Controller in Sales Forecasting*, an unpublished doctoral dissertation (Columbia, Mo.: University of Missouri, 1970), p. 113.

---

[1]James H. Lorie, "Two Important Problems in Sales Forecasting," *Journal of Business*, vol. 30 (June 1957), pp. 172-179.

All approaches to forecasting can be classified as either *quantitative* or *judgmental*.[2] Quantitative forecasting centers upon the application of statistical techniques, while judgmental methods rely upon subjective, but informed opinion. Both are useful in the sales forecasting function. Table 6–2 classifies a number of possible approaches as either quantitative or judgmental; each approach is discussed in the sections that follow.

TABLE 6–2
Classification of Forecasting Methodology

Quantitative Methods	Judgmental Methods
Continuity Extrapolation	Jury of Executive Opinion
Trend and Cycle Analysis	Delphi Technique
Exponential Smoothing	Sales Force Composite
Correlation Analysis	Factor Listing
Lead-Lag Series	Survey of Consumer Buying Intentions
Econometric Models	

JUDGMENTAL METHODS

Judgmental methods can make an important contribution to sales forecasting, since they allow consideration of factors that simply cannot be quantified. These methods also typically make wider use of expertise in all areas of the organization. However, judgmental methods should always be used in conjunction with some other approach, and few executives would condone the use of any of these methods by itself.

Jury of Executive Opinion

The *jury of executive opinion* is probably the oldest approach to forecasting. The basic premise is to establish a jury, panel, or committee

---

[2] An excellent discussion of the various forecasting techniques is presented in J. Allison Barnhill, "Methods of Sales Forecasting," *Sales Management: Contemporary Perspectives*, edited by J. Allison Barnhill (Glenview, Ill.: Scott Foresman and Company, 1970), pp. 247–258. Also see Walter Gross, "An Analytical Approach to Market Forecasting," *Georgia Business*, vol. 30 (November 1970), pp. 1–9.

which is charged with the development of a sales forecast. Typically, this group has a varied membership consisting of qualified and informed representatives from sales, marketing research, accounting, production, and advertising. Each person is asked to provide his best estimate of future sales. A written justification of the estimate is often required. Usually, forecasts are made for only the most aggregate of the sales categories such as district, product groups, and/or customer classes.

The opinions are then pooled and, typically, analyzed at a group meeting. Variations are synthesized through the collective judgment of the validity of individual estimates.

The obvious advantage of such a forecasting procedure is its simplification. However, there are several limitations to this method:

> It must be emphasized that this method of forecasting is only as reliable as the personnel involved and the judgment they express. To use the most qualified executives may in turn add to the work load of highly paid managers. Time that may be required in preparing forecast data may be better spent on the performance of other management functions. Another limitation to this approach is that a forecast made by this method is difficult to break down into estimates of probable sales by products, by time intervals, by customer, and various other common denominators that are so essential to the exact implementation of the sales estimate.[3]

Delphi Technique

A modification of the jury of executive opinion approach is the *Delphi technique* developed by Rand Corporation.[4] According to this procedure, members of the jury make individual anonymous forecasts which are then compiled and returned to the executives for a second round of forecasts. This process continues until a consensus emerges. The Delphi technique has the advantage of eliminating the group pres-

---

[3]Barnhill (1970), p. 249.
[4]See "Forecasters Turn to Guesswork," *Business Week* (March 14, 1970), pp. 130–134. Also see Harper O. North and Donald L. Pyke, " 'Probes' of the Technological Future," *Harvard Business Review*, vol. 47 (May–June 1969), pp. 68–82.

sures of a committee meeting. McDonnel-Douglass; Smith, Kline, and French Laboratories; TRW, Inc.; and the Weyerhaeser Company are examples of firms using this method.

Sales Force Composite

The *sales force composite* is based on the assumption that the individual salesmen are the closest to the marketplace and are the best qualified to provide estimated sales figures for their territories. General Electric Company has used this technique for forecasting the sale of some industrial products. Other users include Pennsalt Chemical, Harris-Intertype, and Otis Elevator.

Perhaps the most important advantage of the sales force composite method is related to the setting of sales quotas. If the sales forecasting exercise is to form the basis of next year's sales quotas, then the salesmen's involvement in the forecast is crucial. A field representative will be more apt to accept a sales quota if he knows that he played a significant role in its derivation.

However, there are several disadvantages associated with the sales force composite. Traditionally, salesmen are sometimes poor judges of future sales levels. Their emotional involvement in the selling activities of their territory may color their forecast. It can be argued that field sales personnel are "too close to the marketplace" to provide a good approximation of future events. Forecasting is also often viewed as a secondary activity by the field force so they do not invest the necessary time and effort. A final disadvantage of the sales force composite is that the salesman may deliberately understate his estimate, if the forecast is to be used in setting sales quotas. Some of the disadvantages can be overcome by requiring the salesman to justify his estimate to his sales manager. However, the quality of the forecast still remains highly dependent upon the quality and interest of the people involved.

Factor Listing

Factor listing is an old method that was originally formulated to alleviate an obvious flaw in the jury of executive opinion and sales force composite approaches. While the latter may ask the participant to jus-

158

tify or explain the reasoning behind his forecast, they do not attempt to analyze the importance of the variables that were considered in the forecast. For instance, an executive of an electrical utility company may justify his forecast of a $10 million sales increase by saying that he expects greater industrial activity in the area and an expansion of new housing starts. Notice, however, that he does not place a dollar value on each explanation. The factor listing method forces one to *quantify* his judgmental reasoning. A balance sheet, showing positive and negative influences on future sales, is set up. Relevant factors affecting sales are then listed, and an estimate of their influences on sales is noted (see Table 6-3). The positive and negative sales factors are then summed and the difference in the sums is added to, or subtracted from, current sales to produce the sales forecast.

TABLE 6-3
A Factor Listing Balance Sheet
Twin Valley Electric Company
Current Sales = $210 million

Positive Factors	Negative Factors
Increased industrial activity (+$6 mil) Expanded new housing starts (+$4 mil) Construction of a large government installation (+$1 mil) Increased sales to neighboring utility company (+$2 mil)	Below average temperature during summer months, thus decreasing usage of air conditioning (−$2 mil)
Total = +$13 million	Total = −$2 million
Forecasted Sales = $210 million + $11 million = $221 million	

While this factor listing approach has the obvious advantage of forcing the forecaster to quantitatively justify his prediction, it still suffers from the fact that its validity is limited by the quality of the personnel involved. This is the primary limitation of most of the judgmental approaches to forecasting.

Survey of Consumer Buying Intentions

Many industrial marketers such as the National Lead Company base their sales forecasts on a survey of consumer buying intentions. This method is particularly applicable to situations in which potential purchasers are well defined and limited in number, such as the markets for most industrial products. In these instances, the forecast has the advantage of being based on direct personal contact with the marketplace. The sophistication of such a survey can vary from the simple recording of customer responses to the application of advanced sampling and probability concepts. In most cases, the survey of consumer buying intentions is conducted by the marketing research staff.

This approach has several limitations. The most obvious is that customers do not always do what they say they plan to do. Second, the respondents to such a survey may deliberately *overestimate* their future needs so as to assure a continued flow of supplies or materials. Finally, buying plans — particularly for industrial goods — can change rapidly in response to changes in the operational environment. Hence, reliance on previous forecasts may be misleading.

QUANTITATIVE METHODS

The use of quantitative forecasting methodology has been greatly facilitated by the advent of computer usage in marketing.[5] Computers have not only allowed sales forecasters to perform their tasks more efficiently, they have also permitted the development of more sophisticated and reliable methodology.

Quantitative methods of sales forecasting have the advantage of an impartial objectivity that does not characterize the judgmental methods (see the cartoon shown in Figure 6–1). The basic disadvantages concern the nature and the validity of the assumptions underlying the quantitative methods used, and the fact that mathematical forecasting techniques tend to *generalize* on the basis of past experience. Sudden shifts in environmental factors, for example, can best be evaluated through judgmental insight.

---

[5]See, for example, Thayer C. Taylor, "The Computer in Marketing — Sales Forecasting," *Sales Management* (January 7, 1966), pp. 45–52.

FIGURE 6–1

"It says today is the tomorrow you worried about yesterday."

Source: Reprinted by permission from *Sales Management*, The Marketing Magazine. Copyright 1968.

Continuity Extrapolation

Continuity extrapolation attempts to extrapolate, or project, the *last increment of sales change* into the future. This could be done on either an *absolute dollar* basis or a *percentage* basis. Again consider the case of Twin Valley Electric Company. Suppose that current sales were $210 million and that last year's sales were $200 million.

On an absolute dollar basis, the *last increment of sales change* would be $10 million. This would then be added to current sales to produce an estimate of $220 million for the next year's sales.

On a percentage basis, the last increment of sales change was $10 million ÷ $200 million, or 5 per cent. Next year's predicted sales would then be calculated as $210 million + 5 percent of $210, or $220.5 million.

161

In most forecast periods, this method will prove to be fairly reliable. Sales do not usually change quickly;[6] sudden, substantial changes are a rarity in most businesses today. But they do occur on occasion. The continuity extrapolation approach, however, assumes that there will be no directional change and the *last* increment of sales change approximates the *average* increment of sales change.

Trend and Cycle Analysis

This approach is based on business cycle theory, and its origin can be traced back to the early 1920s. It determines and then projects the four basic elements of sales variation: trends (long-run changes), cyclical changes, seasonal variations, and irregular factors.[7] This is done by extrapolating the trend with adjustments for the cyclical and seasonal factors. The irregular factor is acknowledged, but not forecasted separately. The interrelation of these variables is shown in Figure 6–2.

FIGURE 6–2
Trend, Cyclical Changes, Seasonal Variations,
and Irregular Factors as Influencing Sales

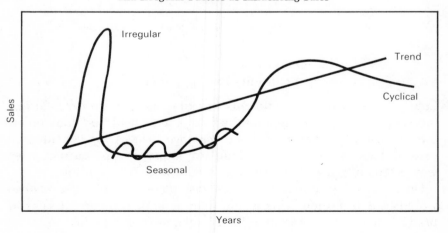

[6]John J. Breen, "Determinants of Future Sales," *Carroll Business Bulletin*, vol. X (Fall 1970), pp. 15–16.
[7]This is discussed in Robert L. McLaughlin, "The Breakthrough in Sales Forecasting," *Journal of Marketing*, vol. 27 (April 1963), pp. 46–54.

Trend and cycle analysis is most applicable to the projection of long-run forecasts and to industry sales projections. The approach assumes a continuation of the firm's sales history and, in fact, *extrapolates the average increment of sales change*. Sears, Roebuck and Company is an example of a company that uses this technique.

Forecasts of sales trends are typically the product of the *least squares method*. The basic formula is

$$Y_F = a + bx$$

Where:

Y_F = the forecasted sales
Y = actual sales
a = the median point in the time series
b = the average increment of sales change (or the slope of the trend line)
X = the number of periods from the median point in the time period

Other relevant formulas include:

$$a = \overline{Y} \text{ or } \left(\overline{Y} = \frac{\Sigma Y}{n}\right) \quad b = \frac{\Sigma XY}{\Sigma X^2}$$

Essentially, the trend extension technique seeks to find the appropriate *starting point* (the median point in the time series) and then extrapolate the average increment of sales change into future periods. This average increment, noted as b, is really then the slope of the forecasted trend line.

The graph in Figure 6-3 shows how trend analysis can be used to forecast sales. If point A represents the current year, then point C would represent this year's *forecasted* sales. The sales figure for some future year (point B) is derived by simply finding the related point on the Y axis (point D).

Consider the example given in Table 6–4.

FIGURE 6-3

The Use of Trend Analysis to Forecast Sales

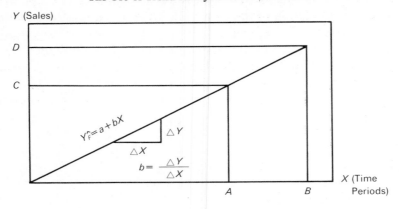

TABLE 6-4

An Example of Trend Analysis in Sales Forecasting

Years	Actual Sales (in Millions of Dollars) Y	X	XY	X²
1972	$16	−2	−32	4
1973	$20	−1	−20	1
1974	$18	0	0	0
1975	$21	+1	+21	1
1976	$25	+2	+50	4
	$100	0	+19	10

$$a = \frac{\Sigma Y}{n} = \frac{100}{5} = 20 \qquad b = \frac{\Sigma XY}{\Sigma X^2} = \frac{19}{10} = 1.9$$

Then the 1977 sales forecast would be calculated as:

$$Y_F \ (1977) = 20 + 1.9 \ (+3) = \$25.7 \ \text{million}$$

and the 1978 sales forecast as:

$$Y_F \ (1978) = 20 + 1.9 \ (+4) = \$27.6 \ \text{million}$$

The year 1974 is designated "O" in the X column, since 1974 is the median point in the time series. The other X column designations refer to the number of time periods (years) away from the median point. If an even number of years of sales history had been available, then the median point would have occurred between years. Hence, the X column designations would have indicated the number of six month periods from the median point.

Years	X
1971	−5
1972	−3
1973	−1
	0
1974	+1
1975	+3
1976	+5

All other calculations would be the same.

The calculations in Table 6–4 show that the forecasted sales in the median year (a) would be $20 million and that the average annual increment of sales change (b) was $1.9 million. This results in a 1977 forecast of $25.7 million sales, and a 1978 forecast of $27.6 million sales. Forecasts beyond this point would be unreasonable since the estimates are being made on the basis of only five years of sales data. As a general rule, one should only forecast a period equal to one-half of the number of years of sales history available.

Actual sales, of course, can vary substantially from the forecasted trend. This variation is due primarily to cyclical and seasonal causes. However, management needs to know the probability that the forecast will be correct.

Standard Error Of The Estimate

An assessment of the probability that the forecast will be correct can be achieved by applying a further concept of statistical analysis — the standard error of the estimate.[8] Its use is based on the premise that

---

[8]See Burton D. Seeley, "Interpretation of Sales Data for Action," *Akron Business and Economic Bulletin,* vol. 3 (Spring 1972), pp. 35–42.

variations from the trend line are distributed in a normal bell-shaped curve (see Figure 6–4).

FIGURE 6–4
Establishing Confidence Limits for Sales Trend Analysis

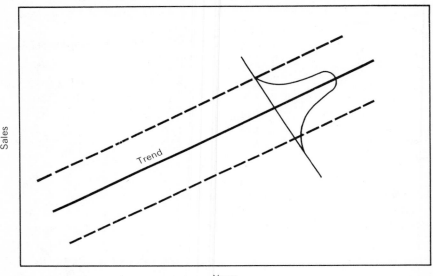

This allows one to apply confidence levels to the sales estimate. For example, on the basis of the data supplied in Table 6–4, the use of a two standard error range would allow us to predict the 1977 and 1978 sales with 95 per cent confidence.[9] The formula for the standard error of the estimate is as follows:[10]

$$\sigma Y = \sqrt{\frac{\Sigma(Y - Y_F)^2}{n}}$$

---

[9]The two standard error range actually allows for about 95.5 per cent confidence.

[10]When n < 30, use $\sigma Y = \sqrt{\dfrac{\Sigma(Y - Y_F)^2}{n - 1}}$

166

Calculations of the sales forecasts for 1977 and 1978, according to the standard error of estimates, are shown in Table 6–5.

TABLE 6–5
Calculation of the Standard Error of the Estimate

Year	Actual Sales (In Millions of Dollars) Y	Forecasted Sales (In Millions of Dollars Y_F	$Y - Y_F$	$(Y - Y_F)^2$
1972	16	16.2	−0.2	0.04
1973	20	18.1	+1.9	3.61
1974	18	20.0	−2.0	4.00
1975	21	21.9	−0.9	0.81
1976	25	23.8	+1.2	1.44
	100	100.0	0.0	9.90

$$\sigma Y = \sqrt{\frac{\Sigma(Y - Y_F)^2}{n - 1}}$$

$$\sigma Y = \sqrt{\frac{9.90}{4}} = \sqrt{2.475} = 1.57$$

Therefore, the 1977 sales forecast would be calculated as:

$Y_F = 25.7 \pm 2\ (1.57) = \$22.56$ to $\$28.84$ million
$\qquad\qquad$ (at the 95 per cent confidence level)

and the 1978 sales forecast as:

$Y_F = 27.6 \pm 2\ (1.57) = \$24.46$ to $\$30.74$ million
$\qquad\qquad$ (at the 95 per cent confidence level)

Exponential Smoothing

A popular modification of trend analysis is *exponential smoothing*,[11] which involves a weighted average time series analysis technique. Actual sales of recent periods are weighted more heavily than the av-

---

[11] Philip H. Siegel, "Exponential Smoothing For Sales Forecasting: Analysis and Application," *Marquette Business Review*, vol. XVI (Winter 1972), pp. 210–217.

erage sales of earlier periods. Exponential smoothing is best suited to short-term forecasting in relatively stable markets. It is particularly useful in updating quarterly forecasts.

Correlation Analysis

Correlation analysis has also been used to forecast sales in such companies as Eli Lilley and Company, American Can Company, Eastman Kodak, Vendo Corporation, and RCA Corporation. This procedure involves the following three basic steps:

1. *Determine the factors that affect sales.* This can be accomplished by plotting a *scatter diagram* as shown in Figure 6-5. Here, a significant relationship can be observed between company sales and gross state product. This is an example of *simple correlation* since there is only one independent variable. (The use of two or more independent variables is called *multiple correlation.*)

2. *Measure the degree of the relationship between sales and the other variable.* This is done through a statistical procedure known as *correlation analysis.* A *coefficient of correlation* (designated as r) is determined. The coefficient ranges from −1.0 (perfect negative correlation) to +1.0 (perfect positive correlation). An r value of +1.0 would mean that for each one unit change in the independent variable, there would be a one unit change in sales *in the same direction.* An r value of − 1.0 would mean a proportionate change in the dependent and independent variables, but *in opposing directions.* For example, if the independent variable went up one unit, then the dependent variable will go down one unit. Assume that the coefficient of correlation from Figure 6-5 was 0.80. This would be considered a relatively high correlation, and the firm would be able to use gross state product as a predictive variable in their sales forecast.

3. *Forecast the dependent variable* (sales) *from the independent variables* (GNP and population are commonly used for this purpose). The statistical procedure involves determining the average increment of change in Y (sales — the dependent variable) resulting from a one increment change in X (the independent variable). Thus, the technique is similar to extrapolating a trend line through the least squares method.

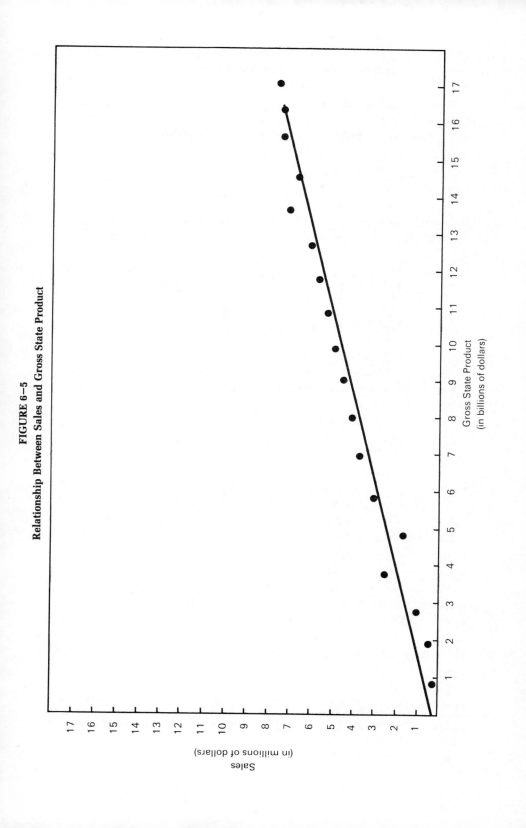

FIGURE 6–5

Relationship Between Sales and Gross State Product

Sales
(in millions of dollars)

Gross State Product
(in billions of dollars)

Effective use of correlation analysis in forecasting requires that the independent variables be causal and that their relationship with sales be stable. In addition, the independent variables should be easily measurable.

Lead-Lag Series

Sales may be correlated with series of data that either lead, lag, or are coincident with changes in sales volume. Data on the number of building permits issued might be a lead indicator of lumber sales. Various companies have used lead-lag analysis in their forecasting work. Its primary value is in the prediction and timing of changes in sales.[12]

Econometric Models

Sophisticated mathematical methodology has also been used to forecast sales in such organizations as the Chase Manhattan Bank. The simplest form of an econometric model is *multiple regression analysis*, where sales projections are based on relationships with several different variables. The general form of such an equation would be:

$$Y_F = a + b_1X_1 + b_2X_2 + b_3X_3 \cdot \cdot \cdot b_nX_n$$

and $X_1 \cdot \cdot \cdot X_n$ would represent the different independent variables.

Consider the variables that might affect the sale of service station equipment. Replacement rate, interstate highway construction, changes in automobile registrations, the availability of capital funds and general economic activity are some of the variables that might be causal factors in the sale of new gasoline pumps.

Various other techniques, such as simulations, can be classified as econometric model building. One of the more complex is *input-output analysis*. The output (sales) of one industry is the input (purchases) of another industry. Input-output models have been developed to show the impact on vendors of increased production in the industries they supply.[13]

---

[12]James Paul Jennings, *The Role of the Controller in Sales Forecasting*, an unpublished doctoral dissertation (Columbia, Mo.: University of Missouri, 1970), pp. 90–91.
[13]James T. Rothe, "The Reliability of Input/Output Analysis for Marketing," *California Management Review*, vol. 14 (Summer 1972), pp. 75–81.

It would appear that most of business's future progress in sales forecasting will come in the area of mathematical model-building. New techniques are being explored every day. The clearly established trend toward sophisticated marketing information systems will provide the impetus and the supporting data for such improved quantitative methodology.[14]

SYNTHESIZING FORECAST METHODOLOGY

For most companies, the best course to follow in sales forecasting is to use a combination of methods. It is particularly important to balance a forecast derived from a quantitative approach with one of the judgmental variety, and vice versa. In some firms, three, four, or more forecasting methods are used.

A combination approach allows the firm to counteract most of the deficiencies inherent in any *single* method. If there is a substantial deviation among the forecasts emanating from each method, then the entire process should be repeated. Forecasters should strive for a consensus among the results of the various methods employed.

SUMMARY This chapter outlined the various methodologies that may be employed in forecasting sales and divided the various approaches into quantitative methods and judgmental methods.

Judgmental methods consist of the jury of executive opinion, the Delphi technique, the sales force composite, factor listing, and surveys of consumer buying intentions. Quantitative forecasting methods include continuity extrapolation, trend and cycle analysis, exponential smoothing, correlation analysis, lead-lag series, and econometric models.

The best course of action seems to be a combination of several of these methods. It is particularly important to balance a forecast derived from a quantitative approach with one of the judgmental variety and vice versa.

---

[14]The status of marketing information systems in industry is described in Louis E. Boone and David L. Kurtz, "Marketing Information Systems: Current Status in American Industry," *Combined Proceedings* (Chicago: American Marketing Association, 1971), pp. 163–167.

DISCUSSION/REVIEW QUESTIONS

1. List and explain each of the quantitative and judgmental methods of forecasting sales.
2. Using the least squares method, forecast 1977 sales for the data shown below:

Year	Sales (in millions)
1972	$ 9
1973	$10
1974	$13
1975	$13
1976	$15

3. Using the data in Question 2, what would your forecast range be at the 95 per cent confidence level?
4. Suppose that 1971 sales of $6 million were also in Question 2. What would be your 1977 sales forecast?
5. Given the data in Question 2, what would your 1977 forecast be using continuity extrapolation

   (a) on an absolute dollar basis

   (b) on a percentage basis
6. Given the data in Question 2, what would you forecast sales to be in 1982 using the least squares method? Comment.
7. "For most companies, the best course to follow in sales forecasting is to use a combination of methods." Discuss.
8. What is meant by input-output analysis?
9. "Exponential smoothing is best suited to short-term forecasting in relatively stable markets." Comment.
10. Outline the three basic steps involved in correlation analysis.

CHAPTER SEVEN
ORGANIZATION OF THE
SALES FORCE

The organization of the sales force is a crucial sales management task, since it has a direct impact on the field sales manager's level of job performance. *Organization* is a management function, activity, or process. It is performed by all managers regardless of their functional responsibility. The controller, personnel director, supervisor of quality control and the sales manager all must perform this organizational task within their own functional area. In addition, top management supervises and coordinates the organizational function for the entire company.

Unfortunately, *organization* is often viewed as the simple determination of *structure*. Some executives treat organization as a one-time decision that is fulfilled as soon as the organizational structure is established. This is far from the case: *Organization is a continuing effort requiring constant management attention.*

THE IMPORTANCE OF ORGANIZATION TO SALES MANAGEMENT

The importance of sales force organization can best be explained by noting that the organizing effort seeks to accomplish three basic tasks:

1. the maintenance of order in achieving sales force goals and objectives;
2. the assignment of specific tasks and responsibility;
3. integration and coordination with other elements of the firm.

173

An effective sales force organization provides the structure for achieving sales objectives. Without it, the sales force will tend to languish in confusion and turmoil; goals and objectives will be misunderstood; the selling effort will be often misdirected; and channels of communications will be blocked and inoperative. The *maintenance of order* is a fundamental task in any organizational structure, whether its province is business, the military, religion, government, or social service.

Organizational structure also permits the *assignment of specific tasks* to a position whose incumbent is then charged with responsibility for accomplishing that task. An effective organization does not permit *buckpassing*, or the shifting of responsibility from one position to another. For instance, one wonders at the circumstances behind President Truman's classic comment that "the buck stops here!"

Integration and coordination is a third aspect of sales force organization. The organizational structure allows the coordination of the various functional areas of the firm. Functional goals and objectives can be integrated so as to accomplish the primary corporate or company goals.

DEVELOPING THE SALES ORGANIZATION

Developing a sales organization requires that management recognizes and then deals with some basic organizational issues. These can be outlined as:

1. formal and informal organizations;
2. horizontal and vertical organizations;
3. centralized and decentralized organizational structures;
4. the line and staff components of the organization;
5. the size of the sales organization.

Formal and Informal Organizations

Every firm has a formal and an informal organization. The *formal organization* is a creation of management, while the *informal organization* is often developed from the social relationships existing in the

174

FIGURE 7-1

The Informal Communication System in a Marketing Organization

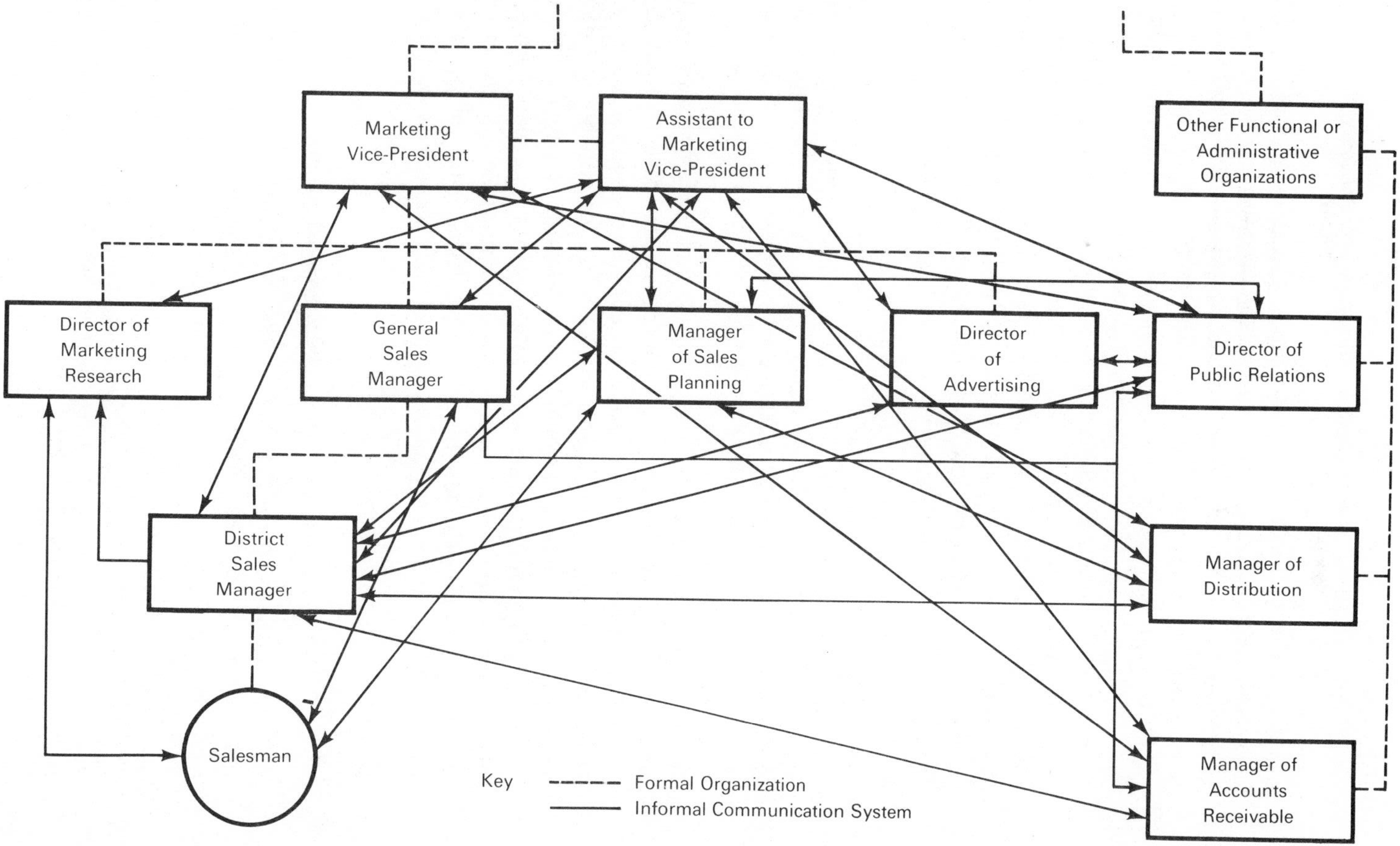

Key
- - - - - Formal Organization
———— Informal Communication System

organization.[1] The informal organization is basically a communications pattern that emerges to facilitate the operation of the formal organization.[2] Most formal organizations would be totally ineffective if it were not for a supporting informal organization.

Figure 7–1 shows the various informal communication patterns that might exist in a marketing organization. Actual communications do not usually follow the formal organizational structure. Some communications cross functional, as well as organizational, lines. This allows the formal structure to operate efficiently. Consider the case of a field salesman who is responsible for collecting certain competitive information such as prices and trade discounts. If he were to forward it through the formal organization, the data would be so dated that it

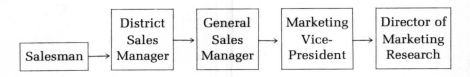

would be useless to management. The informal communication system, however, allows the information to be transmitted directly to the director of marketing research. Similarly, consumer complaints over the *red tape* in correcting billing errors can be mitigated when the district sales manager contacts the manager of accounts receivable directly.

The development of an effective sales organization requires a recognition that informal relationships and communication patterns are useful in accomplishing sales force objectives. They should be nurtured and encouraged to the extent that they improve organizational efficiency.

Horizontal and Vertical Organizations

Sales forces can have either horizontal or vertical organizational formats. The arrangement varies among companies, even within the same industry.

[1]David L. Kurtz and Lawrence A. Klatt, "The 'Grapevine' as a Management Tool," *Akron Business and Economic Review*, vol. 1 (Winter 1970), p. 20.
[2]Informal communication patterns in four manufacturing companies are discussed in R. Clifton Anderson and Edward W. Cundiff, "Patterns of Communications in Marketing Organizations," *Journal of Marketing*, vol. 29 (July 1965), pp. 30–34.

FIGURE 7–2
Vertical Sales Organization

A purely vertical sales organization would be similar to the structure represented in Figure 7–2. In this structure, there are several layers of sales management, all of which report vertically.

The opposite extreme is a horizontal organization, shown in Figure

FIGURE 7–3
Horizontal Sales Organization

7 – 3. Here the number of management levels is reduced appreciably, but the number of managers at any particular level is increased. Instead of two or three district sales managers, there may now be seven or eight.

The factor that determines whether a vertical or horizontal organizational structure should be employed is the effective span of control. The *span of control* refers to the number of employees who report to the next higher level in the organization. Horizontal structures tend to exist where larger spans of control are acceptable, while vertical organizations characterize cases where closer managerial supervision is required.

It is difficult to generalize about setting guidelines for appropriate spans of control. However, one study found salesman performance and turnover to be related to span of control. This study suggested the following optimum spans:[3]

Trade Selling	12/16 TO 1
New Business Selling	10 TO 1
Missionary Selling	10 TO 1
Technical Selling	7 TO 1

This study would suggest that the optimum span of control is reduced as the type of selling becomes more technical or complex. Another survey reported that the median number of salesmen reporting to a supervisor varied by the type of product sold. The reported median rates were as follows:[4]

Services	10 TO 1
Consumer Products	8 TO 1
Industrial Products	6 TO 1

---

[3]See Derek A. Newton, "Get the Most Out of Your Sales Force," *Harvard Business Review*, vol. 47 (September-October 1969), pp. 130 – 143.
[4]Morgan B. MacDonald, Jr., and Earl L. Bailey, "The Field Sales Supervisor," *Conference Board Record*, vol. V (July 1968), p. 34.

The research noted above provides some approximate guidelines for setting reasonable spans of control. Once set, the span of control should be monitored periodically, in order to assure maximum effectiveness.

Centralized and Decentralized Organizations

A related question concerns the degree of centralization in the sales organization. This issue centers around the organizational location of the *responsibility and authority* for specific sales management tasks. In a decentralized organization, responsibility and authority is delegated to lower levels of sales management. In a centralized sales organization, the responsibility and authority for decisions tends to be concentrated at higher levels of management.

The usual rule is that as an organization grows in size, it tends to accept a higher degree of decentralization. The J. C. Penney Company is an example of a firm that has effectively decentralized many managerial decisions. Increased size means that top executives are less able to deal with the range of decisions that they handled when the organization was smaller. By necessity, then, these decisions are shifted downward in the organization.

A decentralized organizational structure is ineffective unless *commensurate responsibility and authority* accompanies the assignment of decisions to a specific level of sales management. The classic mistake is for top management to charge a field sales supervisor with the responsibility to perform a particular task, but then fail to grant him the authority to accomplish the assigned objective. This type of mistake should always be avoided, since it results in poor morale, as well as in failure to perform the task.

Line and Staff Components of the Marketing Organization

Marketing organizations also feature line and staff components. A *line* function is a primary activity, while a *staff* function is a supporting activity. In a marketing organization, the selling function is the line component, while advertising, sales analysis, marketing research, sales planning, sales training, and distributor relations are usually considered staff roles.

While the use of the terms *line* and *staff* has been criticized in many quarters, the basic premise remains applicable to marketing organizations. A modern sales force has to receive various types of support in order to accomplish its objectives. Advertising and sales promotion support is needed to precondition the prospect to accept the salesman's presentation; marketing research and sales planning is required because it allows the field representative to concentrate his efforts on the largest potential markets; internal sales personnel relieve the field force of activities that would detract from their basic effort;[5] and distribution, credit, and maintenance personnel are required to assure that the customer is satisfied with his purchase.

Some firms operate with a simple line marketing organization such as the one shown in Figure 7–4.

Here, the *marketing organization* is simply the *sales organization*. This type of arrangement may be satisfactory for small firms in basic industrial markets. However, if the needs of the marketplace become more complex, or if the company expands, then there is usually a need to add specialists prepared to deal with these problems. Over time, these specialists become the staff departments found in most large organizations (see Figure 7–5).

FIGURE 7–4
A Line Marketing Organization

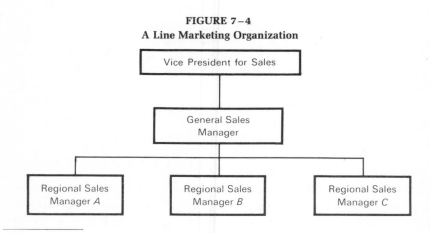

---

[5]The role of the inside salesman is examined in Robert J. Boewadt, "Inside Selling Within the Industrial Marketing Mix: A Role Analysis," 1971 *Conference Proceedings* (Chicago: American Marketing Association, 1971), pp. 172–175.

FIGURE 7–5
Line and Staff Marketing Organization

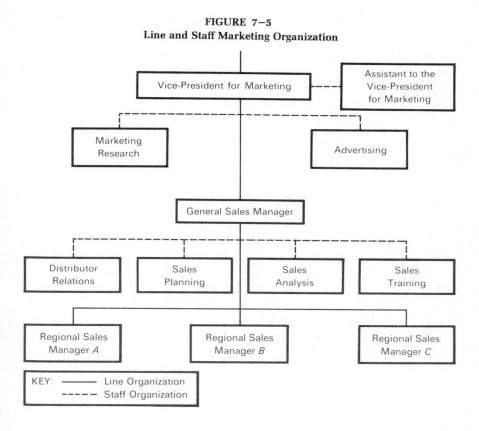

Figure 7–5 demonstrates several key aspects of a large-scale marketing organization. First, the chief marketing officer is typically called *vice-president for marketing* or *director of marketing*, rather than *vice-president for sales*. The title change is indicative of the person's added responsibilities under a line and staff structure. The vice-president for marketing is in charge of more than just the field sales force. The line and staff organization shown in Figure 7–5 indicates that all marketing activities have been grouped together in one organizational structure. It suggests that the basic tenets of the marketing concept have been accepted.

Second, staff activities report to the line position that they support. Distributor relations, sales planning, sales analysis, and sales training are considered to be directly supportive of the field sales effort. Hence, these departments report to the *general sales manager.* By contrast, marketing research and advertising are broader functions, and they report to the *vice-president for marketing.*

Finally, Figure 7–5 shows a position entitled *assistant to the vice-president for marketing.* This is also a staff position. The fact that the position is diagrammed

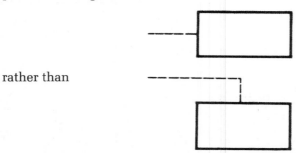

rather than

suggests that this is usually a single individual rather than a department. The *assistant to . . .* is responsible solely to the vice-president; he does not have line authority over anyone in the organization. An *assistant to . . .* is usually someone who performs specific tasks (often nonrecurring in nature) for a line officer.

Size of the Sales Organization

Organizational size is another critical question with which sales management must deal. Traditionally, marketers have paid scant attention to this matter. Field sales forces have expanded and/or contracted with little evaluation on the part of sales management. Smaller firms, for example, are often grossly understaffed, while some large firms have added sales positions beyond the point where it is economically feasible. The importance of this issue has recently been pointed out.

Unfortunately, field sales organization control has not been given nearly the amount of research attention warranted by its substantial contribution to the marketing mix. At the same time, numerous studies have been made of advertising budgets which in contrast are estimated to be less than half the expenditures for only the salary and expense portions of field sales budgets. Contemporary marketing literature contains the results of substantial studies on how to evaluate advertising effectiveness, but few articles have dealt with such an apparently mundane topic as "how large should our sales organization be?"[6]

Organizational size is an important question since it is a prime determinant of organizational structure. Larger field sales forces require more levels of sales management. The number of field sales supervisors is probably more closely related to the geographical expansion of the firm's market than it is to the type of industry or product being sold. For example, one study noted that there was little difference in the "median number of field sales supervisors reporting to the next management level" among product classifications. Industrial and consumer product companies had a median of 5, while service industries reported a median of 6.5.[7]

Sales force size is the derivative of several criteria. One framework for considering organizational size is diagrammed in Figure 7–6 and includes three major criteria:

1. monetary criteria;
2. workload criteria;
3. competitive criteria.[8]

One empirical research study, however, reported that

market potential, number of accounts, geographic basis, and dollar volume were the most frequently utilized criteria. Surprisingly, competitors' salesforce size or outsold units were relatively minor considerations in determining new sales positions. Moreover, present field salesforce size did not appear to have a major bearing on criteria used by firms in allocating sales positions.[9]

---

[6]James E. Bell, Jr., and William O. Hancock, "Optimizing Sales Organization Size," *Business Perspectives*, vol. 8 (Winter 1972), p. 17.
[7]MacDonald and Bailey (1968), p. 35.
[8]Bell and Hancock (1972), p. 21.
[9]Bell and Hancock (1972), p. 19.

FIGURE 7–6
Determining Sales Organization Size

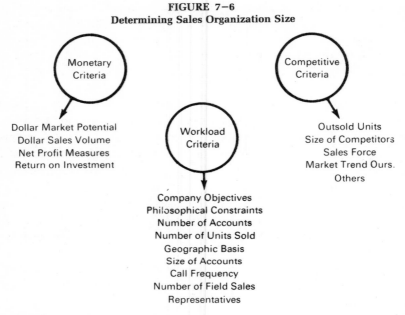

Monetary Criteria

Competitive Criteria

Workload Criteria

Dollar Market Potential
Dollar Sales Volume
Net Profit Measures
Return on Investment

Outsold Units
Size of Competitors
Sales Force
Market Trend Ours.
Others

Company Objectives
Philosophical Constraints
Number of Accounts
Number of Units Sold
Geographic Basis
Size of Accounts
Call Frequency
Number of Field Sales
Representatives

Source: James E. Bell, Jr., and William O. Hancock, "Optimizing Sales Organization Size," Business Perspectives, vol. 8 (Winter 1972), p. 21.

This study also reported that 52 per cent of the firms studied had established procedures for evaluating new position requests.[10] Decisions of this nature also required the approval of several executives.[11]

As noted before, sales managers would be well advised to devote more attention to the matter of sales force size. It is an intricate aspect of organizational planning. Better, formalized methods of making such decisions will be required in the future.

CONCEPTS OF EFFECTIVE ORGANIZATION

The effective organization of sales forces relies on many of the concepts and principles common to the organizational effort in any functional area. A sales organization must provide for a reasonable span of

[10]Bell and Hancock (1972), p. 20.
[11]Bell and Hancock (1972), p. 20.

control for each management position. Responsibility for performing a sales management task must carry with it the authority to take the actions necessary to accomplish the particular goal. These concepts have been discussed earlier in this chapter.

Several other principles or concepts are applicable to sales force organization. Each is important and should be considered in the development, or review, of a sales organization.

Sales Activities Should Be Organized, Not People

The sales organization should be built around activities, rather than around the people involved in the activities.[12] This simple concept allows the organization to be more permanent and stable. One widely cited article argued that there were two basic sales activities: sales development and sales maintenance.[13] Others see a basic division between planning and operating activities. Regardless of the tasks identified, the key factor is that the organization be activity oriented, not people oriented.

This maxim is violated by many firms and exists in a variety of examples: the aggressive executive who is put in charge of several unrelated activities; the chief executive who tends to rely upon his personal friends (at different levels in the organization) for business advice; or a distributor relations department that reports to the vice-president of operations because the chief marketing executive has no interest in such activities. These are common situations to many organizations. The inherent problem is that an organization based on people has to change every time the people involved change. This leads to unnecessary disruption and hinders the effective functioning of the sales force.

Similar Functions Should Be Grouped Together

A corollary to the concept of organization by activities is that like functions should be grouped together. Marketing research and produc-

---

[12]Don H. Scott, "Building the Organization 'Around' People," *Sales Management*, (March 4, 1960), p. 33.
[13]George N. Kahn and Abraham Shuchman, "Specialize Your Salesmen!" *Harvard Business Review*, vol. 39 (January-February 1961), pp. 90–98.

tion should not administratively report to the operations vice-president simply because the chief marketing executive is uninterested in the research activity. Similar functions should be closely linked in a properly defined organizational structure.

Supportive staff activities should be grouped with the line functions they serve, so that the organization can operate with a minimum of confusion and bureaucratic rigidities. Figure 7–5 demonstrated the application of this concept to a sales organization.

Sales Organizations Should Be Coordinated, Balanced, and Flexible

Sales organizations must be *flexible* so that they can adapt to shifts in competitive and operating conditions. A new competitor enters the firm's primary market; several district sales managers are *pirated* away by another firm in the industry; the government releases a report that is negative toward your product; or general economic conditions change drastically. All of these conditions would require that the sales organization be flexible and adapt readily to its altered operating environment.

A *balanced* organization is one that does not allow any unit to become more important than another at the same organizational level. This requires a close *coordination* between the sales force and other departments, both line and staff. Organizational balance and coordination are closely related. An organizational structure that lacks balance is unable to cope with the dynamic forces at work in the modern competitive environment.

BASIC TYPES OF SALES ORGANIZATIONS

A sales force can be organized by *customer, product*, or *geography*.[14] These are the *basic* approaches to organization, but, in actuality, most sales forces are a combination of two or more of these basic types. An industrial products company may have separate sales forces for its two product lines: drills and grinders. Each of these sales forces may

---

[14]Approaches to sales organization are discussed in Andrall Pearson, "Organizing for Profit," *Sales Management* (November 10, 1970), pp. 13–14.

FIGURE 7-7

An Organizational Structure Employing All Three Approaches to Organizing Sales Forces: Organization by Product, Geography, and Customer.

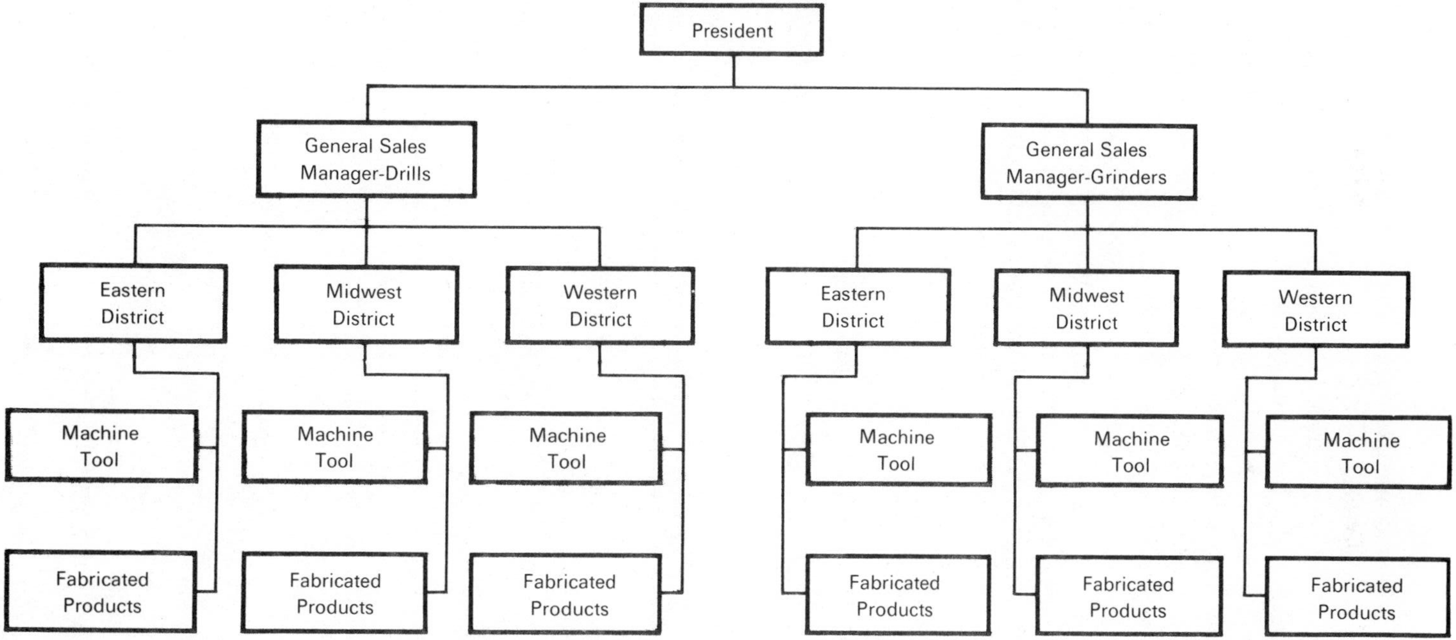

then be organized by geographical location, such as by district or regional office. Finally, within each district, the salesmen may specialize according to the customers the firm serves. Some may call on the machine tool industry, while others may concentrate on fabricated products. This organizational structure is shown in Figure 7−7.

Sales force specialization is very common today. Table 7−1 shows that the bulk of the firms polled in one study had adopted some form of specialization. If geographical location had been considered as a method of sales specialization, it is reasonable to believe that the number indicating no significant specialization would have been substantially reduced. Table 7−1 also shows that many of the firms used more than one approach to sales force organization.

TABLE 7−1
Sales Specialization in Divisionalized and Nondivisionalized Companies

	Product	Sales Speciali- zation by Type of Customer	Both	No Significant Speciali- zation	Total Companies Reporting
Nondivisionalized Companies	16	16	13	29	74
Divisionalized Companies (reporting for the largest division)	20	27	40	16	103

Source: Morgan B. MacDonald, Jr., and G. Clark Thompson, "Specialization in Marketing," *Conference Board Record*, vol. 1 (June 1964) p. 25.

Customer Specialization

Sales forces may be specialized by customer for various reasons. The firm's customers may require that the vendor's salesmen possess specialized knowledge about their industry. IBM is an example of a firm that uses specialized sales forces for different classes of customers. Office equipment manufacturers often have sales specialists who deal only with educational institutions. Some textbook publishers have sales forces that specialize by discipline. One salesman might call only on faculty members in the behavioral sciences, another might specialize in the physical sciences and mathematics, while still another may concentrate his efforts in business administration. These publishers will argue that this type of organization allows them to serve their customers better, because each salesman is a specialist in the area he serves.

Another factor leading to customer specialization in sales forces is that some industries exhibit significant geographical concentration. The petroleum, aircraft, and electronics industries are examples. In such cases, geographical sales specialization is meaningless. Customer specialization may be the best way to approach the marketplace.

The primary disadvantage of customer specialization is that territories typically overlap. There may be three, four, or more of the company's salesmen covering the same geographical area, but serving different customers. The result is often higher selling costs. Therefore, customer specialization should be used only when it is justified by the actual needs of the market.

Figure 7-8 shows several types of customer specialization. This organizational approach can be implemented by industry (as in Figure 7-7), by distribution channel, or by general type of customers.

The first type of customer specialization—by industry classification—might be used by a steel manufacturer who had to deal with diverse industries. The second type—customer specialization by distribution channels—would be useful if customers within the various channels had significantly different needs. Domestic consumers, domestic distributors, and export sales would require specialized product information and sales appeals. Finally, some customer-oriented organizations are based on the type of market in which the consumer operates. A tire manufacturer might specialize its sales force by original equipment market (the automobile companies), by replacement markets (retail stores, garages, petroleum retailers, and catalogue sales), and by institutional markets (fleet sales).

The essential point is that this form of specialization should be used only if it is warranted by specialized customer needs. Excessive sales force specialization means higher selling costs.

FIGURE 7—8
Forms of Customer Specialization in Sales Forces

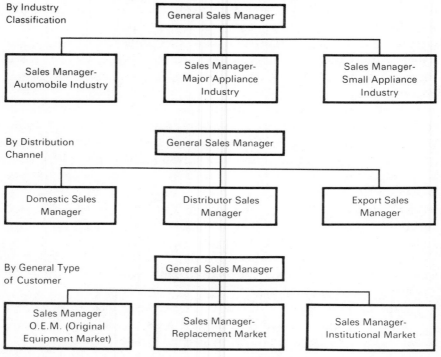

Product Specialization

Product specialization allows salesmen and sales managers to concentrate their efforts on particular product lines, brands, or individual items. Here is the way the president of an apparel firm describes product specialization in his sales organization:

> Our sales effort is organized first by groups: for example, shoes, under apparel, and outer apparel. These groups are further organized by specialized subsections of the particular industry and finally by special product lines within the subsections; e.g., there are six specialty sales forces within the men's shoe classification,

each concentrating on a single brand line, at various price points, or for various product specialty classifications.[15]

The primary disadvantage of product specialization is that in many cases two or more salesmen from the same company will call on the same customer. While the customer will have the advantage of the specialized product knowledge provided by each salesman, he may resent the extra time that must be spent in the purchasing function. Another disadvantage is the expensive duplication of sales effort that results from having more than one salesman operating in the same geographical locality.

In most cases, product specialization in the sales organization implies that the entire sales force is divided by product groupings, such as those shown in Figure 7–9.

FIGURE 7–9
A Sales Force Specialized by Product

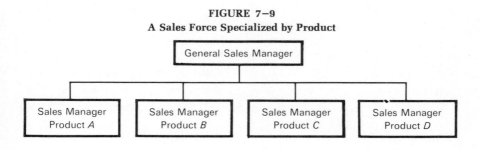

In some cases, however, strict product specialization may not be practical in certain minimum sales areas. These regions may then require the use of a *full-line salesman*. This individual sells all of the firm's products in a given geographical area (see Figure 7–10). Some

---

[15]Morgan B. MacDonald, Jr., and G. Clark Thompson, "Specialization in Marketing," *Conference Board Record*, vol. 1 (June 1964), p. 25.

FIGURE 7–10
Sales Force Employing Both Product Specialization and Full-Line Selling

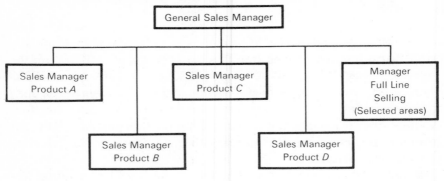

firms prefer to use *manufacturers representatives* in these areas. *Manufacturers representatives* are independent businessmen who act as commission sales agents for several manufacturers of noncompeting products. Their commission, (usually 6 per cent), is a variable selling cost to the firms they represent. Hence, the manufacturer is able to obtain sales representation in sparsely populated, low volume areas.

Another adaptation of product specialization occurs when it is used only for selected products or product lines. The board chairman of a steel company describes his firm's procedure as follows:

> Our field salesmen handle our entire product line with the exception of tool steel, which, because of its highly specialized nature and the fact that we sell it from our own warehouses, is handled by tool specialists. The balance of men handle the complex line of stainless steel products in all forms, silicon steels, and high temperature alloys.[16]

Still other companies prefer to use product classification to organize the staff specialists who assist sales personnel. In other words, the sales force may be organized geographically or by customers, while

---

[16]MacDonald and Thompson (1964), p. 25.

the sales support personnel are organized by product groups. This is often used when sales planning, sales promotion, and advertising are viewed as being product related.

Product manager is the term that is usually used to describe these staff specialists.[17] Proctor and Gamble and Pepsi-Cola are examples of firms using product managers. These staff specialists are responsible for many aspects of product development, sales planning, and the coordination of the total promotional package for a given product(s). This type of organizational arrangement is shown in Figure 7–11.

The advantage of a product manager system is that it allows the product specialization in the area where it is most often needed — sales support activities. At the same time, the system avoids the dupli-

FIGURE 7–11
The Use of Product Managers in the Sales Organization

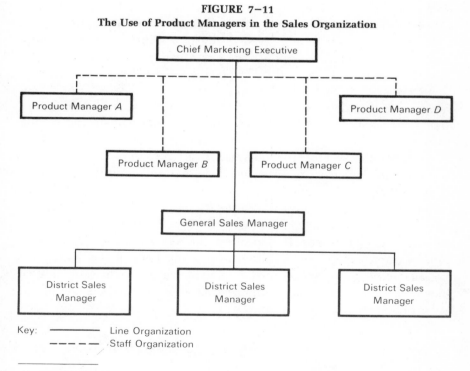

Key: ———— Line Organization
        – – – – Staff Organization

---

[17]Product management can also be a line function if the person is given direct authority over the field sales force. However, this is relatively rare in modern sales organizations.

cation of sales effort that often accompanies strict product specialization.

It is also important to note the growing importance of product specialization in marketing organizations. Many large diversified firms, such as W. R. Grace and Dresser Industries, have chosen to organize their various units under product groupings. The rapid acceptance of the product manager concept lends additional support to the argument that product specialization seems to be the prevalent trend in selling organizations.

Geographical Specialization

Geographical specialization is the simplest and most widely used method of organizing a sales force. Nearly all companies use it at some level in their sales organization. Some firms carry geographical specialization through several organizational levels (see Figure 7 – 12).

Field sales personnel are given the responsibility for direct selling activities in a given geographical area, or territory. The sales representative is responsible for selling his firm's full line of products. Most firms prefer their field sales personnel to function as territorial managers, with complete responsibility for sales in the area. Territories are treated as separate profit centers for purposes of analysis and for the evaluation of sales personnel.

As noted above, geographical specialization is the most commonly used method of sales organization. Customer and product specialization are usually more complex, and they should only be used if their inherent advantages are critical to the firm's sales effort. The simplicity of geographical specialization probably explains its popularity among sales executives. It also offers the advantages of adaptability and of improved coverage at the local level. Even if the sales force uses a customer or product organization at higher levels, geographical specialization is common at the district and territorial levels in the sales organization.

THE FIRST LEVEL SALES MANAGER

Special attention should be given to the first level of management in any sales organization. These managers—with titles such as district

FIGURE 7–12
Geographical Specialization in a Sales Force

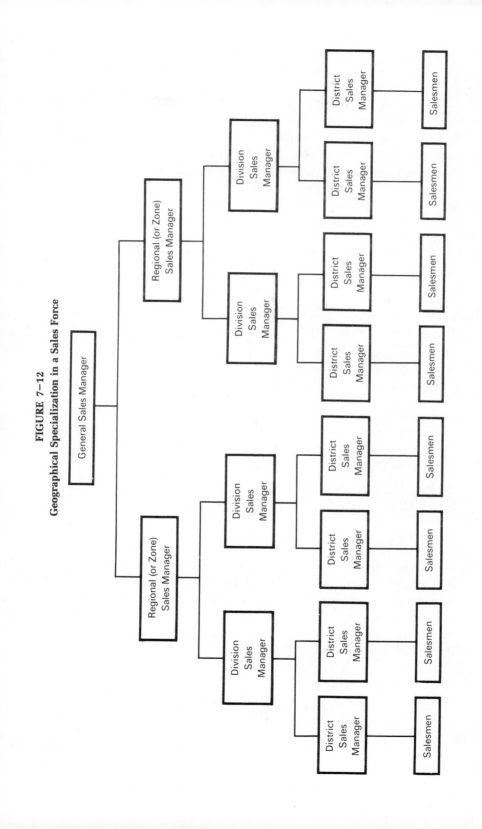

sales manager, branch manager, or field sales manager — may represent the most critical level of leadership and supervision in the entire sales force. They have direct control over the field sales force and have ultimate responsibility in given areas. Their effectiveness and success determines the overall performance of the organization.[18]

Table 7–2 reports the results of a survey of 221 companies concerning the titles of their field sales supervisors. *District sales manager* was the most popular designation, with 31 per cent of the respondents using it.

TABLE 7–2
Titles of Field Sales Supervisors

Title of Field Sales Supervisor	Percentage of Mentions
District Sales Manager (or District Manager)	31
Regional Sales Manager (or Regional Manager)	18
Sales Manager	8
Branch Manager	4
Field Sales Manager	4
Other titles	35
TOTAL	100

Source: Morgan B. MacDonald, Jr., and Earl L. Bailey, "The Field Sales Supervisor," *Conference Board Record*, vol. V (July 1968), p. 34.

Field selling organizations are quite varied. Some may be elaborate district offices with a full complement of receptionists, secretaries, clerks, sales support personnel, and computers. Others may consist of a small, one-room office manned only by an answering service. As a result, the field sales manager's job can range over a wide spectrum. At one extreme he may be a desk-bound executive; at the other he may be a territorial salesman who *happens* to have been assigned some administrative duties.

---

[18]See Eugene J. Kelly and William Lazar, "Basic Duties of the Modern Sales Department," *Industrial Marketing*, vol. 45 (April 1960), pp. 68–74; 78.

The very existence of the field selling organization, as well as the circumstances surrounding its operation, depend on a variety of factors. The *size of the sales force* is a determining factor, since larger sales forces create a basic need for a field organization. Size also determines the extent of the field organization. Firms that place a *higher emphasis on personal selling in their promotional mix* tend to have more comprehensive field systems. The *physical location of the customers* served by the sales force is another crucial factor. Also the *amount of account servicing that is required* partially determines the existence and extent of the field organization. If customer needs require that the account be serviced by a salesman every week or so, then a field organization is almost a necessity.

With the vast range of possibilities, it is little wonder that the first line sales manager is often in a confusing position. If his job were perceived correctly, he would act as a member of management that had direct field contact. Instead, he is usually subjected to pressures from both his superiors and his subordinates. In fact, one study concluded that:

> The field sales executive's position in the corporate structure is not clearly perceived by his superiors. There is a tendency to place the field executive "in the middle," not clearly in management and not clearly in sales.[19]

In addition to their administrative duties, field sales managers are typically required to handle some accounts personally. Accounts serviced by management are often called *house accounts*. The percentage of a sales manager's time spent in personal selling varies according to the size of the sales force. Larger sales forces dictate that the manager spend less time selling and more time in his administrative efforts. This relationship is shown in Table 7–3.

Most authorities in the selling field view the first level sales manager as a vital link with the marketplace and the field sales force. In

---

[19]Rodney E. Evans, "Corporate Management Looks at the Field Sales Executive," *Oklahoma Business Bulletin*, vol. 40 (January 1972), p. 19. Also see Hollister Spencer, "Salesmen and Sales Managers Look at the District Manager," *California Management Review*, vol. XV (Fall 1972), pp. 98–105.

TABLE 7–3

Relationship Between the Size of the Sales Force and the Median Percentage of Time Spent in Selling by Sales Managers

Size of the Sales Force	Median Percentage of Time Spent in Selling
500 or more	20
200–499	25
100–199	30
50–99	30
25–49	30
Less than 25	50

Source: David A. Weeks, "The Sales Manager As An Organizational Orphan," *Conference Board Record*, vol. VII (May 1970), pp. 31–37.

addition to its immediate importance, this level of sales leadership often provides the training ground for executives destined for even higher positions in *all* areas of the marketing organization.

TERRITORY DECISIONS

For the first level sales manager, territory design is the major organizational problem. This issue, as well as its related decisions, has always received considerable attention in the sales management literature.[20] A *sales territory* is a grouping of accounts. Although sales territories are usually thought of as a geographical area serviced by the sales representative, this concept will vary widely if customer or product specialization is used extensively by the firm.

Territory decisions are dependent upon the overall level of selling effort. Once this is set, the sales manager can proceed to make his various decisions and allocations. These decisions include:

1. Should there be a territorial organization?
2. How many territories should there be?

[20]See, for example: Walter J. Semlow, "How Many Salesmen Do You Need?" *Harvard Business Review*, vol. 37 (May–June 1959), pp. 126–132; Walter J. Talley, "How to Design Sales Territories," *Journal of Marketing*, vol. 25 (January 1961), pp. 7–13; J. S. Schiff and Michael Schiff, "New Sales Management Tool: ROAM," *Harvard Business Review*, vol. 45 (July–August 1967), pp. 59–66.

FIGURE 7–13 Conceptual Couplings of Effort and Response Variables

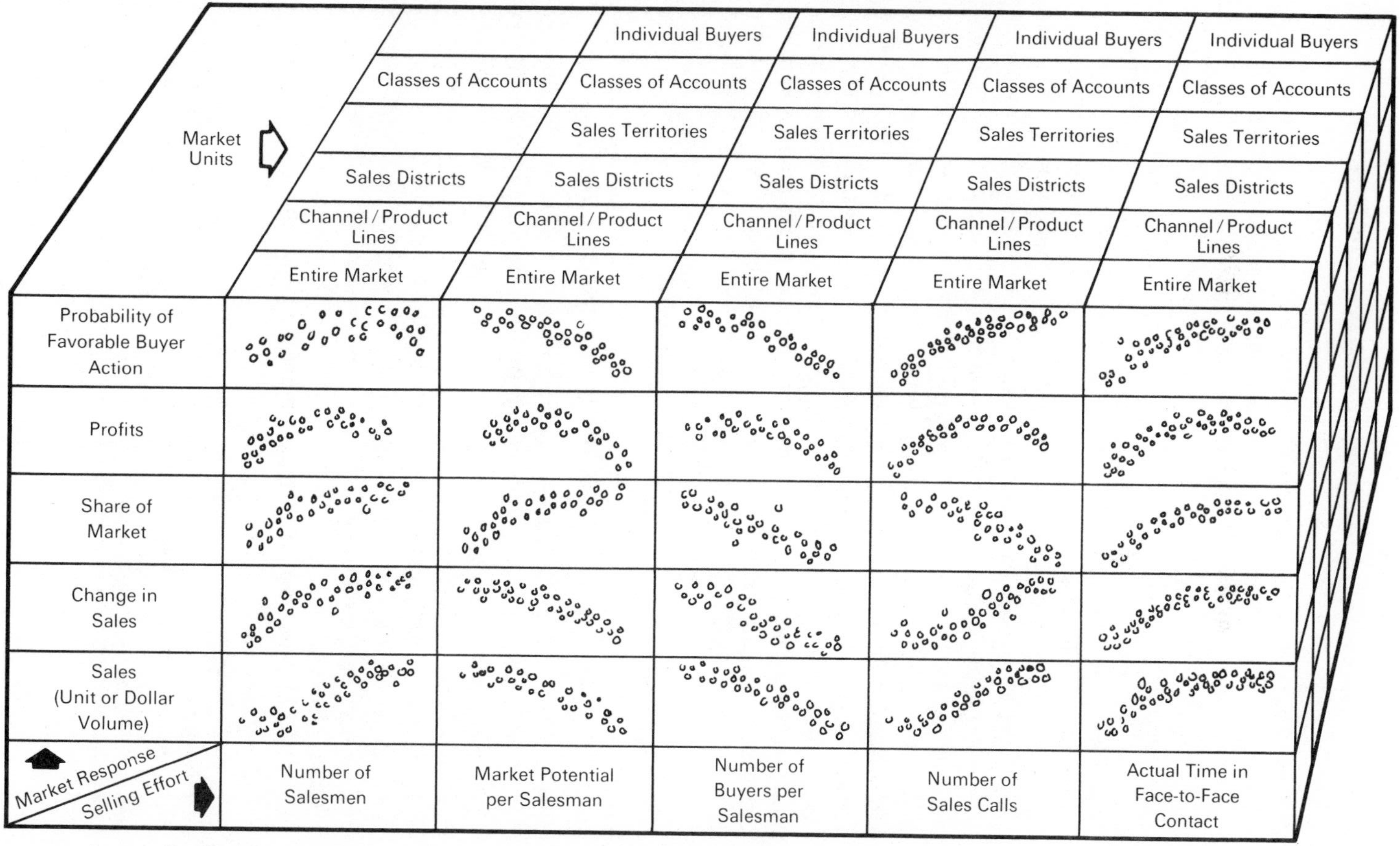

Source: Zarrel Lambert and Fred W. Kniffen, "Response Functions and Their Application in Sales Force Management," *Southern Journal of Business*, vol. 5 (January 1970), p. 5.

3. What are the locations of these territories?
4. How are salesmen to be assigned to territories?
5. How should sales effort be allocated?
6. How should salesmen be scheduled and routed?

All of these questions must be dealt with by the sales manager.

Territory decisions should also be based upon the existing relationship between sales effort and sales volume. One useful tool is the *response function*, which shows how sales volume responds to various sales effort inputs. Many companies use this technique to assist their sales managers. General Electric was one of the early innovators in the field.[21] The application of response functions to sales management is demonstrated in Figure 7–13. Selling effort variables—such as the number of salesmen, the market potential per salesman, the number of buyers per salesman, the number of sales calls, and the actual time spent in face-to-face contact—are shown on the horizontal axis. Market response items—such as sales, change in sales, share of market, profits, and probability of favorable buyer action—appear on the vertical axis.

Establishing Territories

The first step in establishing sales territories is to determine the potential of the area.[22] This requires that the sales manager identify each account and classify it by its potential.[23] A simple A, B, C, D, E categorization is common. The expected value of the account is determined by multiplying its market potential (the maximum possible sales in a given area) *times* the firm's estimated share *times* the appropriate probability. This method of account analysis is shown in Figure 7–14.

Once the accounts have been classified, the sales manager must then set the goals and objectives needed to reach the designated potential.

---

[21]Clark Ward, Donald F. Clark, and Russell L. Ackoff, "Allocation of Sales Effort in the Lamp Division of the General Electric Company," *Operations Research*, vol. 4 (December 1956), pp. 629–647.
[22]This section is based on Robert Vizza, "Managing Time and Territories for Maximum Sales Success," *Journal of Business*, vol. 1 (March 1972), pp. 18–23.
[23]Market and sales potentials are discussed in detail in Chapter 12, "Sales Forecasting."

FIGURE 7–14
Account Analysis and Calculation of Expected Value

1. Account Name	2. Classification	3. Potential by Product			4. Estimated Share By Product			5. Probabilities			6. Expected Value (Col. 3 x 4 x 5)			
		X	Y	Z	X	Y	Z	X	Y	Z	X	Y	Z	Total
Totals														

Classification   Number of Accounts

A   _____

B   _____

C   _____

D   _____

E   _____

Total

Source: Robert F. Vizza and Thomas E. Chambers, *Time and Territorial Management for Salesmen* (New York: The Sales Executives Club, 1971).

Call Frequency

The next step is to determine the optimum call frequency for each class of accounts. The expected value calculated in the account analysis will be an important input into that decision. Executive reasoning and previous call patterns will also play a role in the decision.

One of the classic dilemmas facing sales management is the *small order problem*. Some accounts are simply too small to warrant adequate servicing. ROTI (*Return on Time Invested*) is one way of analyzing this difficulty.[24] It can be calculated as follows:

$$ROTI = \frac{\text{Average Gross Margin per Order}}{\text{Cost per Call Hour}}$$

---

[24]This is suggested in Vizza (1972), p. 20.

where:

$$\text{Cost per Call Hour} = \frac{\text{Salesmen's Direct Costs}}{\text{Call Hours Available}}$$

For instance, if a territory's direct selling expenses were $25,000 annually, and if there were 1250 call hours available per year, then the cost per call hour would be

$$\text{Cost per Call Hour} = \frac{\$25,000}{1250} = \$20$$

Further assume that the average gross margin per order from a particular account was $30. Then the ROTI would be 150 per cent, or 1.5 times the cost of the time invested.

$$\text{ROTI} = \frac{\$30}{\$20} = 1.5$$

A ROTI of less than 1.00 would be unprofitable. Calls on accounts of this size should be minimized, unless the account is expected to increase or unless there are public or legal sanctions involved. The value of ROTI is that it allows the sales manager to rank order his accounts according to their relative profit potential.

Scheduling

After the optimum call frequency has been established, a *call schedule* must be developed. The difference between these two functions has been explained this way: "The call frequencies tell the salesman how often, for what duration, and at what intervals to call; call schedules tell him exactly when to call."[25]

Call schedules are usually made out one or two weeks in advance. In general, longer schedules are a wasted effort, since competitive conditions usually force changes in the intervening time period. The schedule should state the date (and, preferably, the time) of the call, the person(s) to see, as well as the objective of the call. The call schedule is the salesman's basic operating plan for managing his territory. It

---

[25]Vizza (1972), p. 20.

should also be noted that the call schedule should assign the highest priority to those accounts with the highest ROTI.

Routing

Since about 25 per cent of a salesman's time is spent traveling, most effective sales managers develop at least elementary routing plans for their salesmen.[26] The first step is to make a routing pattern analysis. The salesman's actual call pattern should be plotted on a map with times and distances noted. This will allow the sales manager to determine if the salesman has been back-tracking, criss-crossing, or following another costly call pattern.

Generally, the following routing patterns have been found to be most effective:

1. *Straight line:* Starting from the office, the salesman makes calls in one continuous direction to the end of his territory. He may make calls on the way back along the same line, or he may return on another line. Thus he alternates "lines" on each trip.
2. *Circular* patterns involve starting at the home office and prescribing a circle of stops which is completed when the salesman returns to the office.
3. A *clover leaf pattern* is similar to the circular pattern, but instead of covering an entire territory, it circles a part of the territory. The next trip is an adjacent circle, and so on.
4. *Hopscotch* is a practice of starting at the farthest point from the home office and making calls back to the office. A salesman would fly to the outer limits and drive back, for example. On the next trip, he travels in the opposite direction in his territory.[27]

MEASURING THE EFFECTIVENESS OF THE SALES ORGANIZATION

Evaluating the effectiveness of the sales organization is a complex matter at best. In some cases, it is impossible because of the external

---

[26]This section is based on Vizza (1972), p. 21.
[27]Vizza (1972), p. 21.

factors that confuse the traditional yardsticks of volume and profits. But, even if one were able to design a perfectly controlled measurement, volume and profits really say little about the vitality of an organization.

Essentially, the measurement question is heavily influenced by the fact that both people and structure influence organization effectiveness.

$$\frac{\text{Organizational}}{\text{Effectiveness}} = f \text{ (people and structure)}$$

Statements such as "ABC Enterprises is a good organization" reflect this situation. What is really meant is that ABC Enterprises is represented by *good people*. The *structural* aspects of the organization may in fact be very weak. The reverse is also true: many difficulties that are attributed to organizational problems can be in fact people-related problems.

Participants in an organization influence its structure. Owners influence small business situations, while top management influences the structure that exists in larger firms. The most complex problem faced by those who attempt to assess structural effectiveness is to account for the human factor.

The key to evaluating organizational effectiveness is to be able to define what one wants the organizational structure to accomplish. Is it sales maximization? Lowest possible operating cost? Increased market share? The question then becomes, *Has the organization reached these objectives?* If so, then one must question whether the organization is flexible enough to continue satisfying these objectives. These questions are not amenable to easy quantitative assessment; their answers emerge only after careful study and analysis by sales management.

SUMMARY Sales management performance depends in part on the effectiveness of the sales force organization. The organizing effort seeks to accomplish three basic tasks:

1. the maintenance of order in achieving sales force goals and objectives;
2. the assignment of specific tasks and responsibility;
3. integration and coordination with other elements of the firm.

The sales manager must recognize and deal with five basic organizational issues: (1) formal and informal organizations; (2) horizontal and vertical organizations; (3) centralized and decentralized organizational structures; (4) line and staff components of the organization; and (5) the size of the sales organization.

Chapter 7 also identified and discussed several concepts of effective organization: (1) that sales activities should be organized, not people; (2) that similar functions should be grouped together; and (3) that sales organizations should be coordinated, balanced, and flexible. The chapter also presented the basic types of sales organizations, classified according to customer, product, and geography. The final section of this chapter discussed the first level sales manager, territory decisions, call frequency, scheduling, routing, and measuring the effectiveness of the sales organization.

DISCUSSION/REVIEW QUESTIONS

1. Briefly identify each of the following:
   - (a) organization
   - (b) *buckpassing*
   - (c) span of control
   - (d) line function
   - (e) staff function
   - (f) full-line salesman
   - (g) manufacturer's representative
   - (h) product manager
   - (i) sales territory
   - (j) house accounts
   - (k) response function
   - (l) ROTI
2. Explain how an informal organization can assist the operation of a formal sales force organization. Are there any ways in which the informal communication network hinders the formal organizational structure? Discuss.
3. What conditions or circumstances dictate the use of a vertical sales organization? Of a horizontal sales organization?

4. Why is *commensurate responsibility and authority* a requirement for an *effective* decentralized organization?
5. Explain how an *assistant to . . .* position could be used by:
    (a) the president of the United States
    (b) the vice-president for marketing of a large steel company
    (c) a divisional commander in the U.S. Army
    (d) a university president
6. How does the size of a sales force influence its structural arrangement? Discuss.
7. "The sales organization should be built around activities, rather than the people involved in the activities." Comment.
8. Compare and contrast customer, product, and geographical specialization in sales force organizations.
9. Describe the various types of customer specialization in sales forces.
10. Go to your library and read the three most recent articles you can find about product managers. Why do you think so many firms have adopted this concept? Do you believe this trend will continue? Do all product managers perform the same duties? Discuss.
11. "The first level sales manager may be the most critical level of leadership and supervision in the entire sales force." Comment.
12. Should top management require district sales managers to handle house accounts? Why? Why not? Are there any ethical questions involved in the matter of maintaining house accounts? Discuss.
13. What types of territory decisions must be made by a sales manager?
14. How can the sales manager use the ROTI concept?
15. Describe the most effective routing patterns that can be used by salesmen.

PART TWO
CASES

CASE 10
FOOD EQUIPMENT CORPORATION*

The Food Equipment Corporation was founded in 1927. The firm is a pioneer manufacturer of restaurant and automatic food vending equipment. At present, the company is one of the largest manufacturers of vending equipment with annual sales of approximately $100 million, providing after-tax earnings of approximately $5 million. The firm has 3800 employees and 7300 shareholders. Although it is listed on the New York Stock Exchange, the founding family owns or controls a significant percentage of the outstanding common stock.

The Market

Commercial food service equipment sales are limited to the United States. Over fifty models of food, beverage, and tobacco vending ma-

---

*Based on an original case by Professor James P. Jennings of the University of Detroit.

chines are manufactured and sold throughout the United States and in foreign countries. The company has benefited from the rapid expansion of the automatic vending industry. The industry has experienced rapid growth in recent years, because the food service industry has experienced chronic labor problems. The high cost of hiring and training food service employees, in combination with a high employee turnover rate, has provided a ready market for automatic food vending equipment.

The company has developed several major innovations in the vending industry. The combination of an unusually receptive market and the pioneer development of new equipment has provided the basis for a 100 per cent growth in sales over the past ten years.

Sales Forecasting Prior to 1966

Prior to 1966, the company employed a multiple method approach to sales forecasting. The approach combined the sales force composite technique, simple trend extrapolation, and the jury of executive opinion. Late in the fiscal year, each salesman prepared an estimate of his aggregate sales for the following year. Projections of sales by month and by product line were developed by personnel in the marketing department. The detailed forecasts were derived by applying limited historical monthly and product sales statistics to each salesman's estimate of aggregate demand for the year. The detailed forecasts of each salesman were then combined to forecast total sales of each product by month.

Concurrently, the controller's department prepared a twelve-month moving average of unit sales. This moving average was the base employed to project a straight-line trend of sales for the following year. The trend projection was not adjusted for seasonal or cyclical variations, or for the introduction of new products.

The marketing department's forecast and the controller's forecast were presented at a meeting of top executives. At the meeting, the forecasts were discussed and subjectively reconciled to determine an official forecast. Normally, the official forecast was agreed upon as the level of sales at the mid-point between the marketing department's forecast and the controller's forecast. Once the sales forecast was agreed upon, the sales budget was set at an arbitrary figure above the official sales forecast. The sales budget was the basis for setting a fixed operating budget and sales quota. Under this system, wide deviations between forecast and actual sales were common.

Sales Forecasting Since 1966

In November 1966, the first staff economist was employed. The economist employed had extensive forecasting experience with a large manufacturer of consumer goods and as a business economist and market research analyst. The staff economist was initially assigned as an assistant to the treasurer.

The staff economist participated in the preparation of the 1967 sales forecast and prepared the first sales forecast based upon a correlation with Gross National Product. A simple correlation between quarterly Gross National Product and total sales of the firm was computed using historical data. Quarterly projections of Gross National Product for 1967 were employed to project total company sales by quarter for 1967. The projected sales for each division were forecast by applying each division's historical percentage of total sales to the forecast of total sales. Although this approach was crude, it provided a more accurate forecast of sales than either the sales force composite or the controller's trend forecasts for 1967.

In 1967, the economist was promoted to the newly created post of manager of market research and forecasting. The market research and forecasting department consisted of the manager and a staff of three persons and was under the direction of the vice-president for marketing.

Problems in Developing Economic Analysis Based Sales Forecasts

Three fundamental information problems had to be resolved to implement the development of sales forecasts based upon economic activity. First, the accounting system had not been designed to yield detailed sales information on a routine basis. Therefore, nonaccounting sales records were employed to build up a detailed data base which could be employed to yield useful correlations. Second, it was necessary to develop seasonal indices to adjust for the previously ignored seasonal sales patterns. Third, a study was made to determine the external economic factors which influence vending equipment sales.

Regularly published economic statistical series which should logically influence vending equipment were examined. Several statistical series were correlated with published industry statistics and with the recently constructed internal sales statistics. Four series were found to have a coefficient of correlation of 0.96+ over a ten-year period. Vending equipment sales proved to have a high degree of correlation with Personal Consumption Expenditures. Expenditures for New Plant and Equipment—Commercial and Other—proved to be a good indicator of the direction of change. GNP proved to be a good indicator of the magnitude of change. Personal Consumption Expenditures—Food, Tobacco, and Nonalcoholic Beverages—proved to be an excellent indicator of turning points. The latter series correctly indicated turning points in thirty-one of the thirty-four recast quarters.

The market research staff introduced several additional basic analytical techniques to sales forecasting: (1) The product life cycle curve was introduced into the projection of future sales of established products. (2) For the first time exogenous factors, such as the projected level of interest rates, were considered in projecting future sales. (3) A scatter graph of industry sales was prepared to project the trend of industry sales. (4) For the first time company sales were forecast on the basis of market share. (5) Monthly sales were projected on the basis of the precentage of each month's sales to the annual total.

A Comparison of Forecasting Accuracy

Over a seven-year period, the offical sales forecast prepared under the old approach deviated from actual sales an average of ±15.0 per cent. The forecasts developed by the market research staff deviated from actual sales by a ±1.6 per cent average. Normally, the official sales forecast exceeded actual sales. The market research forecast tended to be slightly below actual sales. The pattern of relationships of the various forecasts can be related to one another in the following example.

Current Application of Sales Forecasts for Planning and Control

The sales forecasts prepared by the market research staff have proven to be reliable estimates of future sales. However, sales continue to be budgeted at an arbitrary level above the forecast. The controller's department continues to prepare a fixed operating budget based upon the budgeted level of sales. The use of a fixed budget based upon an

An Example Comparison of Budgeted Forecast and Actual Sales (Actual=100)	
Sales	**Index No.**
Budgeted	120
Controller's Trend Forecast	115
Official Forecast	110
Sales Force Composite Forecast	105
Actual	100
Market Research Forecast	98–102

unrealistic estimate of future sales has contributed to poor financial planning.

The sales forecast is not subjected to a post-audit. Neither the sales forecast nor the budget are reviewed during the year. Both sales forecasting and budgeting are viewed as once-a-year, rather than continuous, activities. Top management's decision to use unrealistic budgets has precipitated human relations problems among the sales force and middle operating managers. Salesmen are assigned unrealistic quotas, and operating managers lack the necessary information to properly plan and control the operations for which they are responsible.

ASSIGNMENT

1. Analyze Food Equipment Corporation's experience in forecasting sales.
2. What factors seem to influence the accuracy of sales forecasting in the company?
3. Does the information presented here suggest that corrective management action is justified?

CASE 11
AGCHEM INCORPORATED*

Agchem was founded in the early 1950s as a joint venture of three major chemical companies. The company is presently an almost whol-

*Based on an original case by Professor James P. Jennings of The University of Detroit.

ly owned subsidiary of one of the founding firms. It is operated as a self-sufficient entity with management effectiveness judged on the basis of rate of return on investment.

Agchem is a leading manufacturer of special purpose agricultural pesticides. The firm's annual sales volume of approximately $50 million is derived from sales throughout the United States and Canada. Major sales categories include (1) agricultural pesticides, (2) bulk sales of pesticides, and (3) animal health feed additives.

The Market

Special purpose agricultural pesticides which are sold to farmers through distributors and dealers constitute the firm's major product line. In recent years the company has experienced a rapid growth in bulk sales of pesticides to firms which produce and market household and lawn and garden pesticides. Also, the company has recently ventured into the animal health field with the production of cattle and poultry feed additives to control animal parasites. This field is expected to provide a major avenue of future sales growth.

Marketing Problems

Agchem faces several major marketing problems which demand the close attention of management. While most of the pesticides produced are patented, the market is highly competitive because of the ready availability of patented substitute products of other pesticide manufacturers. Also there are competing firms which produce substitute pesticides on which patents have expired. In the case of the latter, firms do not have the burden of licensing and research and development costs, and they are able to compete successfully on a price basis. These competitive pressures necessitate the continuous development of new patentable products. New product development is also stimulated by the immunity which insects develop to any insecticide and by the highly specialized applications of products to specific insect control problems.

Marketing problems are compounded by the long lead time between the development of a new product and the placement of a saleable product on the market. Prior to introduction, a new pesticide must (1)

212

be proven to be technically effective, (2) be determined to have a profitable market potential, and (3) pass lengthy expensive tests in order to be licensed by the federal government. Because of the costs involved, licensing applications are not submitted until market research indicates the profit potential of a new product.

Organization for Sales Forecasting

The forecast of unit sales and selling prices is prepared by the market research staff which reports to the vice-president for sales. The market research staff prepares three different sales forecasts: (1) a one-year monthly forecast, (2) a moving five-year forecast, and (3) a new product forecast as each new product is developed and evaluated for licensing.

Each year, prior to the beginning of the next fiscal year, a running five-year forecast is made. The five-year forecast is developed by dropping the year immediately completed, adding a new fifth year, and revising the forecasts for the remaining three middle years. The forecast is prepared on a monthly basis for the first eighteen months and on a yearly basis for the balance of the forecast period. Concurrently, a monthly forecast is prepared for the coming fiscal year. The one-year forecast is the same as the first twelve months of the five-year forecast; however, it is presented in greater detail.

The one-year forecast of prices and sales volume for each product by sales region is prepared by the market research staff. The forecast is then reviewed by the marketing executives; marketing management has the responsibility for pricing. The forecasts approved by the marketing executives are forwarded to the fiscal forecasting section of the controller's department for conversion into revenue forecasts. The approved forecast becomes the sales budget and is used for the short-run planning and control of all operations except research and development.

Forecasting Methodology

Agchem's market research department employs a multiple method approach which combines trend analysis, correlation, and a survey of regional sales managers. Sales of established products are projected on the basis of historical monthly sales as reported for general accounting purposes. Sales revenues are reported by product for each sales district every month. Because the accounting records are computerized, detailed sales information is readily available.

The trend projections are modified by the results of a survey of regional sales managers. Each regional sales manager prepares a sales forecast for his region with special emphasis on local competitive pricing problems and on new applications of existing products. The sales managers work closely with local state agricultural agents to determine new applications of existing products.

The market research staff also studies United States Department of Agriculture crop production and acreage allotment statistics to project the agricultural pesticide demand. This information is made available on computer tapes made by the U.S.D.A. The U.S.D.A. tapes are fed into the computer which stores sales information and a correlation program, to produce a print-out correlation sales forecast.

Weather is a major factor influencing both the volume and timing of sales. Presently the company is experimenting with a computer program weather forecast to improve sales forecasting accuracy.

Sales forecasts of new products to be introduced during the year are prepared separately. New product forecasts are added to the projected sales of established products to complete the forecast of unit sales and selling prices.

Application of the Sales Forecast to Sales Management

Because management is evaluated on the basis of rate of return on invested capital, they are oriented toward profit planning. Consequently, the sales forecast has rather extensive application to the planning and control of operations.

The sales forecast is the basis for establishing sales quotas and is employed to control sales. During the first week of each month, the computer prints out each salesman's quota (forecast sales) and the actual sales for the prior month. Also the total actual and forecast sales for the year to date are printed out for each salesman. The same information is printed out by product for each region. These print-outs are circulated to determine why sales are behind or ahead of the forecast. Also, there is a daily print-out of actual gross sales by product with the budgeted sales for the month, and the cumulative actual

sales for the month to date. The purpose of this print-out is to emphasize the additional sales which must be made during the remainder of
the month to meet the monthly quota.

The sales forecast also guides advertising. Agricultural pesticides
are advertised in farm journals and on local television stations to coin-
cide with the time that the product should be applied. The sales forecast influences the timing of advertising. Further, the advertising budget is determined by the projected sales revenue.

The long-range forecast is employed to project the introduction of
new products and the termination of existing products. Agchem tends
to be self-competitive. Thus, new products often compete more directly with existing profitable products of the company than with products of competitors. The long-range forecast indicates when the
new product should be introduced and the old product should be
eliminated.

ASSIGNMENT

Evaluate Agchem's method of forecasting sales. What improvements
could you suggest?

CASE 12
MIDWEST PUBLIC SERVICE COMPANY*

Midwest Public Service Company is engaged in the generation, purchase, transmission, distribution, and sale of electricity at retail in
approximately 200 communities and twenty-eight rural counties.
Wholesale sales of electricity are made to six municipalities. Retail
sales of natural gas are made in twenty-five communities with an estimated population of 100,000. Three communities with a combined
population of 18,000 are provided water service. The company's service area has an estimated population of 370,000 persons. The company services 70 per cent of a major metropolitan area, from which it
derives 50 per cent of total electric sales revenue. Over the past ten

---

*Based on an original case by Professor James P. Jennings of the University of Detroit.

years, the population of the company's service area has increased 19 per cent. This growth has been concentrated in the major metropolitan service area.

During the past decade, the number of kilowatt hours of electricity sold have increased at a fairly stable rate each year for a ten-year increase of 159 per cent. The company's sales growth is 50 per cent greater than the national average. The sale of natural gas has grown steadily for a 72 per cent increase over the past ten years. Municipal water revenues have remained unchanged over the decade, accounting for less than 2 per cent of the firm's total revenue.

Sales Forecasting Organization and Applications

At present, the sales forecast is prepared in the fall for the following calendar fiscal year by personnel in the finance department under the direction of the vice-president for finance. The two major applications of the sales forecast are the preparation of the annual cash budget for the following fiscal year and estimation of long-range capital expenditure requirements. The sales forecast is not used to prepare the operating budget. Operating costs are determined by "historical formulas." Nor does the sales forecast have direct application to marketing activities since the marketing function is limited.

The marketing department consists of three engineers hired to work with commercial and industrial customers. The sales engineers are primarily concerned with increasing electric heating installations to make more effective use of peak power capacity. Although advertising expenditures were not disclosed, they were described as "rather small." In response to an inquiry as to the extent of marketing activities, the firm was described as "the least marketing-conscious firm you can find."

Sales Forecasting Methodology

The sales forecast is developed via a multiple method approach which combines trend extrapolation and a survey of major commercial and industrial customers. The forecast is developed by calculating a simple moving average of monthly unit sales for each rate classification.*

---

*Sales of electricity are projected in kilowatt hours for each of the following categories: urban residential, rural, electric heating, commercial, and industrial.

The historical unit sales trend is extrapolated and adjusted for normal seasonal demand. The unit sales are multiplied by the expected rates for each rate classification to project the future year's sales by month.

The trend projection is then subjected to modification for anticipated change in demand as determined by surveys of district managers and major customers. Each of the eight district managers is surveyed concerning the rate of new construction in the district. Major commercial and industrial customers are surveyed with respect to anticipated changes in production or plant size which would affect electric power consumption.

Although the present method of sales forecasting has been satisfactory, the sales manager is working with an independent consultant to develop a multiple correlation computer program to forecast sales. The correlation approach is to be implemented to meet the anticipated need for even more reliable forecasts in the future.

Future electric power sales are being correlated with three independent variables: population, weather, and appliance saturation. Major changes in commercial and industrial demand will continue to be treated as special items. If the multiple correlation model presently being developed proves successful, sales forecasting will be computerized, and the responsibility for forecasting will be transferred to the recently established sales department.

ASSIGNMENT

Evaluate Midwest Public Service's sales forecasting organization and methodology. What is your assessment of the proposed multiple correlation method of forecasting sales?

CASE 13
PROFIT CENTER ORGANIZATION*

E. I. duPont deNemours and Company, one of the world's largest corporations, has been the United States' dominant producer of chemi-

*Adapted from DuPont's *Management Newsletter*, February 1970.

cals for many years. In recent years DuPont has faced severe domestic and foreign competition in its major markets. Although sales continued to increase, profit margins shrank. In an all-out effort to improve earnings, many DuPont industrial departments turned to increased delegation of profit responsibility.

This increased delegation of responsibility—and accountability—led to a proliferation of *profit centers* (enterprise units with an operating department which have all functions necessary to making a profit) under the control of one director or manager. Unlike the functional organization (Figure 1)—in which total departmental responsibility below the assistant general manager was shared by directors of manufacturing, research, sales, and accounting—the profit center (Figure 2) concentrated on maximizing the profits of a single segment of a department's business.

FIGURE 1
Functional Line Organization in an Industrial Department

General Manager

Assistant General Manager

Manufacturing

Research and Development

Sales

Accounting and Business Analysis

Personnel and Industrial Relations

218

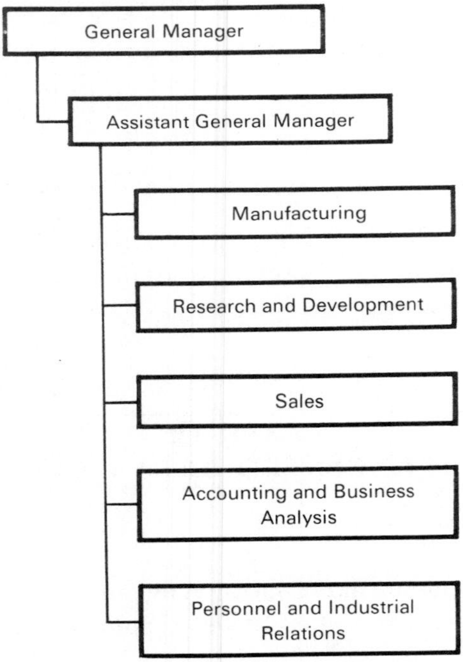

FIGURE 2
Profit Center Organization

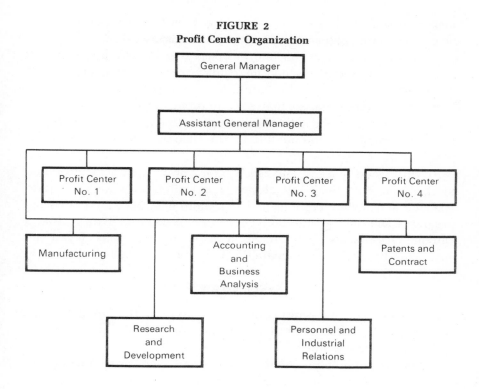

The increasing importance of the profit center to DuPont was attributable to the fact that the magnitude of investment, the volume of business, and the number of customers — on the industrial department level — made it difficult to get quick, well-informed decisions on new products and to take advantage of profitable opportunities in older products. In the profit center, the director, or manager, had full responsibility for the business — whether it was a new venture or an established product line — with a charter to attain optimum growth in earnings and to maintain the highest return on investment. To these ends, he coordinated the functions of sales, research, and manufacturing within his enterprise, in much the same way that a general manager operates in the functional organization.

In its most prevalent form in DuPont, the profit center consisted of a marketing organization, plus manufacturing and research managers reporting to the director. The profit center contracted with the department's manufacturing and research divisions to meet priorities and objectives in those areas. In addition, the director worked closely with the department's accounting and business analysis group to establish cost and business controls, and he regularly received financial data on the state of his business. Other units within the department provided him with necessary market analyses and projections.

In effect—and in fact—the profit center director was an entrepreneur who bore full accountability for the success or failure of his business.

According to general managers, the profit center contributed markedly to the flexibility of the organization. It also resulted in speedier and better decisions and in a more effective job of choosing programs, setting priorities, and controlling costs. As Edwin A. Gee, a DuPont vice-president, put it: "You get better decisions if you put accountability at the level where the man has all the facts."

ASSIGNMENT

1. Compare the new profit center organization to the functional line organization. What are the advantages and disadvantages of each form of organization?
2. What are the implications of the profit center organization for DuPont's salesmen and sales managers?

CASE 14
DELTA, INC. (A)

Delta, Inc., a leading national manufacturer of toiletries and jewelry, was considering the establishment of a new management position, sales supervisor.

Delta's marketing organization is shown in Figure 1. The company's brand managers, who reported to the vice-president for sales and marketing, coordinated sales of jewelry and toiletry products. Other staff positions included the manager for marketing research and sales forecasting, the new products manager, and the chief designer. The national sales manager directed the line sales organization.

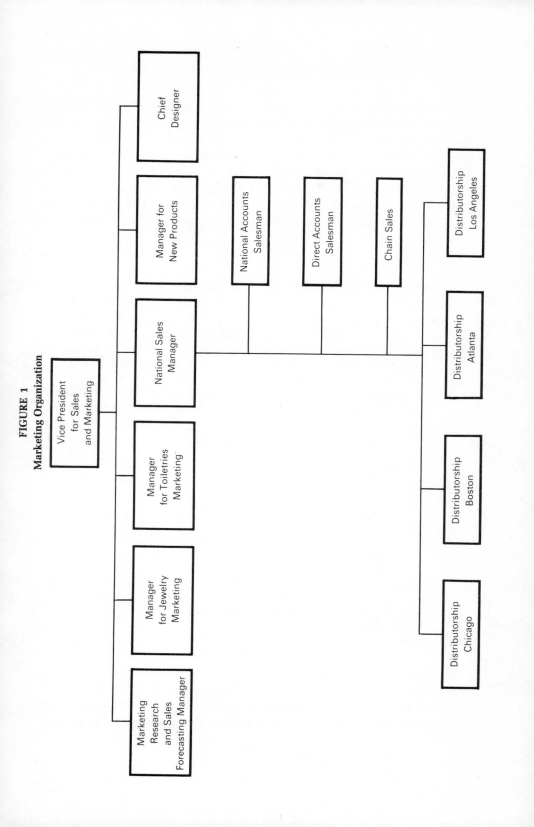

FIGURE 1
Marketing Organization

Delta's sales force was organized into four company owned distributorships. Each distributorship was headed by a general manager who reported directly to the national sales manager. Also reporting to the national sales manager were special salesmen for national accounts, for direct accounts, and for chain sales.

The existing organization of a distributorship is presented in Figure 2. Sales supervisors would assist district managers. The following job description for sales supervisors was prepared by Delta's personnel department.

> Responsibilities would involve personal accountability, assisting district managers (both toiletries and jewelry) in training and merchandising, in the training of all new sales personnel, as well as in recruiting and interviewing. The man would be trained in the internal operations of a distributorship and be given the opportunity of working with the sales, marketing, operations, and accounting departments of Delta's home office, in order to give him a complete picture of Delta's aims and direction. He would be available for promotion to any of the company-owned distributorships, present or future. Compensation would be salary, bonus tied in with distributor sales, plus expenses.

ASSIGNMENT

1. Evaluate Delta's organizational structure.
2. What is your opinion of Delta's proposed *sales supervisor* position? Discuss.

CASE 15
DELTA, INC. (B)

Delta, Inc., a leading national manufacturer of toiletries and jewelry, was recruiting applicants for a newly established position of sales supervisor [see Delta, Incorporated (A)]. After evaluating over thirty applicants for an opening in the Boston distributorship, two appli-

FIGURE 2
Distributorship Organization

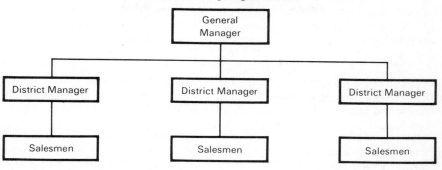

cants were selected for further screening. The resumes of these applicants follow. (Note: These are the actual resumes submitted.)

ASSIGNMENT

1. Evaluate the resumes of the applicants. Do either of the applicants fit the job description for sales supervisor shown in Delta, Inc. (A)?
2. Based upon the resumes, which applicant would you select?

Resume 1

John R. Stevenson
26 Jackson Street
Attleboro, Massachusetts
Phone: 785-1306

Date of Birth—Feb. 2, 1926
Married—one child
Height: 6′ 1″ Weight: 200#
Excellent health

Education   Amherst College—B.S. Chemistry-1948
New York University—Graduate work (no degree) Business Administration

Accomplishments

Through a series of deliberate moves, candidate has been able to gain an uncommon experience in Sales and Management technique and growth.

223

Through diligent application of his abilities, and hard work, he has mastered the techniques of direct, dealer, distributor sales and management. He has steadily risen, in the management area, from Territory Manager to District Manager, Regional Manager, Sales Manager, General Sales Manager, General Manager of Marketing, and presently, Eastern Manager of total P & L responsibility.

Although his titles do not suggest it, his responsibilities have qualified him for a General Manager's title, inasmuch as he has had wide and successful experience in Production and Scheduling, Inventory Control, Purchasing, Manufacturing, Packaging, R & D, Acquisition and P & L.

He is a mature, seasoned individual who is contemplating his final move to a position where he can bring all of his experience and abilities to a focal point. While title of his final position is secondary, the responsibilities and challenge of this final move is of prime importance to the candidate.

The candidate's record of success is outstanding, his credentials are impecable and his intent to make his final move will be of great benefit to the organization that recognizes his worth.

The following, briefly, recaps his record of employment.

1971 to present

Manager, Eastern Region: Nationally known manufacturer of office furniture both steel and wood and accessories. Eastern volume $9,800,000. Dealer, Distributor, Wholesaler operation.

Responsibilities: Marketing, Sales Promotion, Merchandising, Key Account function. Quota and Gross Profit responsibility, 13 company salesmen, Showroom, Office and Office personnel (4). Trade Shows, "Open House" and Product presentation to dealers, dealer prospects, consumers, designers, and architects.

Achievements: Increased sales volume 26 percent to $9.8 million. Increased Gross Profit from 28.9 percent to 32.5 percent. Designed Marketing Show to accomplish above. Set up controls and disciplines for Sales Force, including training sessions, directional guidelines and reporting systems. Realigned territories, hired and fired new sales personnel. Held training sessions, dealer "Open Houses" and brought substantial "Consumer" accounts into Company. Exceeded all quotas assigned.

1969 to 1971

General Manager of Marketing: The leading manufacturer of drafting instruments, stationery and drawing equipment and supplies. Volume approximately $17,000,000. National Sales Force (company owned and representatives). Dealer distribution operation with no direct sales.

Responsibilities: Marketing, Sales, Advertising, New Products, Production Scheduling, Inventory Control, Packaging, Pricing and Key Account Contact and Communication.

Achievements: Designed a Marketing Program that resulted in 20 percent increase in 1969 and an 18 percent increase in 1970 (despite business conditions prevalent at that time).

Initiated priority system to eliminate backlog and developed a production control system to bring production (and inventory) in line with sales demand. Reduced operating costs 16 percent.

Through development of proper sales training, was able to penetrate Company Markets more effectively and was able to develop new markets for his products.

Was able to bring 15 Key Accounts into his sales orbit, some on a negotiated contract basis.

1965 to 1969:

General Sales Manager: Leading manufacturers of standard and special steel fabrication such as office, factory and hospital equipment (as well as specially engineered products). Volume approximately $10,000,000.

Responsibilities: Marketing, Sales, Advertising, Pricing, New Products, Packaging, Direct and Government negotiations, Key Account, Supervisory control of manufacturing plant.

Achievement: Through Marketing design, was able to increase sales 22% for 1966 and held an average increase of approximately 14% for 1967, 1968.

Hired and trained a completely new sales force nationally. Also developed an inside staff. Distributed through a network of franchised distributors that were required to invest from $10,000 to $20,000 to obtain the franchise.

Due to the increase in volume, added 50,000 square feet to manufacturing plant.

1962 to 1965

Regional Sales Manager: Leading manufacturers of fasteners, office and factory equipment, and twist drills. Volume $80,000,000.

Responsibilities: Based in Atlanta, Georgia, was given the responsibility of penetrating virgin territory. Volume at time of takeover was $130,000.

Achievement: Designed a Marketing approach, on a franchise distributor basis, for the Southeast. Set up and serviced a distributor operation (including hiring and training distributor salesmen) that resulted in volume increase to $1,800,000 in 1964.

1950 to 1962

District Manager: Leading manufacturers of office and factory steel equipment. Volume $60,000,000.

Responsibilities: Maintain and improve volume in the Southeastern District. Managed 13 company salesmen and operated district office under company marketing program.

Achievement: Increased volume 10% to 12%. Was given a commendation for his work from company president and special plans were made to bring him along the management ladder speedily.

COMMENT   Candidate has been fortunate enough to successfully expose himself to all areas of management, through both the technical and practical phases, and is fully qualified to accept total responsibility in the General Management, Marketing, Sales and Key Account areas.

*Names furnished on request.

Resume 2

Anthony R. Russo   Telephone: 401-629-3508
75 North Street
Coventry, Rhode Island

PERSONAL   Single, 6′ 2″, 175 pounds, health good.
Military Status 1Y (Allergy)
Date of Birth: May 5, 1947.

GOALS AND OBJECTIVES

Immediate future . . . to be a Director of Admissions and actively participate in the general growth and future of the education process and to assist young people in obtaining the right and proper directions in life.

Long term . . . to work in a sales or sales oriented environment in a managerial or administrative capacity.

EDUCATION

1965 to 1969   Broch and Smith College, B. S. in Business Administration
1961 to 1965   Eastport Academy, Eastport, Massachusetts

BUSINESS EXPERIENCE

May, 1972 to
Present

Broach and Smith College, Associate Director of Admissions
Responsible with the direct management of the entire Admissions operation with the Director of Admissions, including an equal voice in the Senior Administrative process. Duties include all responsibilities of the Assistant Director as outlined below.

1971 to May, 1972

Broch and Smith College, Assistant Director of Admissions
Responsibilities: Admissions budget, advertising, coordination of representatives' high school and college visitations, processing of applications, travel, and in the absence or assistance of the Director of Admissions, all functions pertinent to the general welfare of the department including office management, hiring of personnel, attending trustee and senior staff meetings, and general public relations between the admissions department and the college community.

1969 to 1971

Broach and Smith College, Admissions Representative
Territory assigned: Northeastern Seaboard. Arranged scheduling and visited high schools, community and junior colleges, interviewed students and arranged appointments with parents, students, and guidance counselors on campus. Coordinated advertising for radio and newspapers. Assisted in the preparation of copy for general admissions advertising and publications. Initiated advertising medium for high school guidance counselors through the circulation of a "Fact Folder," including information on campus life and curriculum and admissions prerequisites. Assisted the Director of Admissions in the processing of Applications.

SUMMER EMPLOYMENT

1969   Traveled throughout the United States after graduation.
1968–1969   Colonial Engineering, Cambridge, Mass.—Brakeman, operated 15 ton brake and performed other shop duties.
1967   Encyclopedia Americana, Waltham, Mass.—Salesman.
1966   David Mann Company, Bedford, Mass.—Trainee, Photographic micron scale glass laboratory.

1965	Sears, Lowell, Mass. — Bus boy, short order cook.
1964	Vacationed with parents.
1963	Skip's Restaurant, Chelmsford, Mass. — Bus Boy.

AWARDS, HONORS & MEMBERSHIPS

Appointed to "Who's Who Among Students in American Universities and Colleges."

Award for Outstanding Contribution to the College Community.

Dean's List.

National Association of College Admissions Counselors.

American Association of College Admissions Counselors.

New York State Personnel & Guidance Association.

Westchester, Putnam, Rockland, Personnel & Guidance Association.

Listed with additional Admissions and Guidance organizations.

Assistant Fire Chief for the Small College Fire Department;

250 hours of State Certified Training in Fire Fighting Techniques and Officer Leadership.

INTERESTS AND HOBBIES

Traveling, Fire Prevention, and Skiing.

REFERENCES   Will be Supplied upon Request.

PART THREE: DEVELOPING THE SALES FORCE

CHAPTER EIGHT
ANALYZING
MANPOWER NEEDS
AND RECRUITING
EFFECTIVE
SALESMEN

Staffing, or the manning of a sales organization, is crucial to successful sales management. Any manager—whether he is a general, university president, football coach, or sales manager—must assemble his subordinates carefully. A sales manager is only as good as the salesmen under him. General Eisenhower, Supreme Allied Commander in Europe during World War II, was successful largely because of his faculty for choosing and coordinating the diverse talents of such individualistic military leaders as General Bradley, Field Marshal Montgomery, and General Patton. Consider also the immense difficulties in staffing and managing the highly publicized prima donnas who often typify championship teams in professional sports.

In sales management, staffing is the crucial first step in building an effective sales organization, and the future success of any sales force hinges on how well this task is performed. The sales manager must be both a good salesman for his company and a good judge of the ability of new men on his staff.

Attracting and selecting successful salesmen, however, is only one aspect of the problem. One author has presented the following formula for sales effectiveness:[1]

---

[1]Thomas A. Wotruba, *Sales Management* (New York: Holt, Rinehart and Winston, Inc., 1971), p. 398.

SALES ACCOMPLISHMENT = POTENTIAL CAPABILITY $\times$ TRAINING $\times$ MOTIVATION

The staffing job is related to obtaining sales recruits with the *potential capability* to become good salesmen. Training and motivation are also necessary to develop potentially capable recruits into effective sales personnel.

Basic principles from reliability engineering are applicable here.[2] For example, if there are two central aspects of a project—labeled A and B—then the total reliability rating of the project is the *product* of the ratings for each aspect. If aspect A was 80 per cent reliable, and aspect B only 30 per cent reliable, then the total reliability rating for the project would be only *24 per cent* (80 per cent $\times$ 30 per cent). The same type of reasoning can be applied to the building of an efficient sales organization. All aspects of *sales accomplishment* must be present if the sales force is to meet its goals and objectives. Training and motivation ratings of 90 per cent cannot compensate for a 20 per cent rating in the staffing function. In this case, the total reliability rating would be only .162 per cent (20 per cent $\times$ 90 per cent $\times$ 90 per cent). All features of an effective sales organization must be present if the sales force is to succeed.

STEPS IN THE STAFFING PROCESS

A systematic approach for recruiting and selecting salesmen includes three major steps:

1. The analysis of manpower needs

    Manpower planning has become an essential part of managing the sales force and involves two important activities: the determination of the number of salesmen required and the determination of the type of salesmen needed. Realistic estimates of the size and characteristics of the company's future sales force enable management to develop recruitment, selection, and training programs which will make optimum

---

[2]See William H. Reynolds, "The Fail Safe Salesman," *Business Horizons*, vol. 9 (Summer 1966), pp. 19–26.

use of the company's existing sales force and meet the sales organization's manpower needs of the future.

    2. Recruiting Sales Candidates

    Recruiting involves identifying sources of potential salesmen and attracting these people to the company. In his search for sales candidates, the manager must be aware of the best sources for sales recruits. He must cultivate these sources through personal and indirect recruiting techniques.

    3. Screening and Selecting Applicants

    Screening is a negative process of elimination. Unqualified and undesirable applicants are eliminated until only qualified candidates remain. *Selection* is the positive process of choosing the number of people desired from this group of qualified candidates.

This chapter will examine the first two aspects of the staffing process. Methods for identifying and analyzing sales manpower needs, as well as the recruiting of suitable sales candidates, will be considered in the following pages. Chapter 9 will deal with the screening and selection of new sales employees.

ANALYZING SALES MANPOWER NEEDS

Sales manpower planning has increased in importance primarily because of the shortage of qualified sales applicants. Many young people, for example, are reluctant to consider selling as a career, although statistics indicate that the demand for sales personnel is increasing. Estimates of the annual need for new salesmen vary widely, but generally fall in the range of 100,000–250,000 new sales personnel required each year.[3] This means that the average company shows a 10 per cent annual growth in the sales force.[4] Thus, selling offers numer-

---

[3]See, for example, Cecil V. Hynes, "Sales Personnel: Future Demand and Supply," *Personnel Journal*, vol. 47 (August 1968), pp. 540–546; *Opportunities in Selling* (New York: The Council on Opportunities in Selling, Inc., 1965); T. W. Lyons, "Selling a Career," *Sales Management* (April 1, 1967), pp. 88–90; Richard M. Baker, Jr., and Gregg Phifer, *Salesmanship* (Boston: Allyn and Bacon, 1966), p. 14.

[4]See David L. Kurtz, "Student Attitudes Toward A Sales Career: A Re-Examination," *Journal of College Placement*, vol. 30 (December 1969–January 1970), pp. 85–86, 88.

ous opportunities for meaningful careers.[5] One of sales management's greatest challenges is to convince students and other young persons that selling is an attractive, professional career field.[6]

A second justification for increased manpower planning is the expense of sales recruiting and selection. A company cannot afford to make too many mistakes. Hiring more salesmen than are needed and hiring the wrong kind of personnel are costly errors. Careful planning helps avoid these problems.

Timing is also important in the staffing process. It is wise to forecast needs for salesmen well in advance of the time they will be employed. This allows for a carefully designed recruitment and selection program. It is extremely important to hire sales applicants before they are needed so that there is adequate time for proper training.

Quantitative Requirements

The general approach to determine the number of salesmen needed is explained by a simple equation:

SALES MANPOWER NEEDED − SALES MANPOWER AVAILABLE
= ADDITIONAL SALES MANPOWER REQUIRED

Sales Manpower Needed. Any forecast of sales personnel needs must hinge upon some factual base. The most useful base is a reasonably accurate projection of the firm's long-range sales. Usually, a five- or ten-year forecast is an appropriate planning base.

Trend analysis is one projection technique that can used to predict sales manpower needs.[7] Historical data relevant to sales manpower requirements are obtained from company records and significant trends are identified and projected into the future. The sales manpower forecast is derived from the projected trend.

---

[5]An interesting discussion of this point is contained in William J. E. Crissy and Ferdinand Mauser, "Careers in Marketing: Public Service and Private Rewards," *Sales Management* (March 15, 1967) , pp. 55−60.

[6]Raymond L. Hilgert, "College Students and Their Attitudes Toward Selling," *Marquette Business Review*, volume XII, (Winter 1968), pp. 145−149. Also see Thomas V. Greer, "Improving the Image of Selling: Some Guidelines for Thought and Action," *Marquette Business Review*, vol. XV (Fall 1971), pp. 144−149.

[7]The use of trend analysis in sales forecasting is explained in Chapter 6.

To illustrate this technique, suppose that Alpha Company has collected data on sales and number of salesmen over the last twenty years. The relationship between these two sets of data can be determined mathematically or graphically. Figure 8−1 shows the graphical relationship. By projecting the trend line, management can derive the sales manpower requirements for future sales levels. For example, if sales are expected to be $75 million, 600 salesmen will be required.

A similar approach is to compute the *sales per salesman ratio* and project this trend. For instance, Alpha Company now employs 400 salesmen and has sales of $50 million. The current sales/salesman figure is $125,000 ($50 million ÷ 400 salesmen). The company predicts sales of $75 million at the end of a five-year planning period. An ap-

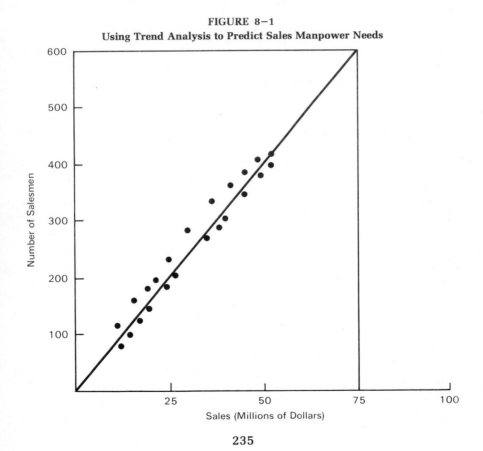

FIGURE 8−1
Using Trend Analysis to Predict Sales Manpower Needs

proximation of the number of salesmen that the firm will require at the end of five years is 600 salesmen ($75 million ÷ $125,000).

The major weakness of trend analysis is that this technique assumes that future operating conditions will remain the same as in the past. This assumption may be unrealistic in today's fast-changing business world. Sales manpower requirements are affected by increases in productivity, by the introduction of new products, by promotional strategy revisions, and by other marketing policy changes.

To illustrate this, suppose that Alpha's management decides to increase the advertising support given salesmen. This is expected to improve the sales/salesman ratio by 2 per cent each year. If this happens, sales per salesman will be almost $138,000 in five years. When this is divided into $75 million, the revised estimate of salesmen needed is 544.

Sales Manpower Available.   The starting point for predicting the number of salesmen available within the firm is a comprehensive inventory of sales personnel. A *man-by-man approach* is recommended, by which the abilities, promotability, and retirement status of salesmen are considered on an individual basis. Vacancies are highlighted, and additional manpower requirements are anticipated. This task has been simplified in recent years by the introduction of computerized payroll and personnel coding systems.

Trend analysis can also be used to predict the number of salesmen available within the firm at some future date. First, historical data on the retirement, turnover, and promotion rates of salesmen are assembled. Then a *total loss rate* is calculated and projected into the future.

For example, assume that Alpha Company's total loss rate is computed as 5 per cent a year. If no interim hiring is done, the company will have slightly more than three-fourths (311 salesmen) of its original sales force available in five years. This year-by-year loss is shown in Figure 8 – 2.

Additional Sales Manpower Required.   The final step is to compare the available sales manpower with the forecasted need for salesmen. To achieve its sales goal of $75 million in five years, Alpha Company will need an additional 233 salesmen. This estimate assumes that the new advertising support policy will be implemented and that the annual loss rate of 5 per cent will continue.

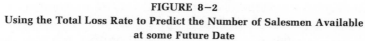

FIGURE 8-2
Using the Total Loss Rate to Predict the Number of Salesmen Available
at some Future Date

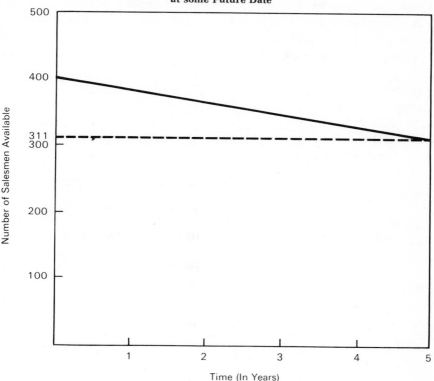

Other Factors. Before leaving quantitative sales manpower planning, it is wise to point out other factors which will modify the number of salesmen needed by a company. Changes in company policies — promotion policies, retirement plans, and transfer procedures — will affect sales manpower planning. For example, if a company stresses maximum promotion from within, the planner must make sure that there are qualified salesmen who can be upgraded to management positions. He must also compensate for this policy when estimating the potential sales manpower available.

External conditions must be considered. Included in this category are the level of economic activity, competitive conditions, labor rela-

237

tions, and government policies. Suppose, for example, that a major competitor decides to double his sales force. It is quite likely that the firm would lose experienced men if the competitor offered higher salaries.

It is also important to relate the concepts of profitability and costs to hiring plans. One method[8] of accomplishing this objective is to hire salesmen up to the point at which

$$S\,(p) - C > 0$$

where

S = Sales volume that each additional salesman will be expected to produce.

p = The expected profit margin on the sales volume.

C = The total cost of maintaining the salesman in the field.

If new salesmen were expected to achieve an $80,000 sales volume with a 15 per cent profit margin, then the firm would continue to hire sales personnel up to the point at which the cost of maintaining the salesman in the field (including salary) was equal to $12,000. Sales force expansion beyond this point would be unprofitable.

Qualitative Requirements

Another part of manpower planning is to determine the type of salesman desired. A job description must be prepared before recruiting and selection can begin. A *job description* is a written, detailed statement of the specific functions the salesman must perform; it should include, as well, guidelines on the relative importance of each function. This enables the sales manager to compile a list of *man specifications*. He then knows what the job demands and what sort of person is needed to do it. It is important to note that:

No standard classification of sales jobs has been established that would provide the means by which uniform criterion measures could be related to a set of universal performance traits.[9]

---

[8]This formula is suggested in Walter J. Semlow, "How Many Salesmen Do You Need?" *Harvard Business Review*, vol. 37 (May–June 1959), pp. 126–132.

[9]James C. Cotham III, "Selecting Salesmen: Approaches and Problems," *MSU Business Topics*, vol. 18 (Winter 1970), p. 72.

A separate job description, therefore, is needed for each type of sales operation. Job characteristics and qualifications cannot be generalized for *all* types of selling activities.

The job description provides the framework for the selection program. It is the basis for preparing application blanks, interview forms, psychological tests, and other selection tools. When these tools are not used, sales managers tend to hire men who are a reflection of their own abilities and qualifications. Selection is often made on the basis of a single outstanding physical, mental, or personality trait.[10] A recruiting coordinator for Mobil Oil Corporation has described the problem this way:

> We've got too damn many people who'll shoot down a candidate as he walks through the door just because he doesn't fit a particular stereotype. But the best salesmen aren't all tall, bright-eyed blonds; sometimes they're little fat guys who stutter.[11]

The job description is an important tool in many areas of sales management. Without job descriptions it is difficult, if not impossible, to do a good job of recruiting and selecting salesmen, to plan and develop sales manpower, to assign salesmen to territories, or to plan market strategy. *Job descriptions are also the key to a good salesman evaluation program.*

Therefore, as the basis for later application of this principle, the following sections set forth the steps in creating a good job description and discusses the characteristics that must be present for the salesman's job description to be a useful sales management tool in the many management areas where it is required.

Job analysis

The first step in creating a good salesman job description is *job analysis*, which is a careful and objective study and written summary of the

---

[10]See, for example, David L. Kurtz, "Physical Appearance and Stature: Important Variables in Sales Recruiting," *Personnel Journal*, vol. 48 (December 1969), pp. 981–983.
[11]"Since 1966, Mobil Man Has Adopted New Look, But Kept Old Pitch," *Wall Street Journal* (April 10, 1972), p. 11.

selling job in question. Through the use of company records, direct field observation, and whatever other supporting information may be available (such as government statistics and trade association studies), the sales job is assessed in light of the following critical issues.

Environmental Factors. What is the nature and extent of the competition the salesmen do, or will, encounter? What are the general business conditions within which they must operate? What industry structure and practices must they take into account, such as traditional channels of distribution and industry credit policies? In short, what is the business and social framework within which the salesmen will have to sell and in which their work will be supervised and evaluated?

Performance Factors. How do the salesmen presently spend their time — traveling, selling, filling out reports, securing sales promotion support from customers, waiting, and entertaining? What specific selling functions do they perform? How much time do they spend on each function and activity? Regardless of how this is finally summarized, it amounts to a *time-and-motion study* much like those used in a plant to study the performance of production workers. When it is completed, it will show in detail just how the salesmen are spending that valuable asset the company has bought for their use — *time*.

Consider the case of a large western liquor wholesaler who handles this job analysis process particularly well. In his annual review of salesman performance, he sends several specially trained supervisors into the field for two days, each with a sample of his salesmen. The supervisors note, on a carefully designed form, everything that the men do and the approximate time required for each activity. These reports are summarized at headquarters and the results are then compared with the salesman job description. This process checks and keeps the salesman job descriptions up to date with environmental and market changes.

Critical Analysis. The last stage in the job study is to analyze *how the salesmen should be spending their time* and to describe this in a meaningful summary. Should they continue to perform the functions that they are currently performing? Should they continue to place the same relative emphasis on the various functions? Are they dealing effectively with competition and other environmental factors? Should they be doing more, less, or the same amount of entertaining?

By combining performance and environmental studies of the salesman's job in an objective, careful, critical analysis of the job, management develops a meaningful summary of what the selling job they are going to describe *should be*.

Working from the systematic job analysis outlined above, a sales manager can produce a detailed, written job description whose purpose is to specify:

1. the precise components of the salesman's job: the functions or specific activities that the salesmen must perform, such as prospecting for new customers, traveling, selling, setting up displays, providing service assistance, and filling out reports;
2. the ideal or desired division of the salesman's time between each function: how he *should* be dividing his efforts among his many activities, *stated in measurable, relative terms*.

Characteristics of a Good Job Description

A good job description has five important features; it must be

(1) written;
(2) accepted;
(3) specific;
(4) inclusive;
(5) detailed — but terse.

Written. The job description must be *written*; it must be committed to paper. Informal, verbal job descriptions are virtually useless in managing salesmen and often lead to misunderstanding and friction. In short, job descriptions that are not written are usually worse than no job descriptions at all.

Accepted. To be of any use at all in their many applications to sales management, job descriptions must be known to, and *accepted* by, salesmen, their immediate managers, and all other sales executives.

241

Unfortunately, this is not always the case. One research study for example, found that 20 per cent of a corporate manager sample indicated indifference toward the question of whether field sales executives should set standards for salesmen performance.[12] Unless the job description is written and agreed upon by all, misunderstanding and friction will result when it comes to using the job description in any of its many applications — in selecting salesmen, in training them, or in evaluating their performance. This is simply because each salesman and each manager will formulate and act upon his own *private* understanding of the job content and of the relative priorities of various job functions.

One example of this kind of problem is offered by the sales manager of a sulphur company:

> My field managers could never agree on whether or not a particular salesman was doing a good job, or for that matter, for any given period, if the whole sales force was doing a good or a poor job. We finally realized why — we didn't have any common standards in our job description. We've fixed that now.[13]

Specific. The job description must be *specific*, that is, it must avoid vague or general statements in its delineation of the men's functions and of the relative emphasis that should be placed on each.[14] So far as possible the salesman's required coverage of each function must be *stated in measurable terms*, such as the number of calls per day, dollars or units sold, number of displays set up, or number of new accounts opened. An example of the kind of statement that is too vague and too general to be of use comes from a plywood manufacturer, who states that "an important part of our salesmen's job is to make regular calls on the trade." Such a description of this element of the salesman's job is useless to management, since no one but the original

---

[12]Rodney E. Evans, "Corporate Management Looks at the Field Sales Executive," *Oklahoma Business Bulletin*, vol. 40 (January 1972), p. 19.

[13]Albert H. Dunn and Eugene M. Johnson, *Managing the Sales Force* (Morristown, N.J.: General Learning Press, 1973), p. 22.

[14]This is suggested in James A. Belasco, "Broadening the Approach to Salesmen Selection," *Personnel*, vol. 43 (January–February 1966), pp. 67–72.

writer knows what is meant by "important," "regular," or a "call." A useful description of the same function comes from a drug manufacturer:

> Our salesmen must call on Class A customers 50 times a year; on Class B customers, 25 times a year, and on Class C customers, as frequently as their other duties allow. Our salesmen do not call at all on Class D customers who are serviced entirely through wholesalers. The classes of customers are established by dollar volume with class A being. . . .

As these examples illustrate, the job description must be specific in order to be useful to management. Vaguely worded phrases such as a "desire to make money" and "must be a hustler" are inappropriate in a well-written job description.[15]

Inclusive. To be useful in the management of salesmen, the job description must be *inclusive*, it must identify and furnish priorities for all functions the salesmen are to perform. None can be overlooked or assumed to be evident. If opening new accounts, or controlling expenses, or maintaining a certain average order size are important functions of a particular sales job, the job description should specifically identify them as such. In addition, it must provide effective measures or standards of performance for the functions, such as an average of new accounts opened per week or month, a ratio of dollar sales, or a dollar range for average order size.

The necessity that the job description be inclusive places a high premium on the careful study of the sales job in the first stage of its development and on the careful study of the results in the development of the job description itself.

Detailed, but Terse. The job description must be *detailed, but terse*—that is, it must avoid the extremes of too much brevity or too much detail. A job description that is too brief will be so generalized

---

[15]See "The Recruitment of College Graduates for Sales Careers," *Journal of Business* (Manhattan College), vol. 1 (March 1972), p. 4.

that is useless for management purposes. The plywood manufacturer's statement cited above is an illustration of this. It describes the function in a very few words, but it says nothing that can be used in managing salesmen's work.

At the other extreme, there is the job description that includes too much detail. In this case, the salesmen's functions are analyzed so minutely that it is difficult or impossible for the salesman or his manager to use it. The job description must be *only as detailed and specific* as is absolutely necessary to provide an effective management tool and to show the salesman what is expected of him.

In summary, the job description is an ideal, but realistic and detailed statement of the salesman's job, in terms of specific functions, activities, and the relative priority of these. The job description is thus a *profile* of the salesman's job, which capsulizes the functions he must perform and the amount of time, effort, attention, and emphasis (however measured) he should place on each activity. Finally, good job descriptions are indispensable in many of the subsystems of sales management, most especially in recruitment and selection, training, motivation, and supervision.

RECRUITING

Once sales manpower needs are projected, plans must be made for recruiting applicants. Recruiting should be viewed as a continuous process which must be thoroughly organized. Too often a sales manager thinks about recruiting only when a vacancy occurs. For instance, one survey found that 58 per cent of the firms studied recruited only when a replacement was needed, or when the firms wanted to expand.[16] (See Figure 8–3 for one cartoonist's view of the results of the recruitment process.)

In his rush to fill the vacancy, the sales manager is likely to overlook an applicant's shortcomings. The effective recruiter always has a list of promising candidates in mind so he will avoid *crash* recruiting efforts.

One study, for example, found that sales personnel hired in the field were below the standard for those hired at headquarters because:

---

[16]*Finding the Superior Salesman* (New York: The Research Institute of America, Inc., 1967), p. 4.

FIGURE 8-3

"Congratulations, Al, on making the team."

Source: Reprinted by permission from *Sales Management*, The Marketing Magazine. Copyright 1971.

1. field executives were willing to settle for the first available
   candidate;
2. field sales managers often hired in *their own image*. In other
   words, they tended to hire salesmen with personal characteristics similar to their own.[17]

---

[17]Andrall E. Pearson, "Sales Power Through Planned Careers," *Harvard Business Review*, vol. 44
(January–February 1966), p. 106.

The way in which hiring in one's own image can be a drawback was described by one author as follows:

> Professional recruiters often say that one of the greatest obstacles to the successful performance of their requirement is the setting by management of arbitrary or unnecessary hiring requirements. For example, a sales manager who is a college graduate might have a preference for hiring graduates as salesmen — may insist on it, in fact. However, a closer look at the type of work may show that graduates are not needed, that the job can be handled equally well by a man who has had, say, two years of college.[18]

The Development of a Manpower File

One way to avoid a hurried search is to maintain a file of potential sales candidates. Every sales manager comes in contact with many potential salesmen. A prudent manager will find out something about these men, record this information, and file it for future reference. When a vacancy occurs, he will have a list of recruits who have been prescreened.

Typically, sales managers have a favorite source of sales recruits. A skillful manager will continue to use sources which have proven fruitful. However, it is desirable to maintain contacts with anyone who might suggest potential salesmen, since *word-of-mouth* is an important source of information when recruiting salesmen. Referrals can come from those outside the company — clergymen, civic leaders, customers, and suppliers — as well as from internal company sources.

Correspondingly, successful sales managers normally discontinue use of sources that have consistently proven to be unacceptable. Equitable Life Assurance Society, for example, discontinued college sales recruiting when they found that many of the new graduates did not remain with the first job.[19]

Sources of Sales Recruits

Company Sources. Other employees within the firm should not be overlooked when searching for sales recruits. In one study, 60 per cent

---

[18]*Finding the Superior Salesman* (1967), p. 6.
[19]"How Do You Find More Salesmen Just Like the Successful Salesmen You Now Have?" *Sales Management* (April 15, 1966), p. 108.

of the firms surveyed recruited from this source.[20] Men in manufacturing, maintenance, or warehouse jobs may have latent sales talent. The company's personnel department should be made aware of sales manpower needs. Since the personnel manager continuously evaluates qualifications of employees, his review may reveal employees with qualifications for sales positions.

The search for sales talent from within can pay handsome dividends. A review of one West Coast company's industrial sales force revealed that five of the nine top salesmen and field sales managers had held production positions. The Research Institute of America study found that 37 per cent of the salesmen surveyed "revealed that their previous jobs were of a nonsales nature."[21] Other advantages of recruiting salesmen from nonsales functions are as follows:

1. The sales recruit is more of a known quantity than an outsider.
2. He requires less training and orientation because he is familiar with the company's products, operations, and policies.
3. Overall company morale is bolstered since employees become aware that opportunities are not restricted to individual departments or divisions.

Company Salesmen. Like a field sales manager, salesmen become acquainted with many potential sales recruits. They should be encouraged to refer qualified applicants to the company. Some firms, of which IBM is one, offer a bonus as an incentive to salesmen to recruit other salesmen. However, referrals from salesmen must be handled tactfully so as not to cause personal animosity if a referral is rejected. Apparently, most sales managers consider this an effective source of sales recruits. The previously cited study by the Research Institute of America found that 76 per cent of the respondents rated present employees and salesmen as a *good* or *excellent* source of new sales recruits.[22]

Suppliers and Customers. Salesmen calling on one's company may be another source. It is possible they may be dissatisfied and looking for a

---

[20]*Finding the Superior Salesman* (1967), p. 6.
[21]*Finding the Superior Salesman* (1967), p. 6.
[22]*Finding the Superior Salesman* (1967), p. 7.

change. Also, distributors, dealers, and other customers may have suggestions about salesmen who call on them.

Local Business and Civic Organizations. Participation in community organizations will often provide recruiting leads. Civic organizations (e.g., PTA, Chamber of Commerce), business associations (e.g., American Marketing Association, Sales and Marketing Executives—International), and service organizations (e.g., Jaycees, Lions, Kiwanis, Rotary) are all possible sources of sales recruits.

Professional Associations. Technical, trade, and sales organizations usually maintain informal employment listings for members. They may also publish and distribute lists of job opportunities. Information can usually be obtained from the executive director of the trade association.

Educational Institutions. All institutions for higher learning—colleges, universities, junior colleges, business schools, adult evening courses, and correspondence schools—are fertile sources of sales recruits. Of course, the type of institution contacted will depend on the job qualifications desired.

If salesmen need a technical background or training in business administration, colleges and universities are the primary source of recruits. Contacts with professors, placement officers, and administrators are often a critical factor. Companies also should not forget alumni as a possible source of sales personnel. Most college placement offices maintain an active alumni file. Experienced salesmen frequently contact the placement directors of their alma maters when they decide to change jobs. Also overlooked are community and junior colleges. These two-year colleges, which are multiplying rapidly, offer a rich source of potential salesmen. The students are often men who recognize the need for higher education, but who are eager to begin work as soon as possible. Many older men, especially veterans, are enrolled in two-year programs.

Other rich sources are evening programs of high schools and colleges. Persons enrolled in these programs are usually employed but are searching for ways to improve themselves. Courses in public speaking, salesmanship, and marketing are logical places to locate people who are interested in selling. One way to meet and interest these people is to speak to their classes about careers in selling.

The Armed Forces.   Placement officers at "mustering-out centers" for servicemen may know of men who are interested in selling careers. Some servicemen may have prior selling experience. Others will have leadership experience and may possess selling potential.

Unsolicited Applicants.   Frequently, sales candidates will contact a company directly. This action shows that the applicant has initiative, but, like everyone else, unsolicited applicants must be checked out carefully. There may be some unusual reason why the applicant is unwilling to go through the normal recruitment channels.

Employment Agencies.   If a sales manager does not have enough time for recruiting, he might consider using a professional employment agency. However, it is absolutely essential that each manager select an agency which is right for him. Employment agencies do not always possess a good reputation as sources for salesmen. Some agencies just refer applicants to clients with no real concern for the client's or the applicant's needs.

Fortunately, not all agencies are this way. Many specialize in sales jobs and render a valuable recruiting service. The following guidelines are suggested for using an agency to the best advantage.

1. Select an agency with a good reputation and with experience in recruiting salesmen.
2. Visit the agency personally. Examine its facilities and personnel to be sure that the agency is able to screen applicants effectively.
3. Make sure the agency knows what is wanted. Provide the agency's recruiters with comprehensive descriptions of the job and of the required qualifications. Supportive literature about the company will also be helpful.
4. Develop continuing relationships with agencies that provide good results and eliminate those which are unsuccessful.

Advertisements. Advertisements placed in newspapers and trade journals may result in responses from many sales applicants. If a technically qualified or experienced man is needed, advertising in trade magazines is an appropriate medium. For more general sales jobs, newspaper advertisements are adequate. Dorsey Laboratories, for example, has reported a 75 per cent "success" rate for salesmen obtained through advertising.[23]

Advertisements in trade journals are usually placed in a personnel or marketplace section. A newspaper advertisement will reach more potential sales recruits if it appears in the personnel section of a Sunday newspaper. In most major cities, one particular paper is usually the marketplace for personnel.

Recruitment ads must be appealing and informative. In one study, it was pointed out that firms sometimes seemed to pride themselves on "a high applicant to job ratio with one firm boasting of a ratio of 120 to 1."[24] However, this is a serious mistake. Unqualified applicants should not be encouraged by vague advertisements to apply for a sales job, since it results in an unnecessary screening and selection burden. High rejection rates can also cause considerable ill will toward the firms involved.

Equal Employment Opportunities. In addition to the above listed sources of sales personnel, it is important to make specific mention of minority hiring for sales positions. While the bulk of the new salesmen from minority groups are obtained through traditional sources, it behooves sales recruiters to make particular efforts to *balance* the sales force. To take only two examples—blacks and women[25]—it is necessary to point out that the balancing concept espoused in *affirmative action hiring programs* has not usually been achieved in sales recruiting. Indeed, this may be one of contemporary sales management's greatest failures.

An early survey by the Equal Employment Opportunity Commission (EEOC) found that of 15,726 sales employees in 204 companies, only 91 (or 0.6 per cent) were black.[26] The number of black salesmen

---

[23]"Dorsey Cuts Salesmen Turnover Rate in Half with Sneaky Test," *Industrial Marketing* (September 1967), pp. 79–80.

[24]"The Recruitment of College Graduates for Sales Careers (1972)," p. 4.

[25]Although women comprise the majority of our population, they are a "minority" group in regard to the composition of our normal labor force.

[26]"The Negro in Sales: Color Him Out," *Sales Management* (February 15, 1968), pp. 32–36.

is growing, but more needs to be done to open up sales as truly an area of *equal employment opportunity*.[27] IBM, Procter and Gamble, General Mills, Hallmark Cards, Inland Steel, and General Foods are often cited as examples of firms that have been active and successful in recruiting blacks for sales positions.[28]

Practices in regard to the hiring of women are equally dismal among sales managers. A survey of 180 sales and marketing executives found that while 72 per cent felt that women — if given the chance — could be as successful as men in selling, 80 per cent said they would not hire a female for outside sales.[29] However, sales managers accustomed to women sales representatives report that they have three advantages over their male counterparts:

1. "The buyer nearly always sees them — even when he has refused to see male reps from the same company."
2. "Women sales reps are highly memorable. Thus their companies and product lines tend to stick in the buyer's mind."
3. "Women tend to be better listeners than men, so buyers often will open up to them about their problems."[30]

Fortunately, many of the artificial barriers to sales employment have begun to fall. Ever increasing numbers of not only blacks and female salespersons, but also Spanish-speaking people, Orientals, Indians, and other minorities are entering the field. The proper role of contemporary sales management is to expedite and facilitate this crucial adjustment process.

TOWARD IMPROVED SALES RECRUITING

An improved sales recruiting function should be the goal of every business organization. The cost of inefficient sales recruiting is too

[27]See, for example, Sampson P. Bowers, "Go to the Ghetto for Marketing Talent," *Sales Management* (January 1969), pp. 7–9.
[28]"The Negro in Sales: Color Him Out (1968)," pp. 32–36.
[29]Eleanor Schwartz, "Women In Sales: Will the Walls Come Tumbling Down?" *Sales Management* (August 15, 1969), pp. 39–40.
[30]Sally Scanlon, "Ms. Is A Hit!", *Sales Management* (February 5, 1973), p. 24.

high to do otherwise. Salesmen, sales management, top management, and most writers on the subject seem to agree on the following general guidelines for improving existing sales recruiting programs.[31]

1. *Improved Coordination in the Recruiting Function.* For many firms, there is a critical need for improved coordination in sales recruiting. The diversification of responsibilities that currently exists often amounts to a bewildering maze of ineffective recruiting activity. In a study of the sales recruiting practices of Michigan-based manufacturers, recruiting directors were asked to specify what they believed to be the weakest aspect of their own programs. Four of the eight factors listed were directly related to the problem of a lack of coordination: (1) deficiencies in the overall organization of the program; (2) lack of feedback to the recruiting department; (3) little continuity in the recruiting staff; and (4) lack of status of the recruiting function within the company. All firms should re-assess their existing procedures with the objective of strengthening the coordination aspect of their program.

2. *Installation of a Periodic Program Review.* In many cases, the adoption of this suggestion would require only that the data generated from existing procedures be analyzed and reported. Offer-rejection questionnaires and exit interviews are examples of procedures that supply meaningful data, which many companies then fail to tabulate, analyze, and report. In the previously cited study of Michigan manufacturers, only about a third of the recruiting directors believed that their follow-up procedure for rejected offers resulted in meaningful data. Several labeled it "just a formality." Consider the case of one large pharmaceutical company which abandoned a requirement that all of its sales representatives possess a biology, chemistry, or pharmacy degree, when it discovered that its highest sales producers were the few business administration graduates they had hired as a stopgap measure to staff some newly created sales territories. Periodic program review is a necessity for improving sales recruiting practice.

3. *Better Qualified and Trained Recruiters.* The need for better trained recruiters is typically evident in the case of college recruiting

---

[31]This section is based on David L. Kurtz, "An Evaluation of the Sales Recruiting Programs of Michigan Manufacturers," *Business Ideas and Facts*, vol. 3 (Winter 1970), pp. 3–8.

for sales personnel. Functional personnel, such as sales managers, often view recruiting as an alien task. Top sales management should stress the need for effective recruiting in their discussions with field sales management and should emphasize this important task in all promotion decisions.

SUMMARY Sales management's staffing job is related to obtaining sales recruits with the potential capability to become good salesmen. The staffing process can be divided into three major steps: (1) the analysis of sales manpower needs, (2) the recruitment of sales candidates, and (3) the screening and selection of applicants. Chapter 8 has examined the first two of these steps; screening and selection will be discussed in Chapter 9.

The general approach to determine the number of salesmen needed is explained by a simple equation:

$$\text{Sales Manpower Needed} - \text{Sales Manpower Available} =$$
$$\text{Additional Sales Manpower Required}$$

Chapter 8 has suggested the use of trend analysis to assess the sales manpower that is needed.

Another aspect of manpower planning is to determine the type of salesman desired. The starting point is a job description which is a written, detailed statement of the specific function the salesman must perform, and which includes guidelines on the relative importance of each function. This enables the sales manager to compile a list of man specifications. The basic characteristics of a good job description are that it is (1) written, (2) accepted by those involved, (3) specific, (4) inclusive, and (5) detailed, but terse.

New salesmen may be recruited from company sources, company salesmen, suppliers and customers, local business and civic organizations, professional associations, educational institutions, the armed forces, unsolicited applicants, employment agencies, and advertisements. Further, sales recruiters should make particular efforts to balance the sales force by providing equal employment opportunities.

Chapter 8 concluded by offering some general guidelines for improving existing sales recruiting programs:

1. improved coordination in the recruiting function.
2. installation of a periodic program review.
3. better qualified and trained recruiters.

DISCUSSION/REVIEW QUESTIONS

1. Evaluate the following statement: "Salesman job descriptions are very useful in hiring the right kind of salesmen, but they are not used elsewhere in managing salesmen."
2. Acquire a copy of an actual salesman job description. Analyze its strengths and weaknesses against the criteria set up in this chapter. How could it be improved?
3. "The salesman's job is to sell products or services at a satisfactory profit. So long as he does this, it's nobody's business how or when he gets it done." Comment on this statement.
4. List the major sources of sales recruits and select the sources which would be most fruitful for a sales position you have chosen.
5. List the major steps involved in the staffing process.
6. A small regional manufacturer of business forms recruits only experienced salesmen from large national competitors. Is this a wise recruiting policy? Can you suggest other sources and methods of recruiting salesmen?
7. Suppose you were looking for a sales job. Briefly list the job features you would want and the qualifications you have to offer. How would you go about looking for a job which meets your demands and qualifications? What does this analysis tell you about sales recruiting?
8. Relate the basic principles of reliability engineering to the building of an effective sales force.
9. Identify and briefly explain the following:
   - (a) screening
   - (b) selection
   - (c) sales per salesman ratio
   - (d) total loss rate
   - (e) job description
   - (f) job analysis
   - (g) time-and-motion study
   - (h) critical analysis
   - (i) manpower file
   - (j) affirmative action hiring programs
10. Explain how trend analysis can be used to determine how many salesmen an organization requires.
11. How can the concepts of profitability and costs be related to salesmen hiring plans? Discuss.

12. "Job descriptions are the key to a good salesman evaluation program." Comment.
13. List and explain the important features of a good job description.
14. Explain how the setting of unnecessary or arbitrary hiring requirements retards effective recruiting. Can you cite any examples?
15. Why have relatively few blacks entered the sales profession? What can be done to alleviate this problem? Discuss.

CHAPTER NINE
THE SALESMEN
SELECTION
PROCESS

Chapter 8 has dealt with the recruiting of sales applicants. Once this pool of potential talent has been generated, it becomes necessary to *select* the individuals who best fit the needs of a particular company. The development of an effective salesmen selection process is the topic of this chapter.

DIFFICULTIES OF SELECTION

Recruitment and selection present a transposition problem to the sales manager, especially to the manager who has advanced from the ranks of selling: he must reverse the roles built into the usual selling situation. *Instead of being a salesman, he must now become a buyer.* He is purchasing the services of men for his company, and as industrial consultant Keith Jewell comments, he "must put aside his usual selling attitudes and become, instead, an astute and careful buyer."[1]

Prediction Is Risky

Like most purchases, the selection of salesmen involves risk. *Prediction is hazardous.* When he chooses a sales applicant, the sales manager is predicting that the applicant will be an effective salesman.

[1]Keith R. Jewell, "Let's Take the Hocus Pocus Out of Hiring," *Sales Management* (February 7, 1964), p. 28.

Both the company and the applicant have much to gain or lose from this prediction. The company will incur costs for recruiting, hiring, and training the man. Sales losses can be expected if the wrong man is chosen. From the applicant's viewpoint, he is gambling a part of his working life. If he selects the wrong job, he has lost a portion of his career which cannot be recovered.

Further complicating the selection process is the complexity of selling. Unlike many jobs, selling does not depend for its success solely upon intellectual qualifications. Sales jobs impose emotional and temperamental demands upon a person, so that the application of simple concepts of management psychology to the selection of salesmen is difficult. Selection techniques must emphasize personality and temperament, as well as ability, experience, and aptitudes.

Art or Science?

Selection is both an art and a science. Predicting an applicant's future performance involves experience and usually more than a little *luck*. This is the art of selection.

Too many sales managers rely solely on their experience and luck. Critics of sales selection argue that most sales managers fail to follow a tested, systematic procedure when hiring. No company can expect to do a perfect job of selection. People are too complex, and not everyone can meet the rigorous qualifications of selling. However, by following a logical procedure, a sales manager can expect to improve his selection performance rating. This is the science of selection.

Responsibilities for Selection

In the past most companies have placed the responsibility for recruiting, screening, and selecting salesmen with field sales managers. This seems appropriate since a field sales manager will ultimately succeed or fail with the people selected. However, many field sales managers have been poor recruiters and selectors.

A busy field sales manager often fails to use proven hiring practices. Because he is diverted by pressing day-to-day operations, he fails to devote sufficient attention to the vital activity of manpower development. Thus, he may settle for the first available applicant to fill a territory opening, or he may hire in his own image and reject those applicants who do not fit his view of a *good* salesman.

Many field sales managers also lack the training and experience for effective selection. The techniques of selection — interviewing, testing, and the like — require a qualified background. Unless a field sales manager has received training in these techniques, it is unlikely that he will be a good predictor of sales success.

Because field sales managers have failed to recruit and select qualified salesmen, many companies have centralized the sales selection activities. Professional recruiters are used to relieve field sales managers of preliminary hiring chores. Applicants are recruited, tested, and screened by trained personnel specialists. However, most companies still leave the final selection to members of sales management.

This shared arrangement is probably preferable. In a large company with a personnel department, recruiting and preliminary screening should be turned over to experts. Of course, they should receive guidance from the sales department. Final selection decisions should remain with sales management. Consequently, it is necessary for field sales managers to understand the complete selection process and to be able to interpret test scores and recommendations of personnel specialists. In a small company, which may lack trained personnel specialists, it is imperative that field sales managers understand the selection process.

EVALUATING A SELECTION PROGRAM

When is a company's selection program in need of revision? If the sales manager answers "yes" to any of the following questions, then his selection program may be at fault. Program revisions and modifications would appear to be justified.

Is Turnover Excessive?

Salesmen turnover is a problem for almost every company and cannot be eliminated entirely. There will always be some salesmen who quit the company for other positions, or who are considered unfit for selling and must be discharged. Some companies lose more than half of each year's incoming sales recruits over a three-year period. Consider the following example:

> More than 35 years ago, the insurance industry embarked on an intensive program to solve the problem of costly, wasteful turnover among its agents. Estimates at that time indicated that there was a turnover of better than 50% within the first year and almost 80% within the first three years. After the expenditure of millions of dollars and 35 years of research, the turnover in the insurance industry remains approximately 50% within the first year and 80% within the first three years.[2]

The point at which turnover becomes excessive varies according to company, industry, and type of selling, although it is possible to offer some guidelines.[3] A study by Derek A. Newton of the Harvard Business School considers a turnover rate of 10 per cent or more *excessive*.[4] Another study of 655 large manufacturers by the National Indus-

TABLE 9–1

Median Quit Rates and Median Discharge Rates Classified by Average Age of Sales Force and by Type of Product Sold.

Average Age of Sales Force	Median Quit Rate (in per cents)		Median Discharge Rate (in per cents)	
	Consumer Products	Industrial Products	Consumer Products	Industrial Products
25 – 34 years	9	6	8	3
35 – 39 years	6	3	3	2
40 – 44 years	2	2	1	1
45 – 54 years	3	0	2	0

Source: David A. Weeks, "Turnover Rates for Salesmen, *Conference Board Record*, vol. III (April 1966), p. 22.

---

[2]David Mayer and Herbert M. Greenberg, "What Makes a Good Salesman," *Harvard Business Review*, vol. 42 (July – August 1964), p. 119.

[3]Turnover rate equals the number of salesmen who quit or were discharged divided by the average size of the company's sales force during a given period of time (usually one year).

[4]Derek A. Newton, "Get the Most Out of Your Sales Force," in *Salesmanship and Sales Force Management*, edited by Edward C. Bursk and G. Scott Hutchison (Cambridge, Mass. Harvard University Press, 1971), p. 123.

trial Conference Board reported that, on the average, 3 per cent of a company's sales force quits and 1 per cent are discharged during a given year.[5] Thus, a turnover rate greater than 4 per cent is cause for concern and a rate above 10 per cent requires immediate action.

It also important to observe that turnover rates can vary according to the type of product sold (consumer or industrial goods), the average age of the sales force, and the number of years salesmen are employed. Table 9–1, for instance, shows that younger salesmen are more likely to quit or be discharged. Median quit rates and median discharge rates also vary by type of product sold (industrial or consumer goods).

In addition, Table 9–2, which was developed from another study by the National Industrial Conference Board, indicates that salesmen retention rates are related to the number of years employed and the type of product sold.

TABLE 9–2
Salesmen Retention Rates Classified by Number of Years Employed and by Type of Product Sold

Years Employed	Type of Product Sold	Median Per Cent Retained
1	Consumer	81
1	Industrial	85
1	Service	86
2	Consumer	66
2	Industrial	75
2	Service	80
3	Consumer	59
3	Industrial	60
3	Service	71
4	Consumer	47
4	Industrial	59
4	Service	66
5	Consumer	45
5	Industrial	57
5	Service	65

Source: "Some Stay and Some Go, But Which Salesmen Stay With You the Longest?" *Sales Management* (May 1, 1972), p. 74. Reprinted by permission from *Sales Management*, The Marketing Magazine. Copyright 1972.

[5]David A. Weeks, "Turnover Rates for Salesmen," *Conference Board Record*, vol. III (April 1966), p. 19.

Is Excessive Dollar Investment Lost on Men Who Have Left the Company?

The out-of-pocket costs of turnover are startling; they include the costs in time, energy, and money of recruiting, selecting, training, and supervising men who ultimately fail to sell. The compensation paid to these salesmen must also be counted.

It is estimated that the average cost of hiring and training a salesman exceeds $10,000. If a firm has 200 salesmen and if turnover is 10 per cent per year, then the firm will incur an expense of $200,000 per year. By cutting the turnover rate in half, this firm could save $100,000 per year.

Turnover costs may also be viewed in another way. Again, assume expenses of $10,000 to recruit, select, and train a salesman. If a company has a turnover rate of 10 per cent, the cost of each retained salesman would be approximately $11,111 (10,000 ÷ 0.9). If turnover can be reduced to 5 per cent, the cost per retained salesman would be reduced by over $500 per man ($10,000 ÷ 0.95 = $10,526).

Are Sales Lost Because Salesmen Leave the Company?

When a salesman leaves, the impact on sales volume is immediate. If the departed salesman has switched to a competitor, he may take old customers with him. A customer's loyalty is often to the salesman rather than to a product or company.

Even if customers remain loyal to the company, excessive turnover may result in lost sales. It is hard to convince a customer that he is dealing with a reputable firm with quality products if he sees a different salesman every few months. Further, the buyer's ordering routine is interrupted during the time that replacements are recruited, selected and trained. These incremental costs of turnover may be more costly in the long run than out-of-pocket expenses.

Figure 9–1 presents a checklist for evaluating a firm's selection program.

Is the Selection Process Too Time Consuming?

When selection programs are too long, they result in numerous indirect costs to the company. Sales management's time is expensive, and its use must be equated with resulting benefits to the organization. In addition, an inefficient hiring procedure can lead to an extensive loss of the firm's goodwill.

Unfortunately, many organizations have an inefficient selection program that is too time consuming. One-fourth of the salesmen in one survey said that their own hiring took between two and four weeks. Another 20 per cent indicated that their hiring took between four and six weeks. Certainly, no one would advocate speeding up the hiring process to the point where previous selection standards were meaningless. Simplification and improvement, however, should be the goals of any salesman selection procedure. In a study of both managers and salesmen, one of the most frequently noted improvements by both groups was the reduction in hiring time.[6]

FIGURE 9–1
Checklist For Evaluating Your Selection Program

Turnover

Number of salesmen at beginning of year	Number of salesmen at end of year	Average sales force
(———————) +	(———————) ÷ 2 =	———————
Number of salesmen who left company during the year	Average sales force	Turnover rate
(———————) ÷	(———————) =	——————— %

Costs

1. Dollar investment per salesman
   - Recruitment and selection $———————
   - Training $———————
   - Supervision $———————
   - Compensation $———————
   - Other $———————

Total ——————— × (———————) = $———————

Number of salesmen who left   Total Cost

2. Lost sales (estimate)   + ———————

Total Costs $———————

[6]*Finding the Superior Salesmen* (New York: Research Institute of America, Inc., 1967), p. 3.

SCREENING AND SELECTION

The final aspects of staffing the sales function are the screening and selection of potential candidates. Various tools and procedures are used to accomplish this end.[7] The effective implementation and use of selection tools has always been of considerable concern to sales management.

For the most part, the following selection tools have been used to select sales personnel:

1. Application blanks
2. Interviews
   a. Screening
   b. Selection
3. References
4. Physical Examinations
5. Intelligence tests
6. Aptitude tests
7. Personality tests

One study of firms with large sales forces asked top sales management to evaluate each of the above tools in terms of

1. helpfulness in selecting salesmen;
2. relative cost in the selection procedure;
3. order of use in the selection procedure.

Summary results are shown in Table 9 – 3. Scores such as 3.5 or 4.5 indicate similar rankings for two of the tools.[8]

---

[7]A good discussion of selection tools is contained in W. J. E. Crissy and Charles L. Lapp, "Sound Selection: First Step in Building an Effective Sales Force," *Advanced Management*, vol. 25 (March 1960), pp. 6–10.

[8]Thomas R. Wotruba, "An Analysis of the Salesmen Selection Process," *Southern Journal of Business*, vol. 5 (January 1970), pp. 41–51.

TABLE 9–3

Typical Rankings of Selection Tools on Helpfulness, Order, and Cost.

Selection Tool	Rankings on		
	Helpfulness	Order	Cost
Interviews	1	2	1
Application Blanks	2	1	6.5
Physical Exams	3	6.5	2
References	5	4.5	6.5
Intelligence Tests	4	3	3.5
Aptitude Tests	6	4.5	3.5
Personality Tests	7	6.5	5

Source: Thomas R. Wotruba, "An Analysis of the Salesmen Selection Process," *Southern Journal of Business,* vol. 5 (January 1970), p. 47.

Application Forms

Properly constructed, a written application is an important source of information about a candidate's background and qualifications. Most companies use application forms for two purposes: to collect pertinent information and to aid personal interviewing. Table 9–3 shows that sales managers typically use application forms as the first step in the selection procedure; that they regard them as the second most helpful selection tool; and that the forms are a minimum cost item.

An application form provides a sales manager with a means of reviewing the applicant's background without being influenced by his appearance or personality. A typical form records facts about an applicant's physical condition, family status, educational background, business experience, military service, and outside activities. Other facts pertinent to job success can also be included. This information is then used to eliminate candidates who are not qualified.[9] Since there are legal limits on types of information that can be requested on application blanks, it is advisable to clear any application form with the firm's legal department.

---

[9]See James C. Cotham III, "Using Personal History Information in Retail Salesmen Selection," *Journal of Retailing,* vol. 45 (Summer 1969), pp. 31–38.

Some companies eliminate applicants deemed unqualified through the use of a list of *knockout factors*.[10] This is an organized list of characteristics, traits, conditions, or experiences that the firm believes would prevent the applicant from being a successful salesman. Klein Institute for Aptitude Testing has developed such a listing:[11]

1. instability of residence or job-hopping (defined as three or more jobs in the past 3 years)
2. failure in business within the past two years
3. divorce or separation within the past two years[12]
4. excessive personal indebtedness (defined as debts — excluding mortgage payments — which cannot be met within two years from the earnings on the new job)
5. too high a previous standard of living
6. unexplained gaps in employment

If any of the above factors are established to be true of an applicant, then that individual is eliminated from further consideration. The danger of this approach is, of course, that a prepared list of knockout factors may not be descriptive of ineffective salesmen in all cases. As a result, some potentially good salesmen may not be hired.

Specific questions for use in a personal interview are determined by carefully reviewing an applicant's written responses. For instance, if he indicates that he is active in a civic organization, one might ask why he joined that organization, what his personal role is, and what he expects his future role to be.

The application form will also point out possible difficulties which should be pursued in the personal interview. Are there gaps of several months between jobs? Has the applicant changed jobs several times during his career? Perhaps he is a *job hopper*. These and similar questions will suggest issues for future inquiry.

---

[10]See, for example: H. Jay Bullen, "How Industry Finds and Hires Salesmen," *Industrial Marketing* (March 1964), pp. 68–69.

[11]Henry R. Bernstein, "How to Recruit Good Salesmen," *Industrial Marketing* (October 1965), pp. 70–77.

[12]By contrast, it is interesting to note that one study of retail sales personnel found married and *divorced* salesmen to be related to high output, while low producers were typically single or *separated*. See Charles N. Weaver, "An Expirical Study to Aid the Selection of Retail Clerks," *Journal of Retailing*, vol. 45 (Fall 1969), pp. 22–26, 82.

Each company must prepare its own application form. Only information which will be used in the selection process should be requested. Some companies have found a short application form useful for initial screening, to be followed by a comprehensive form completed by the surviving applicants. Another variation is a *weighted application form*. These employ specific weights assigned to the information requested. The sales manager can then mathematically determine how an applicant compares to the minimum qualifying score, and unsatisfactory candidates can be quickly eliminated.

References

Character and credit references yield several benefits. First, and most important to the selection process, they provide evaluative information. No matter how promising a candidate may appear, there may be flaws which will go unnoticed.[13] Information from other sources can be verified by checking a man's references.

Reference checks also have public relations value. They indicate that a company has a sincere interest in picking the right men for job openings. The company's name becomes familiar to key persons in the community. Reference checks also reveal to the applicant that the company is sincerely interested in him. When checking references, a sales manager should not just contact an applicant's listed references. These persons may not be objective sources of information. This factor probably explains the relatively low rating for helpfulness in Table 9-3.

The best source of information about a person is his previous superior. More than anyone else, he should know what the person is really like on the job. Previous employers know about the applicant's performance characteristics from personal, day-to-day experience. How well does he get along with others? What are his strengths and weaknesses? What is he especially good at doing? Perhaps the key question is whether the superior would like to rehire the candidate.

For younger applicants who have little or no job experience, education is comparable to work experience. Factual data (dates of attendance, courses, grades, and degrees received) can be verified by the reg-

---

[13]See, for instance, "Self-Made Men: Many Job Seekers Lie About Past in Resumes, but Concerns Are Wary," *Wall Street Journal* (January 22, 1968), p. 1.

istrar's office. Other information about the applicant's character and performance can be obtained by contacting his teachers, guidance counselor, faculty advisor, or major professors.

In general, it is most effective to interview references in person. However, personal visits may be difficult to arrange. If this is the case, a telephone call is more effective than a letter. People are reluctant to say anything bad about someone else in writing. A telephone call is a prompt, efficient way to get an accurate assessment of an applicant. To be sure all items are covered, it is a good idea to have a checklist or interview form to follow. Another method of improving reference checks is to ask the applicant to list five, six, or seven references rather than the usual three. This forces the person to use references who have less personal association with the applicant. Some companies have found that the last two references under such a system are the most unbiased ones.

Credit references provide an indication of the applicant's financial responsibility. Personnel experts suggest watching for danger signs such as unusual debts, slow payment, or nonpayment, of debts, or refusal of credit. Lack of financial responsibility may be symptomatic of other difficulties. Further, a man who is overly concerned with his financial problems will not be able to devote all his efforts to selling.

Interviews

Interviews are the major source of evaluative information about an applicant. The previously cited study of sales managers noted interviews as the most helpful of the selection tools. Screening interviews are useful as a preliminary step, and more extensive interviews are mandatory as part of the final selection process.

An interview is a conversation with a purpose, normally involving two people. The general function of an interview is to exchange information (see Figure 9 – 2).

Interviews will vary in format and style depending on the company involved, the type of salesman desired, and on the specific purpose of the interview (screening or selection).

Each sales manager must decide which interviewing techniques work best for him. A major choice is between the patterned and unpatterned interviews.

FIGURE 9–2

*"As you were governed in college by the 'pass-fail'
system, we here in sales are ruled by a
similar method called 'advance-fired.'"*

Source: Reprinted by permission from *Sales Management*, The Marketing Magazine. Copyright 1973.

The *patterned*, or guided, interview is the easiest to use. This method employs a list of questions which the interviewer asks in order to obtain the required information. The set list serves as a control and helps the inexperienced interviewer to cover all factors relevant to the applicant's history, qualifications, and goals. Written notes are taken of the applicant's responses. As the interviewer gains skill and confidence, he can go beyond this list of questions to explore other areas of interest.

The *unpatterned*, or unstructured, interview requires more skill and experience. This method has no set format or plan. Instead, it involves a relaxed discussion in which the interviewee is encouraged to talk about whatever is on his mind. The interviewer assumes that the interviewee will reveal a lot about himself during the discussion. However, as a fact-finding device, the unpatterned interview is limited by the skill of the interviewer. Unless one is trained in using this sophisticated interviewing technique, he is advised to use a patterned interview.

Screening Interview.   An early step in the selection procedure is a preliminary screening interview. This interview has two purposes: to interest applicants in sales positions with the company and to screen these applicants. An applicant wants to know about the company and the job while the interviewer wants to know about the applicant. The interviewer must maintain a fine balance between generating enthusiasm for the job and questioning the ability of the applicant.

Screening interviews should definitely be patterned. They should be short — thirty minutes or less. The main purpose is to quickly eliminate applicants who are not interested in the job or whose qualifications do not meet the job's basic requirements. This can be done by briefly describing the job and by asking the applicant a few pertinent questions. Frequent reasons for eliminating applicants at this stage are inadequate experience or training, physical disability, and inappropriate personality.

In many companies, screening interviews are done by personnel specialists. Recruiting teams who visit college campuses are trained to prescreen applicants. Higher-level sales executives will enter the selection process only after the initial screening.

Selection Interview.   After a candidate has progressed through the preliminary selection steps, including a screening interview, he will be interviewed in depth. The selection, or employment, interviews are usually conducted by line sales managers. *The final decision should rest with the field sales manager who has the vacancy.*

The selection interview is viewed as a continuation of the screening

270

and selection process. Usually, staff experts have screened applicants and only qualified applicants are sent to selection interviews. During the selection interview, the sales manager tries to make sure the applicant has the intelligence, education, and experience to perform the job. He determines whether the applicant's attitudes and personality will permit him to become an effective part of the existing sales organization.

There are several techniques used for selection interviews. The most common is a *background interview*. The interviewer employs a structured format to discuss the experience, education, interests, and other activities of the applicant. Some sales managers prefer a *discussion interview*. This involves a very informal and flexible interview with no set questions. However, as discussed earlier, this approach must be used by an experienced interviewer.

Two other variations are the job-question interview and the stress interview. The *job-question interview* involves posing a job problem to the applicant and asking him how he would handle it. It is assumed that his response will reveal the way he would handle similar problems on the job. In *stress interviewing* stress is placed on an applicant through interruptions, criticism, or silence. The way the applicant reacts to this stress is analyzed to determine how he would react to stress on the job.

How Not to Interview. Poor interviews are a complete waste of time for the sales manager and the applicant. Nevertheless, many busy sales executives fail to give serious thought to the techniques of interviewing. James Menzies Black, author of a practical guide for interviewing, has identified eight types of poor interviewers:[14]

1. The *conversation capper* loves the sound of his own voice. Unfortunately, when an interviewer is doing most of the talking, he is not obtaining information.
2. The *agile anticipator* thinks he knows the answers before they are given. He breaks in with his own views, thus emerging with a distorted view of the interviewee's replies.

---

[14]James Menzies Black, *How to Get Results From Interviewing* (New York: McGraw-Hill Book Company, 1970), pp. 9–11.

3. The *listless listener* is only going through the motions. His mind is wandering; he hears only what confirms what he already believes.
4. The *prosecuting attorney* is conducting a penetrating cross-examination of a hostile witness. By putting the interviewee on the defensive, he loses the interviewee's respect and cooperation.
5. The *goodwill ambassador* is afraid to ask hard or touchy questions. Because he is unwilling to ask blunt questions, he fails to obtain needed information.
6. The *captious categorizer* thinks he has special insight into the minds of others. He classifies interviewees according to his own prejudices, even to the point of thinking that physical appearance is a clue to character. For instance, the recruiting director for a large manufacturer once told one of the authors that when it came to salesmen selection he believed that "the bigger they are, the better."[15]
7. The *simultaneous question-snapper* is the world's busiest executive. He has calls coming in, he is signing letters, he is giving orders to subordinates, and so on, all while trying to conduct an interview.
8. The *faulty-question framer* does not ask the right questions, asks questions that are too general and vague, or interrupts with additional questions before the interviewee can respond to his original inquiry.

Effective interviewing.   The above examples suggest some of the mistakes interviewers make. Effective interviewing does not come easy. It is difficult to apply any rigid rules to interviewing since interviewing is both an art and a science. However, some general guidelines which will assist one to be a better interviewer are suggested below.

1. *Prepare for the interview.* An interviewer must be able to quickly evaluate a candidate. The interviewer should identify goals for the interview and determine exactly what he wants to know about the candidate. As indicated earlier, the application form can be used effectively as an aid for interviewing. It can be used to prepare questions

---

[15]See David L. Kurtz, "Physical Appearance and Stature: Important Variables in Sales Recruiting," *Personnel Journal,* vol. 48 (December 1969), pp. 981–983.

and to eliminate areas for discussion. Asking the candidate questions which he has already answered in writing is an inappropriate and ineffective use of interviewing time.

2. *Select a suitable environment.* Make sure the setting is appropriate for interviewing. If the interview is in his office, the interviewer should avoid interruptions from others, accept no phone calls, and postpone routine office work. If he is in the field, he should select a quiet room in a convenient hotel or motel and make sure that he will not be interrupted.

3. *Establish rapport.* A pleasant, relaxed atmosphere must be established early during the interview. The interviewer and the interviewee must be at ease with one another. Perhaps the easiest way to do this is to open the interview with a topic of mutual interest. A quick review of the interviewee's application form will suggest a suitable opening question. Another approach is to review the steps taken so far in the hiring process with the applicant.

4. *Listen and observe.* Most authorities recommend that *the interviewee should do about two-thirds of the talking.* To make sure the interviewee does the talking, ask probing questions. Questions which can be answered by a simple *yes* or *no* do not tell one much about the applicant. It is also important not to prejudice the applicant's responses by expressing approval or disapproval. A successful interviewer also learns a lot through observation. Does the applicant project a businesslike appearance? Is he dressed neatly? How does he handle himself? Is he poised and confident? Is he alert? Observation will provide many clues about how the applicant will handle himself in a selling situation.

5. *Take few notes.* Most interviewers will need to refer to notes when evaluating an interview. However, taking notes during an interview distracts the applicant and slows down the tempo of the interview. Try to develop unobtrusive methods of taking notes. Better still, use a simple evaluation form which can be filled out after the applicant has left. An easy-to-use interviewing chart prepared by Professor Black is shown in Figure 9-3.

6. *Use two or more interviewers.* It is unwise to rely on a single interview or interviewer. With only one interviewer a possible danger is the *halo effect.* A single factor may create a favorable or unfavorable impression and influence the interviewer's appraisal of other factors.

273

FIGURE 9–3

Employment Interviewing Chart

Name ——————————

Position sought ——————————

Date of Interview ——————————

Conducted by ——————————

Educational Background

1. Level attained	High school passing marks	— Ph.D. honors
2. Intellectual accomplishments		—
3. Outside activities	None	— Many, varied
4. Athletic abilities	No sports	— Varsity competition
5. Subject taken	Not job related	— Highly suitable

Job Experience

1. Past responsibilities	None	— Heavy, varied
2. Skills	Unskilled	— Competent professional
3. Past accomplishments	None	— Top-flight manager
4. Career progress	None	— Steadily upward
5. Motivation	Happy with routine	— Works under pressure, ambitious
6. Pertinence of past jobs		— Highly suitable

Suitability for Available Position

1. Future ambitions	Unplanned, confused	— Realistic, objective
2. Reasons for applying	No clear reason	— Qualified by past experience and desire

3. Promotion potential   None — — — — — — Highly promotable

Individual Characteristics

1. Appearance   Awkward, homely — — — — — — Poised, cleancut
2. Diction   Grammar bad — — — — — — Well spoken, cultivated
3. Verbal facility   Difficulty express-ing self — — — — — — Excellent
4. Tone of voice   Sharp, unpleasant — — — — — — Well modulated, pleasant
5. Attitude   Timid, nervous — — — — — — Confident, at ease
6. Grooming   Badly dressed — — — — — — Well groomed, in good taste

Social Relationships

1. Family status   Parents divorced, unstable home — — — — — — Enjoys home life
2. Marriage relationship   Unhappy, divorced — — — — — — Successful marriage
3. Social interests   None — — — — — — Outgoing, sociable
4. Outside interests   None — — — — — — Civic leader
5. Hobbies   None — — — — — — Several active hobbies

Final Disposition

(1) Reject (2) Hire on trial (3) Hire with caution if no better candidate appears
(4) Recommend (5) Recommend highly

Remarks: _____

Source: From *How to Get Results From Interviewing* by James Menzies Black. Copyright 1970. Used with permission of McGraw-Hill Book Company.

Unskilled interviewers are especially likely to be unduly influenced by an applicant's appearance or personality. This danger is reduced by requiring each applicant to have multiple interviews.

Interviewing an Applicant's Wife. More and more, companies recognize that a salesman's wife will influence his performance.[16] Therefore, meeting the wife of a sales recruit is becoming an accepted practice in many companies. Admittedly, some sales managers consider this an unwarranted invasion of one's private life, but these executives are probably in the minority. A related situation is interviewing the spouse of a female sales candidate. Currently this is a grey area in the sales management literature.

The interview with the sales candidate and his wife should be relaxed and informal.[17] If possible, the sales manager should include his wife so that the candidate's wife will feel at ease. The conversation should be unstructured. Let the wife talk about her husband. If travel is involved, find out how she feels about her husband being away from home. It is better to identify potential family problems before a man is hired than later. The same rationale holds for spouses of female sales personnel.

Medical Examinations

A complete medical examination is recommended despite its relatively high cost. Table 9–3 indicates that the sales managers studied viewed physical examinations as the third most helpful selection tool. Good health is vital to a salesman. He often travels for long periods of time, numerous calls must be made, and some physical work may be involved. To cope with the stresses of selling a salesman cannot be handicapped by illness or physical deficiencies.

A company doctor should be used, or the sales manager should designate a doctor. To assist the doctor in his examination the company should advise him about the physical requirements of the job. Extraor-

---

[16]David J. Schwartz, *The Relationship of the Salesman's Wife to the Salesman's Selling Performance,* Bureau of Business and Economic Research, Paper no. 16 (Atlanta: Georgia State College, 1960). Also see Marvin A. Jolson, "Managing the Salesman's Wife," *Sales Management* (July 1, 1971), pp. 36–37.
[17]Suggestions on interviewing a sales applicant's wife are contained in "Should You Talk to His Wife," *Sales Management* (April 20, 1962), p. 65.

dinary travel requirements, physical tasks, and the like should be highlighted. The doctor must make sure the applicant has no chronic diseases, heart ailments, digestive troubles, or respiratory difficulties. It is essential that those applicants who will be unable to stand the physical strain of selling be eliminated.

Psychological Tests

Psychological testing is an attempt to measure a person's behavior. Industry uses these tests to predict employment success. The assumption is made that a test will provide a representative sample of a person's behavior, which will be a valid predictor of his future employment behavior. As a sales selection technique, psychological tests are used to measure attributes which cannot be measured by other selection tools. They are concerned primarily with aptitude and interests, mental ability, and personality.

Psychological testing of sales applicants first began soon after 1940. Since then, research into what makes a good salesman has resulted in a proliferation of tests. Some of the reasons for increased emphasis on testing are the greater importance of selection, the rising costs of selection and training, the increased knowledge of psychological tests, and the greater availability of tests for industrial use. Many companies also report that testing reduces turnover by providing an objective means for evaluating sales recruits.

Principles of Testing.   To effectively measure and predict behavior, a test must be constructed using four major principles:

1. *Job analysis* will reveal the type and degree of specific qualifications required for successful job performance. Each test should be designed to match the man to the job.
2. *Reliability* refers to the consistency of the test results. A test is reliable if a person will achieve approximately the same score on the same test under the same conditions if he takes the test again. If results are inconsistent, it is doubtful whether the test provides a true representation of the candidate's behavior. Selection decisions cannot be based on highly variable results.
3. *Validity* refers to the authenticity of the test as a measure of behavior. A test is valid if it actually measures what it is sup-

277

posed to measure. In order to accurately predict job success, a test must be valid.

There are two ways to validate an employment test. One is to give the test to present salesmen and to then compare test results with actual performance. If there is a close correlation, the test will probably be a valid predictor of job success. The second method is to give tests to new salesmen but withold the test scores from interviewers. After the salesmen have been working for awhile, their performance is compared with their test scores. Again, the degree of correlation will reveal the validity of the test.

4. *Standardization* implies a uniform procedure for administering and scoring a test. Any deviation from this procedure will impair the reliability and validity of the test.

Types of Tests. There are many kinds of tests available for screening and selecting salesmen. A sales manager should seek the advice of experts when choosing tests for his company.

1. *Intelligence tests* are useful for determining whether an applicant has sufficient mental ability to become a salesman. Table 9 – 3 points out that sales managers consider them more helpful than the other types of psychological tests. General intelligence tests are designed to show how well a person reasons, thinks, and understands. As such, they provide a rough guide to the applicant's overall mental abilities. Other more specialized tests have been designed to measure certain types of intelligence, such as speed of learning, number facility, fluency of ideas, memory, and verbal skill.

The *Wonderlic Personnel Test* has been designed to measure intelligence quickly. The test is composed of fifty short items which roughly divide the intelligence levels of people. Since only about twelve minutes are required to complete the test, it can be used to provide an indication of an applicant's basic intelligence. This may be all that is necessary for many sales jobs, since the company only wants to know whether the applicant meets minimum intelligence requirements.

2. *Sales aptitude tests* are designed to measure what an applicant already knows about selling. This form of test may be useful if applicants have had some selling experience. Many sales managers doubt whether it is possible to measure a special aptitude for selling. Per-

haps this explains the *low helpfulness rating* in Table 9–3. It is also important to note that an aptitude for selling does not mean that the person will be a successful salesman. He must also have the interest and desire to succeed in selling.

A form of sales aptitude test is the *Multiple Personal Inventory* test, which was developed in the early 1960s by Marketing Survey and Research Corporation.[18] This test assumes that empathy (the ability to know what the other person is thinking) and ego drive (a fierce desire to conquer) are the two traits most vital to successful selling. Forced-choice questions are used to measure these two traits. The designers of the test feel that anyone who has an abundance of these traits can be taught to sell.

One of the most widely used tests is the *Strong Vocational Interest Blank*. This test asks questions about likes and dislikes, in order to measure the similarity between an applicant's special interests and the interests of men and women who are successful in a given occupation. Some companies have found this type of test very helpful in screening. However, such tests can be faked by clever applicants.

3. *Personality tests* have some value if they can indicate persons who will fail in selling because of personality defects. However, personality tests are often not as reliable as other forms of tests. The sales managers survey by Professor Wotruba gave personality tests the lowest rating in terms of helpfulness. Since accuracy of results depends on skillful interpretation, results should never be analyzed by an untrained person.

Jack H. McQuaig of the McQuaig Institute of Executive Development has designed a word survey test which measures one important personality trait—temperament.[19] This test is based on the belief that a salesman will be successful if he has the right temperament for selling, if he is competitive, sociable, aggressive, and independent. A job applicant ranks words within groups of four, first indicating how he sees himself and then how he thinks others see him. Analysis of an applicant's ranking enables the tester to place him on a *temperament scale*.

---

[18]A good discussion of the MPI Test is contained in Leslie Rich, "Can Salesmen Be Tested?" *Dun's Review*, vol. 87 (March 1966), pp. 40–41, 63–65.
[19]"Word Survey Interviews Job Applicants For You in Minutes," *Industrial Marketing*, vol. 54 (March 1969), pp. 53–54.

Using Tests Intelligently.   Psychological tests are helpful, but there is no magical shortcut for finding good salesmen. Tests used for selecting salesmen are relevant only if they are a part of the total screening and selection program and if they are directly applicable to an individual company's needs.

A manager who uses tests should be aware of their limitations. *Perhaps the greatest limitation is that tests are suited for group rather than individual predictions.* Tests which attempt to predict sales success based on what is *normal* are on dubious ground. These tests may eliminate innovative and creative people who do not conform to normal concepts of behavior.

Many tests developed to predict sales success have not been scientifically and statistically proven valid for measuring what they purport to measure. Great care must be used in choosing tests. There are opportunists who have developed tests without basing them on accepted testing principles, and it is very doubtful whether these tests have much value in selecting salesmen.

A problem with many standard tests is that a reasonably intelligent applicant can *fake* his answers to make himself look good. This is especially true of aptitude and personality tests. Since an applicant wants the job, he will answer the questions as he thinks the company wants them answered.

The best advice is for sales executives to *use tests with caution.* They are a tool to assist the sales executive in selecting the right man, but they should not be relied upon to the extent of complete dependency. In general, psychological tests are best suited to the initial screening process.

When used with discretion and with competent professional help, tests may provide a manager with additional information not available from other sources. Test results may help a sales manager avoid a serious error, but they must not make the selection decision for him.

Trial Periods

A recent trend is to *try out* a sales applicant before permanently hiring him. In fact, it may be wise to hire all salesmen on a probationary basis. It is easier to replace a man if he is on trial than if he is a permanent employee.

Frequent progress evaluations should be made to determine whether to continue the employment of new salesmen. At some point a definite decision must be made. This will, however, vary from company to company. Life insurance companies have found that a three-month trial period is usually sufficient to discover whether a salesman will be successful. In a large retail shoe chain the trial period is even shorter. Store managers claim they will know within a month whether a new man will be a good salesman.

SUMMARY Salesmen selection is the final step in the staffing process. Once a pool of potential talent has been generated, it becomes necessary to select the individuals who best fit the needs of a particular company.

An evaluation of a selection program requires that the following questions be answered:

1. Is turnover excessive?
2. Is the dollar investment lost on men who have left the company excessive?
3. Are sales lost because salesmen leave the company?
4. Is the selection process too time consuming?

Chapter 9 concluded with an examination of some common selection tools:

1. application blanks;
2. interviews:
   (a) screening;
   (b) selection;
3. references;
4. physical examination;
5. intelligence tests;
6. aptitude tests;
7. personality tests;
8. trial period.

DISCUSSION/REVIEW QUESTIONS

1. List the major screening and selection tools, and explain how they are used to select salesmen.
2. Given the need for sound selection procedures, identify the difficulties of selection.
3. Obtain information on a company's sales force. How many salesmen have left the company over the last year? How much have they cost the company in out-of-pocket expenses and disruption of selling routines?
4. In discussing salesmen selection errors, a personnel researcher commented: "Many [errors] arise from the emphasis in current selection procedures on the abilities, experience, attitudes, or dexterities needed to perform a particular job." What does he mean by this statement? What other factors must be considered when selecting salesmen?
5. The Jacoby Company began last year with 240 salesmen and ended the year with 260 salesmen, a net gain of 20 salesmen. During the year 60 new salesmen were hired and trained and 40 left the company.
   (a) What was the Jacoby Company's turnover rate for last year?
   (b) Using the following cost data, calculate the total cost of turnover

Recruitment and selection	= $800 per salesman
Training	= $2000 per salesman
Supervision	= $1200 per salesman
Compensation	= $6000 per salesman
(average for 6 months)	
Other costs	= $400 per salesman
Estimated lost sales	= $3000 per salesman

6. A regional sales manager suggested to his director of sales that the company use a systematic hiring procedure employing a weighted application form, reference checks, formal interviews, and psychological tests. The director refused with the comment: "I don't want to be bothered with all that so-called scientific selection stuff. Any sales manager worth his salt knows a good salesman when he sees one." How would you answer him?
7. Assume that you are a regional sales manager for a large national manufacturer and distributor of ethical drugs. Reporting to you are 12 sales representatives who call on physicians, hospitals, and drugstores to promote and sell the firm's complete line of products. A vacancy exists in your region which must be filled immediately. Preliminary interviews and other screening procedures have permitted you to narrow your selection down to three men: Jim Adronis, Tom Barkov, and Bob Carter. Brief descriptions of their qualifications follow:
   (a) Jim Adronis is 24 years old, single, in good health, and was recently discharged from the Army after having served for three years as a corps-

man. Prior to military duty, he left college, where he was a biology major, at the end of his junior year and worked as an office clerk for a large retail chain until he entered the service.

Jim shows interest in personal selling as a career, but he does not appear to have crystallized his personal and career goals. Tests show him to be a self-confident, aggressive, and emotionally stable young man. He is tactful, has a good sense of humor, and appears able to take charge. On the other hand, tests indicate that he is able to think accurately at a rate somewhat below that for a person with his mental capacity.

(b) Tom Barkov is 41 years old, married with three children, in good health, and has been employed as a salesman for 20 years. He left college after two years and began selling real estate. Since then he has sold insurance, securities, and automobiles, and is now a salesman for a local grocery wholesaler. He likes his job, but the pay is relatively poor.

Tom is a professional salesman and make a good impression. He thinks this job is exactly what he has been looking for, and he wants to make a permanent connection. Tests indicate that he is conscientious about his interest in selling and that he has exceptional sales insight. He appears to have a thorough understanding and appreciation of the methods, strategies, and techniques of personal selling.

(c) Bob Carter, the third applicant, is a recent graduate of State College where he was a marketing major. Recently married, he is 21 years old and in good health. He had an outstanding record in college where he was a dean's list student and president of his fraternity.

Tests and preliminary interviews with Bob indicate he has outstanding potential. He makes an excellent impression and gives every indication of having the ability to be a successful leader. He is interested in selling, but he has his sights set on a long-range career goal of top marketing management. Bob openly admits he looks upon selling only as an apprenticeship for his marketing career.

Evaluate the qualifications of each applicant. Which applicant would you choose to fill the vacancy?

8. The Binet-Simon Intelligence Test is based on the assumption that intelligence is a common characteristic—that is, on the assumption that all normal people can think, reason, and understand to some extent. The test's questions are designed to find out how well a person thinks, reasons, and understands. The test is long and requires a professional to administer and interpret it. Do you think this test would be useful in selecting salesmen? Why or why not?

9. Various studies of salesmen turnover have reported that younger men are most likely to quit and are most subject to discharge. Also, consumer product salesmen are more likely to quit or be discharged than industrial product salesmen. What do you think are the reasons for greater turnover of younger salesmen and consumer product salesmen? Can you suggest selection safeguards which might cut down on turnover?

10. Identify and briefly explain the following:
    (a) turnover rate   (i) aptitude tests
    (b) quit rate   (j) job hopper
    (c) discharge rate   (k) knockout factors
    (d) application blanks   (l) weighted application form
    (e) interviews   (m) halo effect
    (f) references   (n) reliability
    (g) physical examinations   (o) validity
    (h) intelligence tests   (p) trial period
11. Differentiate between the various types of interviews. Cite examples of each.
12. Who should be responsible for salesmen selection? Discuss.
13. Discuss the possible guidelines that could be used to determine whether salesmen turnover was excessive?
14. "Recruitment and selection present a transposition problem to the sales manager." Comment.
15. Discuss the eight types of poor interviewers identified in the chapter. Do you agree with this classification?
16. List some general guidelines for improved interviewing. Explain how each of these will aid the interviewing process.
17. Do you believe that a firm should interview a male applicant's wife as part of the salesmen selection procedure? Defend your position on this matter.

CHAPTER TEN
SALES TRAINING
AND DEVELOPMENT

There are two distinct forms of salesman training: formal and informal. *Formal training* in most companies involves carefully planned programs complete with schedules, lesson plans, visual aids and other teaching devices, and systematic reviews and evaluations. There are three distinct phases in formal sales training: designing the sales training program, managing its operation, and evaluating its success. This chapter will examine each of these phases in turn.

Informal training programs are equally important for the maintenance of an efficient sales force. Continuous salesman development is a prime responsibility of the sales supervisor in his personal contacts with his salesmen. This involves working with individual salesmen, guiding their daily activities, and advising on improvements that should be made. This has been characterized as *curb side* training, informal and on-the-spot instruction for performance improvement. Although it does not utilize formal training plans and devices, curb side training plays a vital part in the development of salesmen.

REASONS FOR TRAINING

Many people assume that sales training is necessary and possible only in large companies with many salesmen and large operating budgets. However, although extensive formal programs exist less frequently in smaller enterprises,[1] various types of sales training have been carried

---

[1] This is pointed out in Lloyd R. Saltzman, *Sales Training Programs in Concerns With Fifty Salesmen Or Less* (New York: National Sales Executives, Inc., 1956).

out successfully on a modest scale—in small companies with few salesmen and on small outlays. Whatever the size of an organization, the training of salesmen is virtually universal in American business, and there are two basic reasons for such training:

To Develop the Right Work Habits. Salesmen will learn some pattern of work habits, depending upon how they are taught. They will learn how to cover their territory, to approach customers, in what style to live while traveling, what sort of records to keep, and how to plan and execute their sales calls. Salesmen will learn how to do these things well and efficiently, or poorly and at substantial expense to their company. If sales recruits are trained, they will learn the right work habits and patterns, at the right time and from the right learning source.

To Offset the Effect Of "Detraining." Salesmen are constantly being detrained—that is, taught the wrong things—by their field experience. They adapt undesirable "short cuts," gravitate toward ineffective ways of selling, and often become discouraged and dispirited from the constant buffeting of the competitive marketplace.[2] Both new and experienced salesmen must be trained to offset this negative effect of their field sales experience.

PAYOFFS OF TRAINING

Training of the sales force pays for itself in a number of important ways; if the training is effective, it

1. improves the salesman's relationship with his customers by showing him the right way to do business with them.
2. motivates the salesman to develop himself and raises his morale because he sees his company concerned with his development. Coach Vince Lombardi characterized this as the all-important "second effort."

---

[2]Many authorities argue that salesmen often lack the inner knowledge to cope with sales resistance. See, for example, John Vollbrecht, "Are You Leaving the Customer Out of Your Sales Training?" *Sales Management,* vol. 99 (August 15, 1967), pp. 29–31, 68.

3. reduces the cost and the lost sales that result from a high turnover of salesmen.[3]
4. makes salesmen more flexible and innovative in meeting changing competitive market conditions.[4]
5. reduces the costs incurred by inefficient territory coverage by poor use of company-supplied sales tools, by the wrong application of company policy (credit terms, for instance) or of operating procedures (delivery schedules).
6. increases sales volume.
7. reduces the cost of supervision: a well-trained salesman is more economical to supervise because he requires less supervisory attention from his boss.
8. increases the efficiency of controlling salesmen's activities: a well-trained salesman needs less direct control from his supervisor.[5]

In summary, the net effect of training is to develop proper work habits and to offset the effect of field detraining, so that salesmen's expenses are reduced and their sales volume is maximized. Both of these are critical management objectives. As one sales manager of a plastics company observed: "The company that thinks it cannot afford to, or does not need to train and retrain its salesmen has just thought itself out of business."[6]

THE THEORY OF TEACHING AND LEARNING

Before considering the design of the sales training program, one must understand the characteristics of the process by which people learn. In the basic learning situation, (1) the learner knows nothing about the

---

[3]There is empirical evidence to suggest that unnecessarily long training programs significantly increase turnover among sales recruits. See David L. Kurtz, "High Salesman Turnover: A Function of Lengthy Training Programs?" *Carroll Business Bulletin*, vol. XI (Winter 1972), pp. 3–5. Also see David L. Kurtz, "Relationship Between Training and Turnover," *Review of Business*, vol. 9 (March–April 1972), pp. 4–5.

[4]For instance, the salesman's need for perceptual skills is pointed out in Frederick E. Webster, Jr., "Interpersonal Communications and Salesmen Effectiveness," *Journal of Marketing*, vol. 32 (July 1968), pp. 7–13.

[5]Dunn and Johnson, (1973), p. 77.

[6]Albert H. Dunn and Eugene M. Johnson, *Managing the Sales Force* (Morristown, N.J.: General Learning Press, 1973), p. 78.

subject being taught, and/or (2) he knows something of it but not a sufficient amount, and/or (3) what he knows is incorrect. The mission of the teaching process is thus to transmit knowledge and skills and to create positive attitudes and/or to correct these things if they already exist but are incorrect. Training salesmen to sell effectively and efficiently is, in the last analysis, an industrial application of the basic principles of education, as they have been developed by professional educators in schools and universities. A good training program therefore should be based on sound educational principles.

Clearly Recognized Purpose. It would be a poor trainer indeed who did not clearly recognize the purpose and mission of the training program. But this is not enough. The trainee himself must have a clear understanding of why he is being trained, toward what goals his instruction is directed, how he will use what he learns, and how he will personally benefit from the instruction.[7] Training can never be successful if the trainee feels he is simply being "walked through" the program because it is a matter of company policy. This aspect of a sound training program underlines the value of a carefully planned pretraining orientation period, in which the trainee is shown the purposes and payoffs of the training he is about to undertake and is allowed to question any purpose or method that may be unclear to him. In addition it is useful during the course of the training program to remind the trainee of the purposes and uses of his training.

Clarity of Presentation. Too often, the trainers themselves know the company, industry, products, sales problems, and technical jargon of the business so well that they forget that the trainee does not. Since the trainers assume too much, the trainee is likely to become quickly lost among unfamiliar language, concepts, or procedures. Every effort must be made to make the training material simple and clear and to present the material in terms that are understandable to the trainee.

Planned Repetition. In a learning situation, few people fully grasp a new idea or concept the first time they are exposed to it, no matter

---

[7] The importance of audience orientation is stressed in George Conomikes, "What Kills Sales Training in the Field?" *Sales Management*, vol. 97 (July 15, 1966), pp. 115–119.

how clearly it is presented.[8] This is especially true if the idea or concept is complicated, or if it varies in form or application between different selling situations. In addition, repetition is necessary if the trainee is trying to unlearn some previously learned wrong notions or techniques.

To overcome this difficulty, the good trainer carefully plans restatement and repetition into the program. Important ideas or concepts are repeated at relevant places in the training program, either in their original form or in a different form. In this way the trainee has the opportunity to reinforce his understanding of the concept and to see it in several different applications or contexts. Trainers should not be reticent about planned repetition of key points for fear that it will bore trainees. Planned repetition is a required characteristic of good learning and training, and it will be welcomed by trainees.

Systematic Review. Reviewing, going back over and high-spotting material already covered, has several advantages. It allows the trainee to check his understanding of what has been covered. It shows what he has failed to learn, and where therefore he must shore up his knowledge by extra work. If he has been applying himself, review bolsters his morale because it demonstrates to him what he has learned. Finally, periodic review sets the stage for the training material that is to follow.

Orderly Development of Material. The major difference between learning by experience and learning by training is that training is *orderly* and can be repeated, while experience is *random* and uncontrolled. To illustrate this point, suppose that a sales manager wanted to teach a trainee how to deal with a particular objection that is often raised by customers. If he were to learn how to handle this objection only by experience, he might make dozens of calls before he encountered the particular objection. Even then experience alone is not likely to indicate to him if he handled the objection well or poorly. Orderly training can show him how to manage this objection, demonstrate its

---

[8]B. F. Skinner has noted that the relative infrequency of reinforcement is a critical problem in the teaching/learning experience. See "The Science of Learning and the Art of Teaching," *Harvard Educational Review,* vol. 24 (Spring 1964), pp. 86–97.

proper handling, and allow the trainee to practice the proper response as many times as is necessary to master it.

The training program should be designed so that learning has a logical and meaningful sequence, so that it flows from one topic to a related topic and avoids random skips from one subject to another. In this way the trainee is not confused by being asked to study what appear to him to be unrelated topics, and he is able to relate individual steps or activities to those that logically precede or follow. For example, assume that the trainer wants to discuss how to prospect for new customers. The logical order or flow of this topic would be (1) how to locate new potential customers, (2) how to identify the buyer to be visited, (3) how to arrange to meet him, (3) how to plan the introductory call, (4) how to open a continuing relationship with him, (5) how to follow up.

A Sensible Pace. All people learn at a different rate of speed and it is important to remember that, excepting the genius mentality, the pace at which people learn has no relationship to how well they retain and use what they learn. Fast learners can be quick forgetters or poor users of what they have learned, while slow learners may remember what they have learned for long periods of time and use the information well. This means that the trainer must be sure that:

1. the training is not proceeding at a pace too fast for slower learners;
2. the fast learners are retaining the information they absorb so quickly.

One useful device for checking these conditions is periodic tests — verbal or written — during the training program. These tests should cover not only the material recently learned, but earlier material as well.

Trainee Participation. Research in learning has established that people retain a very small portion of what they see or hear, but a much greater proportion of what they *see, hear and do.* In some way, implementing or performing the thing one is learning reinforces the message that the memory at first receives by sight or sound. Effective trainers explain, then they demonstrate, and then they have the student perform the thing being taught. Skilled sales trainers realize the importance of reinforcing oral and visual instruction by action, and they devise ways by which trainees may participate in their own training by actually doing what they are learning. A later section on teaching aids suggests ways by which this can be accomplished.

DESIGNING THE SALES TRAINING PROGRAM

Clearly the benefits of sales training cannot be attained unless the program is well designed to fit the particular company's needs. In this light the design of a sales training program involves answering four critical questions for each sales group: Which salesmen should be trained and at what point in their careers? What should the training program cover? What should be its form and organization? Who should train salesmen and where does training fit in the organization?

WHICH SALESMEN SHOULD BE TRAINED
AND WHEN IN THEIR CAREERS

Training New Salesmen   The question of when to train new salesmen is difficult for most companies to answer because its resolution is based on a dilemma. On the one hand, training is more efficient and meaningful if the new salesman has had some first-hand selling experience before he begins training. Consider the example of a beginning salesman for a hardware manufacturer. His training is more interesting, efficient, meaningful, and economical if before he begins training, he is familiar with such things as the language of the trade, the problems and practices common to the industry, and the objections often raised by customers.

On the other hand, it is difficult to provide selling experience for an untrained salesman, since the company risks sales losses and damaged relations with customers because of his inexperience. As a result, a minimal amount of field selling experience is usually provided for the sales recruit before he is given the basic sales training.

Retraining Experienced Salesmen. Frequently situations arise that make it necessary to retrain experienced salesmen. Some of these are the following:

1. when new products are to be introduced
2. when new kinds of customers are to be solicited
3. when the man is to be assigned to a new territory
4. when new reporting or other new sales operating procedures are to be introduced
5. when the man is to be promoted to a supervisory position
6. when there is evidence that the salesman has adopted improper selling habits
7. when competition, economic conditions, governmental regulations, or other environmental conditions change in such a way as to drastically affect his selling operations

When these or similar conditions arise to substantially change the required knowledge, skills and attitudes of experienced salesmen retraining is usually indicated.

Even when all of the above conditions are absent, continued training for salesmen has many tangible benefits. A large consumer goods division of a diversified corporation recently evaluated the effects of retraining. Salesmen who had attended a continuing instruction session recorded significant performance gains, including the following increases: 12 per cent in number of calls per day, 25 per cent in new product retail placements, 62 per cent in displays sold, 100 per cent in case sales, and 250 per cent in sales to direct-buying or chain accounts.[9]

WHAT THE TRAINING PROGRAM SHOULD COVER

The successful salesman for any company, regardless of its size or industry, must know his product and his company's policies and procedures. He must possess the necessary sales and territory manage-

---

[9]"The New Supersalesman: Wired for Success", *Business Week* (January 6, 1973), p. 49.

ment skills, and have a positive, constructive attitude toward his products, customers, his job, his company, and himself.

In setting up a training program, the first decision to be made concerns content or, in other words, what the training program should cover. The answer to this question can be put in this way:

The knowledge, skills, attitudes the salesman must have	LESS	Those he already has	EQUALS	What he must be trained in

For instance, salesmen need to know the technical specifications of all of the company's products, and new salesmen will not know them. Hence, new men must be trained in the product specifications. The same sort of analysis applies to all salesmen, whatever their degree of experience.

Limitations on Training Programs

The question then arises, should the *formal training program* undertake to impart all of the necessary skills, attitudes, and knowledge to all of the company's salesmen? The answer is, not necessarily since it depends on prevailing conditions. Consider the following reasoning:

Not All Skills and Attitudes Can Be Trained. Some skills and attitudes are fixed and unchangeable when the man is hired. Others can be trained, but no company can afford to undertake to do it. An electronics company, for example, might require its salesmen to have a graduate level technical training. When certain required skills, attitudes, or knowledge either cannot be trained by any formal program, or when the company cannot afford to train them, the recruiting and selection system must choose salesmen who already possess the qualities that are desired.

Success Requirements Vary Between Sales Groups. The skill and knowledge required for a salesman's success differ according to the

293

product, the industry, and the specific competitive conditions. Therefore the content of training programs must vary also. No single program can fit all selling conditions.

Individual Salesman Training Needs Vary.   Among new salesmen, one can assume a certain consistency of background. For instance, all graduates of reputable business schools can be assumed to have had at least elementary accounting. On this level, one can safely presume that sales recruits will require the same general content in their training. But frequently individual training needs vary, and firms must individualize training to the greatest degree possible.

Informal Training Can Accomplish Much.   As was pointed out earlier, a major responsibility of sales supervision is continuous informal, curb side training of salesmen. Much of the knowledge, skills, and attitudes needed by the successful salesman do not have to be included in his formal training program. They can be imparted on the job by his supervisor's informal instruction.

The Optimum Content: A Checklist

Designing the content of a formal training program for a particular company is a matter of analyzing what knowledge, skills, and attitudes are required for sales success in that company.

The checklist shown in Table 10–1 is used in answering these questions about the content of the sales training program.

TABLE   10–1
Checklist for Designing a Formal Training Program

Product Knowledge
1. How much technical knowledge, of what sort, does the salesman need to know about his products (for example, how they work, what they will and will not do, how they are made, their expected life)? What does he *not* need to know about his products?
2. What does he need to know about how the product fits into the customer's technology, production, use, or resale process?
3. What does he need to know about competitor's products, strengths and weaknesses, characteristics, use features?

Knowledge of Company Policy and Procedures

1. What must the salesman know about internal policies and procedures, such as expense accounting, retirement and sick leave, vacations, transportation?
2. What must he know about the marketing policies and procedures, such as credit, terms of sale, delivery, product guarantees, advertising and promotion support, service and technical assistance?
3. What must he know about marketing operations, such as order and report forms, territory coverage, personal records?

Required Selling Skills

1. Must he know how to prospect for customers?
2. Must he be able to plan each call?
3. Must he know how to handle customer objections?
4. Must he be skilled in identifying customer needs and matching them with product features and benefits?
5. Will he need to entertain his customers?
6. What social skills are required?
7. What communications skills will he need?

Attitudes

1. What positive attitudes must he have toward his customers, company, job, supervision?
2. What sort of relationship will he have with his customers and what attitudes will this require?

Step-by-step analysis of this sort against the job description will show specifically what each sales group's training requirements are and what the skill, knowledge, and attitude content of the training program should be.

It should be noticed that the checklist does not mean to imply that product knowledge and company policies and procedures are more important than selling skills. In fact, most authorities argue that training programs typically overemphasize such factors as product knowledge.[10] There is a need to place a greater stress on effective selling techniques in these programs.

---

[10]Richard C. Chaistian, "Have We Forgotten How to Train?" *Journal of Marketing*, vol. 26 (October 1962), pp. 81–82. Also see Roy C. Brewster, "More Psychology in Selling," *Harvard Business Review*, vol. 31 (July–August 1953), p. 91.

Learning Basis/Training Policy

The next consideration in designing the formal sales training program concerns the learning basis or training policy to be employed.

Sales training is based on one of two basic education philosophies. The best alternative for a particular sales group depends on the specific conditions involved — on the characteristics of the salesmen, products, markets, competition, and customers. Both policies are well suited to certain conditions and are ineffective in others. The first policy discussed below is the historical basis for sales training, while the second policy is relatively new on the business scene.

Conditioned Response. Under the conditioned response approach, salesmen are trained *in advance* in the proper response to any and all problems, conditions, and objections that they may encounter. The selling job is carefully analyzed. Prospecting for new customers, the approach, the sales presentation, the close, and follow-up are carefully combined into a general model representing *all* selling situations. The salesmen are required to learn premade instructions and responses and to adhere to them strictly. In this way, under a carefully prepared conditioned response policy, no salesman ever finds himself in a situation that has not been anticipated and for which he is not fully prepared with a memorized reaction provided by his employer. Conditioned response is a generalized response, and the training program is designed to transmit this response.

Insight Response. Insight response takes an opposing stance: it expects salesmen to respond to selling problems on the basis of their personal insights into the nature of each individual selling situation. The training is aimed at helping salesmen develop their insight and analytical skills. Insight response is an individualized response.

In deciding on which training policy is best suited for a particular sales group, it is useful to consider two completely different selling situations. If the product is atomic power generation equipment for example, the selling situation is complex and highly technical. Customers are knowledgeable and their requirements are varied. Salesmen are highly trained and sales force turnover is generally low. At the other extreme, there are situations such as door-to-door selling, in which the selling job is fairly simple and nontechnical. Customers know little about the products and their requirements are standard. Salesmen are not highly trained and sales force turnover is high.

In the first selling situation, insight response is indicated and in the second, conditioned response is favored. In general, a decision concerning conditioned response or insight response will be based on questions such as:

1. Is it *feasible* to condition the salesman's response? In complex, changing sales situations involving knowledgeable buyers with various requirements, it is not possible to effectively condition the salesman's response, because the customer's individual needs and requirements are so varied that it is impossible to anticipate them. When these conditions are reversed, conditioned response is possible.
2. Is it *desirable* to condition the salesman's response? The kind of customer, his knowledge, and desires dictate the answer to this question. Is the customer best persuaded by a conditioned or an insight response?

In extreme cases, such as the examples given above, the choice between these two training policies is not difficult. But the selling conditions of a great many companies fall between the extremes and do not clearly demand either conditioned or insight response approaches. For these companies the decision involves the weighing of the advantages and disadvantages of the policies as suggested in Table 10–2.

Each sales group must analyze the pros and cons of these two training policies very carefully. As the table demonstrates, each policy has advantages and disadvantages in regard to cost, salesmen's morale, flexibility, and customer reaction.

THE FORM OF A TRAINING PROGRAM

Sales training has adopted a variety of teaching devices and techniques from the field of education. Each has its own special purposes

TABLE 10−2
Advantages and Disadvantages of the Conditioned and Insight Responses

Advantages	Disadvantages
Conditioned Response	
Expert experience and advice is brought to bear on all of the problems the salesman encounters	Salesman may overlook particular interests or problems of individual customers while adhering to the conditioned response pattern
No problem, procedure, or situation the salesman will encounter is overlooked	Salesman is not allowed to adjust to unique selling conditions
Training is economical once the response program has been developed	Customer may resent standardized selling process as manipulation, or as a high pressure tactic
All salesmen in the group react in the same way, making it easy to transfer salesmen between territories within the same company	Some salesmen may resent absence of initiative and opportunity thus affecting morale
Customer is supplied all information the seller wants him to have	
Insight Response	
Salesman is flexible to adjust to changing market and customer conditions	Salesmen's morale is raised by active participation in their own work
Salesman's focus is on an individual situation, not on a generalized situation	Training is slow, difficult and expensive
Customer's individual conditions and problems are central in the sales call	

and applications. Most companies use a combination of these devices and techniques rather than relying on a single method.

Visual Aids. Visual aids include such special devices as films, tapes, flip charts, chalk and flannel boards, film strips, closed circuit and play-back television, and overhead slide projection. The advantages of visual aids are that they add color, motion, and drama to the training. They can be repeated as often as necessary for review and reinforcement of the message and for rechecking by the trainees. Since visual aids are prepared in advance their form, content, sequence, and organization can be completely preplanned and controlled. There need be no unrehearsed presentation mistakes. The main disadvantage of visual aids as a training device is that they should usually be prepared by experts and so are expensive to use.

Often a company's advertising agency can provide the necessary artistic talent and technical competence to produce effective visual aids for training salesmen. In addition there are a number of firms that specialize in the planning and production of visual training aids for specific clients.

Lectures. A *lecture* is a formal, structured, verbal presentation of information to trainees by expert trainers and company executives. This technique is economical of trainees' time and makes top-flight trainers and executives available for training efficiently and at low cost. It is a very effective method of transmitting straight factual information. The difficulties inherent in the lecture method are that unless lectures are carefully prepared, planned, and rehearsed the trainees will "shut off" the lecturer out of boredom or antagonism. In addition, because lectures must necessarily be generalized, the method is poorly adapted to the transmission of the specific information needed for the dynamic, dissimilar conditions of selling.

Discussions. Under the guidance of a skilled conference leader, *discussions* permit trainees to examine a common problem, procedure, company policy, or case history. This training technique is well suited to orientating trainees in selling problems that involve individual judgment, personal decision, and adjustment to specific selling situations. It has the further advantage of directly involving the trainees in their own training. A limitation of discussion as a sales training technique is that it requires skilled and experienced conference leaders. Such people are in short supply, since not everyone can conduct a meaningful training discussion.

Role Playing. In *role playing*, a problem situation is stated and several trainees play out the important roles in the problem, e.g., the roles of buyer and salesman.[11] Other trainees, trainers, and executives observe the role play session and later make suggestions and offer constructive criticism. The advantages of this training technique are that it adds realism and interest to the training and increases the trainees' skills in reacting immediately to selling problems in a face-to-face sales situation. The weaknesses of the technique are that trainees sometimes feel awkward and embarrassed "play acting" in public and that the role playing skills of individual trainees vary widely. Both of these conditions can detract from the effectiveness of this training device.

Panels. The *panel* consists of a small group of trainees and sales managers — or a combination of both — who, under the guidance of a chairman, make short prepared presentations on a training topic. Members of the panel are then questioned by other panel members and by the trainee group. Advantages are that the panel is an economical way to make experts available to trainees; that trainees can ask their individual questions; and that trainers can observe the trainees' responses to the panel. In addition, the panel adds interest to the training program through the give and take between panelists and between panelists and trainees. One weakness of panel discussion is that the differing opinions and points of view of panelists may confuse trainees. In addition, it is sometimes difficult to control the interchange between trainees and panelists so that a clear, consistent message comes across. This is especially true when one panelist monopolizes the presentation or the question and answer period.

Observed Sales Calls. In *observed sales calls*, the trainer makes field calls with the trainee, observing his sales technique and later coaching him on methods for improvement. The advantages of this training technique are that it provides a realistic learning experience as well as the immediate opportunity to correct bad selling habits and techniques. However, it is expensive and the selling situation encountered (and therefore the learning experiences) are random; they cannot be preplanned or fitted into any sort of predetermined sequence of trainee experience.

---

[11]The use of role playing for sales training is advocated in John M. Frey, "Missing Ingredient in Sales Training," *Harvard Business Review*, vol. 33 (November–December 1955), pp. 126–132.

Programmed Instruction. In *programmed instruction,* the total body of knowledge that the trainees are to learn is broken into small segments, each of which consists of explanatory material and questions covering it.[12] These segments are presented to the trainee in sequence, either by a teaching machine or in a printed text. The trainee answers a set of questions on each module of the work and is directed either to study the explanatory material and take the test again or to proceed to the next "lesson." The advantages of this technique are several: it can be used by a single trainee and requires no formal class session; it does not require the presence of a trainer; and the trainee can progress at his own rate of learning. The Warner Brake and Clutch Company of Beloit, Wisconsin, for instance, used programmed instruction to inform 500 distributor salesmen about several complex product line changes.[13] The drawback of this technique is that it is expensive, because it must be planned and written to suit the needs of a specific company and industry. Early pioneers in the use of programmed sales instruction included Schering Corporation, Spiegel, Inc., Eastman Kodak Company, AT & T, Prudential Insurance Company, Mead Johnson, Humble Oil Company, and Shell Oil Company.[14]

Dramas and Skits. In live *dramas and skits,* a script is produced that highlights the training points to be emphasized. Actors in the appropriate stage setting and with the appropriate props act out the script before the trainee audience. The main advantage of this technique is that it can be used to introduce a change of pace and to add interest to the training program. It facilitates learning and allows the trainees to associate themselves with members of the cast of actors. Because the actors are obviously not real people, dramas can be used to introduce humor, criticism, and satire, which might not be acceptable in lectures or discussions. It can be used to lighten the training while still imparting a useful message. The disadvantage of the approach is that the skits are difficult to design and are therefore expensive. It requires a specialist to prepare a script that is interesting, en-

---

[12]The use of programed instruction is described in Leon G. Schiffman, "Programmed Instruction: Its Use In Sales Training," *Industrial Marketing* (February 1965), pp. 82–86.

[13]"Programmed Instruction Pays Sales Knowledge Dividends," *Industrial Marketing,* vol. 52 (March 1967), pp. 62–65.

[14]J. Porter Henry, Jr., "Can Machines Teach Salesmen To Sell?" *Sales Management,* vol. 89 (July 20, 1962), pp. 38–39, 95–103.

tertaining, engrossing and that at the same time gets the message across. Such specialists are usually to be found outside the company. And, since the use of company personnel as amateur actors is a highly risky proposition, the actors also are usually professionals from outside the company. As is the case with the production of visual training aids, however, there are companies in existence that specialize in planning, producing, and presenting training dramas and skits.

Business Games. Alternately called *simulation exercises, business games* can also be utilized in the training program. Competing as individuals or as teams, trainees must make series of decisions which are then scored against the "moves" of competing units. After the complete series of moves, one unit emerges as the "winner," on the grounds of such standards as profit, return on investment, or penetration of new markets.[15] Advantages are that this technique is realistic and interesting and that it gives the trainees a genuine sense of competition in the market. Further, it allows the exposition and demonstration of business and selling problems that are not always readily demonstrable through the use of other teaching techniques. It is, however, usually an expensive technique, and management games that are applicable to some industries and selling situations are not available unless specially prepared.

WHO SHOULD TRAIN SALESMEN AND WHERE TRAINING FITS INTO THE ORGANIZATION

In sales training, as in other forms of education, it is a cardinal principle that the skills of *teaching* are different from the skills of *performing* the subject being taught. There is a prevalent fallacy in all fields of human endeavor that anyone who does something well is automatically an outstanding teacher-trainer of that same skill. In practice, however, the skills involved in *making* a sale are completely different from the skills of *teaching* or *training* the making of a sale.

To be sure, some skilled salesmen and sales managers are topflight trainers, but others are very poor indeed. Some mediocre sales people

---

[15]See, for example, Louis E. Boone and David L. Kurtz, *The Sales Management Game* (Morristown, N.J.: General Learning Press, 1972).

are good trainers. Some professional sales trainers were or would be poor salesmen, others, excellent. This condition has an important bearing on the questions of who should train salesmen and of where the training should take place in the organization.

The Sales Trainers and the Training Location

For the question of who should train salesmen, the alternatives are (1) training specialists, (2) field sales managers and experienced salesmen, or (3) outside training specialists. On the problem of location, training can take place either in a single, centralized location or in decentralized field sales installations. Thus a number of combinations are possible: sales training can be conducted by training specialists in a centralized location, by sales managers in the field, or by outside consultants or field men in a centralized location.

However, for the great majority of companies, only three of the many alternatives are possible because of the excessive cost in time and money of the other approaches. Field sales personnel cannot generally afford the time away from their sales work to participate in centralized training at another location. Outside training experts are too expensive to be employed in decentralized training at a number of different field locations. As a result these alternatives are unrealistic for most companies.

Most companies then must choose between three alternatives: (1) sales training by company training specialists in a central location; (2) training by outside experts in a central location; or (3) training by field sales people at field sales locations. Each of these alternatives has its merits and its limitations which are considered in Table 10-3.

A Compromise Plan. According to a combination plan that is frequently used, the training is done in the field, by field sales people who are assisted in a staff capacity by training specialists from headquarters. In such instances the training specialist assists the field trainers in planning the program, participates in the program, counsels field trainers, and assists in evaluating the program. While this is not necessarily the ideal solution, it does have all of the merits of training in the field by field people. At the same time it lessens the problems posed by the lack of special training know-

303

TABLE 10–3
An Evaluation of Three Training Alternatives, by Type of Trainer and by Training Location

Merits	Limitations
Training by Company Training Specialists in a Central Location	
Provides specialized training know-how and experience	Training cannot be directly related to real-life selling situations and problems
Does not take line sales people away from their work or distract their attention from their sales job	Trainee learns nothing about the market in which he will be working
Training is the main purpose of the operation—hence, there is no dilution of the training activity by the pressures of selling problems	When the trainee is sent to the field after training, his manager may belittle his centralized training as being unrelated to real market conditions
	Adds overhead costs of staff, special equipment, and meeting rooms

Training by Outside Experts in a Central Location

This alternative shares all of the merits and limitations cited above for training by company training specialists at a central location, except that training by outside experts has an additional advantage and two potential limitations.

Merits	Limitations
Provides ideas and techniques from training in other industries and companies; offers broader experience and viewpoint	Danger exists of leaking company trade secrets to the outside training experts
	Expert may not know or may not be able to master important problems or conditions unique to the particular company

Training by Field Sales People at Field Sales Locations

Merits	Limitations
No added overhead cost for training personnel, since line sales people are already on the payroll	Does not provide specialized training know-how and experience
Training can be related to real selling situations	Takes line sales people away from selling and managing
	Training emphasis likely to be

304

Trainee learns about conditions in the actual market	diluted by the pressures of every-day sales activities
Field sales people are themselves involved in the training, so they are less likely to deny or downgrade its value	

how and by the diversion of sales people from their selling jobs. The preceding discussion can be summarized in the form of a model (Figure 10-1), which can be used by an individual sales group to decide what combination of training personnel and location is best for them.

FIGURE 10−1
Model For Training Decisions

Sales Training Program Specification	The Training Program Required		Location and Personnel Alternatives	
	Must Provide This Specifi- cation	**Need Not Provide This Speci- fication**	**Accomplishes Well**	**Accomplishes Poorly**
Training Specification Provide specialized training experi- ence, know-how			CCS COX	DFS
Time Cost Must not take field sales people away from selling			CCS COX	DFS
Emphasis Emphasis must be strictly on training			CCS COX	DFS

Program Expense
   Keep training costs
      at minimum
	DFS	CCS
		COX

Realism
   Training strictly
      related to real-life
      conditions
	DFS	CCS
		COX

Market Orientation
   Trainee shown
      conditions in his
      territory
	DFS	CCS
		COX

Program Creativity
   Provide new ideas,
      concepts, training
      techniques
	CCS
	COX
		DFS

Security
   Safeguard company
      trade secrets
	CCS
	DFS
		COX

Focus
   Directly and ex-
      clusively on
      company
      problems and
      procedures
	CCS
	DFS
		COX

CCS = centralized location by company training specialists
COX = centralized location by outside training experts
DFS = decentralized location by field service personnel

Each sales group must use the kind of analysis summarized in this model in deciding on the optimum training location-personnel choice. This requires weighing the relative importance *for them* of one program specification against each training alternative. For instance, decentralized training by field personnel reduces expense, adds realism to the training, orientates the trainee in his future territory, safeguards company trade secrets, and focuses on company problems and procedures. However, this alternative does not provide specialized training skill and experience, does not utilize full-time trainers, and is not likely to be particularly creative.

FOLLOW-UP AND EVALUATION

The purposes of formal and informal sales training are to transmit required knowledge and skills and to create a positive attitude in the salesman toward his company, products, and job. On one level, evaluation of the success of the training program is not difficult. It is easy to determine if the program has succeeded in imparting the necessary factual information to the trainee. However, in the areas of sales skills and personal attitudes, the evaluation of sales training is difficult and inexact for a number of reasons:

1. skills and attitudes are difficult to observe and to evaluate objectively;
2. one can never be sure which changes are the result of training and which may have existed in the trainee before he was trained;
3. after training, one cannot be sure which skills, attitudes, and knowledge the trainee has learned from sales experience and which have come from the training program itself.

At best, sales training is, like all educational undertakings, an inexact and only semi-measurable activity. Evaluating the effectiveness and efficiency of sales training can never be a completely accurate activity. In spite of the known inaccuracies, the training program must be subject to constant evaluation (and, if necessary, revision), if training dollars are to be spent well and efficiently. The various methods used by companies to evaluate their sales training programs are discussed below.

Observe Salesmen at Work. After training, skilled observers who know the training program and its objectives can accompany recent trainees on their sales calls. They can observe how the trainee-salesman is, or is not, applying what he was taught in the program. They can thus evaluate the training techniques used and change or improve them to better fit market conditions.

Sound out Customers. Customers can be contacted personally or by mail for their opinions about the salesman's performance after training. In some instances customer's reactions indicate strengths or weaknesses in the sales training program.

Review a Man's Performance Against Standards. Some companies establish one set of performance standards—such as new accounts opened or promotions arranged with customers—for salesmen without training, and another set of performance standards for those who have been through the training program. By comparing the performance of trained and untrained men against these standards, they can achieve some evaluation of the training program.

Interview Trainees. Carefully planned pretraining interviews can be compared with matching posttraining interviews, to indicate what effect training has had on attitudes, skills, and knowledge. Another version of this evaluation device employs written tests of the trainees before and after their training.

Management Opinion. The supervisors of salesmen who have undergone training can be a useful source of information about the value of the program. Do the newly trained men have a positive, constructive attitude? The necessary selling skills? The necessary company and market information? Their immediate supervisors can supply valuable information on such questions and thereby indicate the strengths and weakness of the training program.

Recycling the Sales Training Program

What if the various forms of evaluation of the sales training program indicate that it is inadequate? What if evaluation shows that salesmen are not being orientated in the proper attitudes; that their product, company, or industry knowledge is insufficient; or that they lack the required selling skills? In this unhappy event, management is confronted with the necessity to recycle, to redesign the training program. To do this one must begin with a reexamination of the training objectives, program content, teaching methods, location of the training, and training personnel.

But what if evaluation of the sales training program indicates that the program is a good one and that it is satisfactory in all respects? Should a firm discontinue the expense and bother of regular evaluation of the program? Definitely not! The marketplace is in a constant state of change: competitors introduce new products, new uses for the product appear, new competitors enter the market, economic conditions shift, new customers appear, and old customers disappear. Consequently, the skill, knowledge, and attitude required for successful salesmanship are also in a constant state of change, and the form and content of salesman's training is always subject to alteration. It follows, then, that when evaluation shows a training program to be effective, evaluation of it must continue because training that is successful today may be inadequate tomorrow. Evaluation of the sales training program must continue at reasonable intervals. Certainly, at some time market and economic changes will necessitate the recycling and redesign of even the best training programs.

SUMMARY Sales training can occur on either a formal or informal basis. Regardless of the type, sales training is virtually universal in American business, and there are two basic reasons for such training: (1) to develop the right work habits, and (2) to offset the effect of detraining.

A good training program should be based upon the following principles of education: (1) a clearly recognized purpose, (2) clarity of presentation, (3) planned repetition, (4) systematic review, (5) orderly development of material, (6) a sensible pace, and (7) trainee participation.

The design of an effective training program requires that sales management answer the following questions:

Which salesmen should be trained and when in their careers?

What should the training program cover?

What should be its form and organization?

309

Who should train salesmen and where does training fit in the organization?

Chapter 10 also noted the general limitations on training programs and provided a checklist for determining the optimum content of a formal sales training program.

Sales training is based on one of two basic training philosophies. Under a conditioned response policy, the salesman is trained in advance in the proper response to any and all problems, conditions, and objections that he may encounter. By contrast, insight response expects the salesman to respond to selling problems on the basis of his personal insights into the nature of each individual selling situation.

Chapter 10 concluded with a discussion of various teaching instruments and techniques, types of sales trainees and locations, and the recycling of training programs.

DISCUSSION/REVIEW QUESTIONS

1. A manufacturer of mechanical and electrical typewriters, adding machines and other office equipment regularly hires sales recruits from high schools and junior and business colleges. Their job is to call on office managers of business firms, banks, insurance companies, and retail establishments in their assigned territories to sell the company's products. They are also expected to provide simple servicing for machines already sold. More complicated repair jobs are handled by a crew of repair specialists. The company is the third ranking manufacturer in its industry; there are six competitors, some of whom are much larger and have more complete product lines.

   What should the training program for the territory salesmen cover? To be successful do the territory salesmen need any qualities that cannot be trained? What does the training program not need to cover? In this company would it make sense to treat all trainees in the same way? What are your reasons for the answers to the questions above?

2. Justify the cost of sales training to someone skeptical of its value.

3. Recommend which of the two training policies, conditioned or insight response, is better for a particular sales group with which you are familiar.

4. For a particular sales force with which you are familiar, justify centralized or decentralized sales training, by staff specialists or field sales personnel or outside experts.

5. Below is a list of products and services. Indicate whether you believe that the product or service is better adapted to conditioned response or insight response selling, and note the reasons for your decision.
   (a) encyclopedias sold door-to-door
   (b) internal communication system in an office
   (c) low-cost term life insurance
   (d) travel tour packages
   (e) cosmetics sold direct to women in their homes
   (f) refrigerators sold in department stores

6. Which teaching method or combinations of methods would you recommend for each of the following situations:
   (a) to impart technical information about a new product
   (b) to help the salesman understand how his selling work affects the other operations of the company and largely determines the company's success or failure
   (c) to improve salesmen's skills in opening and closing a sales call
   (d) to orientate new salesmen in the company's sales reporting system
   (e) to help an individual salesman overcome some bad selling habit
   (f) to inform salesmen of a complex new delivery, warehousing, and billing system to be introduced
   Why would you choose the training techniques you did in these examples?

7. What principles of learning should underlie every sales training program?

8. Identify which specific knowledge, skills, and attitudes can be improved by sales training.

9. Using a company's sales force with which you are familiar analyze its training needs in terms of the model presented in Figure 10-1. Now assess your conclusions by comparing the training program requirements against each other. What is the relative importance of each requirement? Which are critical, which less important, which not required? On the basis of this analysis, which alternative of sales training personnel and location is the best for the sales force you have analyzed?

10. Secure the outline of a sales training plan. To what extent does this plan follow the training principles discussed in this chapter?

11. What might the following evidence indicate about the effectiveness of the formal sales training program for a company that manufactures hardware products sold by company salesmen to retail hardware stores?

> *Retailer to sales supervisor:* "Your salesmen Lewis did a bang-up promotion job for us last month! He set up a floor display of one of your products and arranged local advertising that more than doubled our usual volume."

311

Recent trainee to his supervisor: "They told us in training that the calls-per-day column in the sales activity report form was to be for the month. Now I get a nasty letter from the controller asking me for weekly figures. What gives?"

Supervisor's report: "Salesman Bonner consistently neglects to use the sales promotion materials we provide."

Retailer to supervisor: "That salesman of yours, Dorre, must be the busiest man you have. Don't see him but about twice a year and when he does come he runs out as quick as he came."

Sales manager to salesman's supervisor: "Before he went through the training program, your man Hunt was the dumbest salesman this corporation ever had. Now I see he's third man in your region."

Observer's report on calls with a recent trainee: "Rushes calls, ill at ease, nervous."

Retailer to sales supervisor: "Your regular products are okay. They're good and I can explain them to customers when they ask questions about them. But those new items you've brought out—I don't know the first thing about them."

12. "Only large companies with many salesmen need to bother with sales training." Comment on this statement.
13. Either for your company or for one you know well, compile a list of the skills, knowledge, and attitudes that are needed by the salesmen but which cannot be trained.
14. For the sales force you used above, draw up a specific list of the product knowledge, company knowledge, selling skills, and attitudes that can be trained. How should this training be done?
15. Take some company you know well:
    (a) make a detailed list of the skills, knowledge, and attitudes the salesmen of this company must have.
    (b) opposite your list, indicate which teaching technique (visual aids, lecture, etc.) would be best suited to training each skill, knowledge, or attitude.
    (c) indicate your reasons for the answers to (b).
16. Contact a sales executive who is involved in some way in sales training for his company. Interview him concerning what that company does in regard to evaluating the effectiveness of their sales training. What is your appraisal of their evaluation activities? What would you suggest that they do to improve them? What are your reasons for this?

PART THREE
CASES

CASE 16
QUESTIONING THE INTERVIEWER*

The State Farm Insurance Companies of Bloomington, Illinois, are one of the world's largest insurers. Included are the State Farm Mutual Automobile Insurance Company—the largest automobile insurance underwriter in the United States—the State Farm Life Insurance Com-

*Used by permission of State Farm Insurance Companies.

313

Interview your interviewer.

Interviewing isn't just a chance to display your talents. It's a chance to get information about employers. Don't waste it. Ask questions. To help you, we've listed some things that could affect how much you enjoy your future job. And finding work you enjoy is what it's all about.

1 Do you have a training program? Describe it.

2 What specific responsibilities are trainees given?

3 What percentage of your management . . .
are products of a training program?
come from a specific area or school?
hold graduate degrees?

4 What percentage of your management openings are filled from within?

5 If I join your firm and decide to change fields, can it be done within your firm?

6 What's the cost of living and the housing situation where I'd be employed?

7 Does your company have any additional benefits such as cost of living adjustments, employee group life and medical insurance, company-paid retirement plan?

8 How does your company's size and growth compare with others in your industry?

9 What is your company doing in the way of public service?

10 How does your employee turnover rate compare with other companies?

11 There must be some negative aspects of the job you're offering. What are they?

Interviewing the interviewer is an important step in selecting your career. And because we're one of the world's largest insurers, a State Farm interview is a good way to investigate a number of career fields. Right now we have opportunities in accounting, actuarial science, claims, electronic data processing, investments, law, management and underwriting. Our recruiter will be on your campus . . . . Arrange an interview through your Placement Office. Then bring your questions.

STATE FARM INSURANCE COMPANIES An Equal Opportunity Employer M/F

Regional Offices: Bloomington, Ill. • Jacksonville, Fla. • Marshall, Mich. • W. Lafayette, Ind. • Lincoln, Nebr. • Newark, Ohio • Salem, Ore. • Winter Haven, Fla. • St. Paul, Minn. • Wayne, N.J. • Scarborough, Ont. • Santa Ana, Calif. • Westlake Village, Calif. • Frederick, Md. • Columbia, Mo. • Springfield, Pa. • Murfreesboro, Tenn. • Dallas, Tex. • Charlottesville, Va. • Monroe, La. • Greeley, Colo. • Birmingham, Ala. • Santa Rosa, Calif. • Tempe, Ariz. • Austin, Tex. **Home Offices: Bloomington, Ill.**

Needham, Harper & Steers Inc.
STATE FARM MUTUAL
1973 RECRUITMENT PROGRAM
NEWSPAPERS ONLY _ 560 lines
AD 1156 R 2

pany, the State Farm Fire and Casualty Company, and other wholly owned companion carriers. Like most large companies, State Farm recruits college graduates. The advertisement shown here appeared in college newspapers prior to the campus recruiter's visit.

Joe Mancini, a senior marketing major, saw this advertisement in his college paper. Since Joe was just starting to look for a job, he began to wonder about upcoming interviews. Joe was especially concerned with preparing for an interview next week with a major life insurance company.

ASSIGNMENT

1. Comment on this advertisement as a recruiting technique.
2. What do these questions tell you about the interviewer's function in salesmen's selection?
3. Put yourself in Joe Mancini's place. Which questions do you consider most important? Can you think of other pertinent questions?

CASE 17
TITAN CORPORATION

Professor Howard Jacoby was engaged in research on the recruitment and selection of salesmen. Part of his investigation involved soliciting general statements from a sample of the sales managers of large companies about their recruitment and selection programs. Extracts from the reply of the Titan Corporation follow:

Dear Professor Jacoby:

Mr. George Bell has asked me to reply to your letter. . . .

As you know, we have been engaged in reorganization and Mr. Bell has been traveling 75 per cent of the time, which has left little time for administration in the office. He turned to me for help and since I do 100 per cent of the recruiting for our sales organizations, he felt that I would be in a position to comment on your letter and to offer you information as to how we proceed in the matter of recruitment. . . .

Starting with our basic recruiting efforts, we use a form . . . called "Making a Career in Sales." This is somewhat out of date in terms of titles, but the format still holds. It is used in various universities to inform graduating students of the opportunities that exist in Titan and its four sales and marketing groups. . . . To some degree we emphasize the masters program and are looking for men who will enter marketing positions, which is an office assignment, and who might later be transferred into the field as line salesmen. We have also felt that in view of today's marketing and in view of today's job situation, many men with M.B.A.'s are interested in line sales as a career with the possibilities of moving into a marketing position later. This material is left at many universities and is also filed with a number of specialized employment agencies so that they can identify our needs with the men that these agencies screen.

Following expressed interest by young men, they are interviewed at universities, preselected and brought into our Detroit office for final screening. Much of the interviewing is done by a "seat of the pants" feeling about men. They seem to mentally and physically fit our picture of what a Titan salesman looks like, although this is not determined by height, weight, color, etc. One of the things we look for in these individuals who express an interest in Titan is their knowledge of the company. It is my personal feeling that a man who comes unprepared for an interview would go unprepared to make a sales call. I have expressed the thought a number of times that when a man is looking for a job, he should do his "homework." He should bone up on the company and know a great deal about our products, our sales activities, our revenue, and our progress from a period of five or eight or ten years ago to the present time. He need not know the intimate details of the organizations, but he certainly should have done some reading before he comes for employment or an interview. Failure to do so gives him several negative points.

We do not feel it is our job to sell Titan, rather, it is the applicant's job to sell himself and he should come to the interview as well prepared as if he were making a sales call.

We do look for neatness, of course; verbal skills, intelligence, ability to hold a conversation, to remain calm and poised under some rapid fire questions, all of which is done informally.

We do not use a salesman's job interview guide as such in terms of a check list, although we do have an evaluation form . . . which is completed by each interviewer and the results are then summarized.

We recognize that our interviewing procedure is unstructured, but we have been most successful in the past because we do not rely on the judgment of one individual, but rather, depend upon several who are in different areas of the business. For example, I may ask a manufacturing man to interview a sales candidate, as well as a marketing man, a sales manager, and maybe even a sales trainee. I like to get all the views I can. I like to have these men scrutinized from several different kinds of business approaches. As a result, we have been about 90 per cent successful in our retention for at least two years of the men we hire for our sales training program."

Sincerely yours,

TITAN CORPORATION

William T. James, Manager
Management Development
WTJ/maj

ASSIGNMENT

1. What general qualities would you expect the average M.B.A. graduate to possess? Which of these are relevant to a selling job? Which are not? Why?
2. How should a company such as Titan go about contacting college students before they graduate?
3. Do you agree with Mr. James that "a man who comes unprepared for an interview would go unprepared to make a sales call"? Why?
4. From the letter, it appears Titan has two main sources of sales recruits: universities and employment agencies. Are there other sources they might consider? Do sources of recruits precondition

the kinds of candidates coming from them? If so, how? If not, why not?

5. Mr. James states that many men . . . are interested in line sales . . . with the possibilities of moving into a marketing position later." If this is the case, what effect, if any, should this have on Titan's recruitment and selection program? Why?

6. Of what value is Mr. James' practice of having candidates interviewed by (1) as many people as possible? (2) nonmarketing personnel? (3) sales trainees?

7. From the letter, does it sound to you that Titan has a good recruitment and selection program? Why?

CASE 18
THE SEVEN-UP COMPANY

In selecting salesmen, the Seven-Up Company uses the following interview appraisal form:*

The Seven-Up Company
Interview Evaluation of _____
Date: _____

Recommend _____
Appearance _____
Intelligence _____
   Reasoning/Flexibility
Personality _____
   Self-Confidence/Social Presence/Poise
Ambition _____
   Motivation/Drive/Interest
Interpersonal skills _____
   Get along with others/Cooperative/Accept supervision
Emotional _____
   Stability/Adjustment

_____

*Used by permission of Seven-Up Company.

Verbal facility _____
Background _____
   (Experience/Education)

ASSIGNMENT

1. *Specifically* how would you plan, as an interviewer, to get adequate information on all of these criteria?
2. How valid do you think your conclusions would be? Why?

CASE 19
CUTTER LABORATORIES AND INLAND STEEL COMPANY

Consider these two firms:

1. Cutter Laboratories is a manufacturer of pharmaceutical products distributed nationally. The bulk of their sales is to the veterinary market.

2. Inland Steel is a large manufacturer of specialty steel shapes and forms.

The following questions appear on Cutter's *Application for Professional Employment* and Inland Steel's *Salaried Employment Application Form:**

  a. Quarter of class standing in high school and college
  b. Extracurricular activities engaged in while in high school and college
  c. Professional and community activities
  d. Primary duty while on military service
  e. Reason for terminating each job held
  f. How did you happen to apply for a position with us?
  g. Do you know anyone employed with us?
  h. How much life insurance do you carry?

---

*Used by permission of Inland-Ryerson Construction Products Company and Cutter Laboratories.

ASSIGNMENT

For each of the above employment questions:
1. What is the purpose(s) of seeking this information?
2. How could this information be used in the salesman selection process?
3. How accurate or truthful do you think the answers are likely to be? Why?
4. How could the company check the accuracy or truthfulness of the answer? Would the results of the check be worth the cost of checking? Why or why not?

CASE 20
GEORGE KRUM

George Krum, an undergraduate in marketing at a large midwestern university, was in his second year as a member of the summer sales internship program of the Caldwell Company. Interns lived near company headquarters for the summer. They were assigned minor research and clerical jobs, but their main objective was to "live with" the Caldwell headquarters sales management group. The interns observed the group at work, attended staff meetings, and read correspondence, in order to acquire an understanding of how a "real life" sales organization operated. One element of the program was a regular Friday meeting between the intern and his company sponsor, at which the intern was free to ask questions that grew out of his week's work and at which both exchanged ideas on a variety of sales conditions and problems. At one such meeting with his sponsor, Mr. William Burns, George raised this question:

"Mr. Burns, I've spent some time this week studying our sales application form. I'm wondering about the three personal references you require. It seems to me this is a waste of time. You let the candidate select his own references, and he certainly isn't

320

going to pick people who don't like him. That's a built-in bias. In addition, you don't know the references, so you can't decide what they are worth. You don't even know if the candidate wrote them himself and had three friends sign them. I just don't see the value in references when we know they're biased to start out with, when we don't know the people writing them, and when we don't know whether they're forged or not!"

ASSIGNMENT

1. Assuming George is at least partly right, why does Caldwell, and so many other companies, continue to require personal references from sales candidates?
2. Does a company like Caldwell have any way(s) to check the validity of sales applicant's personal references?
3. Are there any dangers in a company checking applicant's references?

CASE 21
DELTA, INC. (C)

Delta, Inc., a leading national manufacturer of toiletries and jewelry, was searching for a national account salesman. The job description prepared for this position is as follows:

The man we are looking for would be calling on national accounts selling a heavily advertised consumer product that is the leader in its field. Primary emphasis will be on the drug, discount, and variety store chains. He must have experience calling on national multi-store accounts, with a minimum of three to four years key account selling. He must be a mature individual with a college degree, able to initiate and coordinate not only the selling but the servicing of these multi-store chains. The job will entail extensive travel, and he will report directly to the national sales manager.

Robert Simpson, assistant personnel manager, was responsible for recruiting and screening applicants to decide whether to invite them in for a personal interview, the next step in the screening process.

ASSIGNMENT

1. Evaluate the job description prepared for the national account salesman's position. (These are actual resumes.)
2. Compare the three applicants below. Which, if any, should Mr. Simpson invite for a personal interview?
3. Suppose you must interview each of the applicants. What types of questions are suggested by the resumes?

Resume 1

Resume of: James T. Lester
1250 Oxford Street
Springfield, Pennsylvania

JOB OBJECTIVE Position in Sales

Employment

8/66 – Present   SALES REPRESENTATIVE
A Company, Philadelphia, Pa.

Hired as Detailer and promoted in 3 months to Manager of New York State, working out of Syracuse, N.Y.

Adept at opening new accounts through creative sales and customer relation programming.

Met and exceeded Goals 3 of 5 years. Also had several suggestions accepted and used on a national basis.

Created a warm friendly relationship between all types of accounts. Increased sales by motivating wholesaler salesmen to sell our product using all available monies as motivation. Hurt competition by faithfully detailing all national accounts, such as W. T. Grant, Sears, and Woolworth's.

Doubled income in 5 years as a result of Personal achievement and sincere work.

Can, have and do work with all types of wholesalers (Drugs—Tobacco—Sundry—Sports) and chain stores (Drugs—Dept. Stores—Toys)

Recently been promoted to Philadelphia territory.

10/62—8/66   SALESMAN
              B Company, New York

As Salesman for the second largest tea company in the East, I was responsible for achieving or exceeding sales quotas set by management in such a way as to realize or exceed profit goals, as such:
    Maintaining liaison with all classes of trade.
    Coordinating activities with principals and personnel of chain, and jobbers.
Effective in achieving mass displays and introducing new items.
Writing and paying for contractual agreements on merchandising and advertising.

Reason for leaving was to seek a better sales position and better myself.

3/57—1/61   ASSISTANT MANAGER
              Drugstore, Long Island and New Jersey

As Assistant Manager for the largest drugstore chain in the U.S., I had dealings in sundries, drugs, and such items as carried in today's modern drugstores. Displaying and Merchandising items of all seasons, and managing and maintaining a work force as so needed.

Was promoted twice, both times into a higher volume store, assuming more responsibility each time.

Reason for leaving—to become a sales representative and to better myself.

9/64—10/66   SALESMAN—Part-time Men's Dept.
              Department Store—Babylon, L.I.N.Y.
1/62—7/62   SALESMAN Insurance Company

1949—1953   Freeport High School, Freeport, L.I. N.Y.
              Academic Diploma
10/62   Course for Life Insurance
              Passed N.Y. State Test.

PERSONAL

Age: 37   Height 6': 165 lbs., Married: 2 children, ages 7 & 10.
Health   Good; Last Physical 9/70., Finances: Good order, own
            Home and Camper.
Hobbies: Fishing, Boating, Camping, and all family activities.

AFFILIATIONS

1964 – 1966   Past member & on Board of Governors of American Venice Civic Association
1968 – Pres.   Member of BPOE Elks organization.
1971 – Pres.   Treasurer of Civic Club.
                Tribal Chief of Y-Indian Guides.

Resume 2

Name: John R. Martino

Address: *71 East Street*

            Moorestown, New Jersey

TELEPHONE: 784-5613

DATE OF BIRTH: December 1, 1943

MARITAL STATUS: Engaged

MILITARY   OBLIGATIONS: Completed-Honorable   Discharge,   United States Army

EDUCATION

Temple University	Major:	Marketing
Philadelphia, Pennsylvania		Attending Night School
Villanova University	Attended:	1961 – 1963
Villanova, Pennsylvania		Associate Degree
Ocean City High School	Graduated:	June, 1961
Ocean City, New Jersey		

ACTIVITIES AND OFFICES HELD
1. Dale Carnegie Sales Course; placed second in class of sixty students. Also earned several honors.
2. Participated in football and basketball at Villanova University and Ocean City High School.
3. Member of Student Council at Ocean City High School.

EMPLOYMENT EXPERIENCE
1. 1969 – 1971: A Company, Philadelphia, Pennsylvania *Territorial Manager:* Responsible for all Food Service Sales in New Jersey, Eastern Pennsylvania, and Philadelphia area. Also responsible for maintaining stock in-

324

ventories of four hundred items, holding sales meetings for new and present accounts, calling on government and national accounts, and correcting credit violations.

2. 1966–1969: B Company, Philadelphia, Pennsylvania Account Representative Duties included calling on chain headquarters and selling new products and promotions.

Sales Representative: Duties included sales territory and warehouse control.

Resume 3

Confidential Resume of   Alfred J. Wright
                            803 Rose Avenue
                            Media, Pennsylvania

OBJECTIVE: Challenging position in managing responsibilities in sales or marketing.

EDUCATION: Pennsylvania Military College, Chester, Pa.
                  1956 to 1960 Business Administration

PERSONAL: Born-August 30, 1938-Married-2 children-Height 5'11"
                  Weight 190 lbs.

EXPERIENCE: *A Company*—July 1968 to present

Development Representative-Assumed responsibilities for managing new product marketing of plastic tapes. Make customer and end user calls in the territory with gas and oil companies. Promote products through management and professional meeting presentations, and necessary code regulating agencies. Work with distributors and marketing groups in expanding product distribution which has resulted in sales increase each year. Territory consists of 14 states in the northeast U.S. Salary $12,000.

B Corp. — August 1966 to July 1968

Territory sales of laminated plastics-Development of new customers and product adaptation to meet competition of products manufactured from other materials. Sales were made by working with development and project engineering groups then with purchasing department to complete the project and obtain orders for products. Salary $9,000.

C Construction Co. — April 1963 to August 1966 Co-owner and vice president of small construction company in New Jersey. Work involved construction of water and sewer pipe line in N.J. As co-owner my responsibility included personnel management, field supervision, payroll and sales estimating. Salary $10,000.

D Company—July 1960 to April 1963 Sales representative in the Philadelphia and New Jersey area. Duties involved display merchandising and sales of automotive belts and hose to service stations and fleet accounts.

Summer work during school included working for E Company as a Lab wireman. Duties involved assembly and wiring of prototype electronic equipment.

Other Activities—National Association of Corrosion Engineers.

Hobbies—Electronics, woodworking and Lapidary arts.

CASE 22
TRAINING INSURANCE AGENTS

James Alveres, sales training director for a large life insurance company, received a copy of the following article from his supervisor, Robert Santee, vice-president of sales. Mr. Santee suggested that the results of the study had some implications for the company's sales training program.

A CONSUMER'S VIEW OF HIS INSURANCE AGENT*

Eugene M. Johnson
University of Rhode Island

How does today's consumer feel about his insurance agent? Although this question is complex and not easy to answer, a recent study of

*Originally published in Insurance News, May 1969. Reprinted by permission of the publisher.

buying behavior provides some answers. The findings, which are the result of over 50 in-depth interviews with consumers and a larger number of written responses, prove that the agent is still the key to successful insurance marketing.

What do buyers want? Most insurance buyers want three things from their agent: prompt attention, rapid service, and personal attention.

Prompt Attention

Of prime importance to the consumers surveyed is prompt attention. Whether he is buying a new policy, changing an existing policy, or processing a claim, the buyer expects, and demands, immediate action.

It appears that new patterns of social and economic behavior, which place added stress on the consumers' time, have strengthened his demands for prompt attention. When an agent fails to respond to his customer's requests quickly, he usually ends up with a dissatisfied customer. In fact, several consumers related their displeasure when they had to wait several days to hear from their agent.

Rapid Service

Time is also a factor in the buyer's demand for rapid service. Not only does the buyer expect the agent to respond to his requests immediately, but he also wants satisfaction quickly.

In particular, insurance buyers are concerned with the slowness with which claims are processed. Although this is usually not the agent's fault, he, as the customer's prime contact with the company, must shoulder the blame. It is the agent's responsibility to smooth over customers' complaints about delays.

Personal Attention

Finally, and perhaps most important to the marketing of an intangible such as insurance, is the buyer's desire for personal attention. A satisfied customer talks about "his" insurance agent. He describes his agent as friendly, cooperative, and personable.

The buyer expects his agent to be more than a salesman; he should be a personal friend, a trusted adviser, a financial expert.

The desire for a personal relationship with the seller is common for most buyers of services; this is particularly true for insurance buyers. Insurance is complicated, and it is difficult for the layman to understand the complexities of insurance. In fact, many consumers admit they know very little about insurance.

Also, buyers realize that they are unable to judge the quality of competitive insurance plans. Because he lacks knowledge, the buyer feels his purchase of insurance is risky. To reduce his perceived risk, the buyer tries to select an agent in whom he has confidence. He substitutes trust in the agent for information when he buys insurance. This requires him to become personally involved with his insurance agent.

Guidelines for Selling

This study points to the need to reverse the recent trend to mass merchandising of insurance. Buyers want personalization. In several instances, consumers expressed disappointment with the loss of close personal contact with their insurance agents. They resented the increasing impersonalization of insurance marketing.

Thus it seems that the agent should assume a larger role in insurance marketing, rather than a lesser one. To increase his effectiveness, the agent must know his customers as individuals, he must develop close personal relationships with his customers, and he must be a professional salesman.

Successful selling requires a thorough knowledge of the buyer—his needs, attitudes, buying behavior, and so forth. It is imperative that an insurance agent thoroughly understand his customers. The insurance buyer wants more than a policy. He wants advice, assistance, and extra personal attention. Unless the agent understands exactly what is expected of him, he cannot meet these demands.

Recent developments in insurance marketing strengthen the case for added customer knowledge. Innovations such as homeowner's policies, family plans, and convenient payment plans have been introduced. However, these innovations must be adapted to individual customers. This cannot be done unless the agent knows his customers individually. He must be customer oriented.

Develop Personal Relationships

As noted, the intangibility of insurance raises the value of the agent's personal relationships with his customers. Buyers want to be personally involved in the purchase of insurance. They want a policy tailored to their personal needs.

However, it is usually the personal contact, rather than the actual policy, that leads to satisfaction with an insurance purchase. Nothing is more important to insurance marketing than the personal interactions between the agent and his customers.

The insurance agent must never forget that he is selling a personal service. The buyer actively seeks personal attention. He wants to be treated like an individual, not like just another name on the company's records.

Exhibit Professionalism

For many years the insurance industry and many companies have promoted the agent as a professional financial adviser. This strategy has successfully upgraded the image of the insurance agent. However, advertising is not enough. The agent himself must adopt a professional orientation.

This study revealed that consumers are quite particular about their insurance agent. A majority of the respondents pointed out that the agent's reputation is a major factor in their insurance buying decision. The buyer needs to have confidence in his agent. He expects his agent to be a professional.

Developing a professional approach should be a major goal of an insurance agent. He must strive to create an impression of competency, honesty, and sincerity. He must develop close, professional relationships with customers.

In short, an insurance agent must be more than a salesman. He must be a counselor who advises his customers of their financial obligations and explains the complexities of insurance protection. This requires a well-informed agent and an imaginative, problem-solving approach to selling.

ASSIGNMENT

1. Based upon the information presented in the article, outline a sales training program.

2. What other areas of sales management might be affected by the suggested guidelines for selling?
3. How might a training program for independent insurance agents differ from a training program for company salesmen?

CASE 23
KRUSER COMPANY (A)

The Kruser Company was a medium-sized manufacturer of plastic billets, sheets, and forms. The bulk of its business was in finished forms such as football helmet shells, various surgical implements, trash baskets, automobile gear shift shafts and knobs, bicycle handle grips, and a wide variety of other forms sold to twenty-five different industries. Company sales were $30 million per year.

The company employed what it termed a *mixed* sales and distribution strategy for its national sales force of 200 men. Each salesman was assigned a territory and was responsible for all company sales in his area. In industries where efficient channels of distribution existed, the company relied on established middlemen (such as brokers, manufacturer's agents, and wholesalers) to sell the products. An example would be hospital supply dealers in the clinic and hospital market.

In markets where distribution was diversified, such as trash baskets, the company relied on its territory salesmen to effect mass distribution on the largest and most economical scale possible. In their territories, salesmen were responsible for promoting sales with both types of customers.

The company had about a 15 per cent turnover in the sales force per year, necessitating the training of approximately 30 new men a year.

All formal sales training was done at headquarters under the supervision of a six-man corporate sales training department whose chief was Norman George. In his staff capacity, George reported directly to Phil Manfred, the vice-president of sales.

Recently field and headquarters sales managers had become increasingly dissatisfied with the existing training program for new hires. Mr. George concurred in this. As a result, Mr. Manfred had ordered the sales training department to undertake a thorough field study of training needs and problems and to propose a new salesman entrance training program.

Shortly after he ordered the review and revision of the new salesman training program, Mr. Manfred received a memo from the president. The sense of the memo was that because of the general economic downturn, all costs (including sales) would have to be reduced by at least 10 per cent.

ASSIGNMENT

1. If you were in Mr. George's position, *specifically* what kind of information would you try to get to assist you in the formulation of a new training program proposal?
2. Why would you want such information? How would you plan to use it?
3. Would you consider the *sequence* in which you gathered information to be of any importance? Why, or why not?
4. How, if at all, should the president's memo influence Mr. Manfred's thinking about revision of the sales training program? Why?
5. Should Mr. Manfred let Mr. George know about the president's memo? Why or why not?

CASE 24
KRUSER COMPANY (B)*

After six months of research and study, Kruser Company's training department submitted a sales training proposal which was then put out for analysis and comment by all echelons of the sales force, from salesmen to Phil Manfred. A series of meetings were held at all levels

---

*For company information see Kruser Company (A), the preceding case study.

for the purpose of gathering suggestions and reactions to the proposed new training program.

Mr. Manfred was 63 years old. A high-school graduate, he had worked in the plastics industry since its inception. Starting as a territory salesman with Kruser, he worked his way through territory, district, and regional sales managerships in twenty-five years to become Kruser's vice-president of sales. He was considered "crusty" and "tough and hard-nosed" by his superiors and subordinates. They also considered him the "best salesman in the company," and although not the perfect administrator, a man who was completely sincere, fair, and dedicated to his job. He was respected and liked by all of his associates.

After the final version of the new training program had been reviewed and approved by all levels of the sales force and by management, Phil Manfred and Norman George met on a Friday afternoon session to arrange the details of implementing the new program. About 5:30 P.M. all of the details were wrapped up, and they began to chat while they relaxed. After awhile the following conversation took place:

Manfred: "You know, Norm, I think we've got a winner of a program in this new revision."

George: "I hope so, Mr. Manfred. We've all put enough into it to make it a winner."

(Pause)

Manfred: "But the whole idea of training salesmen to sell has never come across for me. Sure, you have to tell them all about the customers and our products, the competition, our prices, delivery schedules — all that.

"But after that . . . (pause) I'm just not so sure what else you can do for them."

George: "You mean about selling skills?"

Manfred: "That's it. Nobody ever told me anything about how to sell, I learned for myself from the best teacher there is — experience. (Pause.) It doesn't seem I've done too bad learning that way. Guess I was a born salesman who learned from experience. I just don't think any kind of training will make a salesman and there's no fancy training that's as good as knock-em-down field experience. What do you think, Norm?"

ASSIGNMENT

1. Do you think salesmen "are born, not made"? Why?
2. What do you think are the relative advantages and disadvantages of field experience for training? Why?
3. Why do you think Mr. Manfred believes as he does?
4. How should Mr. George reply to Mr. Manfred's question? Why?

CASE 25
TWIN C COMPANY

Charles Callahan was the owner and president of Twin C Company, a small wholesale distributor of power saws, power lawnmowers, and similar equipment. The company had nine salesmen, and Mr. Callahan served also as sales manager.

For several years Mr. Callahan had been concerned over the lack of formal sales training in his organization. Each new salesman was orientated by Mr. Callahan and received on-the-job training, but there was no other initial training program. In addition, monthly half-day sales meetings were held during which some sales training was done.

While discussing this concern with a business acquaintance, Mr. Callahan was advised to contact the marketing department of the local state university for assistance. He called and arranged a meeting with John Pomaski, a professor of marketing and sales management. After discussing his concern for sales training with Professor Pomaski, the two men agreed that Professor Pomaski would submit a proposal for a sales training program.

The following proposal arrived a week later. Mr. Callahan must notify Professor Pomaski of his decision within a few days.

PROPOSED SALES TRAINING SEMINAR

PREPARED FOR
TWIN C COMPANY
MR. CHARLES CALLAHAN, PRESIDENT

SUBMITTED BY DR. JOHN POMASKI
ASSOCIATE PROFESSOR OF MARKETING
STATE UNIVERSITY

INTRODUCTION

The following proposed seminar is a twelve-hour program designed specifically for the salesmen of Twin C Company. It is expected that this program
will partially fulfill this company's need for continued training for its sales
force. As such, the proposed program will benefit both the company and
the individual salesmen.

The importance of the salesman as the company's primary connection with
its customers has long been recognized. The salesman is the man in the
middle; he is responsible for communicating the company's sales message
to its customers, as well as for providing feedback on his firm's products
and marketing program. The objectives of this seminar will therefore be
twofold: to assist the salesman with selling problems and to emphasize the
role of communications in selling. Emphasis will be upon problem solving,
and the student will be presented with situations in which he will be chal-
lenged to think. These problem situations will be designed to compel the
participant to go beyond his role as a salesman and consider problems from
an overall marketing point of view.

334

SEMINAR OUTLINE

The following outline is designed to fit either a two-day format or six evening sessions. It includes six sessions, of which the first is an introduction and orientation period and the last is devoted to conclusions.

SESSION 1   INTRODUCTION & ORIENTATION

  A. *Introduction to the seminar*
    1. Brief description of program
    2. Objectives

  B. *Salesman and his role in marketing*
    1. Nature and scope of marketing and its environment
    2. Marketing concept
    3. Marketing mix
    4. Personal selling as an integral part of the marketing mix

SESSION 2   PERSONAL SELLING

  A. *The selling process*
    1. Understanding the buyer
    2. Salesman as a communicator
    3. What the salesman needs to know

  B. *Sales problems* (utilize case studies of selling situations)

SESSION 3   SALES TECHNIQUES

  A. *Prospecting and preparing sales calls*
  B. *Sales presentation*
    1. Developing an approach
    2. Handling objections
    3. Closing

  C. Follow-up

SESSION 4   WORKING WITH RETAILERS

  A. *Understanding the final stages of the distributive process*

  B. *Basic merchandising strategy of your retail accounts*

335

C. *Positive points of customer relations*

D. *Educating your accounts to sell more*

SESSION 5 CREDIT POLICIES

A. *Credit as a marketing tool*
  1. Part of product "package"
  2. Using credit to sell

B. *Credit problems*
  1. What to look for
  2. Some easy guidelines

SESSION 6 SUMMARY & CONCLUSIONS

A. *Summary of the program and suggestions for fully utilizing the material covered*

B. *Panel discussion — question and answer session with faculty members*

BUDGET

Faculty salaries	$ 700
Books and other materials	150
General overhead	150
Total	$1000

ASSIGNMENT

1. Evaluate the proposed sales training seminar. What are its strengths and weaknesses?
2. Should Mr. Callahan accept the proposal?
3. What should be the role of formal sales training in a small company like Twin C?

PART FOUR: DIRECTING THE SALES FORCE

CHAPTER ELEVEN
LEADERSHIP
AND
SUPERVISION
IN SALES
MANAGEMENT

The most difficult task any sales manager faces is the supervision of his subordinates. The task is exceptionally complex and difficult, because he cannot assume that his personnel are strongly motivated day in and day out. The salesmen may be scattered across a large geographical area, and they may offer a broad product line to serve diverse markets. Their selling job is often technical and highly competitive, and the business expenses they control are large. However, failure to identify the needs of salesmen and to provide effective leadership will result in increased turnover, lower productivity of the sales force, and unnecessary selling expense.[1]

This chapter will examine sales executive leadership and supervision, to provide a better understanding of why salesmen do or do not follow their supervisors well. To lead salesmen effectively, one needs a thorough understanding of human behavior, of the concepts of motivation, and of how to apply them. Chapter 11 also identifies the important human relations skills of good sales leadership and indicates how these skills can be improved for greater efficiency and lower cost in sales force operation.

---

[1]A good discussion of the difficulties of sales supervision is contained in Charles L. Lapp, *Training and Supervising Salesmen* (Englewood Cliffs, N.J.: Prentice-Hall, Inc., 1960). The relationship between sales performance and supervision is examined in W. Cameron Caswell, "Marketing Effectiveness and Sales Supervision," *California Management Review*, vol. 7 (Fall 1964), pp. 39–44.

UNDERSTANDING BEHAVIOR

Human behavior and its causes are complex. One compilation of scientific findings observes that

> Human behavior itself is so enormously varied, so delicately complex, so obscurely motivated that many people despair of finding valid generalizations to explain and predict the actions, thoughts, and feelings of human beings — despair, that is, of the very possibility of constructing a science of human behavior.[2]

Elements of Behavior

Despite the barriers to understanding, behavioral scientists have tried to find valid generalizations about human behavior. Industrial psychologist Harold J. Leavitt suggests that three major assumptions are inherent in human behavior:[3]

1. Human behavior is *caused*, or influenced, by outside forces, primarily the environment and heredity.
2. Human behavior is *directed*; it is pointed toward a goal or desire.
3. Human behavior is *motivated*; some form of "push," "need," or "motive" underlies all forms of behavior.

The principles of causality, direction, and motivation apply to all forms of behavior. For instance, the successful salesman is able to relate the features of his product to the customer's buying motives. *This is purposeful behavior.* From a management perspective, one must recognize that the effectiveness of a person's performance is related to the extent to which performance achieves a goal or is a means to attaining a goal. The role of the sales manager is to influence their behavior by providing his salesmen with a stimulus, or cause, for acting. Figure 11-1 shows this relationship graphically.

---

[2]Bernard Berelson and Gary A. Steiner, *Human Behavior: An Inventory of Scientific Findings* (New York: Harcourt Brace and Janovich, 1964), p. 3.
[3]Harold J. Leavitt, *Managerial Psychology*, 2nd. ed. (Chicago: University of Chicago Press, 1964).

FIGURE 11–1
Operation of the Elements of Behavior

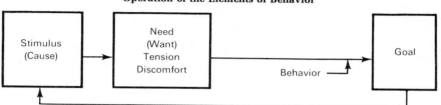

Source: Harold J. Leavitt, *Managerial Psychology*, 2nd. ed. (Chicago: The University of Chicago Press, 1964), p. 9.

Motivation, then, is at the heart of sales management (see Figure 11-2). It is simply the *how to* of getting salesmen to do their job well.

FIGURE 11–2

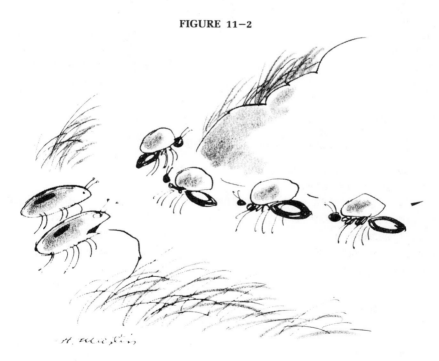

"Find out what motivates them."

Source: Reprinted by permission from *Sales Management*, The Marketing Magazine. Copyright 1968.

Motives are the *whys* of behavior. A sales manager must understand the whys of his salesmen's behavior before he takes steps to lead and motivate them. Incentives, or stimuli, must be developed to fit the specific needs of salesmen.

THEORIES OF MOTIVATION

How can the sales manager identify the specific motives of his subordinates when every person's needs and life goals are unique to the individual? Fortunately, there is general agreement that everyone's needs fall into a universal pattern.

Primary and Secondary Needs

Psychologists differentiate between primary and secondary needs. *Primary needs* are physical needs which must be satisfied immediately. Hunger and protection from excessive heat or cold are examples of these needs. *Secondary needs* are those which can be satisfied at a later time. Frequently, secondary needs are psychological or have been learned from others. The need for recognition and love are secondary needs.

Rational and Emotional Needs

Another useful distinction is between rational and emotional needs. *Rational needs* are based on reason. A person's desire to purchase a Volkswagen because of its low price and economy of operation illustrates the dominance of a rational buying motive. On the other hand, another person's purchase of a Cadillac may result from his *emotional needs* for status and prestige. It is frequently quite difficult to identify exactly which needs are based on emotion and which are based on reason.

A Hierarchy of Needs

Abraham H. Maslow, a professor at Brandeis University and a prominent student of behavior, has developed a theory which arranges needs in order of their importance.[4] He argues that needs on the lowest level must be satisfied before higher level needs become important motivating forces. When a need is essentially satisfied, it ceases to be a motivator of behavior.

For instance, an explorer lost in the desert for several days without food has only one thing on his mind. He is hungry and will do anything for food. Once his desire for food has been satisfied, other needs become important, such as the desire to reach civilization. Likewise, a salesman who has been on the road for several weeks will be concerned only with getting back home. However, after the weekend, he will be ready to resume his calls.

Each of us has his own hierarchy of needs. For an ambitious young executive, personal achievement is the dominant driving force. He may neglect his family, his private social life, and even his health to get ahead. However, his wife's needs may be quite different. Her goal may be social status. She must be a member of the country club; her children must go to prestigious schools; she shops at only the exclusive boutiques.

Often, an individual's needs are in conflict. A salesman wants to make more money which means making calls at night. However, his son is a Little League ballplayer, and the salesman also wants to spend more time at home. He must choose between his conflicting desires for the material satisfactions which additional income will provide and the inner satisfaction from watching his son play ball.

Maslow's hierarchy of needs includes five levels. As a theory of motivation, its contribution is to identify and rank the motivating forces. As shown in Figure 11-3, a person's needs are physiological, safety and security, social, ego, and self-fulfillment.

Physiological Needs. Physiological needs include the basic needs for food, clothing, shelter, and the like. Also called the *tissue* needs, these are built-in needs required for normal functioning of the body. As the first step in the need hierarchy, these needs must ordinarily be satisfied before those needs above will significantly influence a man's behavior. This is to say that praise of a salesman's performance (an

---

[4]Abraham H. Maslow, "A Theory of Human Motivations," in *Motivation and Personality*, 2nd ed. (New York: Harper and Row, 1970).

FIGURE 11-3
Maslow's Hierarchy of Needs

Source: Based on Abraham H. Maslow, "A Theory of Human Motivations" in *Motivation and Personality*, 2nd. ed. (New York, Harper and Row, 1970).

ego need) has no motivating power if he is not earning enough to feed himself and his family at a satisfactory level. Physiological needs are not a motivating force when they are totally satisfied.

Safety and Security Needs. Protection from threat, danger, and deprivation can be primary motivating forces. These are activated when a person is uncertain about his own or his family's well-being or fearful for his job. In today's fast-paced world, many men are especially concerned with being prepared for what the future may bring. Life insurance, pension plans, and health and accident policies are a few of the incentives which appeal to this level of needs.

Social Needs. Social needs are satisfied by relationships with other people. Man is a social animal; everyone has a desire to belong, to be accepted, to give and receive friendship. Company bowling teams, office picnics, and the like all serve to enhance the social aspects of a job.

Ego Needs. Ego needs are directed toward enhancing or gratifying one's ego or one's self-image. One type of ego need is the desire for self-esteem, self-respect, self-confidence, and achievement. A person wants to feel that he is *somebody.* He also desires the esteem of others. He wants status, recognition, and appreciation from his peers. Status in an organization may be conveyed by the man's title, the size of his office, his furniture, and special privileges and responsibilities.

344

Self-Fulfillment Needs. The final level of needs is defined as those desires for continued self-development. Self-fulfillment is the wish to succeed simply for the sake of accomplishment, not for material gain or recognition. Because other needs take precedence, very few people are strongly driven by self-fulfillment needs. Leonardo da Vinci, Paul Gauguin, and others are the exceptions rather than the rule.

Maslow's hierarchy is a useful tool for analyzing human motivation. It shows that a need is an effective motivator only when it is activated; that frustration of an activated need acts negatively on productivity and morale; and that satisfaction of an activated need acts positively on productivity and morale.

THE MANAGEMENT OF MOTIVATION

The ethic or philosophy of American business is subtly but drastically changing. Business at present is witnessing the coexistence of two different kinds of salesmen who, for sake of simplicity, might be characterized as the *Puritans* and the *New Generation.* The *Puritans* are salesmen of the Great Depression generation, who as children witnessed their parents trying to survive the economic disaster or as young adults tried to find jobs that did not exist.[5] The *New Generation* have never known real economic deprivation, or what it is to be hungry and unemployed.

For the Puritan generation of salesmen, various forms of monetary incentives—increased take-home pay, fringe benefits, seniority rights—are still important motivators, although they are influenced also by nonmonetary factors.

For the New Generation of salesmen, various forms of monetary incentives are less important. For them the important motivators are internal drives related to the challenge of the job, participation in organizational decision making, and the relationship between the individual and the company. Traditional incentives are needed primarily to maintain good morale.[6] These various forms of incentives will be further explained so as to more clearly explain what motivates salesmen.

---

[5]The problem of remotivating senior salesmen is discussed in Daniel D. Howard, "What to Do When Salesmen Run Out of Steam," *Management Review* (September 1967), pp. 4–11.
[6]Some managers will argue that the 1970–1972 "mini-recession" served to improve the work attitudes of many younger employees as the number of job opportunities dwindled.

Job Challenge

Whether a person's job is challenging and interesting is one key to motivation. Psychologist Frederick Herzberg observes:

> The argument for job enrichment can be summed up quite simply: If you have someone on a job, use him. If you can't use him on the job, get rid of him, either via automation or by selecting someone with lesser ability. If you can't use him and can't get rid of him, you will have a motivation problem.[7]

Fortunately, the challenge of selling is an effective motivator for salesmen. Being competitive, most salesmen rise to the competitive aspects of selling. They are motivated by factors which are intrinsic to the job—achievement, responsibility, growth, enjoyment of the work itself, and earned recognition. A comprehensive study of 1029 sales executives indicated that *job content* was a major factor affecting performance and turnover.[8]

Participation

One means of providing salesmen with a challenging job is to encourage them to take an active part in decision making. Salesmen should be involved in decisions which affect them. When salesmen are allowed to participate, they are more willing to accept management decisions.

Each salesman should have a part in setting his quota or other performance evaluation standards.[9] Each salesman should have a different quota, based on conditions within his territory. Since he is most familiar with his territory, the salesman should be involved. Also, if he helps to set his goal, he will be anxious to achieve his quota.

---

[7]Frederick Herzberg, "One More Time: How Do you Motivate Employees?" *Harvard Business Review*, vol. 46 (January–February, 1968), p. 62.

[8]Derek A. Newton, "Get the Most Out of Your Sales Force," *Harvard Business Review*, vol. 47 (September–October, 1969), pp. 130–143.

[9]An interesting account of EMKO Company's adoption of management by objectives is reported in James O. Leathers, "Applying Management By Objectives to the Sales Force," *Personnel*, vol. 44 (September–October, 1967), pp. 45–50.

Active participation by field salesmen will have another major benefit: problem solutions will be improved. The old adage, "Two heads are better than one," is true. By encouraging participation, the sales manager will bring the collective thinking of several persons to bear on a given sales problem.

Being a Part of the Company

Equally important to successful motivation is making the salesman feel that he is an integral part of the company. If a salesman is to be motivated, he must be sold on his company, his colleagues, his customers, and the products or services he is selling. If he understands his role in the company, the salesman will make the company's goal his goal. He will think in terms of *my company*. He will relate to the total company, not just to his field sales office.

Morale

Morale and motivation are closely intertwined. *Morale* relates to the salesman's attitudes toward his job—the sum of his feelings toward his supervisor, his pay, his fellow employees, and other job-related factors—and the sum of his attitudes toward himself. In general, morale is determined by needs which are peripheral to the job. Contributions to morale are such factors as company policy and administration, supervision, work conditions, pay, relationships with peers, and the man's personal life.

For example, salesman Ralph Sancho covers a Texas territory in which the weather is especially humid. He has requested an air-conditioner for his company car, but company policy forbids this. Although an air-conditioner is unlikely to greatly motivate Ralph, the lack of one has not helped his overall attitude. He is dissatisfied with his job; he is making fewer calls and spending more time at home; and his sales are beginning to suffer.

As Ralph's situation indicates, successful selling performance depends on good morale. Ralph's sales manager will find it difficult to motivate Ralph until the question of the air conditioner is resolved. Morale has a two-edged impact. *Creating good morale will not neces-*

347

sarily motivate a salesman. However, unless a salesman is generally content with his job, he will not be receptive to attempts to motivate him.

Discipline

Orderly behavior is necessary in every organization. This does not mean that a sales manager must play the role of a strict schoolmaster, but rather that he must establish certain standards for his salesmen. These are related to their conformance with rules, procedures, and acceptable social behavior. In any organization individual desires must generally conform to the wishes of the group.

The methods by which salesmen are influenced to conduct themselves in an orderly manner are negative in nature. It is part of every sales manager's job to take remedial action when a salesman's behavior and performance are not acceptable. He should discipline his men when reports are turned in late, when instructions are ignored, when social taboos are violated, or when dishonest actions are committed.

Every sales manager must have an established disciplinary procedure to follow for specific violations. Negative incentives can take the form of deferred promotion, demotion, transfer to a less desirable position, withdrawing merit pay increases, and deprivation of regular or special assignments. The most drastic form of discipline is discharge. The field sales manager usually has the authority to fire an unsatisfactory salesman. This action is taken only after other alternatives have been exhausted.

In general, negative incentives are not effective motivators of behavior. Disciplinary procedures are intended to prevent salesmen from doing certain things, not to stimulate them. Although absolutely necessary to the smooth running of the sales organization, discipline cannot positively motivate salesmen.

SALES MANAGEMENT LEADERSHIP AND SUPERVISION

Thus far, the chapter has been concerned with the motivation and morale of salesmen. Now let us turn to a closely related condition, that of the sales supervisor as a *leader* of men. This section will deal with such critical questions as:

1. What determines the degree to which salesmen cooperate with their supervisors?
2. What are the conditions under which the supervisor must be an effective leader of salesmen?
3. What *roles* must the sales supervisor play in leading his men?
4. Why do some salesmen follow their supervisor-leaders enthusiastically and to the best of their capabilities while others are stubborn, reluctant, and unproductive?
5. What are the results of poor leadership by the sales supervisor?

The Basic Condition of Sales Supervision

Most sales supervisors rise from the ranks of salesmen, so that their job changes completely when they are promoted from salesman to supervisor.Unfortunately, too many new sales managers fail to make the transition.[10]

Salesmen are evaluated and rewarded, or punished, on the basis of *how they do* — how they sell, cover their territories, service customers, and so forth. In short, they stand or fall on their own personal sales performance record. On the other hand, sales managers are evaluated and rewarded or punished not on how well they themselves sell, but on how their salesmen perform.[11] *The job of the salesmen is to sell. The job of the sales manager is to supervise the selling activities of his salesmen.* If his salesmen do a good job, the sales manager is successful. If they do a poor job, he has failed. A critical element in the success or failure of a supervisor's salesmen is the quality of his leadership.

The Critical Importance of Salesmen's Cooperation

In leading and supervising salesmen, the degree to which they cooperate with their sales supervisor is of immense importance.

One may ask why this is so. What difference does it make whether the salesmen cooperate fully or only partially with their sales man-

---

[10]This is pointed out in R. A. Johnson, "Motivating a Far-Flung Sales Force," *Personnel*, vol. 45 (February 1968), pp. 29–32.
[11]The promotion of a firm's leading salesman to a sales management position is examined through three case studies in "Should a Top Salesman Go Into Management?" *Sales Management* (December 1, 1970), pp. 31–32.

ager? Is not this matter of cooperation an idealistic question more suited to ethics and religion than to realistic, profit-seeking business?
What is the reason for this concern about cooperation in sales executive leadership? Why must salesmen be *led* instead of simply *directed*? Imagine a line that would measure the degree of cooperation a
salesman gives to his manager. The line would extend from zero (no
cooperation at all) to infinity (complete cooperation). Somewhere on
the line would be a *cut-off point*. This point would represent the absolute minimum amount of cooperation that the sales supervisor would
tolerate. If the salesman does not cooperate at least to that degree, he
will be fired. The cooperation scale and cut-off point might resemble
the drawing in Figure 11 – 4.

FIGURE 11–4
Scale of Degree of Salesman's Cooperation

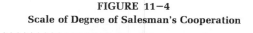
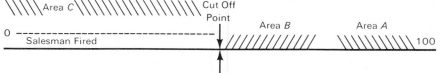

If the salesman cooperates with management to any degree in Area
C, below the cut-off point, he will be fired. If he cooperates to any
degree in Areas A or B, he will be retained. But there are two important observations that illustrate why the degree of the salesman's cooperation in either Area A or Area B is so critical:

1. Within Area A–B (above the cut-off point) *the salesman is
   free to elect the degree to which he will cooperate.*
2. *Where* in Area A–B he elects to cooperate is importantly a
   result of how well or how poorly he is led and supervised by
   his sales manager.

In every sales supervisory situation there is a point at which a salesman will be fired if he does not produce a minimum degree of cooper-

ation with his sales manager. Above that point, however, he is free to choose the degree of cooperation he will deliver. This choice is essentially determined by how well he is led and supervised by his sales manager. When properly supervised, salesmen will *want* to do the things that will achieve the company's goals.

The Costs of Less Than Complete Cooperation by Salesmen

Since salesmen may choose the degree to which they will cooperate with their sales manager (above the cut-off point), does it make any real difference if they elect a low or a high level of cooperation? If there were no dollar-and-cents difference between minimum and maximum cooperation by salesmen, then there would be no need to be concerned with leadership and supervision as an important determinant of the level of the salesmen's cooperation.

The fact is that when the salesman elects to operate at a low level of cooperation, because he is poorly led and supervised, he generates real costs that could be avoided by good leadership and supervision. When a salesman chooses to cooperate with his supervisor in Area *A*, rather than in Area *B*, he generates the costs of

lost business;
damaged customer relations;
impaired corporate image;
increased sales expenses;
poor quality competitive and market intelligence;
high personnel turnover costs;
lowered morale;
absenteeism;
customer complaints;
work completed late.

THE ESSENCE OF SALES LEADERSHIP

Many authors and researchers of executive leadership claim to be able to prescribe formulas or *golden rules* of leadership that are applicable to any and all supervision problems. However, the fact is that all sales leadership problems are essentially unique unto themselves. No two sales supervision problems are exactly the same. Consequently, no leadership *principles* are applicable to every leadership problem. Rather, understanding leadership and developing skill in it depend upon

1. an understanding of why salesmen follow (or do not follow) to the full extent of their capacity;
2. mastery of the skills of creating and maintaining ardent followership, which are the human relations skills of leadership.

The Environment of Sales Management Leadership

The sales manager must exercise leadership under two kinds of conditions, *routine* and *emergency*. In leading and supervising salesmen under *routine conditions*, the sales manager must deal with day-to-day, repetitive conditions. Customers must be called upon, orders written and submitted, customer service must be provided, and reports filled out. This is the daily, undramatic, repetitive business of sales supervision. In other circumstances, a sales manager must lead in *emergency conditions:* a competitor introduces an unexpected new product or cuts his price, a storm or flood destroys a field sales installation, a government agency passes a ruling that challenges the firm's price schedule. These are sudden, unexpected, nonrepetitive, dramatic conditions. The fact that the sales executive must lead and supervise personnel under both routine and emergency conditions places several important requirements on the sales supervisor as a leader.

The sales manager must be skilled in differentiating routine from emergency conditions. Of course, many emergency sales situations are quickly and dramatically known. It requires no special insight to realize that when a competitor cuts his price 20 per cent, an emergency exists that requires prompt and effective retaliatory action. However, not all sales management problems are so obvious and dramatic. Frequently what appears to be a normal and routine sales situation in fact hides an emergency. A change in a competitor's advertising theme may simply be an effort to improve communication with their customers (routine), or it may be the first step in the introduction of a new product (emergency). The leader must be skilled at recognizing what is a true routine situation and what is a seemingly routine situation that is hiding an emergency.

The sales manager must manage routine operations in a way that prepares himself and his salesmen for effective reaction to future emergency conditions. To an important extent the management of routine selling operations is a rehearsal or training exercise for effective reaction to emergency conditions. If routine, day-to-day sales executive leadership is done properly, it becomes an unconscious habit, requiring no special thought or attention by the supervisor. In addition, it demonstrates to the salesmen that the supervisor knows his business. Consequently, when an emergency strikes, the supervisor and his salesmen are prepared, as their experience under routine conditions has geared them for effective reaction to emergency.

The sales manager must not create artificial emergencies, but must save his subordinates' extra effort for real emergencies. Physically and psychologically the human body and mind have special emergency systems built into them. Under conditions of true emergency, one generates extra physical energy, mental alertness, and attention. In emergencies an individual can do things he would never believe himself capable of: a 98-pound woman can lift a stalled automobile off her child, and a computer engineer-salesman can work 36 straight hours to repair a customer's equipment so that the payroll can go out on time. The skillful supervisor, however, recognizes that his followers' extra efforts should be conserved for true emergencies. He does not try to make himself a hero to his superiors by constantly driving his salesmen under self-created emergency conditions.

The sales manager must be skillful in leading under routine conditions. Leading salesmen under routine conditions is extremely difficult. The reason is that emergency conditions usually involve built-in penalties that compensate for a considerable amount of poor leadership. Routine conditions, however, do not usually contain such penalties. Two examples illustrate these conditions. In Company *A*, sales are down and management has decided that unless sales can be substantially increased, retrenchment in the sales force will be necessary. Some salesmen will have to be laid off. To be sure, the sales manager has to exert leadership, but the situation itself contains penalties for the salesmen (they will lose their jobs) that would compensate for a considerable amount of poor leadership by their supervisor. By contrast, in Company *B*, every salesman on the sales force has exceeded his quarterly quota by at least 10 per cent, and there are three weeks remaining in the quarter. The second situation requires considerably more leadership skill from the supervisor than the first, because there is no built-in penalty for poor followership.

THE SALES MANAGER'S LEADERSHIP ROLES

In sales management there is no such thing as the leadership role. Rather, leadership is multi-roled. The supervisor must be capable of playing one of several roles depending on what the situation requires.

Role playing in executive leadership is not unfair, unscrupulous, or double dealing. Quite the contrary, it is the honest and responsible way for a leader to behave. Consider an analogy. What roles does a parent play for his children? Most people would say that the parent must play many roles: those of disciplinarian, encourager, loving stabilizer, an example of what it is to be an adult, provider, advisor, educator, and perhaps several more. Note that these are all different roles. Is it wrong that the parent plays these several roles at different times and under different conditions? Is it immoral, unethical for the parent to shift from one role to another as the occasion demands? Of course not. In fact, when one considers the matter carefully, *it would be wrong for the parent not to play these several roles, not to shift from one to another as the situation requires.*

So it is with the sales manager in the leadership of salesmen. Suppose that one of his salesmen wants advice on how to increase volume with a big account. Should the sales manager refuse to play the role of advisor? Suppose another man is dispirited and discouraged. Should the sales manager refuse to try to cheer him up? Another salesman is having serious personal financial difficulties. Should the sales manager refuse to help him find remedies? Should he refuse to play these and other roles for and with his salesmen? Of course not, no more than the parent should refuse his several roles with his children.

It is this legitimate and necessary role playing aspect of sales management leadership that is under discussion here. When conditions require a particular role response, the leader must play that role and play it well. The major roles the sales manager must be able to play are discussed below.

Effective Performer.   Effective performance is the *competence dimension* of leadership. Because the supervisor-leader is himself a skilled salesman, his follower-salesmen respect his orders and advice.

When he suggests what they should do, or when he directs them to do some activity, they cooperate fully because they know they are receiving instructions or directions from a professional. "Larry, your selling story should emphasize our service policies more than it does now." "Oscar, the man who makes the buying decisions for that customer is John Petrillo not Homer Carter with whom you have been spending so much time." "Chris, you'd do a lot better if you brought out our promotion materials earlier in your presentations." When guidance and advice come from a supervisor, who is himself an effective salesman, the subordinate cooperates fully and willingly.

Inspirational Leader. In his role as inspirational leader, the sales manager is the emotional catalyst for his salesmen. He enables his salesman-follower to attach himself emotionally to his job and his company, to become emotionally involved. Visualize, for example, a medium-sized or large company. Here is an organization of several thousand people, perhaps a dozen plants, and as many or more warehouse and sales installations — sprawling, faceless, impersonal. How does a salesman attach himself emotionally to such an organization so that he is personally motivated to give his last ounce of ability for the company? He does so through his supervisor in his role as an inspirational leader.

Innovator. In his role as innovator, the leader is the source of problem-solving ideas for his followers: how to crack the big account, how to cover the territory more effectively, how to reduce expenses, and how to make better use of promotional materials. When necessary, his salesmen look to him to play this role for them. The innovator-leader must answer or at least help the salesman discover his own answer.

Father Image. In his role as father image, the sales manager is the embodiment of what his salesmen-followers think a father should be: a kindly, loved, respected, fair arbiter, judge, and disciplinarian. In his role of the father image, the manager holds the sales environment steady for followers so that they can learn about it — what the rules are, how people are judged, how success is attained, and what constitutes failure.

Guardian of the Status Quo. Finally, the manager-leader is also a guardian of the status quo, who speaks for and represents the company to his salesmen. He is the source of information about company history, policy, and procedures. When necesssary, he explains and enforces these things.

LEADERSHIP REQUIREMENTS

There are several leadership requirements that follow from the fact that supervisor-leaders must play several roles. These critical requirements can be outlined as follows:

Leadership as Multi-Roled. Since the sales supervisor plays several roles, he must change them as the situation requires. Furthermore, determining the proper leadership role in any given situation is a difficult task. The adoption of the improper role can have serious effects on the salesman.

Role Action and Reaction. Whether he recognizes it or not, when the salesman deals with his supervisor, he is always requesting *some* role response from him. And, on his part, the supervisor is always playing *some* role in his relations with his men. The interaction of the role requested by the salesman and the supervisor's role response will always produce a result—anger, satisfaction, frustration, or pleasure. This makes the matter of role analysis a particularly critical leadership skill.

Role Analysis. The sales manager must give thoughtful attention to what role he should play in every leadership situation, and he must be skilled in making this critical decision. The leader must ask such questions as: What role is the salesman asking me to play? With what roles should I respond?

Role Skills. Good managers are skilled in executing all of the leadership roles. Some roles just *come naturally* because of one's personality, upbringing, background, and experience. Most people can identify leaders who are naturally great father images or innovators. But by this same token, other leadership roles do not come naturally to managers. For example, a supervisor who is naturally a good guardian of the status quo is very likely to be a poor innovator. Hence, the sales manager must carefully analyze each of the leadership roles and deliberately work to improve his performance in those roles that are not natural to him.

THE SALESMAN'S ROLE IN THE COMMAND HIERARCHY

What determines the degree of cooperation a salesman chooses to deliver to his manager? How does leadership affect the degree of a salesman's cooperation? The answers to these questions constitute the subject of this section.

Followership as a Contractual Relationship

A *contract* is, of course, an agreement between two or more parties under which each receives and gives something of value. In this sense, the leader-follower relationship is a contract. It is not a written contract, nor is it sometimes even consciously recognized. But it is, nevertheless, a contract, under which each party — leader and follower — gives and receives certain things of value. This concept of the contractual nature of the leader-follower relationship is critical for understanding why the follower chooses the degree of cooperation he does and why he generates or avoids the costs of low cooperation.

What the Salesman Gives Under the Followership Contract

In the leader-follower relationship, the things the salesman gives that the leader-supervisor wants and values are his time, energy, skills, attention, loyalty, interest, extra effort, imagination, and knowledge. These are what the sales manager *buys* under the leadership-followership *contract*. These values the salesman can give completely or can partially withold (short of the cut-off point) at his own discretion. In a very real sense, these are the qualities and activities the follower *offers for sale* under the *contract*.

The Follower's Prices for His Complete Cooperation

If the salesman-follower gives management the values he has to offer under the *contract* and does not receive the things he requires in return, he is frustrated and dissatisfied. He produces at a low level, gen-

357

erates avoidable costs, and often quits. If, however, he gives his values and receives a full measure of what he requires in return, his job satisfaction and productivity are high. Typically, salesmen require:

To Be Understood. The understanding that a salesman wants from his supervisor is the kind of understanding that can overcome the treacheries of communication, surmount his own inability to understand himself, and occasionally surmount his own deliberate effort to hide his real feelings and meaning.

To Be Valued. If the salesman is to cooperate to the fullest extent of his capacity, one of his *prices* is that his manager-leader value him. The leader has two elements he can value: the *salesman himself* and *the work he does.* Ideally, the sales manager should value both. This is not always possible due to personality differences. But if the supervisor does not at least value the salesman's work, the salesman should be dismissed.

To Contribute. The salesman must also know, or be shown, how he contributes to the work of the company and the sales force. On the surface this requirement appears too obvious to require special attention. A reader might comment, "It should be no mystery to the salesman what he contributes. He contributes sales income to the company." But one must remember the nature of the command hierarchy and the information system in a company.

The *command hierarchy* is a pyramid:

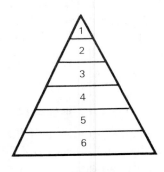

At the top resides the most power, and at this level there are the fewest people (in most companies, just a single man). At successively lower levels of the hierarchy, there are more and more people, with less and less power. At the lowest level are the salesmen. But if one considers the company's organization structure not as a command and power hierarchy, but as an information system, another pyramid or triangle results. However, it would be inverted:

Command Hierarchy

Information System

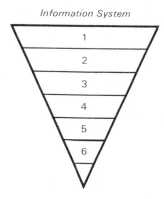

The information system diagram suggests that the most information about the company's policies, prospects, plans, and operations resides at the top and that the least information exists at the bottom. In addition it shows that less and less information is known at progressively lower levels in the organization.

Applying this analysis to the problem of the need for salesmen to know how and why they contribute, the leadership problem is found to be more complex than one might have first thought. When orders and directions pass between levels in the command hierarchy, they also pass between information levels in the organization, as shown on the top of page 360. Therefore, orders or directions for salesmen's participation that are sensible and obvious on the basis of the information available to the sales supervisor on level 5, may make no sense at all on the basis of the information available to the salesman on level 6. The

Command Hierarchy

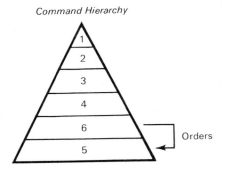

Information System

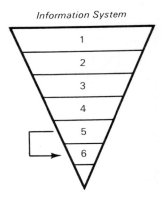

sales manager must never assume that it is clear to the salesmen how what they are asked to do contributes to the overall sales results, simply because it is apparent to the manager on the basis of the information he posesses.

To Belong. Man is a social animal who craves companionship and satisfying social intercourse. At first, it might seem that providing salesmen with satisfactory social relationships is not a particularly difficult task. After all, it could be argued, the essence of their job is to work with people and to interact socially with customers. This is not the case, however. The type of social interaction required by the salesman as a human being is not the salesman-customer relationship, no matter how friendly the salesman may be with a particular customer. In essence, the salesman-customer relationship is competitive in nature, not social. The customer *wins* by getting the best product and the most service at the lowest possible price. The salesman *wins* by getting the highest possible price at the least cost to his company.

If the salesman is to cooperate to his fullest capacity, the manager must find ways to provide him with social satisfactions. Many companies use sales meetings as one means of achieving this end. Other companies encourage company salesmen in adjoining territories to meet regularly with each other to talk about mutual problems and to exchange ideas. When the supervisor visits his salesmen in the field, calls on customers with them, socializes with them after hours, he is adding to the salesman's social satisfaction from his job. When, as is frequently the case, a group of salesmen work out of a single office, there is the potential for various social activities. But whatever form it may take, it is a prime responsibility of the leader-supervisor to see that his follower-salesmen are able to relate themselves to some satisfying social group.

To Be Buffered, Protected. The last price for the salesman's full cooperation is his demand for protection from unnecessary pressures and diversions. At the very least, the salesman demands that his supervisor pass these pressures on to him in the proper amount and at the proper time. He wants his supervisor to act as a screen, not as a magnifying glass.

All organizations, and business is no exception, generate diversionary pressures that distract people from the work they are doing. Some of these diversions, such as special market intelligence reports from field salesmen, are necessary, but many are not. If, for example, intemperate criticism of a salesman is presented by a superior to the salesmen's supervisor, the salesman insists that his supervisor will place this criticism in its proper perspective and not magnify its importance.

The salesman also requires his supervisor to plan the impact of these diversions on his selling work. He requires that his supervisor not pass on to him diversions that he does not need to know about or participate in. He expects his supervisor to make him aware of these pressures only at the time when he needs to know about them.

BASIC HUMAN RELATIONS SKILLS

The supervisor pays the price of a salesman's full cooperation by utilizing the human relations skills of executive leadership. *Human relations is the art of creating and maintaining organizational cooperation for maximum efficiency, low cost, and high personal job satisfaction.*

This section will present four of the more important human relations skills:

(1) perception;
(2) conceptualization;
(3) communication;
(4) self-awareness.

It will also discuss the ways in which managers can develop and improve these skills.

Perception

Because follower's demands are what they are, the executive leader must be skilled at perceiving the meanings and causes of individual and group behavior. In short, *perception is the ability to look and see, to listen and hear.* Without perception, the supervisor will not be able to understand and value his salesmen, to show them how they contribute and belong to a social group, or to buffer them adequately. In short, he will be able to pay none of the prices of their complete cooperation.

To the perceptive supervisor everything has potential meaning that may explain individual and group behavior—no matter how trivial the evidence may seem. Nothing that he might possibly use to understand his subordinates escapes him.

But it is most critical that the supervisor perceive meaning and evidence from the things that are normally expected to transmit meaning, *as well as from those things that are not normally expected to contain messages.* For instance, letters, reports, phone calls, telegrams, and special studies are expected to transmit meaning about the causes of individual and group behavior. The perceptive leader, however, does not stop here. He studies rumors, mistakes, accidents, facial expressions, and tones of voice. He notes what is *not* said or written, as well as what is transmitted. He seeks meaning in new or changed behavior patterns. He gauges his salesmen's morale for perceptive meanings.

Conceptual Ability

Conceptual ability is the process by which people relate and understand everything that happens to them. *It is the way one decodes and*

362

unscrambles experience. The supervisor-leader's conceptual ability is the means by which he understands who he is, who his salesmen are, what his company is, what selling is, why his company is in business — indeed, it is the means by which he understands everything around him. Everyone must have a conceptual scheme. Without one the sales manager would have to invent the wheel every time he faced a transportation problem. There are two critical aspects of conceptualization in high-quality, sales executive leadership: *(1) the mutual understanding of conceptual schemes between individuals* and *(2) the relative accuracy and reality of individual conceptual schemes.*

First, there must be mutual understanding by the leader and the follower of the conceptual scheme on which each is working; that is, they must both decode their experiences in a similar way. Unless they are on the same wave length (conceptual scheme), there can be no effective working relationship, communication, rapport or leadership.

Consider the following example: A large customer has drastically cut back an important order with only vague and evasive explanations. The salesman's diagnosis (conceptualization) of the situation is price. His superior sees (conceptualizes) the situation as a step in the customer's planned product line change-over to a higher quality line. Neither the salesman nor his supervisor bothers to explain his conceptualization of the problem and yet they try together to seek a solution to the problem. Since they are working on two different conceptual schemes, no practical solution is possible.

The second concern is the degree of reality of the individual conceptual schemes. For the effectiveness of the leader-follower relationship also depends upon the realism of the individual conceptual schemes, that is, the accuracy with which the conceptual scheme of each reflects the real world.

The paranoid exemplifies the individual with a wholly unrealistic conceptual scheme: he decodes everything that happens to him as a threat to his life and safety. In its extreme form this conceptual scheme is so strong that society institutionalizes the person because he becomes a threat to his own life and that of others. In a less dramatic, but nonetheless critical manner, a manager's conceptual scheme is pivitol in his leadership. The accuracy with which his conceptual scheme reflects the realities of his own situation and that of his salesmen importantly determines his effectiveness as a leader. One commonly encountered manifestation of an unrealistic conceptual scheme occurs when a salesman is promoted to a supervisory position and refuses to recognize that market conditions have changed since he worked the territory. Consequently he manages his men, evaluates their activities, issues them instructions, and interprets what they are doing against conditions that existed when he was a salesman, not against conditions as they now are.

Human beings are imperfect, and no one's concepts can ever perfectly reflect the real world. But the supervisor-leader must constantly question his concepts of himself and his salesmen to insure that to the greatest degree possible they are realistic and meaningful.

Communication Skills

The leadership *skills of communication* are *the abilities to recognize the differences in individuals and semantics and to use this recognition to transmit and receive messages accurately.*

It is important to recognize two major aspects of leadership communication. First, communication takes place through several media and the supervisor must be skilled in the use of all of them. The sales manager communicates by various written media—reports, letters, memoranda, or telegrams. He also communicates verbally—in face-to-face talks with salesmen and customers and by telephone. *But of equal importance is that the supervisor communicates by his behavior,* by a smile or a frown, by his tone of voice, by a pat on the back, by the firmness of his handshake, by the way in which he conducts himself in the presence of others, and by what he does and does not do.

Second, effective communication is *consistent communication:* one message must not contradict another. If, for example, a sales manager circulates a memo to all salesmen directing them to reduce their expenses, he must not then entertain the salesmen in the most expensive restaurants in town or travel short distances by taxicab. The various media of communication between sales manager and salesmen must reinforce, not contradict, each other.

Self-Awareness

Self-awareness is the leader's ability *to recognize himself as an integral part of the management and leadership process.* The traditional way of executive leadership contends that it is the manager's responsibility to decide what must be done, to direct that it be done, and to check that it is done. This is a *mechanistic* concept of management. It conceives management and executive leadership as an abstract, objective process—in which the follower is directed to do something, and he does it.

But this is no longer a realistic way to understand executive leadership and management. Sales management is not an objective process. *The sales manager is an integral part of his own leadership of his salesmen.* Sales executive leadership does not take place at arm's length. It is not simply a matter of turning the key in the ignition or filling in the right words in the right spaces on the form.

A skilled sales manager must not only realize this condition, but must welcome it and be skilled at managing it. He realizes that the followership conditions and problems with his salesmen are what they are because he is involved with them. He is willing and able to be a part of his own leadership, playing the leadership roles well and delivering the required motivations to his salesmen so they will follow him to the complete extent of their abilities.

In conclusion, it is interesting to note that one study of sales managers revealed that 90 per cent of them believed that their advancement from field selling was attributable to the effectiveness of their own sales managers.[12]

SUMMARY The most difficult task any sales manager faces is the supervision of his subordinates. To lead salesmen effectively, one needs to thoroughly understand human behavior, the concepts of motivation, and how to apply them. The intitial section of this chapter points out that human behavior is caused, directed, and motivated. Then, various theories of motivation are examined. Several aspects of effective motivation are discussed: (1) a challenging job, (2) participation, (3) being a part of the company, (4) morale, and (5) discipline. Basic conditions of sales supervision, as well as the degree of salesmen's cooperation, are also presented.

---

[12]John J. McCarthy, "Establishing a Climate for Sales Force Success," *Sales Management* (May 15, 1967), pp. 73–80.

In sales management there is no single leadership role. Leadership is multi-roled. The supervisor must be capable of playing one of several roles depending on what the situation requires. These roles are (1) effective performer, (2) inspirational leader, (3) innovator, (4) father image, and (5) guardian of the status quo.

Chapter 11 concluded with sections on the salesman role in the command hierarchy and on basic human relations skills.

DISCUSSION/REVIEW QUESTIONS

1. Think of an important purchase you recently made. Did the salesman identify your needs? Was he able to relate his product's features to your specific needs? Did other causal factors (e.g., advertising and personal recommendations) influence your decision? What were your motives for buying this product? What does this exercise tell you about the relationship of motivation theory to personal selling?
2. List in order of importance the major factors that motivate you in a work situation. Examine your list: Which of these are true motivators? Which are related to morale?
3. George Patton, the colorful World War II general, once said: "I don't want [the troops] to like me; I want them to fight for me." Does this statement have any meaning for sales management? Why, or why not?
4. Select a company with which you are familiar and then complete the following *morale and motivation audit* for the firm:

    How does the sales force you chose rate on each of these points?

	Excellent	Fair	Poor
a. Pays wages which compare favorably with those paid for similar sales jobs.	____	____	____
b. Lets each salesman reach as many decisions as possible about his work.	____	____	____
c. Holds sales meetings to discuss the company's benefit program.	____	____	____

   d. Takes every opportunity to be
personally friendly with each
salesman.   ____ ____ ____

   e. Sets quotas and goals *with* a
salesman, not for him.   ____ ____ ____

   f. Encourages the salesman by praising
him for a good job done, even to the
point of being lavish.   ____ ____ ____

   g. Gives each salesman every possible
responsibility consistent with his
experience and ability.   ____ ____ ____

   h. Sets up an attractive program of
fringe benefits (vacations, insurance,
pensions)   ____ ____ ____

   i. Strives to provide opportunities for
advancement for all salesmen
regardless of age or length of service.   ____ ____ ____

   j. Makes sure that every salesman gets
some recognition or praise
occasionally, even if no real reason
exists for giving it at the time.   ____ ____ ____

5. Below are three short leadership problems. Try to decide in each case:
   a. What role does the salesman seem to be asking his manager to assume?
   b. What role does the manager seem to be playing?
   c. What response would you expect from the salesman? Why?

I. The sales manager (SM) has traveled all day in the territory with the salesman (S) whom he sees regularly twice a month. They are having a drink together in the early evening before sales manager's plane leaves.

  SM: "Well, tell me, Howard, what's your overall impression of how things are going in your territory?"

  S: "I guess I shouldn't complain."

  SM: (smiling): "But you are. Is that it?"

  S: "Well, Mike, you get the reports. You know how it's going! I've tried every trick I know—but it's no good. I'm working evenings, Sundays, and holidays; I'm using all of the promotion material you send out from headquarters. I'm calling on customers almost twice as often as I used to. Nothing seems to work. I still can't get the old cases-sold figure up to quota!"

SM: "Well you know, Howard, how I sweat over those quotas in the home office to get them just right, to get them on-target and reasonable. Why I bet we worked a thousand overtime hours revising them on the advice of the field people. It's like our president says, if the quotas are unrealistic, our entire business is based on a fallacy."

II. A salesman has telephoned his sales manager on a matter of some urgency. The following conversation takes place:

S: "Look, Jim, I just called to talk to you about a real urgent matter. I've just come from Consolidated Products and their people say that if we can shave just a half cent a pound off our price for 'Creon,' we can get all of their business. Think of it, Jim. That'll run better than a quarter of a million pounds! Can we do it?"

SM: "Just a half a cent? Why, Norm boy, that should be duck soup for a salesman like you! Put on the old Irish charm! Get in there and sell our research, delivery, and credit story! Make 'em see how it's worth far more than a measly half cent a pound to do business with the leader of our industry."

III. A salesman has come in to see his sales manager and the following conversation takes place:

S: "Last month you said—and I agreed—that we should get Brownell's Department Store to tie in with this promotion. Well, I cooked up a special presentation for their buyers showing them, down to the last detail, why and how they should tie in. I even made up dummy displays for them and roughed out some ads. I gave the presentation three times, they were so hot on it. Everybody said the ideas were great, but the merchandising committee said no dice. And that's that."

SM: "I'm glad you brought this up with me, Alan. I like to know that you feel free to take me into your confidence; to share your troubles with me. When I first started selling with the company, my supervisor was a real super salesman, but not much of a manager. You couldn't get to first base talking out your problem with him. He just told you to go out and solve it yourself. But, I want to be in on my men's problems!"

6. Analyze a recent important action that you have taken. What factors influenced your behavior? What were your goals? What motives guided your actions?

7. Think about a close friend or associate. Do you really understand him?

· What are his needs? Does Maslow's need hierarchy give you a better understanding of his behavior?

8. Assume you were recently appointed district sales mamager. What actions, if any, would you take in each of the following situations?

  (a) Salesman Jeff Heally was married a little over a year ago. Since his marriage, he has gone deeply into debt for clothing, furniture, and household appliances. Several installment payments are due every week, and he has trouble just keeping his books straight. His sales have begun to suffer. He has come to you for help. He claims his many creditors and charge account obligations are taking his mind off his work.

  (b) Salesman Jack Holmes has been guilty of several violations of sales ethics. He has misrepresented the company's products, made false delivery charges, and overcharged his customers. Whenever a customer complained about mistreatment or Jack was caught in an inaccuracy, he has attempted to explain his actions with a half-truth. A customer has just refused to accept one of his orders. Jack insists the factory made a mistake, but the factory's original copy of the order indicates he was wrong again.

  (c) Salesman Lee Fontana was an aggressive young salesman who had a remarkable sales record. For the three years that he has been with the company, he has been the top man in his district and one of the top ten salesmen in the country. Six months ago, the district manager was promoted to a home office position, and you were appointed to succeed him. Since then Lee's sales have slumped, and he is now closer to the bottom than to the top of the district.

9. Identify a poor salesman you know. What avoidable costs does he generate because he is a poor salesman?

10. Have you ever experienced a situation that seemed to be a routine problem, but which actually turned out to be an emergency? Why did you at first consider it to be routine? What alerted you to the fact that it was an emergency?

11. Consider a sales manager you know well (perhaps yourself). What sales management "role" does he (or do you) play best naturally? What role or roles does he (or do you) not play well? How could these be improved?

12. Identify a particular order or direction given by a supervisor to a salesman in a company with which you are familiar. As best as you can, make two lists: one of the background information the supervisor possessed concerning the order, the other of the information the salesman had. Do these two lists match? If not, why and what result would you anticipate because the two sets of information do not match?

13. Briefly identify each of the following:

  (a) primary needs   (d) emotional needs
  (b) secondary needs   (e) cut-off point
  (c) rational needs   (f) "effective performer" role

    (g) "inspirational leader" role   (k) contract
    (h) "innovator" role   (l) command hierarchy
    (i) "father image" role   (m) perception
    (j) "guardian of the status quo" role

14. Distinguish between *routine* and *emergency* conditions in sales management.
15. What do the authors mean by the terms *Puritans* and *New Generation*? Discuss.

CHAPTER TWELVE
THE EVALUATION
OF SALESMEN

This chapter will introduce the subject of evaluating salesmen's performance, while Chapter 13 will discuss the actual operation of an evaulation program.

The study of evaluation programs require that three basic questions be considered:

(1) Do all companies evaluate their salesmen?
(2) Do all companies have formal evaluation programs?
(3) Is formal evaluation expensive?

1. *Yes*, all companies evaluate their salesmen—whether the firm is large or small; whether it is in consumer, industrial, government, or export sales; whether it sells goods or services; whether it employs one or several thousand salesmen. The evaluation may be formal or informal, its form may be simple or complex, and its conclusions based on objective criteria or on executive opinion. Whatever its scope, salesman evaluation takes place in all companies because without it the supervision of salesmen is impossible.

2. *No*, all companies do not have formal evaluation programs. Various studies have shown that the percentage of firms with a formalized salesman evaluation program is usually less than 50 per cent for most industries. While formal evaluation of selling performance is prevalent throughout American business, it is certainly *not universal*.

3. *Yes*, formal evaluation is expensive—in money, time, and effort.

As a rule, the more complex and accurate the evaluation plan is, the more expensive it is. The reasons for this will become apparent in this chapter and the following chapter.

WHY EVALUATE SALESMAN PERFORMANCE?

Thus far, it has been noted that all companies evaluate salesmen; that formal evaluation programs are prevalent, but not universal; and that formal evaluation programs represent an important cost to the company. The reasons *why* a company undertakes to evaluate salesman performance can be summarized in terms of the following important management objectives:

1. To discover how and where each man needs improvement. This makes possible individualized manpower development.
2. To check and evaluate the performance standards for salesmen. Poor performance may indicate poor performance standards.
3. To spot men who are ready for promotion, salary raises, or assignment to new territories and responsibilities.
4. To keep the job descriptions current and on target with changing market conditions.
5. To supply evidence on salesmen who should be fired.
6. To cross-check the salesman compensation plan, training, supervision, recruitment, territory assignments, and operating procedures.

The evaluation of salesmen is dependent upon an effective *sales analysis* program. Sales analysis involves the disaggregation and study of sales performance figures. One widely cited study discovered that the top third of a company's products, orders, and customers account for 70–75 per cent of the firm's sales and profits. Furthermore, the top third of a company's salesmen and sales territories typically account for about 60 per cent of its sales and profits.[1] This illustrates the need

---

[1] Henry Deane Wolfe and Gerald Albaum, "Inequality in Products, Orders, Customers, Salesmen, and Sales Territories," *Journal of Business*, vol. 35 (July 1962), pp. 298–301.

for establishing an efficient evaluation program. Sales managers must be able to identify areas of high and low productivity so as to better allocate their efforts and resources.

Each evaluation plan must be tailored to the individual company in which it is used. For one company calls-per-day may be an important criterion of salesmen's performance, while for another company new accounts opened may be a far more critical standard. One company may evaluate its men annually, another quarterly. Each sales group must design its own evaluation program based on these criteria.

Characteristics of a Good Salesman Evaluation Program

The following are the generally accepted characteristics of a good evaluation program:

1. *Realistic:* it reflects things as they are, the man's territory, competition, experience, sales potential.
2. *Continuous, known, expected:* the salesman knows when and how his work is evaluated.
3. *Constructive, not destructive:* it shows him what needs improvement and how to better his performance.
4. *Motivates the salesman to improve.*
5. *Provides useful information about the salesman and his territory for management.*
6. *Involves the salesman in his own evaluation.*
7. *Objective, not subjective:* based on standards, not on opinions or prejudices (see cartoon, Figure 12–1)
8. *Living, changing, adaptive to changing market conditions.*
9. *Fits the company and the sales group involved.*
10. *Is economical of money and time.*

OBSTACLES TO SALESMAN EVALUATION

Salesman evaluation is a sales management process that is difficult and inexact. It is an art striving to become a science. But as uncertain as it is, industry experience has proven conclusively that if it is used with full recognition of its problems and limitations, it pays real dividends.

FIGURE 12-1

"I'll be damned if I'll submit to pressure, Bascomb.
You'll get a raise when I feel you deserve a raise!"

Source: Reprinted by permission from *Sales Management*, The Marketing Magazine. Copyright 1970.

There are important problems in evaluating salesman performance. So common and difficult are these problems that some companies do not employ formal salesman evaluation programs at all and others use only very simple plans. When sales management creates and operates an evaluation plan, they know that these obstacles will always make any plan something less than perfect.

Isolation of the Salesman

Most salesmen do their work beyond the direct personal observation of their supervisors, who can only rarely observe and evaluate their work as they are doing it. In mass-distributed consumer goods industries—such as food, drug, hardware, liquor, and cosmetics—sales supervisors consider themselves fortunate if they can spend one selling day a month in the field with each of their salesmen. The isolation of salesmen creates two problems in evaluating their work.

1. *Evaluation by Inference.* Since he can only occasionally observe his men's performance, the sales supervisor must *infer* conclusions from indirect evidence. For example, records for the last quarter show that Sam Gulligan's calls-per-day, new accounts opened, dollar volume sold, and gross margin earned are well below his quota. The supervisor must infer that Sam is neglecting his job, and this may actually be true. But conditions might have existed under which these same facts would lead to a quite different conclusion. For instance, during this period the union struck Sam's three biggest customers.

Evaluation by inference can often be damaging, in that it leads to incorrect and misleading conclusions. The evaluator should never forget this. Just as the law courts are extremely careful when they deal with *circumstantial* evidence (i.e., when they undertake inferential analysis), the sales manager should handle inferential evaluations with great care. At every possible place inference should be checked against personal information and observation.

2. *Bias of Direct Observation.* When the supervisor evaluates his men by traveling with them, two potential forces of bias are present. First, the salesman may try to make himself look good by calling on only easy, friendly customers. A sales supervisor of a toy manufacturer became curious about the kinds of customers he was visiting when he traveled with his field salesmen. Analysis showed that 80 per cent of his calls with salesmen were made on customers who represented 75 per cent of the salesmen's volume.

A second bias in field observation is that the presence of the salesman's superior almost inevitably changes the customer's normal behavior in some way. He does not react as he normally does when the salesman calls alone.

Observing salesmen at work is a useful and important evaluation tool, but it should be used by the supervisor in full knowledge of its limitations.

Finding and Relating Criteria

One cannot evaluate a salesman's performance until the functions that he should be performing are known. In even the simplest selling job, it is difficult to identify the specific performance factors that are critical to a salesman's success and then to rate these factors in relation to one other.

Some might ask, "What is the problem? Salesmen are hired to sell goods and services at a profit. Why is it difficult to evaluate their performance?" The problem, however, consists in the difficulty of determining what creates profit for a specific company, territory, or unit: Service? Advertising and promotion help for customers? Technical assistance? Advice on inventory control?

Lack of Control over Some Performance Conditions

Another difficulty in evaluation is that the salesman's performance is always colored—for better or worse—by external conditions over which he and/or his company have little or no control. Competition cuts the price. There is a local business recession. A government agency issues a report that is critical of the product. It is difficult to design an evaluation program that takes all such external forces into account.

Evaluation Facts and Evaluation Judgments

A persistent problem in evaluation is that the information used is of two sorts: fact and judgment. *Fact* is quantifiable, *judgment* is nonquantifiable—while fact can be stated and used in the form of figures or other fairly exact measures, judgment cannot. An example of quantifiable fact is number of calls-per-day; of nonquantifiable judgment, the extent of the salesman's product knowledge.

It may seem difficult to use both fact and judgment in evaluation, as if one were trying to add apples and oranges. However, the difficulty diminishes if it is remembered that the purpose of evaluating salesman performance is for manpower development. The sales manager knows all that is required when he finds out that on a particular performance standard—fact or judgment—a salesman did poorly. *The problem is to find out why.*

DEVELOPING THE SALESMAN EVALUATION PROGRAM

This section will examine the critical problems of designing an evaluation program and of managing it effectively. Each individual sales manager must decide which procedures are applicable to his situation and how complex and sophisticated his evaluation program should be.

There are five distinct steps in the development and management of a systematic evaluation program for salesmen's performance.[2] These are shown in Figure 12 – 2.

FIGURE 12–2
Steps in the Development of an Evaluation Program

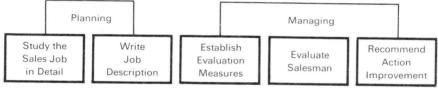

The first two steps were discussed in earlier chapters, the last three are considered here and in Chapter 13.

The third step in the design and management of a good evaluation program is the selection of the measurements that will best indicate how salesmen are doing in relation to the standards established by the job description. These measurements of salesman performance include two types: (1) the salesman's results or output and (2) the salesman's input. Measuring the salesman's results will tell *how* he did. Measuring his input will tell *what* he did. Further, the two types of measurements can be combined, so that by evaluating a salesman's

[2]The development of an evaluation program for measuring sales territory performance is described in David W. Cravens, Robert B. Woodruff, and Joe C. Stamper, "An Analytical Approach to Evaluating Sales Territory Performance," *Journal of Marketing*, vol. 36 (January 1972), pp. 31 – 37. Also see Robert D. Dugan, "Evaluating Territorial Sales Efforts," *Journal of Applied Psychology*, vol. 44 (April 1960), pp. 107 – 110; Allan Easton, "A Forward Step in Performance Evaluation," *Journal of Marketing*, vol. 30 (July 1966), pp. 26 – 32; Frank H. Mossman and Malcom L. Worrell, Jr., "Analytical Methods of Measuring Marketing Profitability: A Matrix Approach," *MSU Business Topics*, vol. 14 (Autumn 1966), pp. 35 – 45.

input, a sales manager can determine the reasons behind a salesman's *output*.

An example of the effective combination of both types of evaluation measures is provided by a large car dealer on the East Coast who employs 60 full-time salesmen. This company regularly evaluates the salesmen's output or results by measuring their gross dollar sales, net dollar sales after trade-ins, number of sales made, gross margin contributed after salesman's commission, and ratio of new cars sold to used cars sold. In order to appraise the output results and understand what might have caused them, so that remedial action can be taken where indicated, they also measure the salesmen's input in terms of number of days worked; number of phone, letter, direct mail piece, and personal contacts with potential customers; salesman's knowledge of his products; company price and service policies; and, number of customer complaints. Using results and input measures together, the company believes that it has an effective method of evaluating the performance of its salesmen.

The Use of a Single Standard

The use of a single standard for the evaluation of salesman performance has the tempting advantages of being easy for salesmen and their supervisors to understand, and of usually being economical to plan and administer. It is likely however to cause more problems and undesirable conditions than it solves. The consensus of respondents in one study of 86 manufacturing firms was that there was "no single, fool-proof method of measuring a salesman's performance."[3]

To demonstrate the kinds of undesirable side effects that can develop from the use of any single standard of evaluation, imagine a salesman whose performance is evaluated solely on a gross dollar sales volume quota. He is expected to bring in X number of dollars in sales in the next quarter to meet or exceed the quota. It would be only natural for him to react to this standard by ignoring other important aspects of his work: to control his expenses, to open new accounts, to resist spending the time to introduce and promote new products, to neglect the lower priced items in the line, to minimize customer ser-

---

[3]Wayland A. Tonning, *How to Measure and Evaluate Salesmen's Performance* (Englewood Cliffs, N.J.: Prentice-Hall, Inc., 1964), p. 54.

vice (unless it was to result directly in a sale), and to skip small or less active accounts. Certainly it is conceivable that this is just what the company wants him to do, but if it were, the company would be a rare exception. In today's changing, sophisticated buying and selling environment, a company hardly wants a salesman to overlook any or all of these important functions.

Single standards of evaluation are used in some companies, but they are always dangerous because they have a strong tendency to create harmful side effects in salesman performance. It is more likely to be the case that several standards must be applied for sensible evaluation and supervision of salesmen and for the avoidance of undesirable behavior by salesmen.

The Use of Several Standards

A great many indices and combinations of performance measures are available to sales management. The emerging information sciences, the explosion of knowledge, and the popularity of computers have made it possible to know — and at great speed and in great detail — virtually anything one might wish to know about salesman performance.[4] The limiting factor are the time and expense of generating, collecting, analyzing, and appraising such information. Management must spend time designing an evaluation reporting and analysis system. The salesman must spend time filling out reports on his activities. And management must spend yet more time collating, analyzing, and appraising the results.

The more measurements that are used in the evaluation of sales performance, the more time is required to process them. Consequently, a company must study carefully what is needed in order to evaluate salesman performance and to employ only the best of those indices and measurements that will give the necessary information.

As no two selling jobs are the same, performance in each kind of selling job must be measured by its own standards. The two basic criteria for the selection of performance measures follow.

---

[4]The adoption of a computer based sales reporting system is described in Lloyd M. DeBoer and William H. Ward, "Integration of the Computer Into Salesmen Reporting," *Journal of Marketing*, vol. 35 (January 1971), pp. 41–47. Also see "Field Managers Go On-Line," *Sales Management* (October 4, 1971), pp. 23–25, 28–30.

What is needed? Because he is evaluated on how well he makes decisions under conditions of constant uncertainty, every manager wants *all* the information before making *any* evaluation or decision. But information costs money, and the more information and the greater the detail, the greater the cost.[5] Consequently, the critical questions in deciding on the performance measurements to be used for a particular sales group are as follows: What information is not essential to the decision? What information can the firm afford to buy? What information can the firm NOT afford to buy?

How Efficient Is the Information Source? Having decided which measures to use in an individual company, critical questions arise concerning the efficiency of the information source: Does it provide the information desired, and only that, or does the source charge for unneeded data? Is the information accurate to the degree needed? If not, what degree of inaccuracy is present? Will the source provide information on time?

Commonly Used Measures of Performance

Table 12 – 1 lists the more commonly used indices of performance along with an indication of what activities or results each measurement can be used to indicate.

ROI – Another Evaluation Tool

In recent years, ROI (return-on-investment) calculations have come to be regarded as an integrating tool for measuring sales performance.[6] It is important to emphasize again that no single standard (including ROI) should form the sole basis of an evaluation. However, ROI is an appropriate tool for reporting territory results to top management. It can also serve as another *input* into the evaluation of individual salesmen or sales managers.

---

[5]The use of the standard deviation in sales evaluation has been suggested as a method for overcoming some of the problems. See James C. Cotham III and David W. Cravens, "Improving Measurement of Salesman's Performance," *Business Horizons*, vol. 12 (June 1969), pp. 79 – 83.

[6]Michael Schiff, "The Use of ROI in Sales Management," *Journal of Marketing*, vol. 27 (July 1963), pp. 70 – 73. Also see Michael Schiff, "The Sales Territory As a Fixed Asset," *Journal of Marketing*, vol. 25 (October 1960), pp. 51 – 53.

TABLE 12–1

Measures of Sales Performance

Index	Salesman's Results or Activity That Is Measured
Dollar or unit sales volume	Output, his dollar or unit "score"
Customer service calls or assignments	Service provided, amount of customer service work done
Share of market attained	Competitive standing in his territory
Number of orders written	Volume of his business, frequency of orders taken
Number of reorders	Frequency of repeat business, customer loyalty, selling skill
Expenses	Selling cost he represents, his interest in expense control
Gross margin on orders	Contribution to overhead, price lines sold
Number of active accounts	Territory coverage, potential
Calls made	Activity rate, aggressiveness
Promotion work done	Rate of nonselling, sales supporting activities
Sales against quota or sales budget	Relative sales results against a standard, standing relative to other salesmen
Sales versus territory potential	Territory coverage, sales record
Average order size*	Nature of business written, size of customer
Number of accounts lost	Territory conditions, sales skills
Ratio of orders to calls made	Time allocation, sales success, territory coverage, sales skill, planning ability
Average of cancelled orders (orders ÷ cancellations)	Sales skill, nature of business written
Number of new accounts opened	Aggressiveness, kind of customers called on, planning ability

Measures of Salesman's Inputs: Quantifiable

Calls per day	Time utilization, application to job, kinds of customers called on, activities on calls, planning ability
Nonselling activities (public relations, etc.)	Attitude toward job, kinds of customers called on
Hours per day worked	Application to job, planning ability
Correspondence, phone calls made	Attitude toward job, selling ability

Continued

Measures of Salesman's Inputs: Nonquantifiable

Problem-solving ideas generated	Creativity in managing himself and his territory
Management of his time	Business ability, efficiency, attitude toward job
Product, policy, and procedure knowledge	Attitude toward company and job, selling ability
Ability as market "intelligence agent"	Value as information source, assistance to company
Personal appearance	Value as company representative, selling ability
Personality traits: judgment, honesty, emotional stability, self-discipline, responsibility	Selling skills, value to company

*Small orders can be a serious problem for many venders since fixed costs such as billing and accounting are the same regardless of order size. See, for instance, William B. Collings, "The Big Small-Order Problem," *Journal of Purchasing* (February, 1966), p. 43.

Historically, sales evaluation emphasized *volume*, and this type of approach is still seen in some less progressive companies. Later, *profitability* became top management's yardstick for measuring sales performance. Both of these suffer from obvious limitations: volume is not necessarily related to net income, and profitability typically varies with the firm's investment in the region or territory. The logical next step was to calculate ROI.

The ROI formula can be shown as:

$$\text{ROI} = \frac{\text{Net profit}}{\text{Sales}} \times \frac{\text{Sales}}{\text{Investment}}$$

or

$$\text{ROI} = \text{Rate of Profit} \times \text{Turnover}$$

A sales territory with sales of $200,000, with net profits of $10,000, and with an investment (assets managed[7]) of $40,000 has an ROI of:

$$ROI = \frac{10,000}{200,000} \times \frac{200,000}{40,000}$$
$$ROI = 0.5 \times 5$$
$$ROI = .25$$

Whether 25 per cent is an acceptable ROI depends upon results in other sales territories and upon the alternative uses of investment funds. However, it is interesting to note that a survey of *Fortune's* largest 500 industrial firms indicated that "the average discounted rate of return for sales management below which projects would not be undertaken was 13.0%."[8] By comparison, the figures for projects in the other functional areas of marketing were 12.3 per cent for distribution channels, 13.4 per cent for advertising, 14.0 per cent for new product development, and 15.0 per cent for marketing research.

Information Sources for Evaluation

Once the proper measures for evaluating salesman performance have been selected, questions arise concerning the sources of such information: Where does one find the indices and measurements that he has decided to use? What are the advantages and weaknesses associated with each information source?

Company Records. The company's own history is often a useful source of data on which performance norms are built. Invoices, historical volume experience by territory or by customer class, complaints, bills of sale, volume-cost-profit experience with various kinds of promotions and lines, the history of individual salesmen, and other aspects of company experience are useful in establishing performance standards for salesmen.

---

[7]The term "assets managed" is sometimes used instead of "investment." See J. S. Schiff and Michael Schiff, "New Sales Management Tool: R O A M," *Harvard Business Review*, vol. 45 (July–August 1967), pp. 59–66.

[8]Richard T. Hise and Robert H. Strawser, "Application of Capital Budgeting Techniques to Marketing Operations," *MSU Business Topics*, vol. 18 (Summer 1970), pp. 69–76.

A tire manufacturer wished to expand from regional distribution in the Midwest into the New England market. The firm sought to establish dollar sales volume quotas as performance measurements for salesmen in the new area. Investigation showed that the social, economic, and competitive characteristics of the proposed New England sales territories were similar to those of selected midwestern territories in which the company had sold for years. So the company's historical sales volume in these comparable midwestern territories was used to establish sales quotas for the new territories.

Potential advantages of company records as an information source include:

1. Information is not generalized to a whole industry, as some other kinds of evaluation data are, but is particular to the company using the information.
2. Data source is known, and in most cases the information is easy to get and does not require much time to recover.
3. Some kinds of in-company evaluation information are very economical to get and to use in comparison with other sorts of information.
4. The degree of accuracy and relevance of the data are known.

Potential weaknesses and risks of company records include:

1. The necessary evaluation information may not be available in past company records.
2. In some important respects company history as represented by company records may not accurately reflect present market conditions.

Customer Contact. Customers themselves are often fruitful sources of data on salesmen's performance. Because customers are in close and frequent contact with salesmen, they are therefore a valuable source of evaluative information about salesmen's performance.

Potential advantages include:

1. Customers can provide fresh, vital, up-to-the-minute evaluation information.
2. Information is firsthand and not therefore subject to distortion by being transmitted through several senders before reaching the supplier's management.
3. The customer is reminded that the supplier company is concerned with him, his operations, and his problems.
4. The customer can provide new ideas on how to better service.
5. Customers can provide useful comparisons of a firm's salesmen with competitor's representatives.

The potential weaknesses and risks include:

1. Information from customers on salesmen's performance is random and unweighted. If a salesman pleases or displeases a customer, his manager may or may not hear about it; he may hear promptly, or a long time later; he may get an accurate or a garbled account of the event. He never can be exactly sure how to appraise the information, because most often he receives a specific judgment that the customer has extracted from the total event. For instance, if and when it comes, customer evaluation of salesman performance is likely to take such forms as: "Your salesman certainly got us out of a bad spot on that one" or "Your man goofed on that shipment."
2. Seeking evaluative information on salesmen from customers can boomerang on the sales manager. Unless it is done carefully and with the salesman's complete knowledge and support, collecting evaluation evidence on him from his customers will appear to him as an unfair intrusion into his relationships with his customers. Under such conditions his morale and effectiveness will certainly suffer.

Salesmen's Reports. Perhaps the most widely used source of evaluation evidence is the information that salesmen themselves furnish through reports, both written and oral.

The potential advantages include:

385

1. Salesmen have intimate, current knowledge of their territories and of their own operations.
2. If the reporting system is designed carefully, salesmen can furnish territory coverage information for supervision purposes along with evaluation data in the same report, thus saving the expense of double reporting for the two purposes.

The potential weaknesses and risks include:

1. The sales manager must handle such information with care. Salesmen as a group are no more or less honest, self-seeking, or ego-centered than any other group. Like everyone else, salesmen will do what they can to protect themselves from criticism, to make themselves "look good," to make the job as easy as possible, and to maximize their incomes. This is not to say salesmen in general will be dishonest or will deliberately distort their activity and result reports. However, when a manager discovers a salesman cheating on his reports, strong disciplinary action or dismissal should follow quickly.
2. But more important and prevalent than outright cheating on reports of his activities is the subtle tendency for a salesman to favor himself in all instances where *he has a legitimate choice on what to report*. For instance, in one company, calls-per-day is an important performance evaluation factor. A salesman has made ten bona fide calls on customers and has run into another customer in a restaurant; they have lunch and discuss baseball the whole time. How many calls does he report for the day? He is likely to report eleven. This tendency is one good reason why so many companies try to collect evaluative evidence on all important job performance factors *from more than one source*. When an evaluation factor is critical, and when one important source of information is what the salesman reports about himself, other collaborating sources should be used.

Manager's Field Visits. Even though most managers cannot find time to travel with and observe their men frequently, visits to the field are important information sources. They particularly offer cross-checks with other data available to the manager.

Potential advantages include:

1. The ability to cross-check other evaluation information with field observation.
2. If properly done, the field visit demonstrates to the salesman and to customers that management is interested and concerned with their operations.
3. It reinforces to the salesman on a personal level the importance of evaluation.

Potential weaknesses and risks include:

1. The salesman may deliberately or unconsciously bias the field observations by calling only on easy accounts or those without current problems.
2. Further, there is a strong tendency for the customer knowingly or unconsciously to change his normal behavior pattern, to become tougher or easier than he usually is, or to bring up matters that he normally does not discuss with the salesman when he calls alone.

The Manager's Personal Insight. Although he usually cannot state it in figures or symbols, charts or graphs, the good sales manager has a sixth sense in evaluating the performance of his men. He himself has usually been a salesman. He is experienced in the industry and his company, and he knows his men as professionals and as individuals. From this knowledge comes a valuable instinct to be used in his evaluation of their work. One study of the brewery industry and the college textbook industry indicated that 66.3 per cent of the respondents considered the "manager's own thought" as an important source of information to be used in establishing salesman evaluation criteria.[9]

---

[9]Bill R. Darden and Warren French, "An Investigation Into the Salesman Evaluation Practices of Sales Managers," *Southern Journal of Business*, vol. 5 (July 1970), pp. 47–56.

Some sales management experts disagree with this contention, by advocating that the evaluation of salesman performance can and should be completely objective and scientific, with no room for subjective instinct by the manager. The great majority of salesmen and sales managers, however, support the view that instinct can be as useful in evaluation as any of the other scientific measures: Instead of giving instinct precedence over science in evaluation, or science precedence over instinct, the two are seen as complementary.

Potential advantages to personal insight include:

1. It brings the priceless ingredient of experience to the evaluation process.
2. It humanizes evaluation, making it more understandable and acceptable to salesmen.
3. It serves as an important cross-check with other objective evaluation data.

Potential weaknesses and risks include:

1. Manager's instinct may be biased.
2. Manager may come to rely too heavily on his own judgment, in preference to other objective evaluation standards.

External Sources.   External forces also influence salesmen's performance. Shifts in buying power in his territory, in population, in economic activities, and in number of potential customers can all influence his performance and thereby influence his evaluations. To take these forces into account, the effective evaluation program includes performance measures that often must be based on information coming from outside the company. For instance, if a manager thinks that his salesmen's expense ratio is high, he would compare it with industry statistics on selling expenses.

There are a variety of sources of such information available at little or no cost, often in the local library. These sources are of two general types: *governmental* and *private*. The governmental sources consist of federal and state agencies and bureaus. The private sources are trade, industry, and professional associations and groups.

The potential advantages include:

1. Much outside information is free, or very inexpensive.
2. In some cases outside sources provide useful information the company could not itself afford to gather.
3. Outside sources provide information that a company itself could not always get, even if it could afford to.

Potential weaknesses and risks include:

1. Data may not be applicable to the company's operations, although they may at first seem to be.
2. Information available outside may not provide the needed facts, or it may not be in the required arrangement or detail.

SUMMARY This chapter introduces the subject of evaluating salesmen. Salesmen evaluation is universal, whether it is formal or informal, simple or complex. It was also noted that formal evaluation programs are very expensive in money, time, and effort. Chapter 12 also described the reasons why sales performance should be evaluated, and discussed the numerous characteristics of a good evaluation program.

There are several major problems in salesman evaluation: (1) isolation of the salesman, (2) evaluation by inference, (3) bias of direct observation, (4) the finding and relating of criteria, (5) lack of control over some performance conditions, and (6) the use of fact and judgment.

The chapter also discussed various measures of sales performance, with particular attention devoted to calculating return on investment. Chapter 12 concluded with a section on the information sources in which the advantages and weaknesses of each source were outlined.

DISCUSSION/REVIEW QUESTIONS

1. What steps should a company go through to design a good salesman evaluation program or to review one already in use?
2. What obstacles stand in the way of designing a good evaluation program? How can these be avoided?
3. Discuss salesman evaluation with a sales executive of a company with a formal program. List the reasons and conditions he cites as favoring and not favoring the use of *any* salesman evaluation system in his company. Do you agree? Why?
4. What performance indices does the company you studied in question 3 use in evaluating salesman performance? Do you think these are the right measures? Why? Would you make any changes in the measures used? Why?
5. Why should firms not use a single standard of evaluation (such as gross dollar sales) when measuring sales performance? Comment.
6. If a territory with an investment of $45,000 produces a net profit of $9,000 on sales of $135,000, what is its ROI? Would the ROI for this territory be acceptable if you were the sales manager?
7. What is meant by *sales analysis*? How is it used in sales management?
8. Identify the characteristics of a good salesman evaluation program.
9. How does the sales manager use both fact and judgment in his personnel evaluations?
10. What performance measures would be appropriate for these sales results or activities:
    (a) service provided
    (b) territory coverage
    (c) contribution to overhead
    (d) the salesman's interest in expense control
    (e) size of the customer
    (f) sales skill
11. Identify and discuss the various information sources for evaluation.

CHAPTER THIRTEEN
OPERATION OF THE
EVALUATION
PROGRAM

Chapter 12 introduced the subject of evaluating salesman performance. This chapter will consider several important questions relating to the successful operation of an evaluation program. These will include who should evaluate salesmen, how frequently evaluation should take place, the follow-up, a salesman's involvement in his evaluation, and the training of evaluators.

WHO SHOULD EVALUATE SALESMAN PERFORMANCE?

There is an important distinction between who should design the evaluation program and who should operate it. The evaluation plan should be designed by those in the company who have the widest sales experience; who know the company, its products, and markets in the greatest detail; and who are experienced in evaluation programs. In most companies, these requirements mean that the evaluation program is originally designed, and periodically reviewed, by top sales management and their staffs. But who in the company should actually make evaluations and work with them once the plan has been designed? Should it be headquarters sales executives and their staffs? Regional sales managers? Field sales managers? Corporate staff evaluation specialists?

Industry practice varies with the level in the company on which salesman evaluation takes place. However, the weight of the evidence supports the conclusion that evaluation of a salesman's performance should be done at the lowest possible level of supervision, preferably by the salesman's immediate supervisor.

There are a number of reasons to support this conclusion.

Strengthening of the Salesman-Supervisor Relationship. Evaluation of his performance by the salesman's immediate supervisor throws the two of them into a closer working relationship. They must *work together* on the man's problems, and they share the satisfaction of improving the man and his work. If well managed by the supervisor, participative evaluation brings the supervisor closer to his men thereby making his other supervisory responsibilities easier and more effective. The salesman's morale is bolstered because he sees the direct interest his supervisor has in his work.

Mutual commitment. When the salesman and his supervisor share in his evaluation, they are both personally and publicly committed to improving the man's performance, to solving his problems. This greatly improves the effectiveness of evaluation and its follow-up.

Supervisory Responsibility. The supervisor is responsible for the performance results of his salesmen. He himself is judged and evaluated by how well or poorly his men perform: through their work he stands or fails. Consequently, it is only sensible and fair that he play a major role in evaluating his men's performance and in working out remedial action with them based on the evaluations. When he does not have an important part in evaluation of his salesmen's performance, the classic administrative mistake is likely to occur — that of assigning the supervisor responsibility for his salesmen's performance without assigning the necessary authority to remedy their mistakes.

Communication of Goals and Remedies. Perhaps the most important reason why the salesman's immediate supervisor should play a major role in the evaluation is so that both parties can clearly understand what is right and wrong with the salesman's performance and what remedial actions must be taken. If someone other than the salesman's immediate supervisor evaluates the man's performance, a third party is introduced and communication is immediately made more difficult. Resentments can quickly appear. Both the salesman and the supervisor begin to wonder about the third party. What standards is he using? What does he mean? Why did he decide that? What information is he using? Why did he recommend that I do that to solve my problems, rather than something else? What right does he have to judge my work?

But when the evaluation of a third party is not imposed upon the salesman and his manager, when they are forced to interpret themselves the meaning of the evaluation, each of them knows precisely what the situation is. Evaluation communication is clear. (See cartoon, Figure 13–1.)

FIGURE 13–1

© *Copyright Sales Management, Inc., 1968*

Source: Reprinted by permission from *Sales Management,* The Marketing Magazine. Copyright 1968.

FREQUENCY OF EVALUATION

By the frequency of evaluation is meant the frequency of *formal* evaluation, exclusive of the routine evaluations that are made almost daily in normal sales operations. Clearly, when a salesman is judged (evaluated) to have made a mistake of some significance, it should be brought to his attention as soon as possible and not stored up against some future formal evaluation date. But apart from individual, routine corrections, how often should salesmen be evaluated under a formal evaluation program?

To answer this question, think of the two extremes of frequency that are theoretically possible. At one extreme management could formally evaluate salesmen after every call; at the other, it could evaluate a man's work only on the day he retires. These extremes can be rejected immediately as impractical and useless. Of the first, one might say that "no company could afford a formal evaluation plan with such frequency." Of the latter, that "it would do no one any good, not the salesman, the company, or the sales manager."

Refinement of this analysis leads to the critical questions that must be answered in order to decide what frequency of evaluation is optimum for any individual sales group.

Time Required to Evaluate. Each formal evaluation plan operates on its own evaluation time cycle. The *time cycle* is the sum of the amount of time necessary, with any given evaluation plan, to complete all the steps in the evaluation program. With simple plans the evaluation time cycle is short — perhaps a matter of only a week or so. With more elaborate plans the time cycle may run to months.

Consider the example of a time cycle analysis made by an office equipment manufacturer. With the evaluation standards that have been selected, data collection requires 90 days, information processing 10 days, and supervisors work with salesmen 5 days. The total evaluation time cycle thus includes 105 days. Of course, this does not mean that this company spends 105 full-time days on each evaluation cycle, but rather that 105 days are needed to complete an evaluation cycle. Another company might require a month or two weeks.

Now one answer to the question of evaluation frequency emerges from this example: that one cannot formally evaluate any more frequently than the evaluation time cycle will allow. If the cycle requires 105 days, management cannot formally evaluate any more frequently than that. The evaluation time cycle sets a bottom limit on the frequency of formal evaluation that is possible under any given evaluation program.

Intrusion of Evaluation. The salesman's and supervisor's jobs are made up of current and future activities. *Current activities* are those that are performed in the present to achieve immediate results. *Future activities* are those that are performed in the present to achieve future results. For the salesman, selling, calling on customers, opening new accounts, providing service, and filling out reports are current activities — functions that must be performed now. For the supervisor, traveling with salesmen and calling on customers are current activities — today's responsibilities for immediate pay-offs.

Evaluation, however, is a future activity for both the salesman and his manager. It is performed not to gain immediate benefits, but to achieve desired future gains. All future activities are based on the concept of delayed gratification: the giving up of something of value in the present in the expectation of receiving something of greater value in the future. The college student gives up present income in the expectation that his education will produce greater returns (personal, social, and economic) for him in the future. In short, future activities *intrude* on current activities; they drain time, money, energy, and attention from current activities. When evaluating past performance in order to improve future performance, the sales manager cannot be selling, calling on customers, or performing any other current activity.

In answer to how frequently to evaluate, then, one criterion becomes the amount of intrusion that can be tolerated. How much time can salesmen and managers spend away from their present activities in order to evaluate? There is no all-inclusive answer. This is a judgmental decision to be made by each company in light of its own needs and conditions. One company may decide that for the sake of future performance their salesmen and supervisors must forego a considerable amount of present activity in the expectation of more substantial future gain. Others may severely limit evaluation, preferring to emphasize present gains over potential future payoffs. The use of time studies in selected British firms increased sales calls per day by 10–40 per cent after it was discovered that their salesmen spent only 20 per cent of their time actually selling.[1] These firms apparently had plenty of time for evaluative purposes.

Time Required for Remedial Action. The last criterion that should be applied in answering the question of evaluation frequency is the length of time it takes for the salesman (1) to solve problems that are indicated by the evaluation and (2) to perform the functions on which he is evaluated.

It is pointless to evaluate salesmen more frequently than they are able to react to the evaluation. If, for example, an important performance criterion is the number of new accounts opened and if it usually takes six months to open a new account, it makes little sense to formally evaluate this activity more often than twice a year, since only at that interval can any significant results be observed.

In summary, it can be seen that the best frequency of formal evaluation for a particular sales group is the frequency that *is established in relation to the evaluation time cycle; is no more intrusive on present selling and management activities than is acceptable; and takes into account the time required to remedy mistakes, solve problems, and perform the activities being evaluated.*

EVALUATION FOLLOW-UP

If the formal evaluation plan is a good one, it will show the specific selling activities that each man did well or poorly, and it will provide, either directly or through deduction, the reasons and causes behind these results. Essentially a good evaluation program indicates *where changes are and are not required to improve each man's selling performance.* Therefore, unless something is done about the evaluation, unless it results in worthwhile change, it will have been a waste of money, time, and effort. The evaluation process must continue through *follow-up,* which is the identification of the remedial actions to be taken and the check by the supervisor that the remedial plan is being followed.

---

[1]Reported in *Sales Management* (July 1, 1969), p. 13.

Follow-up is necessary because the indicated remedial activities frequently involve a change in work habits or make the job more difficult or less pleasant. When left to his own devices, everyone tends to resist change by returning to old habits, to the old ways of doing business, or to the easiest, most pleasant way of working. Without follow-up, the salesman will often revert to his old ways and repeat the same mistakes.

Some procedures companies use to ensure evaluation follow-up include a regular post-evaluation report from the sales supervisor to his superior, which summarizes the steps a salesman will take to improve specific aspects of his performance; subsequent progress reports; and special entries on the salesman's regular activity report, which state the problem(s) his last evaluation showed, the plan for correction, and the steps he has taken to solve it and his results to date. Further, when traveling with the salesman, the supervisor is careful to review the salesman's progress and status on particular problems that appeared in the evaluation. And finally the salesman submits special reports to the supervisor, concerning the specific problems uncovered by the evaluation, as well as reviews at the company sales meetings.

Degree of Salesman Involvement in His Own Evaluations

The degree of the salesman's involvement is the extent to which he is allowed or required to participate in the evaluation of his own performance: how much he is consulted in the process and how much detail he is given about his results.

Firms have typically adopted one of three policies toward salesman involvement: complete participation, no participation, or selected participation.

The *complete-participation policy* is based on the propositions that the salesman and the company share a common interest in the performance evaluation, that the salesman has useful information to contribute, and that the evaluation is for the guidance of all those concerned.

The *no-participation policy* is based on the premises that management is best qualified to set standards and evaluate results and that the results of salesman evaluation are the property of management to be used in any way they see fit.

The *selected-participation policy* seeks a middle ground between these two extremes.

The best policy for a particular company is the one that best suits its needs. These policies cannot be judged, nor choices made between them, on ideal, social, or ethical grounds. One policy is not better or worse than the others because it is more' *democratic*, or *humane*, or *considerate*. Rather, selection must be made on the basis of the particular market, products, competition, customers, and sales force. In some companies, for example, a restricted budget for evaluation, a need for constant and speedy evaluation, or the necessity for the performance of current activities will not only justify a no-participation policy, but will make it the only policy possible. Each policy is applicable to particular sets of conditions and is a *good* or *bad* policy only in relation to how well it fits the conditions in which the policy operates.

Table 13−1 analyzes the advantages and disadvantages of the two extreme policies. The middle ground policy of selective participation shares, of course, advantages and disadvantages with each of the extremes.

TABLE 13−1
**Advantages and Disadvantages of No-Participation
and Complete-Participation Policies**

No-Participation Policy		Feature or Condition	Complete Participation Policy	
Advantages	**Disadvantages**		**Advantages**	**Disadvantages**
Not taken from present activities by participation in evaluation		*Salesman's Time*		Taken from present activities by evaluation
Salesman cannot debate evaluation because he		*Salesman's Relation with Super-*		Salesman can challenge, debate standards and results

Advantages	Disadvantages		Advantages	Disadvantages
knows nothing about it. Cheaper because there are no data from salesman to process and evaluate Less time because less data		visor *Cost of Evaluation* *Time of Evaluation Cycle*		Cost of collecting, processing, and analyzing salesman data More time because more data
	Less complete, no salesman data	*Completeness of Information*	More complete, because of salesman data	
	Less complete, so data are usually less accurate	*Accuracy of Data*	More complete, so data are usually more accurate	
	Can be used to some extent only	*Usefulness of Evaluation for Salesman Development Purposes*	Can be used to a large extent	
	Secret, high-handed, unilateral, and difficult to use in self-development	*Morale: Probable Attitude of Salesman Toward Evaluation System*	Open, Democratic, Cooperative, and Helpful in their self-development	

The choice among these policies depends on the condition and situation of each sales group. However, many companies now operating on a no-participation policy would be well advised to review this policy to see if its modification—in the direction of selective or even complete participation—might deliver the substantial advantages of the other policies. Both the selective-participation policy and the complete-participation policy have the following advantages:

1. They avoid the negative effect on a salesman's morale, when he sees his evaluation as secret, unilateral, and high-handed.
2. They provide the evaluation with an extra ingredient: the salesman's intimate knowledge of his territory and customers and of his own operations and habits.
3. They do not reward or punish a salesman according to standards that he does not fully understand or with which he does not fully agree.
4. They make it easier for the salesman to see specifically how he can improve his performance, because he knows precisely how and why he is evaluated.
5. They improve the communication of job requirements between the salesman and his supervisor.
6. They communicate a genuine interest on the part of management in what the salesman is doing.

METHODS OF INVOLVING
THE SALESMAN IN HIS EVALUATION

Companies that involve their salesmen to some degree in their own evaluations use a variety of techniques to accomplish this purpose.

Evaluation Interviews

Many companies require that their sales supervisors review each man's evaluation with him in a personal interview after each evaluation cycle. This interview is intended to (1) transmit evaluation results to the salesman; (2) allow him to clarify any necessary points, to object, or to raise questions; and (3) allow the supervisor and the salesman to agree upon the action that must be taken. Companies using this technique report that it is a very important management activity. They point out that it translates the evaluation into meaningful action by the salesman and reemphasizes the company's performance standards to him. Further, the evaluation interview is a strong motivator for the salesman and a source of detailed market information for the supervisor. It provides the supervisor with an additional chance to evaluate the salesman and with an opportunity to further train the salesman.

Evaluation of the Program by Salesmen

Involvement is also achieved when the supervisor solicits the salesmen's appraisal of the evaluation system itself, either informally or formally. Informally, when traveling with his sales personnel, he seeks their reactions to, and comments about, the evaluation program. Is it measuring the right activities? In the right terms? Over the proper time period? Is there something the salesman wants to report about his performance that the plan does not allow him to do?

Self-Evaluation by Salesmen

Another device that is used to increase salesman participation in formal evaluation programs is to request that the salesman evaluate himself at the same time and on the same standards as his superior. The two evaluations are compared and form the basis for a salesman-supervisor conference and planning session. Interestingly enough, when this technique is employed, the salesman is usually tougher on himself than his supervisor is. Such a technique draws the salesman's attention to specific aspects of his performance and highlights clearly for him what changes must be made. When properly managed, this technique also makes it easier for the supervisor to work with the men on their evaluations and to attain their enthusiastic, constructive cooperation for improving their performance.

TRAINING THE EVALUATORS

Since evaluation is such a complex process, the supervisors and other executives who undertake it must be trained and guided in its use. It is not true that because a person is skilled at doing something, he is

401

thereby well qualified to appraise another person's performance of that task. A man who is a top-flight sales executive is not necessarily a great evaluator of other men's sales performance. He must be trained, counseled, and guided on how to evaluate the performance of others effectively. Good evaluators have the skills, experience, and insights to know:

1. The significance of each performance measure being used (for example, that the number of promotions secured with customers is in part a measure of the man's aggressiveness).
2. How to spot meaningful patterns of results (for example, a man's calls/day have been trending steadily up or down).
3. The significance of the interrelationship between several performance indices (for example, the relationship between the number of new accounts opened and the man's expenses).
4. How to use performance measures to infer conclusions about the man and his selling skills (for example, that most of his accounts and orders are small may at least imply that he is not skillful in handling large accounts).
5. How to cross-check his evaluation evidence by placing one set of observations against another (for example, the comparison of salesman activity reports with his field visits with salesmen).
6. How to explain problems and deficiencies to the salesmen and work out remedial action with them.
7. How to be as objective and unbiased as possible, by evaluating a salesman against established performance standards; how to avoid judging a salesman on the basis of one's own record or according to personal likes and dislikes.

The skills and insights of the evaluator do not come naturally, nor are they necessarily the result of normal field selling or supervisory experience. They must be deliberately transmitted to evaluators by some form of training. Some means used to impart the necessary knowledge and skills to evaluators are as follows:

Evaluation Manual. Collective company experience is assembled in a how-to instruction manual which new evaluators are expected to master and experienced evaluators to review periodically.

Seminars. Supervisors who are about to assume evaluation respon-sibility are gathered in a group for a seminar. There, under the direc-tion of skilled evaluators, they study cases, problems, and exercises in salesman evaluation. They hear lectures and instructions and ex-change their views and insights with experienced evaluators and with their contemporaries.

Observation and Critique. An experienced evaluator is assigned to a new evaluator, and together they work through a number of individu-al evaluations. The experienced man advises the other on the actual evaluations he must make of his personnel.

SUMMARY This chapter was a sequel to the introduction to sales-man evaluation presented in Chapter 12. Chapter 13 described the operation of an effective evaluation program.

Performance evaluations should be conducted at the lowest possible level of supervision, preferably by the salesman's immediate supervi-sor. There are several reasons for this approach: (1) it strengthens the salesman-supervisor relationship, (2) there is a mutual commitment, (3) the supervisor is responsible for the performance results of his salesmen, and (4) there is a better communication of goals and reme-dies.

Chapter 13 also pointed out that the best frequency of formal evalu-ation for a particular sales group is the frequency that (1) is estab-lished in relation to the evaluation time cycle; (2) is no more intrusive on present selling and management activities than is acceptable; and (3) takes into account the time required to remedy mistakes, solve problems, and perform the activities being evaluated.

Evaluation follow-up and the degree of salesman involvement in his own evaluations (complete-participation policy, no-participation pol-icy, or selected-participation policy) was also examined in this chap-ter. Chapter 13 concluded with discussions of the methods of involv-ing salesmen in their evaluation and the training of evaluators.

DISCUSSION/REVIEW QUESTIONS

1. With a friend thoroughly discuss the question: Should college students take an active part in evaluating their own class and course performance and in setting their grades? Take notes on this discussion organizing them in "yes" or "no" columns. Now study your lists. How, if at all, do they apply to the question of salesmen participating in their own evaluations?

2. What is meant by:
   (a) no-participation evaluation policy?
   (b) complete-participation evaluation policy?
   (c) selected-participation evaluation policy?

3. How frequently should salesmen be evaluated? Discuss.

4. "Evaluation of salesman performance should be done at the lowest possible level." Comment.

5. Make a list of the specific skills and knowledge managers have to possess in order to be good evaluators of their salesmen's performance. Identify which of these would have to be "trained into" an evaluator and which he knows by experience or common sense. What does this analysis indicate about training evaluators? Why?

6. A friend of yours with ten years experience as a salesman with two companies has just been hired by a third company as national sales manager. In discussing his new job with you, he says, "What a challenge! You know, neither of the companies I worked for before had evaluation programs for their salesmen. One of the first things I'm going to do on my new job is design and put into operation a good, hard-hitting salesman evaluation program. It'll be easy and quick to set one up. I should have it working in a matter of weeks after I get started. What do you think?" Outline your reply to him.

7. Why is evaluation described as a *future* activity?

8. Describe how salesmen may be involved in their own evaluation.

CHAPTER FOURTEEN
SALESMEN'S
INCENTIVES
AND COMPENSATION

Through his day-to-day contacts, the field sales manager is perhaps the most effective motivator of his personnel. He sets the style and tone for their relationship with the company. However, personal supervision is limited by the time available to the manager, and other incentives, including compensation, must also be used to motivate salesmen.

In establishing incentives, the first task is to discover what each individual salesman needs or wants. A manager cannot motivate his men unless he understands their desires. Although part of his task is to develop a general awareness of human behavior, this alone will not suffice. The sales manager must also identify the individual needs of his men. Tom Stasizak has four children and a mortgage; he is concerned with security. Bob Clifton is a bachelor; he is motivated by the potential for high earnings. Obviously, Tom's needs and Bob's needs are different. The incentives used to motivate these two salesmen must also be different.

Sales trainees and older salesmen present special motivation problems. It is hard to motivate sales trainees who must undergo long breaking-in periods before they are productive. It is difficult to give them a feeling of accomplishment. It is especially tough to generate enthusiasm for selling when sales trainees are technical college graduates who have no sincere desire to sell.

The older salesman presents a different challenge, since there are sometimes limits on what he can earn, and since he sometimes feels that his own personal growth is restricted. Often, the older salesman feels that his occupation lacks prestige and acceptance within the company. He no longer sees a clear opportunity for advancement.

Talking with and observing the sales personnel will provide insights into each salesman's behavior. The sales manager must then choose the proper incentives to motivate his men. He must provide the conditions for motivation — opportunities for growth, achievement, participation, responsibility, and recognition. The manager must also make sure that the basic conditions for good morale are provided — adequate pay, attractive physical surroundings, social opportunities, and the like.

TYPES OF INCENTIVES

In addition to personal supervision, there are two other major ways to motivate salesmen, *financial* and *nonfinancial* incentives. Like good leadership, well-chosen incentives will stimulate salesmen to use their existing energies and resources more effectively. In designing the incentive, one can choose either a *special-effort* or a *continuing* format. A sales contest is an example of a special-effort incentive, since a contest is designed to achieve a specific, short-term goal. On the other hand, compensation and promotion are related to the achievement of continuing (long-term) objectives.

Nonfinancial Incentives

Nonfinancial incentives for salesmen include a variety of techniques used for specific, special-effort situations. Sales conventions and meetings, sales contests, honors and recognition, and communication are the major forms of special incentives.

These incentives are usually designed to achieve one or two specific, short-range objectives. However, they must be coordinated with the company's long-range marketing goals and overall motivation program. For example, if a company has an overall goal of balanced sales, it would be foolish to introduce a sales contest that would encourage salesmen to emphasize a specific product line.

Financial Incentives

Business organizations provide two forms of financial rewards. Financial incentives may be *direct* monetary payments, such as salaries and wages, or they may be *indirect* monetary rewards. These indirect rewards, commonly known as *fringe benefits*, include paid vacations, insurance plans, pension plans, and the like.

The financial incentive is the most widely used and misunderstood technique for motivating salesmen. Some sales managers feel strongly that money is the only way to stimulate salesmen. Admittedly, financial renumeration is an important motivator, but nonfinancial incentives cannot be ignored. In particular, money as a motivator decreases in importance once a satisfactory level of earnings has been reached. However, up to that point, a salesman will strive hard to reach and maintain a satisfactory standard of living.

Financial incentives have changed in recent years. More salesmen are now paid through a combination plan of salary and commission or bonus. Such plans provide stability of earnings and a direct incentive. Also, fringe benefits have become a more important part of the average salesman's income. These and other trends will be discussed in a later section.

SALES MEETINGS AND CONVENTIONS

Almost every sales manager is involved in planning and conducting a sales meeting or convention. Local meetings attended by salesmen from one sales office or district are usually held weekly or monthly. Conventions, which are held once or twice a year, are national or regional gatherings of salesmen.

Sales meetings and conventions should be designed for specific purposes. For example, a sales meeting or convention can emphasize training material — such as explaining the firm's advertising campaign, assisting salesmen to improve their sales techniques, and providing new product information. Or a meeting can be used to communicate changes in company policies or information on current market trends. Whatever the purpose, it must be specific; a meeting which is designed strictly for motivation will often be rejected by salesmen as a glorified "pep" talk.[1]

---

[1]The need to make sales meetings a learning experience is pointed out in Martin Everett, "Running Out of Time," *Sales Management* (January 10, 1972), pp. 25–30

Certainly, a poor sales meeting is one of the biggest mistakes a field sales manager could make. Effective conventions and meetings are strong motivators, but poor meetings are simply a waste of everyone's time and of the company's money.[2] The keys to a good meeting are planning and participation.

Planning

The first step in planning a sales meeting is to formulate an objective for the meeting. The objective must be set in conjunction with the company's overall marketing and sales objectives. Major automobile manufacturers, for instance, orient their annual dealer meetings toward the goal of introducing the new models to the dealers and the press.

Once the objective for the meeting has been established, the sales manager must consider the theme, the time and place for the meeting, the agenda, timetable, and the administrative arrangements.

Theme. Every sales convention should have a theme. This will serve as a guide in planning the agenda and will stimulate enthusiasm. For the salesmen, the theme indicates the basic purpose of the meeting. It is not necessary that each weekly or monthly sales meeting have a distinct theme. However, a general theme for the month or quarter may provide effective orientation for the regular sales meetings.

Themes for sales conventions are almost unlimited. Frequently, sales conventions are run in conjunction with sales contests, and a joint theme is used for both. Sports, college life, events, and exotic places are commonly used themes for sales conventions. For example, the Graduate School of Sales Management and Marketing, Sales and Marketing Executives — International, uses a college theme. The faculty director is the dean, students elect class officers, athletic competition is held between classes, and a graduation ceremony is conducted.

Time and Place. It is essential that arrangements be made far in advance so that a sales meeting or conference will not conflict with

---

[2] Some guidelines for improving sales meetings are suggested in Arlo Jensen, "Commonsense Guide to Better Sales Meetings," *Marketing World* (December 1970), pp. 17 – 21.

other activities. It is best to schedule meetings at times when they will not interfere with the salesmen's selling activities. Monday morning or Friday afternoon is a good time for weekly or monthly sales meetings. Annual conventions should be held when business is slack, perhaps during the summer or during the Easter or Christmas seasons.

Selecting a meeting place involves many considerations. The location usually indicates whether the purpose of the meeting is work or pleasure. For example, a Las Vegas or Miami Beach meeting would probably be viewed by the salesmen as a pleasure-oriented meeting.

The size of the group will be a major factor in selecting the type of facility. It is often important to get the men away from their normal surroundings. This rules out company facilities. Other considerations are convenience, type of accommodations desired, equipment and meeting room facilities, food service, and reputation of the facility. Airport motels are especially popular as meeting places because of their easy accessibility and their willingness to cater to business groups.

Agenda and Timetable. The agenda and timetable establish the basic structure and timing of the meeting. It is essential that a written agenda and timetable be developed during the planning stages. As plans progress, these will be revised.

The final agenda and timetable serve as the program for the meeting. Topics, speakers and discussion leaders, times and places of sessions, and recreation activities are included. A printed program should be given to salesmen ahead of time so they will know exactly what they will be doing.

Administrative Arrangements. There are many details to attend to when planning and conducting a conference. Space arrangements, food, speakers, recreation facilities, and the like must all be considered in advance. Establishing effective communications with the staff of the facilities is critical. They need to be informed of a meeting's specific requirements. It is especially important to inform the convention site's sales and catering staff of any special services, personnel, or facilities which will be needed. During the meeting the sales manager should continue to work closely with the staff.

Participation

The second key to a successful sales meeting is participation by the salesmen. It is important for the sales personnel to have an active part in the meeting. An exchange of ideas and experiences is vital. Unless the participants feel that they are free to express their ideas, they will not become actively involved in the meeting.

There are many ways to effect participation from salesmen. One technique is to have salesmen prepare special presentations in advance. One company has its top salesmen prepare and talk about how they closed the most difficult sale of the year, the most unusual sale of the year, or the most important sale of the year. The presentations are made to the entire sales force at the national sales meeting, and humorous gifts are awarded to the presenters. For this company, the opportunity to tell his personal success story is a potent motivator for the salesman.

Other techniques for obtaining participation are skits, panel discussions, debates, case studies, and role playing. Each of these techniques makes the salesman feel he is a part of the meeting. They also provide a flow of ideas that may not be forthcoming from a formal presentation. One of the authors vividly remembers a role-playing session with chain saw salesmen. After the session, many in the audience said that more was learned from the participation of an older salesman than from anything else. This man was an excellent salesman, but he was closed-mouthed about his sales techniques. When he was put in the role-playing situation, he willingly demonstrated why he was such an outstanding sales person.

Evaluation of Meetings

Sales conventions and meetings are expensive. Transportation, accommodations, entertainment, speakers, and the costs of planning for large numbers of salesmen involve major expenditures. Also, meetings take salesmen away from selling. Unless the conference results in improved sales effort, the time spent may have been a waste. For instance, if salesmen are at a convention solely for a company-paid vacation, the training time will be wasted.

A Dartnell survey indicates that the average sales and marketing executive attends 20 meetings annually. He travels thousands of miles and spends $2100 on these conventions, workshops, and seminars. However, the important point is that 75 per cent of these sales executives thought the meetings were worth the expense and effort.[3]

SALES CONTESTS

Sales contests are an established technique for stimulating salesmen. They are most popular with firms specializing in consumer goods, such as food and drugs, and least popular with companies selling big-ticket items to industrial buyers. The type of sales contest will depend on the job to be done. Sales contests will vary according to prizes awarded, methods of determining winners, and themes.

Sales contests help to achieve company goals by satisfying some of the salesman's personal goals — recognition from his peers, awards for performance, personal esteem, and respect of his family.

Companies use sales contests to accomplish numerous organizational objectives. One survey of 323 firms analyzed the objectives of their sales contests; the results are shown in Table 14–1 (see page 412).

Planning the Contest

Planning sales contests requires expertise, and it is wise to seek outside help when developing a contest. Sources of help are the sales promotion manager and advertising manager, the advertising agency, sales premium representatives, major companies who have a premium organization, and trade associations in the premium field. In recent years specialized sales incentive firms, such as E. R. MacDonald and Maritz, have become widely known. An incentive house will help the sales manager develop a contest program which coincides with the company's sales goals.

Theme. A good sales contest theme is necessary to provide the play element, to sharpen competition, and to enhance promotion of the contest. Sports themes are often used since they provide the contest

---

[3]Reported in *Sales Management* (November 10, 1970), p. 33.

TABLE 14−1
Objectives of Sales Contests

Objective	Percentage Listing This Item As an Objective
Increase overall sales	85.4
Find new customers	64.7
Promote special items	44.0
Obtain greater volume per call	41.8
Overcome seasonal sales slump	40.6
Introduce a new product, line, or service	36.8
Get better territory coverage	31.9
Stop or slow a sales decline	28.5
Get better balance of sales	26.6
Get renewal of business with former customers	24.5
Develop new sales skills	23.5
Ease an unfavorable inventory position	20.4
Improve sales service to customers	19.2
Sell higher quality products	16.7
Build better product displays	12.1
Do self-training	11.8
Lower selling costs	10.2
Reduce selling time	4.3
Get better sales reports	3.7
Other	6.5

Source: Adapted from Albert Haring and Malcom L. Morris, "Sales Contests As A Motivating Device," *Southern Journal of Business*, vol. 4 (April 1969), pp. 178–183.

with a competitive atmosphere. Themes with an element of chance, such as poker or roulette, are also effective.

Prizes. Prizes are frequently the key to a successful contest. Money is still used extensively, but there is a growing trend toward noncash incentives. (See cartoon, Figure 14–1.) Merchandise catalogs offer the winners a choice and appeal to all members of a salesman's family. Trading stamps do the same thing and have the additional advantage of an immediate payoff at a redemption center. A large manufacturer increased appliance sales 400 per cent when it rewarded salesmen with S & H green stamps for selling accessories on service calls.

Travel is a good prize because it has a strong appeal to the spouse and is easy to dramatize. The buildings materials division of Owens-Corning Fiberglas boosted sales 20 per cent during a slow season by giving top salesmen and their wives a trip to the builders' convention in Las Vegas. The Kirby Division of Cleveland-based Scott and Fetzer Company has sent their 30 top sales personnel and their spouses to Hawaii.[4] While exact figures on the extent of incentive travel are

FIGURE 14–1

*"Mr. Jackson says it's time to
take your incentive prize home."*

Source: Reprinted by permission from *Sales Management*, The Marketing Magazine. Copyright 1968.

---

[4]William S. Hieronymus, Jr., "Expense-Paid Junket Beats Mere Money As A Sales Incentive," *Wall Street Journal* (June 25, 1973), pp. 1, 21.

413

elusive, United Air Lines estimates that U.S. companies spent about $500 million for such trips during 1973. This includes both travel expenses and land arrangements. The 1973 total more than doubled the approximately $200 million spent in 1970.[5]

Also gaining popularity are prizes which offer more practical rewards. Several companies are offering an all-expenses-paid college education for a salesman's child. Life insurance policies are also a popular prize. Finally, honors can and should be used in conjunction with tangible prizes.

Length. Sales managers disagree on the optimum length for a contest. In general, a contest should last long enough for every salesman to make a complete cycle of his territory. This will vary, but most sales managers feel that three months is sufficient. Peak excitement can be maintained for only short periods of time. After three months, enthusiasm typically diminishes.

Promotion. A sales contest should be launched with fanfare. It must immediately generate excitement and enthusiasm. For this reason contests are often introduced during a national sales convention or at regional sales meetings. Follow-up promotion is also necessary; the excitement cannot be allowed to taper off. The salesmen should be sold continuously on the prizes, the winners should be recognized, and losers should be reminded that they are behind.

Criticisms of Sales Contests

As a sales stimulation technique, contests have received much criticism. Some of these criticisms are aimed at poor management of sales contests, while others are concerned with the value of contests as a motivating force.[6]

Poor Contest Management. Sales contests sometimes fail because the sales manager has not carefully planned his contest. The timing may be off, the wrong prizes may be offered, and the goals may be unrealis-

---

[5]Hieronymus (1973), p. 1.
[6]The dangers involved in sales contests are pointed out in David R. Hampton, "The Sales Contest: Fragile, Handle With Care," *Sales Management* (September 10, 1969), p. 62.

tic. Too often sales contests offer a very few prizes attainable by only the top salesmen. Sales contests should allow every participant who reaches his own goals to earn prizes. All salesmen must have a chance to win or negative morale will result. When salesmen compete for a limited number of top prizes, there are only a few happy winners and many unhappy or apathetic losers. For this reason, trading stamps are sometimes used as prizes since they allow every participant to obtain some form of reward.

Another reason for failure is inadequate promotion of the contest. Poor internal communication will result in a salesman's not knowing about a contest. The contest must be well publicized to everyone involved. One writer has suggested that the "10 Biggest Mistakes" made in sales contests include:

1. Failure to set goals
2. Bad timing
3. Complicating the program
4. Setting quotas too high
5. Awarding the wrong prizes
6. Insufficient promotion
7. Excluding managers from rewards
8. Poor "scorekeeping"
9. Neglecting sales support personnel
10. "Forgetting the little woman."[7]

Value of Contests.   The problems mentioned above can be overcome by careful planning. A more serious concern is the question of the value of sales contests as a sales stimulator. A frequent complaint is that sales contests distort the normal sales pattern. It is argued that a contest does not really raise sales over the long run, but that it merely provides a short-term sales expansion.

An example will illustrate this criticism. A major oil company ran a sales contest to increase sales of oil to motorists. During the contest period, sales rose substantially. However, at the end of the period, sales were about what they had been the year before.

---

[7]Zenn Kaufman, "10 Biggest Mistakes Incentive Managers Make," *Sales Management* (October 1, 1970), pp. 26–27.

A related criticism is that contests distract salesmen from their main job of selling. They are encouraged by the contests to concentrate on winning prizes. For example, one company ran a contest aimed at encouraging men to set up dealer displays. The contest was successful; displays were placed in stores. Nevertheless, sales did not increase accordingly because many salesmen neglected to sell the products.

Why Contests Work

Despite the qualms of many sales managers, contests are widely used. And they work for most companies. Various studies have shown that executives generally consider special sales contests to be an effective motivating force. Contests work because they provide recognition, excitement, and rewards.

Recognition. Everyone wants recognition. Salesmen want to feel important; they want status. A sales contest provides salesmen with an opportunity to earn recognition.

Excitement. A sales contest puts a game element into what may otherwise be just a job. The contest is a challenge to which a salesman usually responds. It provides new excitement, and it helps to overcome the routine of selling.

Rewards. The prize is an effective motivator by itself. If every salesman feels that he has a chance of winning, and he should, the prize is usually a reward worth seeking. This is particularly true if the prize is something the person would not normally buy for himself.

HONORS AND RECOGNITION

Special honors and awards are inexpensive and have considerable appeal to salesmen. Frequently, honors are given in connection with tangible rewards. They provide the salesman with the recognition he desires.

There are many types of honors and awards used to stimulate salesmen. These include trophies, plaques, certificates, membership in honorary organizations, such as the Salesmen's Advisory Council, and titles, such as "Salesman of the Year." Salesmen can also be honored through news releases to local newspapers and trade magazines. The life insurance industry's Million Dollar Roundtable is a widely publicized honor.

Recognition can be given through special privileges. One manufacturer of consumer durables has his top salesmen arrive a day before the national sales meeting. They meet with market researchers and with research and development personnel to discuss new product ideas. These top salesmen are recognized for their achievement by being asked to express their opinions. The company also gets the added benefit of receiving salesmen's ideas which are based on their extensive contact with customers.

COMMUNICATION

It is also important to emphasize the role of communication as a motivating force. Salesmen may be out in territories that are hundreds of miles from an office. They need frequent recognition and reinforcement. Continuous communication can be maintained through written communications, phone calls, meetings with field sales managers, and visits to salesmen in the field.

Personal contacts are the most effective form of motivation. But continuous personal contacts are impossible. A field sales manager cannot be with every salesman at the same time. Planned phone calls are an acceptable substitute. One sales manager keeps in touch with his men by calling at least once a week. The manager carefully plans his calls and writes down the main points he wants to cover. The calls usually include praise for some worthwhile accomplishment.

Bulletins, announcements, letters, and other forms of written communication are also useful in motivating salesmen. A congratulatory letter from the boss may be remembered longer and valued more highly than a routine monetary reward. The sales bulletin is an ideal place to use honest praise. Contest winners should be spotlighted in sales bulletins and company publications. The salesman knows that his colleagues and the home office are aware of his accomplishments.

It is also a good idea to mail sales bulletins to a salesman's home as well as to his office. Spouses should be included in communication plans.

COMPENSATING SALESMEN

A sound compensation plan is essential to the successful management of the sales force. However, there is confusion and disagreement about the role of financial incentives as motivators. At one extreme is the sales manager who feels that his personnel are motivated strictly by financial considerations and who is unwilling to recognize their other needs. At the other extreme are the proponents of internal growth needs. They argue that a salesman is entirely concerned with factors related to his job and that financial compensation is relatively unimportant as a true motivator of behavior.

An accurate view of money as a motivator lies somewhere between these two extremes. Financial compensation has several functions in motivating salesmen. It is the determinant of a salesman's purchasing power; it is a symbol of status; it is an indication of equitable treatment.

Further, an inadequate compensation plan can adversely affect all aspects of sales force operation. Depressed pay rates create dissatisfaction and lead to low morale. Turnover of salesmen is often directly related to low compensation. Other symptoms of a poor salesmen's compensation plan include rising field sales expenses, declining sales, growing numbers of customers' and salesmen's complaints, product imbalance, and excessive loss of old accounts.

On the other hand, an effective salesmen's compensation plan can be an important motivator. Increased sales are stimulated by a well-conceived compensation plan. In part, this is true because compensation is more than simply a payment for services rendered; it is related to recognition as well. A salary increase is a reward, but it is also a form of recognition for a job performance.

Trends in Salesmen's Compensation

Compensating field salesmen is more difficult than paying most other employees. The conditions under which most salesmen work are less standardized and less easily controlled. Therefore, salesmen's compensation plans are continuously undergoing change. Several studies reveal three major trends in compensating salesmen.

Shift to Combination Plans. Fewer companies are paying salesmen on the basis of salary or commission alone. One study reported a 55 per cent relative decline in straight commission plans over a recent twenty-year period.[8] The use of incentives and/or bonus payments, to supplement salesmen's salaries has grown rapidly since the end of World War II. Approximately 64 per cent of American companies now use a form of salary plus incentive compensation to pay salesmen.[9]

Combination plans are used more because they provide greater flexibility. The modern salesman's job is more complicated. He must be a problem-solver as well as a seller of goods and services. Incentives can be related to the accomplishment of specific marketing objectives and sales volume. In addition, combination plans satisfy the salesman's desire for some stable base income.[10]

Emphasis on Profitability. Many companies are now trying to relate salesmen's compensation to some measure of profitability. For instance, compensation is sometimes tied to gross margin.[11] The goal is to motivate salesmen to sell not just volume, but *profitable* volume.[12] Sales compensation should be keyed to the more profitable products. Unfortunately, there is no easy way to incorporate profits. Most companies try to do this through some sort of combination plan.

Fringe Benefits. The third major trend in salesmen's compensation is the increased availability of fringe benefits. In most companies, even salesmen on straight commission are now eligible for such benefits as pensions and insurance.

---

[8]The declining use of pure commission plans is reported in Burton E. Bauder, "Changing Patterns in Sales Compensation," *Sales/Marketing Today* (February 1970) pp. 12–13.

[9]Jack R. Dauner, "More!" *Sales Management* (December 13, 1971), p. 27.

[10]An interesting discussion of this point is contained in John W. Bany, "Achieving Balance in Salaries and Incentives," *Sales/Marketing Today* (July 1970) pp. 11–13.

[11]See Ralph L. Day and Peter D. Bennett, "Should Salesmen's Compensation Be Geared to Profits?" *Journal of Marketing*, vol. 26 (October 1962), pp. 6–9. Also see John U. Farley, "An Optimal Plan For Salesmen's Compensation," *Journal of Marketing Research*, vol. 28 (May 1964), pp. 39–43.

[12]See Michael Reynolds, "Keying Compensation to Profits," *Sales Management* (November 10, 1970), pp. 20–21, 53–54.

Changes in the nature of selling are largely responsible for this trend. Salesmen are no longer considered self-supporting free agents. They have closer ties with their companies. Companies have to offer a range of health, welfare, and pension benefits to attract good men.

Salesmen receive "hidden income" from fringe benefits. Usually, the benefits that are available to nonsales personnel are also available to salesmen. Most firms provide paid vacations, group life insurance, hospitalization, and major medical insurance. Pensions for salesmen are now accepted as normal, and salesmen receive paid holidays. Based on a survey by *Sales Management*, Table 14–2 shows the extent of coverage for salesmen, as reported by 169 sales and marketing executives.

TABLE 14–2
Salesmen's Fringe Benefits

Benefit	Percentage of Firms Reporting:		
	Full Coverage	Partial Coverage	No Coverage
Vacation	90	3	7
Life insurance	56	40	4
Hospitalization	50	47	3
Major medical	51	44	5
Pension plan	50	31	19
Personal use of company car	53	24	22
Tuition reimbursement	35	36	29
Profit sharing	28	24	48
Stock options	8	16	76

Source: BASED ON A SURVEY OF 169 SALES AND MARKETING EXECUTIVES See "The Ante Goes Up," *Sales Management* (August 1, 1969), p. 33. Reprinted by permission of *Sales Management, The Marketing Magazine.* Copyright 1969.

Criteria for a Sound Compensation Plan

Designing a sound compensation plan for salesmen is difficult. In perhaps the most complete study of salesmen's compensation ever done, the authors stated:

There is no one best compensation plan for any one size of firm or for any one type of industry. There is no nice solution to the problem of compensating salesmen of all sizes and types of firms, even in a single industry.[13]

A sound compensation plan for salesmen will consider the needs of both the company and its salesmen. From the company's standpoint, the basic consideration is to get salesmen to do what management wants done as efficiently as possible. Salesmen's compensation is a major sales expense. The dilemma for sales management is how to stimulate salesmen to maximize profitable sales volume and yet keep sales expenses at a minimum.

From the salesman's point of view, the basic concern is to maximize earnings. He wants a level of compensation which he feels is fair in comparison with the incomes of his peer group, of other company employees, and of the relevant labor market. The salesman also wants a balance of security (a steady income) and payment for extra effort (incentive income). Achieving the proper balance presents another dilemma for sales management.

An effective compensation plan represents both points of view. General characteristics of a good plan are described below.

Incentive. Financial rewards are an important form of motivation. A sound compensation plan will stimulate salesmen to achieve the firm's goals. In particular, it must motivate salesmen to generate net profit rather than mere sales volume. A good plan will encourage salesmen to accomplish what management decides it wants done.

Simplicity. An effective compensation plan is easily understood and relatively simple to operate. Salesmen should be able to calculate easily what their income will be. A plan which salesmen cannot understand loses its value as a motivator. Further, a plan should not attempt to motivate salesmen to achieve more than two or three important selling objectives. Incentive components must be based on measur-

---

[13]Harry S. Tosdal and Waller Carson, Jr., *Salesmen's Compensation*, vol. 1 (Boston: Harvard Business School, 1953), p. 316.

able, clear factors. Complex salesmen's compensation plans simply do not work.

Fairness. An essential element for any sales compensation plan is equity. The plan must be fair to both the company and its salesmen. The company should be able to keep selling costs in line with volume. The compensation plan should also protect against windfall gains to salesmen in abnormal times.

Salesmen expect a plan to reward ability and productivity This requires a constant scrutiny and a willingness to revise the plan if necessary. Special care must be taken to even out inequities resulting from territorial differences.

Flexibility. A plan should be sufficiently flexible to take into account the rapidly changing needs of the company and its salesmen. Changes in the supply of salesmen, products, and customers, as well as changes in the competitive situation, will require adjustments in sales compensation. For instance, a good plan will operate effectively through the ups and downs of the business cycle.

Control. A salesman tends to do what management pays him to do. The salesmen's compensation plan should provide control and direction over salesmen's activities. A sound plan will strengthen the sales manager's supervision of his personnel. However, no compensation plan can ever take the place of a good sales manager or act as a substitute for good leadership.

Competitiveness. The level of compensation must be competitive with the levels offered by other companies. As the payment for services rendered, a salesman's compensation must be adequate. Attractive pay is needed to attract, keep, and develop effective salesmen. Peter Drucker, a leading management consultant, comments: "To attract and hold the kind of [sales] people we need requires, above all, ability to pay what they can earn in competitive jobs which are easier and less demanding than selling."[14]

---

[14]Peter Drucker, "How to Double Your Sales," *Nation's Business* (March 1967), p. 80.

DEVELOPING A COMPENSATION PLAN

Rarely is a field sales manager called upon to design a salesman's compensation plan. However, he is usually responsible for administering the plan. He may also be asked for recommendations when a plan is being revised. For these reasons, it is important for the field sales manager to understand the process by which a compensation plan for salesmen is developed.[15] The basic steps in this process are as follows:

1. Review the salesman's job;
2. Determine specific objectives;
3. Establish the level of compensation;
4. Choose the method of compensation;
5. Implement the plan.

Job Review

The first step in designing or revising a compensation plan is to carefully review the salesman's job. The preparation of the job description was discussed previously. It is sufficient at this point to reemphasize the value of the job description as a planning tool. Careful analysis of the job description will reveal what a company must pay to acquire and satisfy the salesmen it wants.

For example, education and experience are the two prime qualities which will require above-average compensation. If a college education is a requisite for a sales job, compensation must be competitive with other college-level jobs. Likewise, if a company must hire only experienced salesmen because it lacks a sufficient training program, it must be prepared to pay more for experienced men.

Establish Objectives

Sales compensation objectives must be related to the company's sales and marketing goals. They must also be realistic. One cannot expect

---

[15]The development of sales compensation plans is discussed in Frederick E. Webster, Jr., "Rationalizing Salesmen's Compensation Plans,' *Journal of Marketing*, vol. 30 (January 1966), pp. 55–58.

the salesmen's compensation plan to overcome basic weaknesses in sales supervision.

The objectives will indicate what the plan is expected to accomplish. Richard C. Smyth of Smyth and Murphy Associates, a management consulting firm specializing in the financial management of marketing, suggests three prime objectives for a salesmen's compensation plan.

1. It will motivate the salesman to plan ahead and use his time to maximum effectiveness.
2. It will motivate the salesman to do what sales management wants done, when sales management wants it done, and in the way sales management wants it done.
3. Most important of all, the properly designed salesmen's incentive plan will result in lower direct selling costs and increased profits for the company, and in higher personal incomes for the better salesmen.[16]

Specific objectives will depend on each company's resources, needs, and marketing goals. Developing new accounts, minimizing sales expenses, full-line selling, meeting quotas, and developing new territories are a few examples.

Level of Compensation

Compensation should be set at a level sufficient to attract, retain, and stimulate the type of salesmen desired. This usually involves paying about what other firms are paying for similar selling jobs. However, a smaller company may be forced to pay a premium to attract competent salesmen. This is especially true if the smaller company has a limited sales training program and is required to hire only experienced salesmen.

The level of sales compensation depends upon several factors. Pay must be attractive enough to appeal to sales recruits. There must be a

---

[16]Richard C. Smyth, "Financial Incentives for Salesmen," *Harvard Business Review*, vol. 46 (January–February 1968), p. 117.

fair correlation between salesmen's compensation and the pay of other employees. Competitors' pay plans must be examined as must the company's own past history of sales compensation. Finally, careful attention should be given to the relationship between sales compensation and profits. Management must estimate what salesmen's compensation will cost the company. Overpaying or underpaying salesmen must be avoided.

Dangers of Overpaying. Although many companies overpay their salesmen, this is a bad practice.[17] One result is the adverse effect on company profits. Salesmen's compensation is usually the largest single element of selling cost, so that excessive pay levels will unnecessarily reduce profits.

Personnel problems are also created by overpaying salesmen. The morale of sales managers will suffer, since they will resent the fact that their salesmen earn more than they do. Further, it will be difficult to persuade top salesmen to take management positions, if the latter involve cuts in pay.

Dangers of Underpaying. It is also important to guard against underpaying salesmen. Two conditions may result if this is done. First, the company may attract only poor salesmen, and poor performance will result. Second, if good people are hired at low pay, there will be excessive turnover. Good salesmen will be vulnerable to *pirating* by other firms.

Method of Compensation

The major methods for paying salesmen are salary, commission, and bonus. Most firms now use some type of plan that combines these methods. The method of compensating salesmen is just as important as the level of compensation. In fact, many sales managers feel that it is the method of compensation, not the level, that influences the performance of salesmen. When choosing a method of compensation, three factors must be considered — motivation, control, and cost.

---

[17]This problem is discussed in Kenneth R. Davis, "Are Your Salesmen Paid Too Much?" *Harvard Business Review*, vol. 34 (November–December 1956), pp. 52–60.

Motivation. Different methods of compensation will stimulate salesmen in different ways. Commissions and bonuses provide a direct
incentive to achieve, while salaries are less directly related to a salesman's performance.

Control. Each method of compensation also provides a different
form of control. When a salesman is on straight salary, he is directly
responsible for his actions. A sales manager has direct control and can
ask his personnel to perform extra nonselling duties. The commission
form of payment has the opposite effect. The salesman considers himself more independent than the salaried salesman and often performs
only those activities which are immediately related to sales success.
The bonus form of compensation provides control by inducing salesmen to point their efforts toward a particular goal.

Cost. The various methods of compensating salesmen affect selling
costs in different ways. Salaries are a fixed expense; commissions and
bonuses are variable expenses. When business is good, a straight salary plan may provide higher profits. However, in a business slump,
fixed selling expenses may cause losses. With commissions and bonuses, selling expenses vary with performance. They will be high
when sales are good and low when sales are poor.

FIGURE 14–2

**Relationship Between Selling Expenses and the Methods of Sales
Compensation**

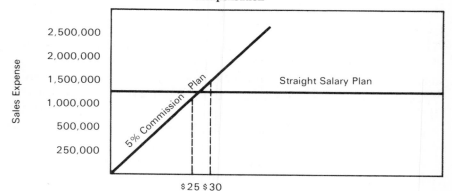

Sales (in millions)

Figure 14–2 illustrates this relationship. Assume that a company has a choice between paying its 100 salesmen a salary of $12,500 a year or a commission of 5 per cent of net sales. If sales are $25 million or less, the company will minimize selling expenses by paying salesmen on commission. If sales are more than $25 million, a salary form of compensation will minimize selling expenses.

A word of caution is in order, however. Cost is an important factor, but cost is not the only consideration. Sometimes the least expensive method of compensation may not be the best. Motivation and control are equally important. For instance, if projected sales in the above example are $30 million, it may be wise to still use a commission form of payment. The greater selling effort generated by a direct financial incentive may have important extra benefits.

Salary

A *salary* is a fixed sum of money paid at regular intervals. A salesman might be paid $200 a week, $800 a month, or $10,000 a year. The amount paid is related to *time* rather than to the work achieved.

A straight salary is used when salesmen's actual work function is not directly related to sales volume or to other quantitative measures of productivity. This is often true when a salesman is expected to perform many nonselling activities, such as market investigation, customer problem analysis, servicing, and sales promotion. The salary compensates the salesman for these nonselling duties. The level is based on many factors such as length of service, living requirements, general performance, and competitive salaries.

Straight salary plans are also found in companies and industries in which an engineering orientation is needed for selling, such as aerospace and industrial chemicals. A salary is needed because of the extended time required to close complex industrial sales. A salary also encourages the salesman to emphasize continued service after the sale.

Salaries are appropriate when a new product is introduced, when a new market is developed, or when a new salesman is being trained. These situations are all characterized by uncertainty for the salesman. A salary provides him with a steady income while he gets his feet on the ground.

The prime advantage of a straight salary is direct control. Salesmen can be required to perform activities which do not result in immediate sales. There is also more flexibility for management. It is easier to switch customers and territories. Finally, the plan is simple to operate and easy for the men to understand.

These advantages are often outweighed by the disadvantages associated with the lack of a direct financial incentive. Only routine motivation is provided by a salary. This may lead to limited individual initiative and drive.

Commission

A *commission* is a payment for the *performance* of a unit of work. A salesman might be paid 3 per cent of net sales, 5 per cent of gross profits, or $1.25 for each 100 pounds sold. Straight commission plans are often used by firms in industries such as leather products, furniture and fixtures, and apparel.

Straight commission plans are based on the principle that earnings of salesmen should vary directly with performance. Salesmen are paid for results. Usually, commission payments are based on dollar or unit sales volume. However, more and more companies are beginning to compute commission rates as a percentage of gross profit.

Direct motivation is the key advantage of the commission method of compensation. A strong incentive is provided to increase productivity. Salesmen are encouraged to think and conduct themselves as if they were in business for themselves. Strong performers are attracted and encouraged; marginal performers are eliminated.

Loss of control over salesmen's activities is the major limitation of the straight commission. The strong incentive to sell more may encourage overstocking, misrepresentation of goods, and other bad selling practices. Customer service and goodwill may also be neglected. Another weakness is the insecurity that the salesmen may face because of irregular earnings. Salesmen's wives often object to the irregular earnings that result from a commission system.[18]

Several modifications of the straight commission plan have been designed to overcome these disadvantages. Three of the most popular are commissions with drawing accounts, sliding commissions, and varied commissions.

---

[18]Marvin A. Jolson, "Managing the Salesman's Wife," *Sales Management* (July 1, 1971), pp. 36–37.

There is a trend toward providing salesmen who work on commission with a *drawing account*. Money is regularly advanced to salesmen and is later deducted from their earned commissions. This gives salesmen some of the security of a salary, and it allows management more control over a salesman's activities. The only problem arises when a salesman fails to earn enough commissions to repay his draw. When this happens, the man may quit or be fired, and the company must absorb the loss.

Sliding commission plans use a changing rate. When a *progressive plan* is used, earnings of salesmen increase more than proportionately with increases in sales volume. For instance, a salesman may be paid 1 per cent of net sales for sales from $0 to $50,000, 1.5 per cent for sales from $50,000 to $100,000, and 2 per cent for all sales over $100,000. This type of commission plan provides a strong stimulus to increase sales.

A *regressive plan* works in reverse. Earnings decrease proportionately with increases in sales volume. For example, a salesman may receive 1.5 per cent of net sales for net sales from $0 to $100,000, 1.0 per cent for sales from $100,000 to $150,000, and 0.5 per cent for all sales above $150,000. This plan gives a strong financial incentive to achieve initial sales and encourages goodwill activities.

Varied commission plans promote sales of the most profitable items. Higher commissions are given for selling products with high gross profitability and lower commissions for products with smaller profitability. Although this plan is not as simple as a straight commission plan, it is more flexible. Further, it is one way to relate selling expenses to profitability.

Bonus

A *bonus* is a payment made at the discretion of management for a *particular achievement*. It is usually a reward for special effort and provides direct motivation. However, in contrast to commission payments, which relate directly to some measure of the salesman's performance (usually sales volume), bonuses are only indirectly related to sales volume. They are considered an additional incentive rather than part of the basic compensation plan.

Attainment of sales quotas is used frequently to determine eligibility for bonus payments. A department of one large corporation in the

Midwest developed an incentive plan based on quotas for four product categories. These were first set by negotiation between salesmen and their supervisors. Incentive payments were set up for sales in excess of quotas. The incentives emphasized sales of the most profitable products rather than sales volume alone. To encourage balanced selling, salesmen receive a bonus only if they meet quotas in three of the four product groups. If they meet quotas in all four categories, bonuses are doubled.

Bonuses are also paid for other forms of extra effort related to the company's sales goals. These include bonuses based on number of new accounts opened, on performance of certain types of promotional work, and on reduced expenses. For example, a salesman might receive $100 for each new customer or $10 for setting up a floor display.

Most bonus payments are in cash, but merchandise gifts and other nonfinancial rewards may be used. One pharmaceutical manufacturer has a plan that pays bonuses to salesmen in company stock. The goal is to create a common interest in profitability by making the salesmen stockholders. Salesmen are offered shares of stock if district sales forecasts are met and if individual quotas are achieved. Regional sales managers, district sales managers, and detail men are also eligible for stock bonuses if their performances exceed expectations.

Combination Plans

Most salesmen and sales managers prefer a compensation plan which combines the security of a fixed base with incentive payments. In a Research Institute of America study, 76 per cent of the salesmen surveyed favored combination plans.[19]

The proportion of incentive pay depends on the company's objectives and on the nature of the selling task. When a salesman's selling skill is the key to sales success, the incentive part of the salesman's pay should be high. However, when the product has been presold and the salesman is little more than an order receiver, the incentive proportion of the salesman's gross income should be small.

Table 14–3 shows some of the variations in incentive payments. Companies selling specialty products that are relatively high priced

---

[19]Research Institute of America, *Sales Compensation Plans* (New York: Research Institute of America, 1965), p. 3.

and keenly competitive (e.g., furniture and machinery) usually pay their salesmen a small guaranteed salary plus a commission based on sales volume. On the other hand, the cigarette industry does not offer bonuses or commissions, since cigarettes are largely presold and since the selling task requires little direct incentives.

Combination plans often fail because they provide too little financial incentive for the salesman to achieve the desired objectives. As a general rule, at least a quarter of the average salesman's gross income should be in the form of incentive pay. If not, the sales incentive plan will not be truly effective.

Salesmen's incentive earnings are paid annually, semiannually, quarterly, or monthly. In general, the shorter the time interval between performance and payment of the reward, the stronger the stimulus to the salesman. However, payment of earned incentives may sometimes be deferred for several years. The standard life insurance plan, for example, involves paying the agent half of his commission when a policy is sold and the rest in regular payments over the next ten years.

TABLE 14-3
Variations in Incentive Payments, by Industry

Industry	Bonus or Commission Payments as a Percentage of Annual Gross Earnings
Household furniture	52
Special industrial machinery	39
Household appliances	35
Molded plastic products	27
Machine tools	23
Pharmaceutical preparations	16
Electronic components	11
Industrial chemicals	7
Portland cement	3
Cigarettes	0

Source: Adapted from Richard C. Smyth, "Financial Incentives for Salesmen," *Harvard Business Review*, vol. 46 (January-February 1968), pp. 109-117.

There are many forms of salesmen's combination pay plans. One variation is the *point plan*. Points, or credit, are given for selling various products, for performing certain special duties, or for intangible contributions such as cooperativeness, interest in the job, and initiative. At the end of the month, quarter, or year, the points are converted into monetary values and a bonus is paid to each salesman who qualifies. This bonus plan complements a firm's basic compensation plan.

Another variation is to give seniority increases. One manufacturer provides a gradual increase in the incentive rate for each year a salesman stays with the company. After twenty-five years of service a salesman receives about 25 per cent more incentive income for the same performance as a man just joining the company. This type of plan provides incentive rewards for salesmen's loyalty and persistence.

Implementing the Plan

Implementation of the salesmen's compensation plan involves pretesting the plan, selling it to the sales force, and evaluating the plan.

Pretest. Any new or revised compensation plan must be pretested. One method is to apply the new plan to the historical performance of selected individual salesmen and sales districts. If the results of this test are satisfactory, the plan can then be tested further by introducing it in one or more sales districts. These results must be carefully reviewed to determine if any modifications are required before the plan is introduced to the other sales districts.

Sell. It is essential that the new or revised compensation plan be properly introduced to the salesmen affected. This is a change and there is always resistance to change, especially one as vital as a change in compensation. The success of the plan as a motivator will depend primarily on how well it is introduced.

Introducing the plan is a selling task. One must keep in mind the guidelines for good salesmanship. Most importantly, management must be "customer-oriented." Emphasis must be on the benefits to the salesmen. However, it is better to go slow and understate the benefits rather than overstate them so as to avoid possible future disappointment.

Evaluate. Once the plan has been sold and put into operation, it should be evaluated. The field sales manager should have major responsibility for administering the plan. A careful periodic appraisal of each salesman's activities and performance under the plan is of major importance. Although drastic changes should not be necessary, minor adjustments may be required.

SALES EXPENSES

Salesmen's expenses have a significant impact on a salesman's effectiveness and on the company's profits. From the salesman's viewpoint, sales expenses are part of his real income. He tends to think of expenses and compensation as similar since both affect his financial status. A poorly administered expense plan will hurt a salesman's morale, especially if he feels the plan reduces his income.

Need for Control

Sales expenses are a major cost factor. Recent studies reveal that the average cost of a sales call made by a manufacturer's salesman is over $40. One survey of several hundred companies revealed a median annual expense account of $4200 across all industry groups.[20] There is every indication that selling costs will continue to rise.

Management often regards sales expenses as a "necessary evil." This is unfortunate because *sales expenses are an investment.* Their purpose is to generate sales in the same way that any promotional expenditure does. Salesmen's expenses must be properly supervised, but they must also be liberal enough to permit salesmen to do their job effectively.

Another management concern is the federal income tax law. The Revenue Act of 1962 eliminated many abuses associated with business expenses. Although the law is mainly concerned with limiting

---

[20]Dauner (1971), p. 27.

excessive entertainment and business gift expenses, it also requires more detailed recording of expenses. The major impact of the law on companies has been more detailed recordkeeping and closer managerial control over expenses.

Current Practices

Most companies have adopted a liberal sales expense policy. A majority pay all *reasonable* expenses rather than set allowances for various expenses or for certain time periods. Expense items that companies usually pay for include travel, automobile mileage and upkeep, lodging and meals away from home, job-related entertainment, promotional expenditures, telephone calls, telegrams, and postage. However, few companies will pay for *borderline* expenses, such as personal telephone calls or telegrams, personal entertainment, laundry, and valet service.

Like compensation, the salesmen's expense plan must be fair to both the salesmen and the company. There should be no net gain or loss to either party. The expense plan must not hamper selling activities in any way. It should be simple and economical to operate and should provide an effective means of controlling expense accounts. One way to do this is to have salesmen use credit cards. Along with avoiding the necessity for carrying large sums of cash, credit cards provide the company with better records of salesmen's expenses.

SUMMARY There are two major ways of motivating salesmen — *financial* and *nonfinancial* incentives. Nonfinancial incentives for salesmen include a variety of techniques used for specific, special-effort situations. Sales conventions and meetings, sales contests, honors and recognition, and communication are the major forms of special incentives. Chapter 14 outlined the ways in which each of these techniques can be used to motivate salesmen. Particular attention was given to the methods of implementing these incentives.

Financial incentives may be direct monetary payments such as salaries and wages, or they may be indirect monetary rewards. These indirect rewards, commonly known as fringe benefits, include paid vacations, insurance plans, and the like. Financial incentives are the most widely used and misunderstood techniques for motivating salesmen.

Several studies have revealed three major trends in the compensation of salesmen: (1) shift to combination plans; (2) emphasis on profitability; and (3) increased availability of fringe benefits.

A sound compensation plan should have the following characteristics: (1) incentive, (2) simplicity, (3) fairness, (4) flexibility, (5) control, and (6) competitiveness. The basic steps in developing such a plan are as follows:

1. Review the salesman's job
2. Determine specific objectives
3. Establish the level of compensation
4. Choose the method of compensation
5. Implement the plan.

The final section of Chapter 14 considered sales expenses. A salesman tends to think of expenses and compensation as similar since both affect his financial status. A poorly administered expense plan will hurt a salesman's morale, especially if he feels that the plan reduces his income.

DISCUSSION/REVIEW QUESTIONS

1. Assume that you have been asked to plan a sales convention to introduce a company's new advertising campaign to the salesmen. Prepare a proposal for this convention.
2. Have you ever participated in a sales promotion contest for a consumer product? How did the objectives of this contest differ from those for a contest for salesmen?
3. Assume that you are a district manager for a medium-sized insurance company. Your company has been having difficulty recruiting qualified

agents, and you have been asked to develop a sales contest to encourage your agents to recruit new agents. Prepare a plan for this contest.

4. Suggest the method of salesmen's compensation which would be appropriate for the following companies. Explain your answers.
   a. a manufacturer of men's and boys' apparel
   b. a manufacturer of machine tools
   c. a furniture wholesaler
   d. a real estate agency

5. The Green Manufacturing Company has recently changed from a straight salary compensation plan to a salary plus commission plan. Although most salesmen will soon earn more under the new plan, they have strongly resisted the change. What do you think are the reasons for this resistance? What can Green's sales manager do now to insure the success of the plan?

6. Listed below are a number of typical sales objectives. Indicate which form of non-financial incentive you would suggest to encourage achievement of the objective?
   Objective
   a. To encourage dealers to use more cooperative advertising.
   b. To improve selling techniques.
   c. To introduce a new product.
   d. To achieve greater coverage in present channels of distribution.
   e. To familiarize salesmen with product changes.
   f. To induce dealers to use special display materials.
   g. To reduce selling expenses.
   h. To recruit qualified salesmen.

7. Obtain a copy of a company's compensation plan for salesmen. Does it meet the criteria established in this chapter? What changes, if any, would you make?

8. "The older salesman presents a critical motivational challenge to a sales manager." Comment.

9. List and discuss the "10 Biggest Mistakes" made in sales contests.

10. Discuss how the life insurance industry's Million Dollar Roundtable functions as a sales incentive.

11. Evaluate the major trends in sales compensation programs.

12. What are the basic steps involved in developing a sales compensation plan?

13. Several modifications of the commission plan have been developed: (1) drawing accounts, (2) sliding commissions, and (3) varied commissions. Explain each of these variations.

14. Why do you think the authors included a discussion of sales expenses in this chapter? Discuss.

PART FOUR
CASES

CASE 26
SHOULD YOU GET YOUR FIELD SALES
MANAGER OUT OF SELLING?*

Consider the following article by one of the authors.

ASSIGNMENT

1. What does the writer say, or imply, are the main reason(s) why sales managers engage in selling?
2. What situations can exist where the sales manager must engage in selling?
3. Do you believe that it is true that a supervisor must be good at, and continue to engage in, the activity he supervises? Why or why not?

---

*Source: Albert H. Dunn, "Should You Get Your Field Sales Managers Out of Selling?" *Sales Management* (October 1, 1966), pp. 37–40. Reprinted by permission from *Sales Management, the Marketing Magazine.* Copyright, 1966.

4. If you were the superior of five sales managers and wanted them to reduce the amount of selling they did, what would you do? Why? How?

SHOULD YOU GET YOUR FIELD
SALES MANAGER OUT OF SELLING?*

Yes, argues Professor Albert Dunn, whose extensive work in sales-management seminars leads him to conclude that many district sales managers take to the field to escape their real responsibilities. What can top management do about it?

If Casey Stengel had taken to pinch hitting every time his teams were in trouble, baseball's Hall of Fame would doubtless be minus one of its greats today. Of course, the idea is absurd; in athletics as in most other fields, the line between management and operations is clearly and realistically drawn; yet, in sales, it is crossed so often by the field manager as to make it almost meaningless. Today's better-trained and -educated sales manager is beginning to ask new and pointed questions about himself, his economic and social function. He wants to know where he fits, not only in his company and industry but in the larger society around him. And he will not be put off by platitudes. One important question raised by the modern manager, a question that bears not only on the nature of his job but on the very economic reason for his being, is: How much selling should a sales manager himself do? The answer, heretical as it may seem, is that with only a few exceptions, the sales manager should get out of selling altogether.

A firm grasp of just what management is (and more important, how it differs from selling), is crucial to an understanding of this position. The manager participates in planning goals and in the selection of facilities to accomplish them: financial, human, and technological. He directs and motivates the activities of others in the attainment of these goals and evaluates the performance of his subordinates against corporate objectives. Thus, management, all management, is the process by which goals are achieved through the activities of others. The manager plans, oversees, directs, motivates, and evaluates. He does not do operations. Operations are done for him by subordinates.

With this distinction, it is possible to contrast management and operations in several ways that bear on the question of how much, if any, selling field managers should do. For instance, selling is an intimate, personal activity; management is a vicarious process in that it gets things done through others. Unlike the salesman, the manager does not derive his job satisfaction from what he himself does, but from what his subordinates do. He is evaluated, rewarded, or punished not on his salesmanship but on his department's performance. In this way, the manager's job can be meaningfully compared with that of a coach. The football coach, for example, does not punt, pass, or block, and he is not evaluated on these abilities. He may, in fact, be utterly incompetent in mechanical skills and yet be an eminently successful coach. Walter Kipputh, noted Yale swimming coach, could barely stay afloat, yet he turned out winning Olympic teams.

How, then, does the great coach or manager make great performers and winning teams without being a participant, or perhaps not even technically proficient. This is not a stupid question. Part of our Yankee business folklore contends that to learn and grow, one must do and experience. The danger of this truism is that experience alone never leads to wisdom or high competence. In fact, unaided experience is a treacherous and bigoted teacher. For wisdom, confidence, and high management competence, two other abilities are necessary: conceptualization and communication. As the manager matures to great responsibility, these skills replace his direct, personal participation in operations.

The great coach or manager used three main administrative skills:

1. An ability to see the skeleton beneath layers of muscle and tissue, which means a basic understanding of how people are persuaded to react as the seller wishes them to.
2. An ability to understand how selling fits into the body chemistry of his company, industry, and society.
3. An ability to communicate concepts, to transmit company goals, practices, and policies to subordinates so that they understand, support, and act on them.

Thus, the competent sales manager must use detail meaningfully, but not be hypnotized by it. He must understand and be instructed about his problems by trained insight and concept, rather than by personal experience; mesh all functions under his control with related corporate functions; and teach subordinates by and through concepts and not personal demonstration. The proper function of sales management, it is clear, is management. But some sales managers object. "Don't we need to sell to keep our hand in, to keep abreast of field-selling developments and problems? How are we going to get our knowledge of market conditions, without doing some selling ourselves?" The answer to these questions is that if these are the only reasons why sales managers sell, they are poor reasons. After all, General Eisenhower did not need to lead an infantry attack every few weeks to keep informed of what the Germans were doing.

The fallacy lies in ignorance of the communication networks that exist in every company for the express purpose of keeping management informed on what is happening in the marketplace. Any reasonably mature company is replete with reporting procedures designed to be the eyes and ears of its commanders. The field manager must learn to use this indirect information system and to shift from gathering market information firsthand (a function of doing) to gathering and appraising it through others (a function of management). If the information system is inadequate, it should be redesigned.

It might then be asked why it is that so many sales managers actively engage in personal selling. If so many companies (many of them big and successful) have selling managers, what can be wrong with the practice? Doesn't their success endorse the validity of "working" sales managers? Not so. There are, in fact, only two good reasons why sales managers must sell. In certain industries, such as grocery, drug, and soft goods, customers' organizations have gone in the direction of decentralized purchasing and operations. Such a structure necessitates the contact of higher-level buyer personnel by higher-level supplier people, not infrequently sales managers. There is no bucking this trend, and the necessity for sales managers to sell such customers cannot be debated. But there is a nagging question here: Is this the kind of selling meant when it is asked how much selling a sales manager should do? Does it mean selling those customers who are the sales manager's assigned accounts? Not really. When it is asked how much selling a sales manager should do, the reference is to trouble-shooting selling; the selling that tries to do for salesmen what they don't seem to be able to do for themselves.

The need to train new men is another valid reason for the sales manager selling himself. Demonstration is required to show proper techniques, response and behavior patterns of customers. It is important to note here that a small portion of the sales manager's job is usually concerned with training new salesmen.

There are, however, a number of bad reasons for the manager selling. In some companies, of course, the field sales manager is, in fact, not a manager but a senior salesman who has been assigned reporting responsibilities for other salesmen in his area. These are not real field sales managers. Therefore, it makes no sense to devalue these sales managers in name only for spending the bulk of their time selling. Also, too many companies have fostered a tradition in which their field sales manager is expected to be a sort of supermanager *and* supersalesman.

This simply cannot be! If there is a real sales management job to be done, the skills, time, energy, and attention required to do it cannot be shared part time with any substantial amount of personal selling. This common but improper tradition is the formalization of a misconception of the true nature of management. But the prevalence of this philisophy in industry should not be allowed to hide the fact that it is wrong. The sales manager often continues personal selling simply because of the very human predilection to do what he knows best. Consider a not-untypical situation, the promotion of a top salesman to a sales management position in which he is confronted by a new set of requirements and responsibilities. Where previously he was asked "to do" and was evaluated on "how well he did," now he is required to direct the doing of others. As a salesman, he was told where to go, how frequently to get there, and what to do when he got there. He was face to face with his customer.

But in his new management job, the world is quite different. Now he must plan and direct his subordinates. He no longer deals on a face-to-face basis with customers. He must evaluate the doing of others and he himself is ultimately evaluated on how well they do. This can be an extremely difficult, frustrating, and maddening business. Plans don't work out, subordinates misbehave and are lazy or misunderstand directions. Customers are stubborn and uncooperative. Competition systematically disrupts plans and operations. Communications are not so efficient as they should be. And while management breathes down his neck for results, most of the things that go wrong with his operation are caused by forces largely beyond his direct control. And what is the natural, instinctive reaction to this difficult and maddening

441

business called management? How does he want to solve the sales problems of his subordinates? He is likely to revert to those activities he knows best and in which he has proven his skill: personal selling. Therefore, with the exception of dealing with companies with decentralized buying structures, or for training purposes, there is no justification for the sales manager to be selling. Company tradition and personal reassurance notwithstanding, selling is not the job of the sales manager. What, then, can be done to set the situation right?

Top marketing management should begin by answering these questions:

1. How much personal selling are the various levels of field sales managers doing?
2. Specifically, what are the functions of the various levels of field sales management? Are they really performing these functions?
3. From a dollar-and-cents point of view, is it wise to have field sales managers do the amount of personal selling that they are doing at the expense of their managerial functions?
4. What is being done to indoctrinate and train the lower levels of field sales management and the upper levels of the field sales force for future management jobs?

A systematic job analysis should be an important result of any reappraisal. It should include these five steps:

1. *Functional analysis:* Specifically and in detail, what must the field sales manager do so that sales show a profit now and in the future?
2. *Operational Analysis:* Specifically and in detail, what is the field sales manager now doing?
3. *Remedial action:* What specifically needs to be done to bring the operational analysis (with special reference to personal selling time by field sales managers) into line with the functional analysis?
4. *Follow up:* How is the implementation of the program succeeding?

The field sales manager, for his part, must appraise himself and his management in light of:

1. To what extent is his personal selling based on need, and to what extent is it done to reassure himself?
2. What is he doing now, and what has he done in the last few years to improve his management skills? What development programs has he attended? What other avenues of management development has he explored?
3. Does he really like management? Would he be happy doing more of it?
4. What steps can he take to encourage his boss to help him develop management skills?

In summation then, it should be seen that one of the most prevalent irritants to the morale of the field sales managers is the question of how much time he should spend selling. Yet the answer in most cases is that he should spend as little time as possible selling. The manager must sharpen his command abilities and draw job satisfactions from them. He must resist the natural temptation to flee the frustrating world of management to the old familiar world of selling.

Top management, too, must take a hard look at its attitudes and traditions in this area, and the field manager must use his influence to gain general acceptance as a manager and not as a salesman. Only then can the field sales manager realize his full potential, for himself and for his company.

CASE 27
PROFESSOR JOHN LUBANY

Professor John Lubany was an instructor in the National Sales Executives' training program for field sales managers. The program lasted a week and was attended by about 100 sales supervisors from many companies and industries, all of whom were in charge of from ten to several hundred field salesmen for their companies.

One of Lubany's assignments was to lead a role playing session on the subject of the motivation of salesmen. On the morning that the incident with William Dolan occurred, the role playing involved a good salesman who had started to drink more heavily than he should. After the two role players — one taking the part of the salesman and the other the part of the sales manager — had performed for about twenty minutes, the whole class took over, acting first as interviewers and then as observers and critics. This session lasted two hours and generated considerable interest among the group.

A coffee break of fifteen minutes followed the role-playing session. As Lubany was leaving the conference room to get coffee, he was stopped by William Dolan. The following conversation ensued:

"John, I was very much interested in that session. It comes very near to a problem that is driving me crazy."

"I guess the problem of the drinking salesman is one you all must run across now and then," Lubany said.

"Yes, I know it must be so. But my problem is in reverse, so to speak.

"You see, I've just been made division sales manager for my company. I've worked for my company for twenty-three years, incidentally. Before that I was eastern regional sales manager. Now I have the eastern, southern, and midwestern regions. I've got about a hundred men under me."

"That's quite a step up. Congratulations!"

"Thanks. I worked hard for it. But my problem comes right out of that promotion. I don't drink, smoke, or use profanity. A long time ago I had a cataclysmic experience which turned me to religion. Matter of fact, I studied a while for the ministry but the depression cut that short. My father was a minister, and during the 1930s he didn't have enough to see me through school so I quit and went to work.

"I'm not only against smoking and drinking but I have a very hard time to keep from suggesting that others — salesmen and friends — also should abstain. That bothers me. Should a good sales manager try to be one of the boys or not?"

Lubany hoped the question was rhetorical, but it wasn't. So he replied, "My feeling has always been that a manager has to be himself, if for no other reason than that a few of us are good enough actors to fool

444

anybody very long about any false character we may try to assume."

"I'm glad to hear you say that," Dolan replied. "That's about what I've decided, but my boss, the national sales manager, goes around under-cutting me every chance he gets. When he visits our region he makes it a point to go out on the town with my salesmen after meeting in the evenings. It almost seems he tries to get them extra drunk just to spite me. I go along with them for a while and then excuse myself and go to bed. I can almost see them breathing a sigh of relief when I get up to go.

"I don't know how much longer I can take this. I like my company and I've spent many years in getting up the ladder in it—I started as a draftsman apprentice in the shop. But I don't know how much more I can take. What do you think I should do?"

ASSIGNMENT

1. Specifically, about what leadership problems is Mr. Dolan talking to Professor Lubany?
2. Why is Dolan behaving as he is? Why is his boss behaving as Dolan says he is?
3. How do you think Dolan's salesmen regard him? Why?
4. What should Lubany advise Dolan to do? Why? How? When?
5. As far as the case evidence allows you to conclude, what is your personal appraisal of Dolan's sales executive leadership? Why?
6. What do you think Dolan will do about the problem when he returns to his office after the program? Why?

CASE 28
THE ECONO-CLEAN FRANCHISE

Stan Kamanski acquired the Econo-Clean franchise for Allentown, Pennsylvania in 1964. The company offered a unique, patented process of cleaning carpets and upholstery. Stan, a native of Allentown, has many close personal friends in the area. These friends provide a major stimulus to his franchise's sales.

Prior to assuming the franchise, Mr. Kamanski worked in the main Econo-Clean plant for a year. The plant is located in Baltimore, Maryland.

Stan was trained through the company's centralized training program. A loan was arranged to start the franchise which he is repaying in monthly installments. It took $7000 to obtain the franchise, a truck, and the equipment needed for complete carpet and upholstering cleaning.

Promotion

The franchise has business cards printed by the telephone company. These cards are provided without charge as a service to Yellow Page advertisers, and help to promote goodwill and business contacts. An answering service is utilized to take emergency cleaning requests after hours and when the office is unattended. Enlarging the answering service operation to include a free stain removal telephone questioning service was considered but never implemented.

Advertising

At present, advertising utilizes radio, the Yellow Pages, and flyers. On Sunday morning, a half-hour gospel show is sponsored on a Country-Western radio station. Mr. Kamanski was advised that it would take about thirteen weeks of radio advertising on this program before its true effectiveness could be evaluated. Later, when the advertising did not come up to expectation, Stan still decided to continue his sponsorship.

Yellow Pages advertising consists of a quarter-page ad describing the unique cleaning process. At periodic intervals, youngsters are hired to canvas neighborhoods distributing flyers telling of the process and offering 300 free Top Value stamps with each free estimate. Salesmen sometimes also distribute flyers and canvas door-to-door. They are also encouraged to seek new business by contacting commercial establishments and offering low commercial rate estimates.

446

Personal Selling

Last summer, Jack Sterling, a college student, was hired by Mr. Kamanski as a salesman. Jack received no training other than accompanying Fred Keiser, the sales manager, for two days on his sales rounds. This gave him a little insight into the selling process, but it seemed quite inadequate. Jack's product knowledge was very weak and when he requested additional information, he was amazed to find that it consisted of only two pages of literature. After asking Fred for more information, he was advised that it would be necessary to write to the main office in Baltimore.

Selling for Econo-Clean was a sink or swim affair. Salesmen received a 20 per cent commission on cleaning jobs and cleaning products sold. There was no salary, drawing account, car allowance, gas allowance, or expense account. Jack made $5 during his first week on the job and used $6 worth of gas. His enthusiasm for the summer job was at best diminished.

In addition to his low earnings, Jack was disappointed over Econo-Clean's method of selling. Each salesman was given an area which was to be his private sales domain. Calls to the answering service were provided to each salesman according to these areas. From this information one would expect salesmen to be "order receiving" types. But, this was far from the truth. Salesmen averaged approximately five calls a day. This was hardly sufficient for a salesman to survive financially since most of these calls were for free cleaning estimates and not definite job orders. The main requirement for the job seemed to be endless amounts of enthusiasm and initiative.

The sales manager was mainly concerned with his own sales, and with insuring his subordinates' attendance and punctuality. As for inspiration, he was definitely not an emotional catalyst. Poor sales were looked upon as an everyday occurance and nothing was done to remedy this.

ASSIGNMENT

1. What can Jack do about his situation?
2. Is the inefficient sales function of the franchise symptomatic of an even more basic problem?

3. What would you suggest Mr. Kamanski do to correct the problems outlined here?

CASE 29
KITCHEN DELUXE, INC.

On January 23, 1973, a Kitchen Deluxe franchise was granted to Warren Field and Nick Alfinakis by Phil Somili, division manager (California). Field and Alfinakis were both attorneys in a medium-sized California city. Although the franchise agreement did not restrict their operations to the city, where the franchise was set up, the bulk of the sales would come from this area.

In addition to their law practice, Field and Alfinakis were both active in other professional and community activities. Field was the director of the local amateur playhouse and chairman of the alumni fund drive for the local state college. Alfanakis was a lieutenant colonel in the California National Guard and actively involved in volunteer work with the boys club. Both Field and Alfanakis were well known throughout the community.

Products

The Kitchen Deluxe multiple products line was recognized as the most inclusive in the field. It included china (Bavarian and Japanese), flatware, a complete line of cookware, and top quality cutlery (guaranteed for life). A major selling appeal of the company is the building of "hope chests" or planning for future marriages. The product line is also sold to prospects at houseware parties and demonstration dinners.

The Franchise

The Kitchen Deluxe Corporation was founded in 1951 in St. Louis, Missouri. The company's founders had introduced some distinctive devices. As operations expanded, the product line widened.

Today, the company manufactures none of its own products. It is solely a distribution operation. However, it does own some of its own machinery and dies so that rigid controls can be maintained on the quality of its products.

The Kitchen Deluxe franchise plan had been in the development stages many months before it was test marketed and put into operation. The goal of the corporation was to develop the best dealership offered in America. The parent company cooperated with the dealer in several ways:

1. The home office offered assistance in many aspects of the business.
2. The sales promotion staff was highly developed. The company felt they were the most aggressive in the United States in the area of sales promotion. Materials available were training films, product brochures, and contests. The company felt that vigorous sales promotion was perhaps the most important aid to assisting the salesmen in success.
3. The company had a national advertising program. Annual expenditures on national television and publication advertising amounted to $750,000.
4. Order books, premiums, and literature were offered to the dealer at cost.
5. The company supplied prizes for dealer salesmen who produced outstanding sales results.
6. The company would drop-ship merchandise to local customers.
7. Each salesman was required to purchase his own set of samples. The company said that this was to allow the salesman a freedom in his work. By purchasing his samples, the salesman would have some incentive so as to get a return on his capital investment in the company.

Soon after the franchise was granted, the owners began to develop a sales organization under Somili's direction.

Somili recommended that because of the location in a college town, the sales force should be made up of college students eager to gain business experience. The first step was to select a supervisor who would aid in recruiting and training a sales force, as well as participate in personal selling. Les Whyte, a 25-year-old graduate student was selected to fill the position. Whyte was single, ambitious, and in need of the money this position could provide. He had had some sales experience at a retail level, and he was confident of success in his new position. Whyte was paid by a commission of 30 per cent of his total weekly sales, with a $25 bonus per sales recruit.

Field and Alfinakis were anxious to get the dealership into operation and gave Whyte three weeks in which to recruit a sales force of eight to ten men.

Field and Alfinakis felt that it would be best if the recruiter could demonstrate enthusiasm by showing the prospective salesman how easy it was to make money "the Kitchen Deluxe way."

To this Whyte agreed, but after many unsuccessful attempts, which he blamed on his inability to close the sales, his own enthusiasm dwindled. His knowledge of the company was limited. All he knew about Kitchen Deluxe was what he read in the sales manual and what he saw from one unsuccessful sales attempt by Phil Somoli. After this unsuccessful sales presentation, Somoli excused himself and told Whyte that he would return in three weeks to give Whyte and the newly recruited sales force intensive training.

Final exams interrupted the recruiting and when Somoli arrived to train the sales force, only Whyte and one recruit were present. Field and Alfinakis were busy and could not attend the meeting.

Somoli returned occasionally to make personal sales and train a few new recruits. He assured the franchisers that everything would "work out in the near future." But after four months, sales were still low and Whyte had secured only two qualified salesmen. These recruits were making only an average of five calls per week with few results. The salesmen viewed their training as highly inadequate and stated that Field and Alfinakis had done little or nothing toward keeping in contact with them. What they had gained from Somoli in his few trips to the city was not enough to motivate and aid them in successful sales presentations.

ASSIGNMENT

1. List and explain the basic sales management problems facing the franchise.

2. How would you suggest Field and Alfinakis handle these problems? Why?

CASE 30
THE LUTRY COMPANY

The Lutry Company is a large manufacturer of packaged, canned and frozen foods. The line consists of about 200 items and is sold direct to chains and through wholesalers to independent grocery stores. The sales force of 2000 men does missionary work with independent stores and works with wholesalers. First, second, and third level sales supervisors call on the local and regional offices of chains in addition to managing their men.

All independent stores order and receive their Lutry merchandise through their local wholesaler. Lutry does not distribute to independent retailers in any other way. In their calls on retailers, Lutry salesmen check that the stores are in-stock of Lutry products (if out-of-stock, they try to get the retailer to approve an order through his wholesaler). They also deliver emergency stocks from the wholesaler; service Lutry stock on the shelves; answer complaints; and seek to have retailers tie-in with Lutry's national promotions through local advertising and in-store display.

Each salesman is assigned a territory. The typical territory contains about 150 retailers and 10 wholesale customers. Salesmen are expected to call on their larger retail customers (about 15 per cent of their total) at least once a week and on the others every month, in addition to maintaining regular contact with the wholesalers in their territory.

ASSIGNMENT

From the information that is available:

1. Do you think Lutry should have a formal evaluation program for their salesmen? Why or why not?
2. What difficulties or obstacles do you foresee in their setting up and operating an evaluation program?

3. Sketch out a job description for Lutry salesmen.
4. What evaluation criteria would you use in appraising their performance? Why would you use these rather than others that are available?

CASE 31
BLACKWELL COMPANY

Blackwell Company had a salesforce of 200 representatives selling its men and women's fashion products nationally. The company was founded fifteen years ago and has grown very rapidly. All levels of management were occupied by young men and women who had risen from the lower ranks of the company. The company's reputation in the industry was one of aggressiveness, imagination, and growth. In the trade, it was considered a mark of status to be a Blackwell employee.

Blackwell's sales management had become dissatisfied with their salesmen's compensation plan. After careful study, it was decided to engage an outside consultant (who specialized in the design of sales compensation programs) to investigate and make recommendations for a new or revised compensation plan.

As one part of his survey, the consultant held informal, unstructured discussion sessions with selected groups of Blackwell sales persons. One such meeting included ten sales representatives, all of whom were under 28 years of age and had been employed by Blackwell for less than four years. The only ones present were the consultant and the salesmen.

After placing the participants at ease, the consultant announced that he wanted their honest, personal attitudes on the role of financial remuneration in their immediate and short-term life plans and expectations. He suggested such "kick-off" questions as: How much do you want to make—enough? A lot? What are you willing to give up in your personal life to attain your ideal level of financial remuneration?

452

The discussion began slowly, but quickly gained momentum. Some of the consultant's taped notes on the meeting follow:

Man A: "I want to make a lot of money—a great deal! I'll work as hard as I have to in order to get it, go anywhere, do anything to get it. But I won't continue until I'm so old that making money is all I can do and I'm completely oriented to making money as a life style. I want to quit or slow down while I still can enjoy what I've earned—maybe 45 or at least 50."

Woman A: "I like the fashion business. I'm in love with it. Maybe someday I'll get married, but I sort of doubt it. Fashion is my life. I want enough money to live tastefully. Beyond that, money doesn't matter if I can really live this business, and move up to where I can help create in it."

Man B: "You asked what I'd be willing to give up for a good salary. My answer is I'd give up a lot, *almost* everything, providing—and this is critical—providing I could see the end to it. I mean, going from the end of one pay treadmill to the start of another, and so on all my life, is not for me. Somewhere I've got to be able to see the end of the tunnel!"

Woman B: "Well, since we're all being so frank, I'd honestly say that all I want is to have an interesting job and enough money to live the way I want to live."

ASSIGNMENT

1. How do you analyze each response above?
2. What kind of personality does each response suggest to you? How are all of them saying that they respond to financial remuneration as an incentive? Why?
3. If these four sales people are typical of Blackwell's total salesforce, *specifically* what problems face the company in devising a new sales compensation plan? What ideas do you have for solving these problems?

CASE 32
ELLIS BROTHERS TRUCKING CO.

Mr. Ivan Daniels, sales manager of the Ellis Brothers Trucking Co. of Chicago, was attempting to evaluate proposed changes in the compensation and size of his sales force.

Ellis Brothers Trucking Co. was founded as a partnership in 1930. At present, it is the largest common carrier in Illinois. It is now governed by a board of directors, and its stock is held by past and present executive employees. A large portion of the firm's sales comes from the large manufacturers in the Chicago metropolitan area. Ellis Brothers has terminals in eight Illinois cities — Chicago (headquarters), Rockford, Springfield, Peoria, East St. Louis, Danville, Kankakee, Champaign, and Macomb. Sales volume generated by this common carrier has been growing rapidly and last year reached an all-time high of nearly $14 million.

The compensation of salesmen has always been on a commission basis, and in recent times this has been the source of considerable controversy in the sales department. Of the 17 salesmen employed by Ellis Brothers, 5 are located in the Chicago metropolitan area; the remaining 12 are distributed throughout the state in the various terminal locations. One salesman, Worthington Booth, is in complete control of the steel division which earned revenues of $1 million last year. Mr. Booth receives the same 2 per cent compensation as the remaining 16 salesmen. This leaves only $13 million to be split among 16 salesmen.

A basic problem arises, when, for example, a salesman in Peoria finds a new account. The goods are to be shipped to a manufacturer located in Chicago. The commissions from this sale often end up in the hands of a Chicago salesman, since the Chicago manufacturer, the final destination, is paying the shipping charge. The company paying the shipping charge can specify which carrier they prefer to deliver the freight. In doing so, the Chicago salesman covering that territory receives the 2 per cent commission.

This fact is a negative motivating factor for the salesmen in the other areas of the state. Very little sales originate from Chicago and go to the other areas. Because of the fact that so much of the total freight shipped ended up in the Chicago metropolitan area, the 5 Chicago salesmen received much more in terms of income than did the remaining 12 men located outside of the metropolitan area.

All 17 of these salesmen had started in the out-state areas, and gradually, through expansion and others' retirements, worked their way into the metropolitan area.

Company sales had risen 55 per cent in the past five years, but dissatisfaction of its sales personnel was also increasing. Mr. Daniels felt that the sales rise was due primarily to expansion of the company into other markets. The new salesmen hired for this expansion showed great potential, but because of their location in the out-state areas, compensation was a problem. In fact, three of the younger salesmen were considering leaving the company.

In a study done by Mr. Daniels, the only correlation between income and other job factors was the length of service—not productivity or performance. Daniels believed that the only inroad to increased sales was through taking business from other companies. But because of ICC regulations and rate structures, no real price discounts could be granted. The only promotional variable was considered to be service. Daniels also realized that any additional costs incurred as a result of his decision in the compensation issue were to be associated with offsetting gains in sales volume.

The decisions facing Daniels then are (1) how to compensate the salesmen and (2) whether the size of the sales force is adequate.

One proposal being considered is to pay the sales force straight salary. While the Chicago salesmen will oppose the plan, the out-state salesmen will probably favor the idea. It was felt that this method would alleviate the problem of the older employees automatically receiving the higher pay due to their location advantage.

Daniels also held another alternative—that being a base salary of $9000 and an annual bonus based on merit according to guidelines set down by top management. The total bonuses granted would not exceed 1 per cent of sales.

Daniels also felt that more salesmen would be needed to adequately cover all the customers' needs. If service was going to be stressed, he felt that this was the proper way to do it.

ASSIGNMENT

What would you decide if you were in Mr. Daniels' position?

PART FIVE: EPILOGUE

CHAPTER FIFTEEN
THE FUTURE
OF SELLING
AND OF
SALES MANAGEMENT

Chapter 2 dealt with the historical development of the professional sales force. Other chapters have discussed the dynamic nature of sales management. In fact, a consistent theme of this book has been that the personal selling function is always in flux. It is subject to an endless variety of environmental stimuli that push it first one way, then another. But, the sales function is more than just a passive ingredient of marketing. Salesmen and sales managers have played an active role in determining the contemporary direction of their field.

It may be trite to say that significant changes are in the offing for sales management. *This has always been the case.* But, it is important to note that it is extremely difficult to predict the direction and intensity of these changes. Some trends are a part of the overall changes occurring in the marketing discipline; others are related strictly to sales management. In any case, the future of the personal selling function is a critical aspect of the continued vitality of a firm's marketing effort.

THE ADVANCEMENT OF MARKETING THOUGHT

Many of the changes in selling have resulted from changes in the concept of marketing activity. Figure 15–1 shows that marketing thought, as we know it, has actually gone through several stages to reach its current emphasis on consumer orientation. The diagram also shows that a further extension of the discipline is likely.[1]

Specialization and division of labor allowed early economies to achieve a production surplus. This necessitated an *exchange process*, in which one person's surplus of farm produce was traded for another person's surplus of clothing items. This exchange is known as *bartering*, the face-to-face exchange of goods or services. It still characterizes some types of transactions.

The development of monetary systems permitted the emergence of *selling*, by which goods and services were exchanged for some form of currency. Later, the institution of *selling on credit* emerged. This further expanded the personal sales function. For most of history, selling has dominated marketing thought. From the first widespread use of money to the advent of the marketing concept (following World War II) — a span of several thousand years — selling was the basic thrust of marketing thought and activity.

The *marketing stage* indicated in Figure 15 – 1 points out that eventually marketing support activities were recognized. Staff activities such as advertising, research, distribution management, and dealer relations were acknowledged to be important segments of the total marketing program.

The *marketing concept's* emphasis on a company-wide consumer orientation characterized the emergence of marketing as the premier function within any business enterprises. Customer satisfaction was recognized as the prime objective of the organization. The marketing concept has been widely accepted by industry,[2] and a consumer orientation has become the basic premise of most business philosophies.

Concern for consumer satisfaction will certainly remain a critical ingredient of marketing. But, in recent years, several proposals have been suggested that would advance or extend the concept of marketing beyond the traditional limits of the business organization. The *broadening concept* is a pervasive societal activity that goes well beyond the selling of toothpaste, soap, or steel. As proposed by Professors Kotler and Levy, the broadening concept views marketing as

---

[1]See Sidney J. Levy, *Promotional Behavior* (Glenview, Ill.: Scott, Foresman and Company, 1971), pp. 85 – 87.
[2]Richard T. Hise, "Have Manufacturing Firms Adopted the Marketing Concept?" *Journal of Marketing*, vol. 29 (July 1965), pp. 9 – 12.

FIGURE 15-1
The Advancement of Marketing Thought

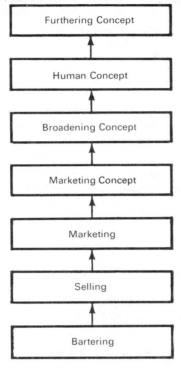

being an important activity of nonbusiness, as well as business, organizations.[3] The ideas, philosophies, and concepts espoused by museums, departments of government, the American Cancer Society, a labor union, or a college or university can also be *marketed*. It can be argued that many worthwhile social projects have failed simply because they were not marketed effectively. While some have disagreed with the Kotler-Levy contention,[4] the *broadening* concept has been generally accepted by society. Marketing has played an increasingly larger role in the administration and operation of many nonbusiness

---

[3]Philip Kotler and Sidney J. Levy, "Broadening the Concept of Marketing," *Journal of Marketing*, vol. 33 (January 1969), pp. 10-15.

[4]For example, see David J. Luck, "Broadening the Concept of Marketing—Too Far," *Journal of Marketing*, vol. 33 (July 1969), pp. 53-55.

enterprises. The Advertising Council, for instance, provides the services of marketers to various nonbusiness causes.

Another extension of marketing thought is the *human concept* proposed by Leslie M. Dawson.[5] The viewpoint holds that management should adopt a human orientation. Professor Dawson has observed that:

> The contribution of the human concept lies in focus and commitment, it can extend the vision of management into those areas of corporate involvement where social purpose beyond profit can be found. Every business organization, regardless of size, can find genuine social purpose in its attitudes and actions concerning employees. Most firms, in alliance with local, state, and federal agencies and institutions, can find genuine external social purpose.[6]

Much of what the human concept proposes has been implemented under the banner of *social responsibility in marketing decisions*. But, few sales managers would deny that much more needs to be done.

The *furthering concept* is another extension of marketing thought and actions.[7] *Furthering* has been defined as "the overall concept encompassing the determination of audience needs and the generation of audience interest and supportive response to one's aims."[8] The furthering concept subsumes marketing, but is applicable to noneconomic objectives. Essentially, this idea treats *marketing as a generic function* of any organization regardless of its goals and objectives.

Professor Kotler has taken his broadening proposal even further to include any transaction between an organization and its publics.[9] Kotler's *generic concept* (or furthering concept) of marketing proposes that marketing applies to any social unit which seeks to exchange val-

---

[5]Leslie M. Dawson, "The Human Concept: New Philosophy for Business," *Business Horizons*, vol. XII (December 1969), pp. 29–38.

[6]Dawson (1969), p. 38.

[7]Sidney J. Levy and Philip Kotler, "Beyond Marketing: The Furthering Concept," *California Management Review*, vol. XII (Winter 1969), pp. 67–73.

[8]Levy (1971), p. 86.

[9]Philip Kotler, "A Generic Concept of Marketing," *Journal of Marketing*, vol. 36 (April 1972), pp. 46–54.

ues with other social units. Thus, products include organizations, persons, places, and ideas, in addition to goods and services. These products are marketed by a wide variety of business, political, social, religious, cultural, and knowledge organizations. Kotler concludes that all marketers face the same tasks in all forms of marketing.

To conclude this examination of the advancement of marketing thought, it is interesting to point out that marketing—and its line component, personal selling—has always been based upon a consumer orientation. The only things that have changed are the *definition of the consumer* and what is believed to be *the best method(s) of reaching one's target market*. For example, the broadening, human, furthering concepts seek to expand the generally accepted definition of the consumer. There seems little doubt that this revision will become an accepted reality in the next decade. This will mean that the sales manager must find new ways of coping with these added dimensions of marketing.

A CHANGED ENVIRONMENT FOR SELLING

The personal selling function faces a different marketing environment than that which existed ten years ago, five years ago, *even* two years ago. It is impossible to identify all of these alterations, since they too would have changed by the time one finished studying the list. So, without detailing specific changes, let us briefly comment on the *general areas* in which change has occurred.

Consumer Education

As noted in the summary of Chapter 2, modern consumers are better educated, and they are more knowledgeable about the products and services they buy. If nothing else, this has forced contemporary salesmen and sales managers to adopt a more professional approach to their job. Admittedly, most of the increased professionalization of sales has come from *within* the selling profession. But, a better educated consumer is a safeguard that will eventually eliminate those salesmen exhibiting marginal professionalism.

All indications are that consumers will be even better informed in the future. Adult education classes, Junior Achievement, DECA Chapters (Distribution Education Clubs of America), the American Marketing Association, improved business coverage in the popular press (in magazines and newspapers), the Sales-Marketing Executives clubs, and consumer economics classes in the public school system are examples of how our economic and business knowledge is being furthered. The consumer educational process is expanding, and its various forms now reach many people, from the preteen to the adult. Effective sales managers applaud this trend since one of its important by-products is an improved sales function.

Societal Changes

Numerous changes in our societal framework have also affected personal selling. Society is now demanding that marketers consider *quality* as well as *quantity* dimensions in their decisions. To cite a simple example, one only has to remember when sales managers could justify somewhat questionable sales tactics on the basis that the maintenance of sales volume preserved employment for many employees. This is a *quantity* dimension. Contemporary society seeks as well a *quality* dimension in marketing decisions, and it questions whether certain sales tactics are ethical *per se*.

A policy statement from the Committee for Economic Development highlights these changing public expectations:

> The expectations of American society have now begun to rise at a faster pace than the nation's economic and social performance. Concentrated attention is being focused on the ill-being of sectors of the population and on ways to bring them up to the general well-being of most of the citizenry. Fundamental changes are also taking place in attitudes, with greater emphasis being put on human values — on individual worth and the qualitative aspects of life and community affairs.[10]

The public's attitude toward marketers (and toward sales managers

---

[10]Committee for Economic Development, *Social Responsibilities of Business Corporations* (New York: Committee for Economic Development, 1971), p. 12.

in particular) is that they should adopt a more socially responsible orientation. This philosophy is reflected in the human concept discussed earlier in this chapter. In fairness to the sales profession, it should be noted that most sales managers have already done this to some extent. But even greater strides will be required in the future.

Increased Government Regulation

It seems reasonable to expect that the next decade will see direct government intervention in many areas of marketing decision-making. Price-setting is a good example. Continued inflation will surely lead to a public outcry for increased government controls in regard to this sensitive issue.

Sales management should play a leading role in self-regulation. This is particularly true in some of those grey areas of sales ethics. Effective self-regulation by industry will eliminate the need for government intervention in conspicious trouble spots.

An essay in Time entitled "The Future of Free Enterprise" predicted that capitalism will take on some features of socialism.[11] Specifically, Time expects the federal government to increase its influence on the private economy, by strengthening its role as:

1. a goal setter and rules maker for business;
2. a stern policeman of private enterprise;
3. a supervisor of wages and prices.

More effective government planning is needed to coordinate the resources of businesses with the spending and taxation policies of federal, state, and local governments, Time argues, if free enterprise is to be more responsive to the nation's needs.

Technological Changes

Rapid technological changes will make today's most modern equipment and products obsolete by tomorrow! The one dominant charac-

---

[11]Donald H. Morrison, "The Future of Free Enterprise," Time (February 14, 1972), pp. 50–51.

teristic of the modern technological revolution is its rapidity of change. New products are being born at an extremely fast pace. Many new products fail, and others become obsolete as quickly as the relevant technology improves.

Sales management provides a vital input into product introduction decisions. This role will probably expand in the future. In addition, sales personnel must remain constantly aware of the prevailing, and proposed, technology in their field. Their customers depend upon them as an information source on new innovations related to their business. An uninformed or technologically obsolete salesman is a poor investment for his firm. Sales management must provide the *educational leadership* needed for a vital, modern sales effort.

Expanded Competition

Sales forces face increased competition both domestically and internationally. Contemporary selling does not merely pit one steel salesman against another. Modern competition is concerned with alternate uses of available funds. Alcoa is as much a competitor of U.S. Steel as is Bethlehem Steel. The savings department of the First National Bank is in competition with Humbolt's Ford Agency and with Margolis's Travel Center.

The consumer's purchasing decision really concerns how to best allocate his funds among numerous alternative uses. This new concept of competition may be the most significant change that has influenced the selling environment in several years.

Not only is domestic competition keen, but international marketers have also proven to be formidable foes. SONY, German steel, Volkswagen, and Datsun have all made sizable inroads into American markets. Today's marketer must also learn to compete effectively in rapidly developing foreign markets.

Increased Selling Costs

As noted earlier in this book, increased selling costs are a fact of life in our business system. Sales management's task is to find new ways of coping with this problem. As selling costs escalate, so must sales productivity. So, the real job is how to make the sales effort more effective. This will necessitate better sales training, new sales strategies and tactics, and the adoption of the latest competitive technology.

Need for Better Sales Intelligence

There is a growing need for better sales intelligence from the field. One of the most interesting aspects of the current selling environment is that today's salesman is regarded as a prime information source for his company. While salesmen have always provided competitive data from the field, much of this information was never formalized, systemized, or very effective. The salesman's role as an information-gatherer has been much expanded in recent years.

Some field representatives claim that this new aspect of their job takes too much time away from selling activities. This may be true in some cases. But if it is, these situations should be corrected immediately. However, it seems reasonable to believe that most salesmen can devote some part of their time to collecting sales intelligence for analysis by skilled staff personnel. This process is a *two-way street*. Once the data have been analyzed, it is assumed that relevant facts will be communicated back to the field force in order to improve their selling efficiency.

DEALING WITH A CHANGED SELLING ENVIRONMENT

The previous section outlined several aspects of the changing nature of the sales environment. Selling, however, is not completely at the mercy of environmental factors. In fact, today's salesman has several advantages over his counterpart of an earlier day. While the modern selling environment is perhaps more dynamic, contemporary sales forces have the important advantages of better communication, better transportation, and additional sales support personnel.

Better Communication. The wide availability of quick, inexpensive telephone service is a significant improvement over the telegraph and mail services used by earlier salesmen. If a customer complains about a delay in his delivery, the salesman can probably resolve the difficulty with a three-minute call to headquarters.

The telephone has also proved an effective aid in making initial sales contacts. With the rapid rise in the cost of sales calls, the telephone has helped firms improve their salesmen's productivity. Other communications devices, such as audio and visual cassettes, special slide projectors, and portable computer terminals, have also become effective selling tools.

Better Transportation. Yesterday's *drummer* would never have understood what the automobile could do for more effective selling. The drummer's territory was dictated by the location of railroad tracks, while today's salesman covers a far wider area. Of particular importance is the emergence of the jet airliner as the primary means of intercity business travel. Sales representatives can now crisscross the country with ease. Air travel has greatly expanded the selling horizon.

Additional Sales Support Personnel. In former times, the field salesman was essentially a loner. He had infrequent contact with his field sales manager, and virtually no personal contact with other employees of his firm. Many a salesman's story is told about how a representative was *lost out there in the field*. The basic point is that the salesman was in a peculiar position. Although he constituted the firm's only marketing effort, he was typically isolated from his own company.

Better communications and transportation helped alleviate this problem. But something else also happened. Companies began to expand their marketing effort by adding staff personnel that provided vital support activities to the sales force. Marketing research, distributor relations, market planning, dealer relations, sales promotion, and inside selling are examples of activities that now assist the direct selling effort.

Herbert D. Eagle, marketing vice-president for Transamerica Corporation, has described this change.

A few years back, it was usually the salesman out there alone, pitting his wits against the resistance of a single corporate purchasing agent. Now, more and more companies are selling on many different levels, inter-locking their research, engineering, marketing, and upper management with those of their customers. This way, today's salesman becomes a kind of committee chairman within his company. Some manufacturers call them "account managers."[12]

All of the improvements discussed above have permitted the field salesman to better cope with his changing environment. One has difficulty in speculating what would have happened if these advantages had not been available to the sales function. It is certain, however, that without them sales management would not have reached its current advanced state of achievement.

TRENDS INFLUENCING THE SALES FUNCTION

Some may argue that this final section of the book is an unwarranted attempt at long-term forecasting. Perhaps it is. But it seems reasonable to identify trends that may have a pronounced effect on future sales management efforts.

Most of the following trends are clearly identifiable and have been pointed out in earlier chapters. All of them will have a significant influence on how sales managers will operate in the future.

Minority Groups. This volume has previously noted that blacks and other minority groups have not traditionally been assimilated into sales forces. However, this has changed rapidly in recent years. Minorities are now viewing sales as an area presenting excellent employment opportunities. Sales has always been a vehicle of occupational and social mobility. It is now fulfilling that important function again. Thus, minority groups will increasingly see sales as an equal opportunity field.

Women. Field selling was always viewed as a man's world, and it still is to a large extent. Yet, women are now beginning to make important inroads that will no doubt broaden in future years.

A study by the Sales Executives Club of New York found that 75 per cent of the sales executives surveyed employed women in their field sales force. The majority of those who employed women believed that

---

[12]Quoted in "The New Supersalesman: Wired for Success," *Business Week* (January 6, 1973), p. 45.

their sales performance equaled or bettered that of the men in the field force. Currently, the best sales career opportunities for women are in service and consumer product marketing,[13] but it is obvious that industrial selling opportunities will increase in the future.

Perhaps a later edition of this textbook will use the term *salesperson* rather than *salesman*. Equal employment opportunity — *regardless of sex* — is a goal worthy of the sales manager's prompt and considered attention.

Societal Role of Sales Managers. As noted earlier in this chapter, society is demanding that all marketers implement *only* socially responsible decisions and strategies. This trend will affect several areas of sales management and will expand the societal role of sales managers.

The Computer. The computer will have a significant impact on future sales management decisions. Computers have already had a sizeable impact, and this trend is likely to continue *and accelerate*. Traditionally, marketers have been slower than others to adopt the computer. But now that it has been accepted, marketers have become some of the computer generation's strongest proponents. The computer is now used in sales analysis, in promotional budgeting, in the aligning of sales territories, and in the routing of salesmen. One of the most important contributions will be in the implementation of a marketing information system (MIS). *A marketing information system* is a designed set of procedures and methods for generating an orderly flow of pertinent information for use in making decisions. The MIS provides management with the current or conditional future states of his market, and it also provides indications of market responses to company action as well as to the actions of competitors.[14] The computer provides the means for implementing the marketing information system. A 1971 study reported that 39 per cent of the firms studied had

---

[13]"161 Sales Executives Rate Women in Selling." *Sales Management* (February 15, 1973), p. 26.
[14]See Donald F. Cox and Robert E. Good, "How to Build a Marketing Information System," *Harvard Business Review*, vol. 45 (May–June 1967), p. 146; and Richard H. Brien and James E. Stafford, "Marketing Information Systems: A New Dimension for Marketing Research," *Journal of Marketing*, vol. 32 (July 1968), p. 21. The current status of marketing information systems is reported in Louis E. Boone and David L. Kurtz, "Marketing Information Systems: Current Status in American Industry," *1971 Combined Proceedings*, Fred C. Allvine, ed. (Chicago: American Marketing Association, 1971), pp. 163–167.

an operational MIS, while another 38 per cent were in the process of installing an MIS.[15] Expanded use of the computer is expected in many areas. As a result, persons planning a career in sales management should become familiar with the uses of the computer and of related data processing equipment.

Sales Productivity. Sales costs are rising rapidly. Many types of products can no longer be promoted via personal selling, because the possible margins are exceeded by the actual cost of selling the item. Finding ways to deal with this cost escalation may prove to be one of sales management's greatest challenges in the coming decade.

Professionalization. As noted in Chapter 2, it is certainly reasonable to believe that the professionalization of the sales function will continue. Several significant issues remain to be solved. There is no widely accepted *Code of Professional Ethics.* Not all sales managers recognize a standard level of educational prerequisities. Marginal, and *unprofessional,* sales operations still exist in many lines of business. All of these problem areas will have to be dealt with if sales is to ever truly achieve professional status in the minds of consumers.

Sales Management as a Stepping Stone. A final point is that sales management is in a position to be coveted by an aspiring marketer. In addition to putting the person at the hub of the firm's competitive effort, sales management acts as a *stepping stone* to other types of managerial positions. A first-level sales manager has several options: he can advance to the next level in the sales organization; he can move to a higher position in one of the other parts of the marketing organization; or he can enter a general management position. The essential point is that sales management prepares the person for advancement in many areas of the firm's hierarchy.

SUMMARY This final chapter has briefly examined the future of the personal selling function. The authors do not pretend to be seers or

---

[15]Boone and Kurtz (1971), p. 10.

oracles. However, we do argue that concepts and trends described here will have a substantial influence on sales activities of the coming decade.

Marketing thought has developed beyond the marketing concept. The broadening concept views marketing as being an important activity of nonbusiness, as well as business, organizations. This contention has generally been accepted by society. Beyond this, there is the human concept with its emphasis on a human resource orientation, and the furthering concept that treats marketing as a generic function of any organization regardless of its goals and objectives.

The environment of the personal selling function has changed considerably over the past few years. Chapter 15 has discussed the implications of the following issues: (1) consumer education, (2) societal changes, (3) increased government regulation, (4) technological changes, (5) expanded competition, (6) increased selling costs, and (7) the need for better sales intelligence. However, today's salesman has several advantages over his counterpart of an earlier day: (1) better communication, (2) better transportation, and (3) additional sales support personnel.

Chapter 15 concluded by identifying some trends influencing the sales function:

1. Minority groups will increasingly see sales as an equal opportunity field
2. More women are entering sales careers
3. Sales managers are expected to fulfill an expanded societal role
4. The computer will have a significant impact on future sales management
5. Sales productivity will be increased
6. There will be a further professionalization of the sales function
7. Sales management will act as a stepping stone to even higher levels of marketing management

DISCUSSION/REVIEW QUESTIONS

1. Briefly identify each of the following:
   a. bartering
   b. selling
   c. marketing
   c. marketing concept
   e. broadening concept
   f. human concept
   g. furthering concept
   h. marketing information system
2. "Many changes are in the offing for sales management." Comment.
3. Trace the evolution of marketing activity. Describe each step in this development.
4. Differentiate between the broadening, human, and furthering concepts of marketing. Cite examples of each.
5. Design a promotional campaign for:
   a. the Navy
   b. American Automobile Association
   c. your church
   d. the Boys' Club
   e. a local hospital's cancer research fund.
   What role does the sales function play in the promotional campaign?
6. Describe the various changes that are occurring in the environment for selling.
7. What factors have allowed salesmen and sales managers to compete with a changed selling environment? Discuss.
8. Identify the major trends influencing the sales function.
9. What is your own assessment of the personal selling function?

PART FIVE
CASES

33
Thursday Evening Is Only Three Days Away
34
Bill Conant Thinks Out Loud
35
Stein Realty Company

CASE 33
THURSDAY EVENING
IS ONLY THREE DAYS AWAY

Reed Granger, the vice-president for sales at Similex Pharmaceuticals, Inc., has just returned to his home in upstate New York from a lengthy business trip to the West Coast.

While relaxing in the family room, he begins to tell his wife, Jennifer, about the West Coast trip:

"You know, Jennifer, we were so rushed with those sales negotiations that I sometimes had to have Carl, the zone sales manager in California, tell me where we were going next!

"Speaking of getting caught up in the rush of things—that reminds me that Ray Parsons asked me to speak to the Sales Executives Club on Thursday evening.

"Oh brother, that is only three days away, and I haven't given any thought to the talk.

"Let me see, as I recall, Ray wanted me to discuss future trends in sales management. He was particularly interested in areas where the sales manager could update and improve his skills so he could better deal with future events.

"Jennifer, what am I going to say for twenty-five minutes?"

474

ASSIGNMENT

1. Prepare a brief outline for Reed Granger's talk to the Sales Executive Club.

CASE 34
BILL CONANT THINKS OUT LOUD

Bill Conant, a district sales manager for Lombard Corporation, and his neighbor Sam Spence, an accounting supervisor for a large insurance company, were sitting in Bill's back yard one Sunday, drinking beer and talking about many topics. The conversation turned to young people's attitudes toward business and careers in business. Bill said:

"Sam, business has really fallen out of favor with the kids. Here we have a cornucopia of wealth, the highest standard of living the world has ever seen, the lowest death rate, more art, music, theater, books than most of the rest of the world put together — all because of American business. And what happens? The kids, our kids, want no part of it. It's dirty, immoral, and polluting, they say. It's money-grabbing, and stomping on people and selling people what they do not want — that's what they say!"

Sam replied:

"You're right, Bill, but you've got to remember we brought a good deal of it on ourselves by saying one thing and doing something else."

Bill:

"You're right. Take my field. The big companies tell everybody how straight and good and efficient they are, and then they get caught by the government rigging prices."

Sam:

"And the packages that are only partly filled, the hidden interest charges in the price the consumer pays. . . ."

Bill:

"Unsafe automobiles and household cures that are dangerous. . . ."

Sam:

"Lousy service for cars and washing machines. . . ."

Bill:

"And all the time we're shouting to everybody, but especially the kids, how honest and clean we are."

ASSIGNMENT

1. What other examples can you cite of commercial deception and error in products, advertising, price, credit, delivery?
2. Are you aware of any company programs designed to facilitate communication between the company, customers, and general public? If so, why do you think these programs were established? If not, should there be such programs? With what objectives? Why?
3. How would you recommend that a company (or an industry) go about communicating with the younger generation?
4. If in fact the younger generation views American industry and selling as Bill and Sam describe, is there any chance at all that it can be changed? Why? How?

CASE 35
STEIN REALTY COMPANY

Marvin Stein, president of Stein Realty Company, was considering whether his firm should participate in Homelist, a computer real estate service.

Stein Realty Company was founded in 1959 by Samuel Stein, Marvin Stein's father. Initially, the business was a one-man operation, and Mr. Stein rented office space in a major San Francisco bank. After a few years, the business prospered enough to permit Mr. Stein to employ Marvin as a salesman and his wife as a secretary-bookkeeper. In 1964, because of continued growth, Mr. Stein purchased two attached buildings in a suburban area and converted these into modern office facilities. The year 1964 also brought further expansion of the company's sales staff and division of the sales force into a commercial-industrial sales department and a residential sales department.

Mr. Stein passed away in 1968, leaving an established firm with ten salesmen. Marvin Stein became president of the company, and his mother assumed a more active management role. Stein Realty Company continued to grow and prosper in the residential and commercial markets.

Homelist, a real estate listing system, used a centralized computer to store information on available residential properties. The information system permitted a realtor to select quickly those properties which met his client's requirements of price, style, location, and features. In addition to providing a complete list of properties currently available for sale, Homelist also provided a list of comparable properties recently sold so that the real estate agent could assure either buyer or seller that the homes listed were reasonably priced.

Among the advantages claimed for Homelist were that salesmen would be able to devote more time to selling since Homelist eliminated much time consuming "book work"; that customers would receive better service by being provided with a complete, up-to-date list of available homes; and that customers would be attracted to a firm which used the latest scientific advances to meet their needs.

This service would cost Stein Realty Company $50 per month plus $10 each time the service was used. An additional cash outlay to change the firm's phone system from dial to touch tone would also be necessary, so that a special terminal could be used to communicate with the central computer. Edmund Jacobson, residential sales manager, prepared a cost statement (Table 1, page 478). This statement was based on estimates of the average number of yearly sales and the average number of prospects who used this service and did not purchase a home from Stein Realty. After reviewing this statement, Mr. Stein agreed that it was a realistic estimate of sales and costs.

Mr. Stein then met with Mr. Jacobson and Mrs. Stein to discuss the adoption of Homelist. Mr. Jacobson strongly urged participation in the computer service. He noted the selling benefits and the relatively low cost of the service. However, Mrs. Stein was against the proposal. She emphasized that purchasing a home is a very personal decision for the buyer, and she expressed concern that the computerized Homelist service might affect Stein's customers adversely. She cited recent

TABLE 1
Homelist Cost Statement

Yearly membership fee: $50 per month	$ 600
Average yearly sales:	
175 @ $10 service charge	1,750
Prospects who do not buy:	
260 @ $10 service charge	2,600
Telephone changeover expenses	240
TOTAL	$5,190

newspaper and magazine articles which discussed the fears of Americans about the depersonalization of society. Mr. Stein was especially interested in his mother's opinion since she had displayed an uncanny ability to predict advertising and promotion success in the past.

ASSIGNMENT

1. Evaluate the Homelist proposal.
2. What is your opinion of the fears expressed by Mrs. Stein?
3. As a student of sales management, what benefits do you see for Stein's sales program?
4. What does this case suggest to you about the potential advantages and disadvantages of the computer as a sales tool?

NAME INDEX

I

IVEY, Paul W., 94

J

JENNINGS, James Paul, 140, 143, 155, 170, 207, 211, 215
JENSEN, Arlo, 408
JEWELL, Keith R., 257
JOHNSON, Eugene M., 242, 287, 326
JOHNSON, H. Webster, 94
JOHNSON, R. A., 349
JOLSON, Marvin A., 276, 428

K

KAHN, George N., 185
KASSARJIAN, Harold H., 66
KAUFMAN, Zenn, 415
KEGERRIS, Robert J., 61
KELLEY, Eugene J., 196
KELLEY, William T., 30
KIRKPATRICK, Charles Atkinson, 93, 94, 102
KISER, G. E., 91, 92
KLATT, Lawrence A., 176
KNIFFEN, Fred W., 199
KNOPP, Jacky, Jr., 51
KOTLER, Philip, 68, 460, 461, 462
KRACMAR, John K., 48
KURTZ, David L., 27, 49, 55, 65, 171, 176, 233, 239, 252, 272, 287, 302, 470, 471

L

LAMBERT, Zarrel, 199
LAPP, Charles L., 264, 339
LAZER, William, 132, 133, 196
LEATHERS, James O., 346
LEAVITT, Harold J., 340, 341
LEE, Stewart Monro, 52
LEVY, Sidney J., 460, 461, 462
LIPPITT, Vernon G., 143
LORIE, James H., 139, 155
LOUDON, David, 115
LUCK, David J., 461
LYNN, Robert A., 51
LYONS, T. W., 233

M

McCARTHY, John J., 365

SUBJECT INDEX